Historic Sites Along
THE OREGON TRAIL

Publisher's Note

Readers who wish to refer to extremely detailed maps of any specific site may do so by ordering maps issued by the United States Geological Survey, as detailed for the sites listed in this book. A list of USGS quads, along with ordering information, begins on page 446. These maps, for the most part, are on a scale of about 2⅝": 1 mile (1: 24,000).

All affected state highway departments offer county highway maps for sale. These are less costly than the USGS maps, and are also detailed with township, range and section. They are printed to a scale of ½: 1 mile, and show road systems with considerably more legibility, but do not show topography.

The Patrice Press offers a complete book of these maps showing the Oregon Trail and its principal alternates on a base of county highway maps. The trail data was compiled by Gregory M. Franzwa and a host of colleagues who are considered experts on the Oregon Trail.

The subscript letter **p** appears after the name of each site which is located on private property, where it is necessary or advisable to obtain permission prior to visiting the site. It is not just a matter of common courtesy, but of extreme urgency to seek such permission. There is still much rustling in the American West, and the perpetrators often take livestock in what appear to be recreation vehicles. Trespassing could cause the sites to be closed to all visitors. Moreover, it could invite one hell of a charge of buckshot. **Please** respect the property rights of our friends who are, after all, helping to preserve these irreplaceable links with those who traveled the Oregon Trail long ago.

Although the site itself might be on private property, access roads usually are public, so the visitor may drive almost to the site itself without trespassing.

The Patrice Press
1810 W. Grant Rd., Suite 108
Tucson AZ 85745

Historic Sites Along
THE OREGON TRAIL

Aubrey L. Haines

The Patrice Press
Tucson, Arizona

Library of Congress
Cataloging in Publication Data

Haines, Aubrey L.
   Historic sites along the Oregon Trail.
   Bibliography: pp. 426
   1. Historic sites—Oregon Trail. 2. Oregon Trail. I.
Title.
F597.H177 1981 917.8 81-9628
ISBN: 1-880397-03-X AACR2

The Patrice Press
1810 W. Grant Road, Suite 108
Tucson, AZ 85745
1-800-367-9242

Printed in the
United States of America

To
Paul C. Henderson
1895 — 1979

whose devotion to Oregon Trail research
has been an inspiration and a help
to many who have followed
its fading trace.

Contents

MAPS

Foreword

The United States enjoys a unique security in the world of nations, due to the fact that its boundaries extend from sea to sea. The longer we enjoy this security, the more difficult it becomes to understand how it came to be. It is an incredible story, one which deserves to be remembered forever.

In the mid-19th century, between 200,000 and 300,000 of our forebears sold their farms and bade farewell to friends and relatives. They struck out over the boundless prairies in their covered wagons in a hazardous journey to the American West.

Had they not done so when they did, it is probable that the West would have flown another flag. Because of their courage, America now has a natural geographic unity that protects us all.

This volume focuses on the celebrated highway taken by the great emigration—the Oregon Trail. The book is of uncommon importance for it locates the sites of hundreds of historic features along that trail—some still here but most gone forever.

It also points out some of the extant segments of the trail. Some of those ruts today are in great peril. Of the 1,900-plus miles of the original route, only about 15 percent remains intact and pristine today. The rest has bowed to "progress"—pipelines, highways, agricultural uses. More is being lost almost every year.

Only through awareness by the American people can this destruction be arrested. Therefore, it is with enthusiasm that we prepare the foreword for this book.

The pleasure is heightened by the fact that the author is "one of our own"—now retired from a distinguished career as a ranger, engineer and historian with the National Park Service. In fact, the work itself was commissioned by the NPS. Economic constraints prevented inclusion of nearly half the original study in the NPS publication, and those same problems kept the press run to only 100 copies.

Author Haines has worked diligently with The Patrice Press to ensure publication of his entire study, and in a handsome volume that is readily available to all Americans. We commend his work. It is a fitting monument to those pioneers who moved over the trail, and a noteworthy service to Americans of today and tomorrow. Should it result in the saving of just one historic site, or the preservation of just a few yards of our priceless Oregon Trail, it will have been well worth the effort.

Russell E. Dickenson

Director, National Park Service
Washington, DC
August 15, 1981

Introduction

A S PRESENTED HERE, *Historic Sites Along The Oregon Trail* is
a revision of a contract study made by the author for the
National Park Service in 1972-1973. The study was performed to
provide basic historical data for use by the Bureau of Outdoor
Recreation in formulating recommendations relevant to inclusion
of an Oregon Trail component in the nationwide system of
trailways authorized by Federal legislation in 1968 (Public Law
90-543).

Ideally, such a study should have taken the form of a complete
inventory of all remaining evidences of the Oregon Trail, but
the subject was very large. Almost 400 potential sites are scattered
along a route more than 1900 miles long, without considering
alternates. A very extensive literature contains thousands of
pertinent items. Therefore, some preliminary deletions had to
be made to bring the work to manageable proportions. Also, the
eight months of available time (of which a minimum of three
would be consumed by field work) precluded a consideration of
the Oregon Trail in all its ramifications. Nor did that appear
necessary in view of the mandate under which the Oregon Trail
Study was initiated. In its essential intent, the legislation
authorizing the study proposed future establishment of a trailway
marked in a manner to make it readily retraceable, in whole or
part, by interested persons. Visitors would be provided with such
facilities and interpretive means as would make their pilgrimage
a worthwhile physical and emotional experience. Thus, a study
contributing to that purpose was indicated, rather than a
comprehensive effort.

The desirability of creating a single interpretive route was evident, and the problem of limiting the study became essentially one of selecting the typical routing. It must be kept in mind that the Oregon Trail was hardly a thoroughfare in the modern sense, but more of a "travel corridor." The selection of the route upon which to focus the study was determined by the commonly held impression of the Oregon Trail as the route followed by emigrant wagons bound for the Oregon country. This, taken with the necessity for an uncomplicated route, established the trail under consideration in the original study as *the principal route followed by emigrants traveling westward from the Independence-Westport vicinity in Missouri to Oregon's Willamette Valley, from 1841 through 1848.* That limitation was approved by Merrill J. Mattes, project supervisor, and later by the group of study participants who met at Cheyenne, Wyoming, on November 9, 1972.

The practical result of the foregoing decision was to eliminate:

1. The Trapper-Missionary-Mormon Route (Council Bluffs Road).
2. Several "feeders" brought into prominence by the California bound forty-niners (the Fort Leavenworth, St. Joe, and Nebraska City roads).
3. Child's Cutoff, along the north bank of the North Platte River, above Fort Laramie.
4. The Lander Road, a product of the late 1850s.
5. Several minor cutoffs in the Green River Basin, and
6. That main stem of the forty-niners—Hudspeth's Cutoff.

Three termini of the trail in the Oregon country—the Applegate Trail, Meek's Cutoff and the Naches Pass Road—were likewise eliminated because they did not qualify as portions of the principal route.

The alignment considered to constitute the principal route, shown on the six route maps included in the text as a heavy solid line, was determined by others who were eminently qualified to delineate the trail in their particular areas. The alignment from Independence, Missouri, across Kansas, Nebraska and Wyoming to the Idaho boundary, is that of Paul C. Henderson. Retracement of the Oregon Trail and careful recording of residual evidences was his hobby for more than 40 years, and it is due largely to his interest and efforts that the eastern half of the Oregon Trail is so well-known. The Idaho portion of the trail was relocated by Dr. Merle W. Wells, with the assistance of Max Bruce and Walter Meyer of the Bureau of Land Management. Their work was enhanced by the use of a helicopter, which simplified following the fading traces of the trail across the rough, sagebrush-covered land along the Snake River. The Oregon portion of the trail was mapped by personnel of the Oregon Park and Recreation Section of the Oregon State Highway Department. Evidences reported by field engineers were correlated with markers placed in former years, and the partial alignment so obtained was then checked by low-level aerial photography which was able to "see" traces of the emigrant route otherwise hidden by cultivation and modern use of the land.

Tracings from all sources were transferred to the best available topographic maps as the basis for the route maps which accompanied the original report, and they are also the basis of the six route maps presented here. The maps show the route mileage, in 50-mile multiples, as scaled along the principal Oregon Trail alignment from its origin at Independence Square, Missouri, to Oregon City.

The idea of providing route mileage markings as a useful adjunct to an Oregon Trail map is not a new concept, for it appeared first in Capt. John C. Fremont's work. His able, German-trained cartographer, Charles Preuss, compiled a "Topographical Map of the Road from Missouri to Oregon," which was published in 1846 as a seven-section strip map, at the scale of 10 miles to the inch. It may be America's first sectional road map. It is interesting to note that the route mileages used in this work agree closely with those set down by Preuss 135 years ago. His mileage for Fort Walla Walla, on the Columbia River, the last point on his strip map, is 1718½. After corrections for slight differences in routing, this is only 8.9 miles more than the figure obtained from modern mapping—1709.6 miles. The difference is one-half mile for each 100 miles of the trail.

Of course, such route mileages, based as they are on map or "flat" distance measurements, do not agree with odometer mileages tabulated in early guidebooks. For instance, a popular guidebook of 1845 lists Fort Walla Walla as 1,903 miles from Independence—long by 193 miles.

Such a detailed discussion of route mapping is important because it is the control for the inventory of sites. They are arranged consecutively by route mileage, with a further designation of the distance right or left when a site is not directly on the principal alignment. For instance, Chimney Rock is left of the trail 1½ miles at Mile 575 (Mile 575 L1½). Please note that the arrangement used occasionally brings sites on different route segments into juxtaposition. For example, Cape

Horn on the Columbia River follows Barlow Pass on the Barlow Road alternate. Such incongruity could not be avoided without greatly complicating the arrangement of the site information.

Because of the necessity for completion of the field work during the summer and fall of 1972, that phase of the work was begun with less than adequate preparation. The search for sites should have been preceded by considerable library research. However, with the project becoming viable July 1, 1972, there was all too little of the season's good weather remaining, and the preliminaries to the field work had to be brief. When the examination of sites began on July 6, the information on hand was just that which had been gathered in three working days at the library of the Oregon Historical Society in Portland, a day with the Parks Division of the Oregon State Highway Department at Salem, and two days with Dr. Merle Wells at Boise, Idaho. The informational base was later bolstered further by a day at the Wyoming State Historical Library, Cheyenne, and two days with Paul C. Henderson at his home in Bridgeport, Nebraska. Although the preliminary research was limited, the assistance received was so great that the field work progressed with a minimum of bumbling.

Retracement of the Oregon Trail began at Gothenburg, Nebraska, weather conditions and prior scheduling dictating an east-west progression of the work. The decision to omit the first 380 miles of the trail was discussed with Mattes and Henderson, who agreed that the added time involved in traveling to Independence, Missouri, and back again to the Platte River Valley would not be well invested because intensive agricultural use had eradicated almost all evidence of the trail. Also, the availability of Mattes' excellent study of the trail's eastern reaches (published by the Nebraska Historical Society as *The Great Platte River Road,* and covering the overland trail routes east of Fort Laramie), compensated for this omission in the field work.

The data gathered covered 501 sites of historic interest. Of those, 308 were related to the Oregon Trail, although not all referred to the primary route and its time frame (1841-1848). For that and other reasons the number of sites considered in the original report was limited to 190. In this volume, all the sites related to the Oregon Trail are included, regardless of their significance.

The information presented for each site includes its accepted name or descriptive phrase; mileage from Independence, Missouri; location in general terms and specifically with regard to the Public Land Survey; a brief description, including relevance to the Oregon

The spelling and grammar of the diarists is unchanged from the original drafts. In some cases vicinity maps have been included to clarify or elaborate local situations.

Virtually all the photographs were taken by our son, C. L. Haines, during the summer of 1972.

The site descriptions presented in this volume represent conditions as they were in 1972, except where subsequent alteration is known to have occurred or recent investigation has added to the knowledge of the site. Such changes are appropriately noted.

Some mention has already been made of the particularly generous help which preceded the field work, but nothing has been said of the assistance from other sources. A host of writers on the Oregon Trail were helpful, among them two who wrote more as explorers of dim paths than as scholars—Irene Paden and Gregory M. Franzwa. Also, there were the many kind and informed people met by chance along the way. There was a banker who left his desk to conduct us personally to a well-preserved Pony Express station. A rancher insisted on taking us in his truck across fields too rough for our passenger car, so that we might see several remote gravesites. One man put aside his Sunday dinner to give us explicit directions. They all helped, for, as Mrs. Paden once said: "The telltale marks are easy enough to see—always providing someone shows you where they are."

Aubrey L. Haines
August 1, 1981

A "prairie schooner" which once traveled the Oregon Trail. This restored vehicle is on display in the museum of the Oregon Historical Society, Portland.

Historic Sites Along
THE OREGON TRAIL

The Background

THE FOLLOWING REVIEW of the Oregon Trail from the viewpoints of its historic development, the geography of the country traversed, and the variations in its routing is provided as a basis for the central discussion of historic sites.

History

Although the Oregon Trail has been defined, for the purposes of this study, as the route followed by emigrants from the vicinity of Independence, Missouri, to the Willamette Valley of Oregon during the period 1841 through 1848, its history has roots in nearly a half-century of prior American interest in the trans-Mississippi West. Discovery of the Columbia River by Capt. Robert Gray, master of the ship *Columbia*, of Boston, on May 11, 1792, accomplished more than the mere finding of that elusive "River of the West;" it also laid a basis for an American claim to the Oregon Country, and, through the financial success that attended his triangular trade between New England, the Northwest Coast, and China, it turned our national attention in that direction. It has been said of his voyaging that "empire followed in the wake."[1]

American vessels trading upon the Northwest Coast monopolized the business there during the decade following Gray's epochal visit. It was due largely to this national interest that President Thomas Jefferson sent the exploring expedition under Captains Lewis and Clark beyond the limits of the territory acquired from France by the Louisiana Purchase of April 11, 1803, and on to the mouth of the Columbia River, where they over-wintered within sound of the breakers of the Pacific Ocean. The expedition's route across the Rocky Mountains was hardly an acceptable thoroughfare, but as they moved westward from the mouth of Snake River, for 180 miles of the voyage down the Columbia they pioneered a segment of the overland route that many emigrants would later follow.

Another segment of the route was pioneered by the overland contingent of the Pacific Fur Company sent westward by John Jacob Astor to found a trading post at the mouth of the Columbia River. Leaving St. Louis on March 1, 1811, under Wilson Price Hunt, they began their journey by way of the Missouri River. They left that familiar approach to the Rocky Mountains at the Big Cheyenne River, turning westerly across present South Dakota and Wyoming to the headwaters of Green River, from where they crossed the Teton Range to their "Mad-River"—the Snake. They continued down that stream, suffering greatly during their passage through the inhospitable region between the Great Plain of Snake River and the crossing of the Blue Mountains of Oregon, but they added 500 miles to the route that would become the Oregon Trail. The experiences of this party have been described by Washington Irving.[2]

The following year—1812—a group of homeward-bound Astorians led by Robert Stuart retraced Hunt's trail as far as the western flank of the Wind River Range. There they became confused and turned southwesterly along the foot of the mountains, going beyond South Pass before managing to cross the continental divide. Upon regaining the Sweetwater River below the Three Crossings, they were able to follow that stream and the Platte River to the Missouri River, upon which they drifted down to civilization in a skin boat obtained from traders. They had made use of yet another 500 miles of what would become the Oregon Trail, but had not, as P. A. Rollins implies by the title of his book, opened the Oregon Trail.[3] A 350-mile gap remained—between the Great Plain of the Snake River and the Sweetwater River—an area for which contemporary geographic knowledge was inadequate to the point of uselessness.

The situation remained so for a decade, for the War of 1812 curbed American enterprise west of the Mississippi River. No serious ventures were undertaken until 1822, when William Ashley and Andrew Henry recruited trappers for service in the northern Rocky Mountains. They were unsuccessful on the Missouri and Yellowstone rivers, but moved southward into the beaver-rich triangle between the head of Wind River, the Great Plain of the Snake River, and the littoral of the Great Salt Lake, and there they prospered. While searching out the haunts of beaver, Ashley's men also came to understand the geography of that area, and were able to trace out practical routes through it in 1824.

A first fruit of these explorations appeared in 1825, when William Ashley brought a pack train of supplies to the trappers who had wintered in the Rocky Mountains, traveling to the rendezvous on the Green River by way of the Platte River-South Pass route.[4] The Oregon Trail was thus rounded out. The last essential gap was closed, and the route was ready for wheeled traffic.

The first wheels upon this natural route to the Oregon Country were those of a six-pounder cannon that Ashley dragged, in 1827, to the fort built on the shore of the Great Salt Lake[5] and that led to the use of wagons for the hauling of trade goods and supplies consigned to the annual rendezvous held on Wind River in 1830. The success of this venture was reported to Secretary of War John H. Eaton in a joint letter written by Jedediah S. Smith, David E. Jackson, and William L. Sublette, on October 29, 1830. In it they reported how they had taken 10 wagons, pulled by five mules each, and two Dearborns pulled by single mules, by the Platte River route—the wagons carrying loads of 1,800 pounds and progressing 15 to 25 miles each day.[6]

The fur traders used a mule train of 14 wagons in 1831, and Capt. B.L.E. Bonneville went to the Rocky Mountains with 20 ox-drawn wagons in 1832 (the first use of such motive power on the Oregon Trail). His wagons were also the first to cross the South Pass, and their wheels—except for Ashley's little cannon—were the first to reach the Green River. This was as far as the fur traders advanced the development of the Oregon Trail. It remained for another class of persons to take up the pioneering of the wagon track to Oregon—the missionaries.

In 1836, Dr. Marcus Whitman, his wife Narcissa, the Rev. and Mrs. Henry H. Spalding, and William H. Gray went out to the Oregon Country under the auspices of the American Board of Foreign Missions. This party traveled with traders of the American Fur Company as far as the annual rendezvous, but began the journey in recognizably emigrant style, their wagons being accompanied by driven cattle. Whitman's wagon broke down before it reached Fort Hall and had to be rebuilt as a cart, which was taken as far as Fort Boise before the idea of breaking a track to the Columbia River was given up for the season.[7]

The cart was abandoned at Fort Boise, but three wagons completed the journey to the Columbia River in 1840. "Doc" Newell, a mountain man, had guided a missionary party as far as Fort Hall, there accepting two wagons in payment for his services, and Caleb Wilkins had obtained a small wagon abandoned at Fort Hall by Joel Walker. The two, with Joseph L. Meek and Francis Ermatinger, decided to use the vehicles for moving their Indian families to the Willamette Valley, and they did manage to get through to Whitman's mission that fall with the running gears. In 1841, Newell took his wagon on down the Columbia, and it became the first to make the entire overland journey.[8] The Oregon Trail was open.

The fact that a way for wagons had been opened to the Columbia River did not become common knowledge for several years. Those of the Bidwell-Bartleson party of 1841 who elected to go to Oregon did not attempt to take wagons beyond Fort Hall, and the Elijah White train of 1842 likewise changed to pack animals there. It was not until 1843, and the "Great Migration," that wagons were taken through to the Dalles of the Columbia. Travel beyond this point was precluded by rugged terrain until Samuel K. Barlow opened his toll road around the southern flank of Mount Hood in 1846.[9]

The following figures indicate the numbers of emigrants who reached the Willamette Valley by way of the Oregon Trail prior to 1849 (when the pattern of trail use was altered radically by the California Gold Rush):

1841 —	32	1845 —	3,000
1842 —	197	1846 —	1,500
1843 —	875	1847 —	4,500
1844 —	1,750	1848 —	1,000 [10]

The total for the early, or pre-gold rush, period of Oregon emigration is 12,764 persons, but it is not known if that number includes those who arrived by the Applegate Trail opened into southern Oregon in 1846.[11]

Other figures indicate that emigrant use of the Oregon Trail during the late period (1849 through 1863) was approximately 30,500 persons, distributed as follows: 1849 — 500; 1850 — 5,000; 1851 — 2,500; 1852 — 1,500; and 1853 — 8,000.[12] It is stated, without particular substantiation, that the totals declined thereafter—an inevitable result of the Indian unrest that followed the Ward Massacre and related events. For more than a decade the Oregon Trail was kept open only by military force, and it was unsafe for travel by small parties until the end of the Snake War in 1868.[13] By that time its importance as an emigrant route had dwindled to insignificance.

Hardly anything has been said of the economic and social forces that led to the establishment and use of the Oregon Trail. There was a profit motive behind its initial development, but its use was later dictated by religious fervor, rampant nationalism, and, most important, the common man's restlessness—his desire to escape from frontier poverty, the debilitating illnesses then prevalent in the Mississippi Valley, and his all-too-familiar neighbors. And there was the concomitant hope of finding wealth, health, and happiness in the Oregon country—surely these things should follow as a matter of course where rich land was free for the taking. So, they succumbed to the "Oregon Fever" and went trekking westward with children, goods, and cattle—some dying en route of illness or violence, and many arriving worn-out and impoverished, only to find that their new homeland was not an instant Eden. But in the long run the dream proved true for most.

Geography

It was the character of the country through which the Oregon Trail passed that made it a generally satisfactory emigration route; and a cursory understanding of its nature, in terms of physiography, climate, vegetative cover, and life forms is absolutely essential to an understanding of the route and the migration that passed over it.

The migration corridor—for that is what the Oregon Trail was—traversed four regions, which, though similar in some respects, were so different in others that each presented the emigrants with particular problems. Almost immediately upon leaving Independence, the familiar Missouri River bottomlands were left behind and the route entered the Great Plains, which were crossed to Fort Laramie. Beyond that way station, the Rocky Mountains were traversed to Fort Hall, where the route emerged upon the Columbian Plateau, crossing it to The Dalles of the Columbia River. The remaining distance to the Willamette Valley was forested terrain typical of the northern Pacific Coast.

Considering these regions in greater detail, the Great Plains have been described as a debris apron descending from the Rocky Mountains on a uniform slope toward the Mississippi River.[14] The eastern portion is the humid, tall-grass region—the "low plains"—where light sediments, rearranged by wind erosion, lay in loess deposits of great depth. Streams were deeply incised, and, because it was a region of predominantly summer rainfall, were apt to be swollen with floodwaters during the emigrating season. These streams—even the insignificant ones—were difficult to cross because of the eroded, caving banks created in unstable soil. The low plains were singularly treeless except along the larger streams, where ash, elm, cottonwood, and similar broad-leaved trees were found in local abundance; otherwise the vegetation of the region consisted of such grasses as blue-stem (both sod and bunch) and several varieties of wild wheat. Flowers were abundant in the spring and early summer.

At the beginning of the emigration, large game was already scarce on the low plains. The buffalo were gone, and only an occasional antelope on a prairie rise or a deer in a streamside thicket remained. The Kansas Indians, who had not settled down to a "civilized" existence like the Shawnees and the more recently resettled Potawatomies, were forced to hunt far afield, bringing them into frequent conflict with their Pawnee neighbors.

While crossing the low plains, the emigrants' main concern was necessarily with sudden, violent storms and their effect upon stream-crossings, the management of their stock where there were no natural bounds to random movement, and the petty thievery of Indian bands. Grass and water were available everywhere, wood could be obtained along the streams, and the road was naturally good—neither steep nor hard on the hooves of the cattle.

The meridian of 98 degrees west longitude roughly approximated the beginning of the "high plains." This sub-humid, short-grass region abutting on the Rocky Mountains contained the uneroded fragments of the ancient debris apron, which, with progress westward, became increasingly apparent as bluffs and highlands until they finally gave way to outliers of the Rocky Mountains. Upon these firmer sediments the streams were not deeply incised, but flowed shallowly in broad valley bottoms. Stream-crossing, however, remained difficult because the shallowness concealed a sandy, fluid bottom requiring enormous motive power to pull vehicles through. There, the only trees were cottonwoods and willows, on islands in the larger streams, and ash and cedar trees in coves and canyons back of the bluffs. The lesser vegetation was grama, galleta, and buffalo grass, with an increasing amount of sagebrush as the mountains were approached. Further evidence of aridity existed in the appearance of small cactuses.

During the period of the emigration, buffalo were found in numbers on the high plains. Those who cared to risk horses in a chase (dangerous because of burrows made by the inhabitants of extensive prairie-dog towns) could usually have fresh meat. Antelope were plentiful, also rattlesnakes and wolves. In the early days the Sioux Indians encountered along the Platte River were often helpful, and at worst only a begging nuisance; but in the sixties they became extremely dangerous, after the Grattan Massacre of 1854.

Thus, the route across the high plains was not particularly bad. Stream-crossing became less of a problem, water and grass remained sufficient, and the road was good—although some heavy pulling was required in the sand hills along the Platte River, and there were a few steep grades. The worst hazard was the declining humidity that shrank the wood of wagon wheels until they became rickety; yet the same dryness made the heat of the day more bearable. The lack of firewood, for which *bois de vache*—dry buffalo dung—was substituted for cooking, was the great privation, for, without wood, there was no bright fire to alleviate the chill of evening, or for drying out after the frequent thundershowers.

Fort Laramie marked the end of the Great Plains and the entrance into the Rocky Mountains. The crossing of the range, in its strictest sense, was accomplished easily at a broad sag in the continental divide known as South Pass (so-called in contradistinction to the more northerly pass used by Lewis and Clark.)[15] However, the passage of that 7,550-foot gap was anticlimactic after the long approach by way of the Platte-Sweetwater Valley. Also, the highlands that lay beyond it—between the drainages of the Green and Bear rivers—certainly presented greater difficulties.

Immediately upon leaving Fort Laramie the character of the country changed. The Black Hills, outliers of the Rocky Mountains proper, crowded upon the North Platte River, and the minor streams flowing down from the hills interdicted the route of travel to create many steep ascents and descents. Individually, these grades were not particularly bad, but their frequency, combined with a rocky soil, wore out vehicles and beasts alike. Forage and water were readily available in the tributary drainages all along the North Platte River, and, while rounding the Black Hills (now known as the Laramie Range), there was wood also. Toilsome traveling was balanced by good camping conditions.

The Sweetwater Valley, which was reached by crossing the North Platte River (a dangerous stream which seldom could be forded), was a better natural road, but the rugged, barren ridges paralleling the stream nearly to South Pass created a far greater hazard than did a merely rough track. Erosion of the flanks of the ridges provided a granitic detritus that broke down into alkali compounds, and, rather than leaching away in that dry climate, it accumulated in dusty deposits and bitter waters. Such irritants were hard on people and stock; skilled management was required to get through without the loss of essential draught animals.

The aridity of the region beyond the Black Hills was reflected in its vegetative cover. Grass was sparse—even absent in places— and such plants as greasewood, creosote brush, and sagebrush became dominant. The last plant, which often grew to very large size, was the principal source of camp fuel. Prior to the gold rush, buffalo could usually be found along the emigrant route through the Rocky Mountains, antelope were common, and elk and grizzly bear were occasionally met in the adjacent hills. The little ground squirrels, called "picket-pins," and large jackrabbits formed the essential understory of the fauna, supporting a very vocal population of coyotes. Buffalo wolves were ready enough to pull down an abandoned horse or ox, quickly reducing such casualties of exhaustion, lameness, or alkali sickness to scattered, bleaching bones.

Westward of the South Pass the broad drainage basin of the Green River could be traversed by wagons almost at will, yet lack of water between streams sent most early emigrants looping southward around the Little Colorado Desert. The forty-niners—and others traveling in haste—often preferred to cut directly across that Rocky Mountain wasteland, frequently paying a high price for their temerity. Either way, there was another seldom-fordable river to cross—the Green—and a last barrier of rough hills to negotiate before the Rocky Mountains were left behind, and the lush valley of the Bear River was reached.

In addition to its dryness, the climate along this portion of the emigrant route was notable in another way: the variation in temperature between day and night was generally very great. Scorching days were followed by uncomfortably chilly nights, and ice might form in the water bucket in any summer month.

The Sweetwater-South Pass-Green River locality was essentially a middle ground between the Indian tribes. Hunting excursions were made here from the east by Sioux, Cheyenne, and Arapaho; from the north by Crow and Gros Ventres; from the west by Shoshoni and Bannocks; and from the south by Utes. War parties were also frequently abroad in search of horses, scalps, and glory; and yet, the emigrants suffered less here from Indian thievery than they had on the Great Plains, and were subjected to fewer Indian attacks than in the Snake River Valley farther west.

The valley of the Bear River provided a pleasant interlude

between two stark landscapes. Behind were the Rocky Mountains, and ahead, the Columbia Plateau. This "intermontane," which occupies the trench between the Rockies and the Cascade Range, from the northern rim of the Great Basin into the Province of Alberta, is an uneven area of mainly volcanic origin. It varies in elevation from 1,000 to 5,000 feet and is ruggedly eroded, with mountainous spurs and highlands interrupted by valleys.[16]

A succession of such river valleys—those of the Snake, Burnt, Powder, Grand Ronde, Umatilla, and Columbia rivers—provided a practicable route through an inhospitable region dominated by the recent-appearing lava flows. Only the crossing of the Blue Mountains was otherwise; here, rounded landforms carried a forest of pine and fir, with an understory of grass and brush. These timbered heights were a delightful contrast to the stony benches, thinly covered with sagebrush, over which the emigrant route passed below Fort Hall.

The Columbia Plateau was a harsh, barren land in other ways. Forage was scarce—more so than anywhere else along the emigrant route; water was often difficult to reach due to the precipitous nature of the canyon walls along the streams; and game was nearly absent. The many buffalo that once roamed the Great Plain of Snake River had disappeared by the end of the fur trade period around 1840,[17] leaving only a few antelope and mule deer. This scarcity was somewhat offset by the cheapness of fish taken by the Indians at the Salmon Falls and other fishing sites on the Snake River, and by occasional opportunities to purchase potatoes and beef from the semi-civilized Cayuse Indians living along the Umatilla River.

Food-wise, the Snake River country was an impoverished land even from the Indian viewpoint, and the ostentatious wealth of the emigrants, with their edible horses and cattle, presented a great temptation to the hungry Indians. So it was here that small parties were in the greatest danger. At first, depredations took the form of arrows surreptitiously shot at cattle in the hope they would die or be abandoned by the trail; later, when guns had been obtained, direct attacks were made upon small wagon trains for the purpose of plundering them.

After crossing the Blue Mountains, the emigrants were faced with less brutal terrain, but it was still a dry, sterile land as far as the Dalles of the Columbia, where that great river began its passage of the Cascade Range. This last mountain barrier did not equal the Rocky Mountains in elevation but exceeded them by far in ruggedness; there was no easy way through or over it. The

Columbia River breached the range through a gorge, a mighty rent extending to the foundations of the volcanic rock. Halfway through the gorge were the Cascades, where the river foamed over and around great blocks of basalt (according to Indian legend, the ruins of a prehistoric bridge), forcing all but expert rivermen to make a laborious portage. For those who did not care to go by water from the Dalles, there was but one alternative prior to 1846: they could pack over the Indian trails, which were equally wearying. A road through that formidable terrain was beyond the simple means of the emigrants.

In 1846 a road over the Cascade Range south of Mount Hood was opened. It was a rude track cut through such forest as the emigrants had never seen, crossing glacial rivers with a gradient that made them powerful beyond their size (compared with an equal flow in a prairie or Rocky Mountain stream), and negotiating grades steeper than those met with anywhere else on the nearly 2,000-mile trek.

Neither rough terrain nor mean rivers were any novelty, but the forest was. Beginning with a light stand of oak and a scattering of yellow pine on the eastern flank of the range, the forest became increasingly denser and the trees mightier to the west. As the emigrants descended into Willamette Valley, they passed through a forest such as they had never known—a dim, damp world beneath great Douglas firs, western hemlocks, red cedars, and Sitka spruce trees, where the ground cover was moss and the infrequent natural openings were choked with bracken fern, sallal brush, or devilsclub, and openings made by fire were tangles of laurel scrub or vine maple. Stock starved in that forest or sickened on the laurel, and the emigrants, worn down by their prolonged journey, fell sick from the dampness.

It was a misfortune of the emigration that the arrival at the Cascade Mountains coincided with the onset of the wet season (the coastal summer is typically dry), bringing leaden skies and those persistent rains sometimes described as "Oregon mist."

Whichever way they came—down the Columbia River by raft, scow, or canoe, usually piloted by Indians; scrambling over the rough pack trails through and around the gorge; or up over the Barlow Pass by wagon—the emigrants arrived at last in their valley, described as follows by one who came in 1842:

> You who have never seen what is called a prairie country, can form but a faint idea of the beauty of its scenery. A diversity of oak-covered hills, cleared of underbrush as if by the hand of art, and plains covered with the most

luxuriant verdure, intersected with small streams from the mountains, whose serpentine courses divide them into convenient farms, which are supplied with wood and timber from the narrow groves along their banks, or the oak groves on the intervening hills, constitute the face of this valley as viewed from my residence eastward until the sight is lost in the smokey atmosphere thirty miles distant. . . .[18]

Route

The Oregon Trail began in the town of Independence, Missouri, at the southwest corner of Courthouse Square. From there one branch went south, down Liberty Street and along the Blue Ridge, following the trace of the Santa Fe freighters; and another went west, on Lexington Street, pointing generally toward the neighboring town of Westport, which is now in the city of Kansas City, Missouri.

Those emigrants who went south crossed the Blue River about 15 miles out at a ford, until the Red Bridge was built over that stream. This structure is remembered today in the name of Red Bridge Road. Beyond the crossing was a flour mill—Fitzhugh's, operated by Watts after 1837—where emigrants could purchase flour ground by waterpower; and there was also a campground just short of the Missouri state line. The latter was crossed at New Santa Fe, also known as Little Santa Fe. Here, 17.9 miles from Independence, was the beginning of the Indian Territory where the sale of whiskey was forbidden by law; hence, New Santa Fe was a mere collection of "doggeries." The first place of importance west of the line was the Lone Elm Campground, 32 miles from Independence, where the Santa Fe-Oregon Trail was joined by a feeder route from the town of Westport.

Emigrants who went west out of Independence found numerous wagon trails crossing the 10 miles to Westport[19]—another jumping-off place, but to a lesser degree than Independence. Whether Westport was a starting place or merely a way point, the emigrant could leave it by going either south or southwesterly. This route, which probably developed as a supply route to New Santa Fe, had a cross-connection outside of town to the second route. This brought most of the emigrants going the Westport way onto one track a few miles beyond the Shawnee Mission. Farther on, there was a fork in the road that allowed emigrants to join the Santa Fe-Oregon Trail at Lone Elm Campground, or near the junction of the Santa Fe and Oregon routes, about 39 miles from the town of

Independence.

At that major junction, west of present Gardner, Kansas, the Oregon- and California-bound emigrants stuck to the right-hand track. Nearly eight miles beyond the junction, the trail passed around Observation Point, which many emigrants climbed for the view—it was the highest hill these flatlanders had ever seen.

About 54 miles from Independence the Oregon Trail reached the Wakarusa River and it was forded either there, which is southeast of present Lawrence, Kansas, quite near another eminence called the Blue Mound, or four miles upstream. Most traffic went over at the first crossing, and it was there that an Indian by the name of Blue Jacket later established a ferry and roadhouse.

Once across the Wakarusa, the emigrants followed the high land south of the Kansas River, continued westward to Coon Point—71 miles from Independence—and Big Spring at the head of Coon Hollow. There, 76 miles out, the track forked, the right branch heading for a crossing of the Kaw, or Kansas River, and the left continuing on to a crossing near the agency for the Kansas Indians. Those who took the nearer crossing, at present Topeka, had first to cross Shunganunga Creek, and then usually found it necessary to ferry across the Kansas. This crossing, 88 miles out, was improvised in the earliest days; later, Pappan's Ferry solved the problem there. The alternate to this lower crossing was to continue on the south side of the river, past the Baptist mission and the site of Chouteau's trading post to an "upper crossing" near the agency village of Union. The river could be forded there at low water, but because emigrants usually arrived with the spring rise, ferriage was again a necessity. There was a commercial ferry there after 1846.

A few miles beyond the upper crossing the two routes joined again, 110 miles out, where travelers after 1848 found the Catholic mission of St. Mary's. Ten miles farther, at the crossing of the "Red" or Little Vermillion, a toll bridge operated by a Michigan Potawatomi Indian, Louis Vieux, appeared soon after 1848. The emigrant was now on the frontier of the "civilized" Indians—the Shawnee, Kansas, and Potawatomi—all of whom had adopted many of the ways of the white man—including sharp trading.

The "Black" or Big Vermillion was crossed 152 miles out, and there was—after 1849—a branching of the track on the north bank. The left fork crossed the Big Blue River near Alcove Spring, at what was called the Independence Crossing, because it was predominantly used in the days when most traffic on the trail originated from that town. The other fork continued up the east bank of the Big Blue to a junction with the St. Joe Road at present Marysville, Kansas, where the river could be crossed on Marshall's Ferry. During the early Oregon Trail period, all traffic originating in the Independence-Westport area used the Independence Crossing, 165 miles out—an uncertain prospect, because fording might be practicable one day and entirely impossible for days afterward, according to the volume and frequency of the spring rains.

There was a "Junction of the Ways" 180 miles from Independence, where the St. Joe Road came into the older Oregon Trail. It is worth noting that there was some early emigrant use of the route that became the St. Joe Road—perhaps even before 1846—but it was in the nature of shortcutting, and was not established as a distinct route until the gold rush traffic substituted more northerly jumping-off places for the cholera-ridden Independence-Westport area.

It was on or near the St. Joe Road that the Pony Express and the Overland Stage lines were later operated, and one of the stations-Cottonwood, now Hollenberg State Park—lies just north of the "Junction of the Ways." An alternate to the St. Joe Road, the Oketo Cutoff, comes into the original emigrant route 193 miles out—about three miles north of the Kansas-Nebraska state line.

The Oregon Trail continued northwesterly on the east side of the Little Blue River, past the interesting Rock Creek Station-Fremont Springs area—201 miles out—and soon turned west toward "The Narrows" near the headwaters of the river. Thereafter the trail crossed a low divide into the sandhill country on the "Coast of Nebraska," a land so openly dreary that a single cottonwood tree—the Lone Tree—was a monumental landmark. In the early days of the trail, this country was a battleground for Kansas and Pawnee Indians. The emigrants were generally safe from all but petty thievery, but in the 1860s, it was an area where only defensible points and strong parties were safe from Sioux and Cheyenne warriors.

Some 310 miles from Independence, as the Platte River was approached, the Nebraska City, or Old Fort Kearny, road was joined—after 1848—at a place that came to be known as "Dogtown." During the gold rush and later periods, considerable military, emigrant, and freight traffic was fed into the Oregon Trail at this point, which lay outside the Fort Kearny military reservation.

Fort Kearny—the city's name, Kearney, is a misspelling of the name of Stephen Watts Kearny of Dragoon fame—was begun in 1848 as the result of an earlier decision to garrison key points along the Oregon Trail in order to protect and assist the emigrants. Situated in the river bottom 230 miles from Independence, the second Fort Kearny was better placed, logistically, but in an unhealthful location. Its role was essentially that of a base from which the posts and stations farther west could be supplied.

Three miles beyond the fort and close to the line of the military reservation, was "Doby Town," which performed all the necessary functions of a red-light district; and 11 miles farther on lay a fording place that cross-connected the Oregon Trail with the fur trader-missionary-Mormon trail along the north bank of the Platte River. This last route originated in the Bellevue-Council Bluffs area on the Missouri River.

Another ford of importance—the Platte River could be crossed at many places here—lay at the forks, 418 miles from Independence. Here it was possible to cross over to the north-side route, or, as Fremont had done, to get upon the point of land between the forks. However, few emigrants followed his example; usually they preferred to move up the South Platte River to one of a number of recognized crossings. The major crossings were at 444 miles (Ford No. 1, opposite O'Fallon's Bluffs); at 453 miles (Ford No. 2, opposite Paxton); at 463 miles (Ford No. 3, near Roscoe); at 485 miles (Ford No. 4, past Brule—the famous Beauvais, or Lower California, Crossing); and at the mouth of Lodgepole Creek (the Upper California Crossing of the late Oregon Trail period). Fords 1, 2, and 3 led to direct crossings of the sliver of land between the forks, feeding into a track up the North Platte, but the Lower California Crossing led to a broad plateau, from which it descended to the North Platte 20 miles farther on. The route by way of the upper crossing made a long detour before joining the North Platte between Courthouse Rock and Chimney Rock.

But it was the Lower California Crossing that was most used, and the evidence of this is still plainly visible on "California Hill," where the trail climbed up from the South Platte; and on "Windlass Hill," where it dropped into Ash Hollow, near the North Platte. Ash Hollow, 504 miles from Independence, was the place where the track from the fords below the Lower California came back into the principal route. Wagons coming up the North Platte River Valley could sometimes come all the way to Ash Hollow along the bank, but in wet seasons they had to leave the river at Cedar Grove and cross a ridge into Ash Hollow several miles above its mouth.

Above Ash Hollow, the Oregon Trail continued up the bottom land on the south side of the North Platte, passing Courthouse Rock at 561 miles, and joining with the alternate by way of the Upper California Crossing at 571 miles. Thus, the Oregon Trail was, for a few miles, essentially a single track. It is worth mentioning that this junction was 10 miles beyond a crossing of the North Platte—a ford that was later the site of the Camp Clarke bridge, near present Bridgeport.

But the Oregon Trail followed one track for only 20 miles. After 1848 it split at 591 miles, with the northern track following a new route through Mitchell Pass, close behind Scotts Bluff. The earlier route, by way of the pass that now bears the name of Joseph Robidoux, continued to be used for some years, although in lessening degree. The two were reunited 615 miles from Independence at Horse Creek, the scene of treaty negotiations with many Indian tribes in the summer of 1851.

From Horse Creek to Fort Laramie, 650 miles from Independence, the Oregon Trail was a single track again but, in the vicinity of the fort, a very complicated pattern developed. This resulted from the numerous stream crossings here and from the several route possibilities to the west. Fort Laramie was the hub of a transportation network oriented essentially east-west in the pre-railroad days, but north-south after 1868. Only the earlier pattern is of interest here.

The trapper-missionary-Mormon trail on the north side of the Platte River paralleled the Oregon Trail from Fort Kearny to the Laramie River. At the latter, it crossed the North Platte opposite the site of Fort William, about three-quarters of a mile above the mouth of the Laramie River. In 1847, the Mormons who came by this route varied the crossing by ferrying opposite Fort Platte, three-quarters of a mile above the early crossing. In 1849, the army established a ferry 0.2 mile below the Mormon Ferry site that remained the crossing until an iron bridge was built between the two ferry sites in 1876. Until 1850, all traffic coming up the north side of the river crossed above the junction with the Laramie—at the trapper's ford, the Mormon Ferry, or the army Ferry—because it was not considered possible to continue up the north bank of the main stream (the North Platte) with wagons. However, the opening of Child's Cutoff in 1850 made crossing the North Platte an option instead of a necessity.

On the south side of the river, the Oregon Trail first approached the Laramie River as two branches. One was on the bottom land and the other on slightly higher ground. Both crossed the Laramie nearly opposite Fort William. Later, after Fort William was replaced by Fort John (Fort Laramie) a mile to the east, another approach on even higher ground was developed, and it descended in trident fashion to a number of crossings scattered along the Laramie River.

The tracks leading west out of Fort Laramie were equally complex. The early Oregon Trail left the vicinity as a hill road, which stayed on the dry benchland to Warm Spring, at mile 662. The Mormons who ferried the North Platte River in 1847 at the site of the abandoned Fort Platte, opened a new route to Warm Spring along the south bank of the North Platte, past Register Cliff. Later traffic used both routes by starting out along the ridge and dropping down to Register Cliff by way of "Mexican Hill."

After merging near Warm Spring, the route west divided again at mile 666. The hill road, to the left, went up Cottonwood Creek and appears to have been the original route. It was also the one followed by the Mormons in 1847. It also served, to mile 677, as a part of the haul road the army used to begin bringing timber from the Laramie Range, in 1849. The river road, which stayed closer to the North Platte as far as the crossing of Horseshoe Creek at mile 683, came later, but was better known because of its connection with the stage, Pony Express, and telegraph lines. Horseshoe Creek was also the point at which the latter day Bozeman Road diverged from the Oregon Trail.

The hill and river roads through the Black Hills came together at mile 700, and remained a single track to the Deer Creek Crossing at mile 739, at present Glenrock. There was a crossing of the North Platte River at the mouth of Deer Creek that the forty-niners popularized, and in 1851, a man known to the emigrants simply as "Reshaw" (John Richard) built a flimsy bridge there to connect with the road on the north bank. The structure lasted less than two years, and was replaced by another, built by Reshaw and his partners, near mile 761.

The most notable crossing of the North Platte was on the outskirts of the present city of Casper, at mile 766. It was there that the earliest emigrants forded or improvised a ferry until the Mormons went into the business of ferriage and continued a seasonal service at that point until construction of the Reshaw bridges made the ferry unprofitable. The construction of Louis Guinard's "Old Platte Bridge" at the same point had a disastrous effect on the Reshaw enterprise, and this third was the crossing until the abandonment of Fort Caspar in 1867, when both were burned by Indians. Thereafter, the principal crossing was a bridge at Fort Fetterman, reached by a spur off of the Oregon Trail at mile 716.

When the North Platte River was not fordable, there was an alternate crossing near the Red Buttes (Bessemer Bend), which could be reached by continuing on the south bank for an additional eight miles. It was here that the trappers had customarily crossed.

Most emigrants crossed at the Casper site, going from there along the north bank of the river until they rounded Emigrant Gap Ridge. The route through the Gap was a later development. All the tracks—whether from the Fort Caspar crossing by the river road or from the Red Buttes crossing—came together again in the vicinity of the Poison Spring at mile 776, and continued west as one through Rock Avenue, past Willow Spring, and over Prospect Hill to Independence Rock, at mile 815. This was also the place where the Sweetwater River first was crossed.

The Oregon Trail continued up the Sweetwater Valley as a single track to mile 831, where there was a seven-mile-long alternate that stayed farther south of the river as far as Split Rock (mile 838). There also were branches near Three Crossings. At mile 848, a left fork bowed around the southern end of the Sweetwater Rocks, and at 851 miles the route split again, with a variant branching to the left to go up through a sandy gap, while the main route went through a rocky canyon and included the difficult Three Crossings of the Sweetwater River. The route returned to a single track at mile 860, east of the Ice Slough.

At mile 872, the Seminoe Cutoff branched to the left, remaining on the south side of the Sweetwater River as far as the Burnt Ranch, at mile 905. The Burnt Ranch was also the origin of the Lander Road, built westward close to the Wind River Range in 1857-1858. It offered a more direct route to Fort Hall. By taking the Lander Road, one saved 73 miles, but at a cost of passing through the rugged mountains that flank the Salt River Valley.

The Oregon Trail continued as a single track through South Pass, mile 914, past Pacific Springs and the Dry Sandy Crossing, to the Parting of the Ways. There, at mile 932, the Sublette Cutoff, which should be known as Greenwood's Cutoff, branched right and headed across the Little Colorado Desert for the Bear River. The Parting of the Ways referred to here is not the one marked by the monument alongside Wyoming State Highway 28. That monument was mistakenly placed where the Green River-South Pass stage road crossed the Oregon Trail at mile 924. There was also a connection to the Sublette Cutoff at mile 942.

Near the Big Sandy Station site were two alternate connections.

To the left, at mile 965, was a cutoff to a lower crossing of the Green River. The other, known as the Slate Creek connection to the Sublette Cutoff, split off to the right at mile 966. Four miles farther, the Kenney Cutoff, also headed toward the Sublette Cutoff, turned left and followed closely up the north bank of the Green River. There were a number of fords and ferries over Green River above and below the mouth of Big Sandy, creating an elaborate maze of cross-connections.

At the crossing of Hams Fork, in mile 996, two cutoffs branched off to the right from the main route. One approached the Sublette by way of Hams Fork, while the other went by way of Blacks Fork and Muddy Creek, across to the Fort Bridger-Fort Hall leg of the principal route, coming into it again at mile 1046. Three miles beyond the Hams Fork crossing an alternate to the principal route was opened by the Mormons in 1847. They had stayed closer to the Green River after they had crossed it at mile 977.

The rest of the route to Fort Bridger remained uncomplicated until the area around the trading post was reached. Then one fork—the older track—turned northwest from the site of the first trading post. And with the opening of the Salt Lake trail and the relocation of the trading post a mile to the south, the Oregon Trail soon shifted in that direction.

The trail from Fort Bridger toward the Soda Springs forked at mile 1067, on the Bear River divide, with the left track descending by way of Bridger Creek into the Bear River Valley, and the principal route continued along the high ground to come down into the valley at mile 1083. A mile beyond the latter was reunited with the Bridger Creek alternate.

At mile 1093 the principal route was rejoined by the Sublette Cutoff—that shortcut had saved 47 miles over the southern, Fort Bridger route—and the Dempsey Cutoff came in at mile 1097. The travelers who chose the Dempsey saved a few more miles, at the cost of a little more rough country. Thereafter the trail was again essentially a single track to the crossing of the Thomas Fork, mile 1109, where an alternate starting at mile 1118 swung past Smith's trading post near the outlet of Bear Lake.

Beginning in 1849, there was a very important junction beyond the Soda Springs. At the foot of Soda Point, where the Bear River turns sharply to the south, Hudspeth's Cutoff branched from the Oregon Trail at mile 1159 and continued westward through the mountains toward a junction with the California Trail in the Raft River Valley. There was also a track down the Bear River from Soda Point.

Continuing on the Oregon Trail, the Lander Road rejoined it at mile 1194, and the California Trail pulled away at the crossing of Raft River at mile 1265. The main trail continued along the south bank of the Snake River to the Three Island Crossing. There was also a crossing of the Snake River above Salmon Falls, although the actual route on the north bank is not clear.

At the Three Island Crossing—mile 1397—emigrants had the option of fording or ferrying, provided either could be managed. There was no commercial ferry service until Glenn's Ferry was established several miles upstream in the 1860s. They also could have stayed on the south bank, where the terrain was much more difficult. This south alternate was seven miles longer. The two routes came together again opposite Fort Boise, at mile 1517. The Snake River was crossed at Fort Boise by fording or ferrying, depending upon the stage of the river. Commercial ferry service was established there in the early 1850s.

The Malheur River is crossed at mile 1527—it was there that Stephen Meek left the trail to lead a wagon train into the eastern Oregon desert, a disastrous trek over a shortcut that was totally unsuited to wagon travel. That was also the point of departure of at least one more "lost wagon train" in 1853. The Oregon Trail remained uncomplicated—albeit rough—from the Malheur Crossing to the valley of the Grande Ronde River.

There were three routes—probably based on Indian trails—out of the Grande Ronde Valley. Branching off at 1640 miles, the westernmost track passed over the ridge behind present LaGrande, descended to the Grande Ronde River where Hilgard State Park is today, and continued over the Blue Mountains along the approximate alignment of old U.S. Highway 30. The middle route climbed the slope on the north side of the canyon by which the Grand Ronde River debouches into the valley, and then swung into the first route at mile 1658. just how important this alternate was is not certain, but it was recorded in 1883 as the "old emigrant wagon road."[20] Both of these tracks passed Emigrant Springs, and their distances are the same. The third, or easternmost route, is the one opened by John C. Fremont in 1843. It passed over the Blue Mountains at the northern end of the Grande Ronde Valley, but had no evident advantage over the route by which the Cayuse Chief Sticus guided the emigrants in 1843. However, the sectional map prepared by Fremont's cartographer for the use of emigrants probably led at least a few to follow his trail.[21]

In the Blue Mountains, subsequent development of the emigrant tracks into freight and stage roads, particularly during the Idaho

Gold Rush, tended to obscure the original routes. However, the resultant confusion is inconsequential compared to the destruction wrought by more recent agricultural uses, of all evidence of the roundabout loop by which the emigrants of 1843 (and to a lesser degree those of the years up to 1848) maneuvered in order to include Whitman's mission in their route.

William Ghent has corresponded with President B. L. Penrose of Whitman College concerning the early route beyond the Blue Mountains. Dr. Penrose thought there was no doubt the wagon trains of 1843 came down Cabbage Hill, but, beyond Cayuse Post Office at mile 1687, he could only describe the route as "at first going north to Athena, Weston, and Walla Walla, but later continuing down the Umatilla past Pendleton."[22] That is where the matter stands up to the present. Excepting the Whitman Mission site, at mile 1710, the entire route is in question—from the foot of the Blue Mountains to Fort Walla Walla, at mile 1730. From that point some emigrants embarked on various craft to descend the Columbia River, but more traveled with difficulty along the sandy south bank of the river.

The unnecessary deviousness of the Whitman loop was at once evident, and an emigrant of 1844 recorded that his party went west along the west bank of the Umatilla River to Butter Creek, where "Whitman sent an Indian to pilot us thru this place to Well Spring then to Willow Creek, where we again struck the Emigrant Road from Willow Creek to Rock Creek, where we crossed the John Day river. . . ."[23]

From the above it would seem that those emigrants of 1843 who elected to follow the south bank of the Columbia River had turned inland at the mouth of Willow Creek, proceeding up that stream and Eight-mile Canyon to what eventually became the established Oregon Trail, and that the route across the dry benchland, from the Umatilla River to Willow Creek by way of Well Spring, was only a logical shortening of the route—particularly desirable after some emigrants began descending the Umatilla River to the Columbia instead of taking the Whitman loop.

The route beyond the Blue Mountains was stabilized by 1846. After descending from the mountains, the emigrants turned westward, crossing the Umatilla River in the vicinity of present Pendleton, mile 1690, and again at present Echo, mile 1712, from which the route crossed over the drainages as follows: to Butter Creek, mile 1722, and Willow Creek, mile 1752—a long, dry pull somewhat alleviated by the presence of Well Spring; to the John

Day River, mile 1775; and to the Deschutes River, mile 1804, where the route touched briefly on the Columbia River. Another 15 miles over the basaltic bluffs above Celilo Falls brought the emigrants to the Dalles of the Columbia—that rock-bound gutter through which the Columbia River raced with such power and majesty. Some stopped at the Methodist Mission, mile 1819, but most continued on to the mouth of Chenoweth Creek, at mile 1822, which place marked the end of wagon travel until 1846.

The mouth of Chenoweth Creek provided a snug harbor where rafts and scows built with timber from the neighboring hills could be launched, and where Indian canoes or Hudson's Bay Company bateaux could be obtained for the trip down the Columbia River.

Although there was no road through the Columbia River gorge to accommodate wagons, there were several trails. One, the Jason Lee cattle trail, by which the missionaries had taken cattle from the Willamette Valley to their stations east of the Cascade Range, was traveled in the opposite direction in order to bring emigrant stock into the valley. It climbed over the ridges projecting from the north side of Mount Hood, going by way of Lost Lake, and then down Sandy River. Another, and equally rugged trail kept closer to the south bank of the Columbia. An alternative was to cross the river—with Indian help—above the Cascades, and to then descend the north bank to Fort Vancouver. All three trails were used by emigrants, packing their possessions on the backs of beasts—or on their own backs—to get past the last mountain barrier and into the Willamette Valley.

Those who did not want to abandon their wagons and heavier possessions rafted or boated down from Chenoweth Creek. They arrived at the Cascades, mile 1862, where there was a three- to five-mile portage. Indian help was available there. Then they floated on down the river on the rafts or scows that had been run over the rapids empty and caught below. Once past the fearsome Cape Horn, at mile 1877, the voyage could be terminated at the mouth of the Sandy River, mile 1887, or continued down to the mouth of the Willamette River and up that stream to Oregon City, with Indian helpers poling against the sluggish current. Those who disembarked at the mouth of the Sandy were able to put their wagons together and travel overland the few remaining miles to Oregon City.

After 1845, the opening of the Barlow Road over the Cascade Range provided a wagon road all the way to Oregon City. Some emigrants of 1845 were so discouraged with the prospect of the slow and expensive transit of the Columbia River gorge that they decided to attempt a passage over the range south of Mount Hood. Traveling south to Tygh Valley, mile 1846, the train waited there while Samuel K. Barlow led a scouting party westward over an Indian trail. A practicable crossing was located via Barlow Pass, but the lateness of the season prevented completion of a road that year. Wagons were left near the head of White River, mile 1872, and they completed the journey afoot. The road was roughed through the following spring and was used by emigrants thereafter.

The entire journey from Independence to Oregon City—by the standard route touching Fort Bridger, but not Whitman Mission— was 1,932 miles via the Columbia-Willamette Rivers, and 1,930 miles via the Barlow Road. Of course, up to 75 miles could be saved by using various cutoffs, many route combinations were possible, some advantageous and others not noticeably so.

This discussion of the route to Oregon has not included the Applegate Trail, by which some emigrants reached Oregon through its southern door, because that approach, like the two one-shot routes across the eastern Oregon desert, does not warrant the effort required to trace it out.[24] The cutoff just west of the John Day River to a connection with the Barlow Road at Tygh Valley has also been left out. It was a late development, opened in 1864 by freighters after the building of Sherar's Bridge provided a crossing above the mouth of the Deschutes River.

Admittedly, such a brief overview as this does not do justice to so complicated a route as the Oregon Trail. It is offered only as a device for relating historic sites to each other and to the overall route.

Endnotes

[1] Oscar O. Winther, *The Great Northwest* (New York: Alfred A. Knopf, 1948), 29-30.

[2] Washington Irving, *"Astoria"* in *The Works of Washington Irving* (New York: Pollard & Moss, 1882), II: 331-85

[3] Phillip A. Rollins, ed., *The Discovery of the Oregon Trail; Robert Stuart's Narrative... 1812-1813* (New York: C. Scribner's Sons, 1935). For a more recent presentation of the Stuart narrative, see Kenneth A. Spaulding, ed., *On the Oregon Trail; Robert Stuart's Journey* (Norman: Univ. of Oklahoma Press, 1953).

[4] LeRoy R. Hafen, *The Mountain Men and the Fur Trade of the Far West* (Glendale, Calif.: Arthur C. Clark, 1965), I: 79.

[5] U.S. Congress, *The Old Oregon Trail* (Washington: 1925), 84.

[6] J. Cecil Alter, *James Bridger* (Columbus: Long's, 1951), 110.

[7] Walter E. Meacham, *Old Oregon Trail* (Manchester, N.H.: The Clarke Press, 1948), 6-10.

[8] "'Doctor' Robert Newell," in *Oregon Historical Quarterly*, 9 (June 1908): 103-26.

[9] Walter E. Meacham, *Barlow Road* (Portland, Oreg., 1947), provides general information.

[10] The figures for 1841-42 are from Winther, 122; and those for the remaining years are from Phillip H. Parrish, *Wagons West* (Portland, Oreg.: James, Kerns & Abbot, 1943), 7, 18-19.

[11] Walter E. Meacham, *Applegate Trail* (Portland, Oreg., 1947), provides general information.

[12] Parrish, 19.

[13] Information on the effect of these events is in the Idaho Historical Society's Reference Series leaflet, No. 236.

[14] W. P. Webb, *The Great Plains (Boston: Ginn & Co.*, 1931), 10

[15] Reuben G. Thwaites, ed., *Early Western Travels*, 21: 58, fn.

[16] Winther, 4

[17] Osborne Russell, *Journal of a Trapper* (Portland: Oregon Historical Society, 1955), 123.

[18] Ibid. 187-88.

[19] Archer B. Hulbert, ed., *The American Transcontinental Trails* (Colorado Springs: Stewart Commission on Western History, 1926), I: Map No. 2.

[20] From a compilation prepared from General Land Office Survey plats in the Whitman-Wallowa National Forest Office, Pendleton, Oregon. (A copy was made August 10, 1972.)

[21] Charles Preuss, compiler, "Topographical Map of the Road from Missouri to Oregon" (Baltimore, Md.: E. Weber & Co., 1846), 7 sections.

[22] William J. Ghent, *The Road to Oregon* (New York: Tudor, 1934), 147.

[23] William D. Stillwell, Letter, 1916 (Oregon Historical Society, Misc. Overland Journeys to the Pacific), concerning his experiences enroute to Oregon in 1844.

[24] Information on the Applegate Trail is available in Meacham, *Applegate Trail*, 27; and Meek's Cutoff, through eastern Oregon, in Roland K. Clark & Lowell Tiller, *Terrible Trail: The Meek Cut-off*, 1845 (Caldwell, Ida: Caxton, 1966).

1

Independence to Fort Kearny

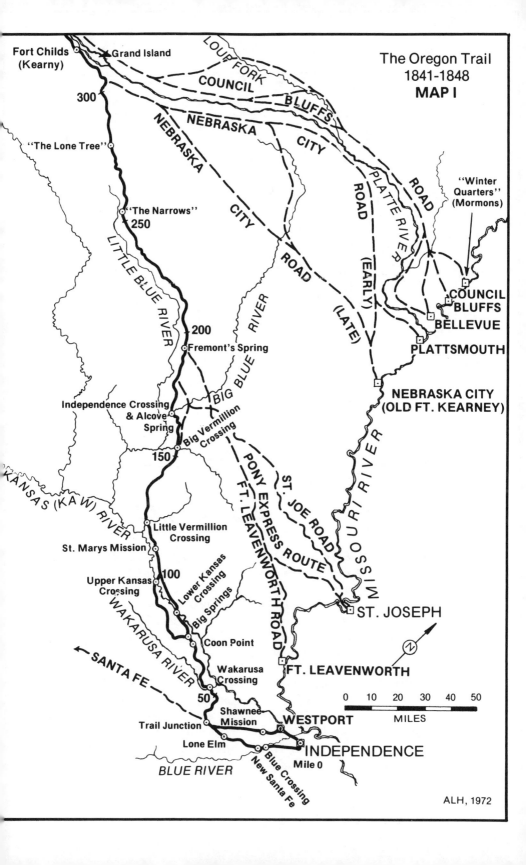

The Oregon Trail
1841-1848
MAP I

Fort Childs (Kearny)
Grand Island
LOUP FORK
COUNCIL
BLUFFS
300
NEBRASKA
CITY
PLATTE RIVER ROAD
"Winter Quarters" (Mormons)
"The Lone Tree"
ROAD
COUNCIL BLUFFS
NEBRASKA CITY
(EARLY)
BELLEVUE
"The Narrows"
250
ROAD
PLATTSMOUTH
LITTLE BLUE RIVER
BIG BLUE RIVER
(LATE)
200
Fremont's Spring
NEBRASKA CITY (OLD FT. KEARNEY)
Independence Crossing & Alcove Spring
BIG
Big Vermillion Crossing
150
KANSAS (KAW) RIVER
PONY EXPRESS ROUTE
ST. JOE ROAD
MISSOURI RIVER
Little Vermillion Crossing
St. Marys Mission
FT. LEAVENWORTH ROAD
Upper Kansas Crossing
100
Lower Kansas Crossing
ST. JOSEPH
WAKARUSA RIVER
Big Springs
SANTA FE
Coon Point
FT. LEAVENWORTH
Wakarusa Crossing
50
N
Shawnee Mission
0 10 20 30 40 50
Trail Junction
WESTPORT
MILES
Lone Elm
INDEPENDENCE
Blue Crossing
Mile 0
BLUE RIVER
New Santa Fe

ALH, 1972

OREGON TRAIL

INDEPENDENCE, MO., VICINITY MAP

Key: 1. Present City Hall; 2. Original Courthouse; 3. Site of the Weston Blacksmith Shop (1840s); 4. The Younger Cabin (1837, and now the Independence Visitor Center); 5. Present Hotel Independence (on the site of an 1834 hotel replaced by the Nebraska House, 1837-1840); 6. Marshal's House (1859); 7. The Old Jail (1859), now a museum; 8. Col. Noland's Tavern and Inn (1846); 9. Independence Spring (now covered over); 10. Independence Spring (city water, not spring water, but presently located in a charming sunken garden); 11. The road to Independence Landing, 3½ miles north; 12. Original Santa Fe Trail (used by Oregon-bound emigrants for nearly 40 miles); 13. Independence-Westport Road, an alternate route for Oregon traffic. The southwest corner of Courthouse Square—The intersection of Liberty and Lexington streets—is taken as the origin of the Oregon Trail, and mileage shown on the route map is reckoned from there. The National Frontier Trails Center is located at Spring and Pacific streets, a half-mile southwest of Independence Square.

Independence Courthouse as it appeared in 1855. The Oregon Trail began at the southwest corner of the square.

INDEPENDENCE COURTHOUSE SQUARE
Mile 0.0 — Lexington and Liberty Streets

The square is the center of the town of Independence, around which clustered establishments catering to the needs of emigrants (provisioning and equipment stores, blacksmith and wagon shops, inns and saloons, and markets selling oxen, mules and horses). See Independence, Missouri, Vicinity Map for identified sites.

Being both the last significant point of supply and the place of convergence of early routes from the Mississippi Valley, this square stood at the beginning of the Oregon Trail up to 1849. Emigrants camped on the outskirts of the town and wagon trains commonly formed up along Liberty and Lexington streets, adjacent to the square.

George McKinstry, May 21, 1846: "I find that the best place to fit out is at Independence oxen can be had at 25 $ pr yoke mules & Horses from 30 to 40 $ pr. head flour this year 4 $ pr bbl. . . ." [275: 1, 205]

James A. Pritchard, April 22, 1849. "Indipendence is a handsome flourishing town with a high situation, three miles from the Missouri River on the South side And Surrounded by one of the most beautiful & fertile countries of any Town in the

Nation . . . The Emegrants were encamped in every direction for miles around the place awaiting the time to come for their departure. Such were the crowded condition of the Streets of Ind by long trains of Ox teams mule teams men there with stock for Sale and men there to purchase stock that it was all most impossible to pass along. . . ." [317: 54-55]

WPA Writers Project, 1939. "In Courthouse Square is the brick Jackson County Courthouse, part of which was erected in 1836 . . . The first Jackson County Courthouse . . . 107 W. Kansas Ave., was built in 1827 at the southeast corner of Lynn St. and Lexington Ave. The building cost $150 and is of white oak and walnut logs cut by a slave. Weatherboarding, put on the west end to preserve the structure, and a porch, have been added." [146: 43]

Merrill J. Mattes, 1969. "Independence became the third and most important point of overland departure [after Fort Osage (1808) and Chouteau's Landing (1821)] . . . A modern shopping center surrounding a splendid brick courthouse, built on the site of the 1849 courthouse, now dominates the square which once echoed to the braying of mules, the bellowing of oxen, and the blasphemies of their drivers. The only tangible links with the past are a protected 'emigrant spring,' a log cabin dubiously represented as the original 1827 courthouse, and the restored Jackson County jail and Marshal's House, of 1859 vintage." [249: 106] (See 107-08 for a description of the town during the Oregon Trail period.)

Gregory M. Franzwa, 1972. "Henry Page, moving west in 1849, stopped in Independence long enough to describe the courthouse which, with its fanlight over the door and its cupola, made him think of the college chapel at Middlebury, Conn. He noted that the green grass of the square was kept from the livestock of the emigrants by a rail fence." P. 93: "Return to the south side of the square, along Lexington. This, according to Mrs. [Pauline] Fowler [archivist of the Jackson County Historical Society], is the location of the famous drawing of the square at Independence, showing the courthouse of the 1840s [See 146: 37] . . . It was Mrs. Fowler who discovered only in 1971, the substantial evidence that the courthouse shown in that old drawing is the third courthouse, and not the second. . . . The second is thought to have been razed and the third built on at least part of the original foundation, which is still in evidence in the basement of the present building. The third courthouse, shown in the picture, is inside the fourth, and the fourth is inside the fifth and present courthouse." [141: 91, 93] (See 82-95 for additional information on the town during the Oregon Trail period.)

See Independence, Mo., Vicinity Map for other sites and structures of historical importance near the Courthouse Square.

USGS map, Independence, Mo., 1:24,000, 1964 ed., rev. 1970.

INDEPENDENCE SPRING
Mile 0.0L⅓ — SE corner, Dodgion St. & Truman Rd.
Independence, Missouri

One of the two great Independence springs was located across Dodgion Street from this site, a few yards to the west. Outflow from that spring now is piped directly into the storm water main below Truman Road. The water oozing from the rocks at the bottom of the grotto actually is city water—it is turned off in winter.

Merrill J. Mattes, 1969. Mentioned as a tangible link with the past. [249: 106]

Gregory M. Franzwa, 1978. ". . . the old Younger cabin . . . was relocated from Walnut Street in the 1970s. Just past it is the open air stone garden area. Stairs lead down to a sunken space, and at the bottom is a stone wall, out of which flows a stream of water. This is said to be one of two principal springs which supplied water to the families moving west. It is said that, without those springs, Independence could not have survived. The spring originally rose in the berm just west of the present location, later was piped beneath Truman Road. At one time Independence had three other springs of major size and 16 smaller ones." [141: 94]

James T. Barrett, 1961. "In the Independence-Kansas City area cholera was severe as early as May [1849]. In Independence there were seven and 10 deaths respectively in the Independence and Nolan houses [inns, or hotels; see Independence, Mo. Vicinity Map] within 24 hours. Of 300 Belgian immigrants living in the East Bottoms, nearly half died of cholera, which later spread to the city and took 400 more. . . ." [26: 348]

Author's note, 1991. The original Independence Spring was on the west side of Dodgion Street at a point about 120 feet south of Thomas Road. It has been covered over, with its water disposed of through a storm drain, but there is a replica across the street. There, on the edge of the parking area which serves the Oregon Trail Visitor Center (located in the large building to the south) is a sunken garden in front of a log cabin (the Younger Cabin, an 1837 building relocated from its original site on Walnut Street). Steps lead down from the sunken garden to a stone wall from which piped water flows. It is potable water from a city main and not spring water.

USGS map, Independence, Mo., 1:24,000, 1964 ed., rev. 1970.

SHAWNEE MISSION
Mile 15.0 — Mission Road at 51st St.
Kansas City, Kans. — SW¼, Sec. 3, T12S, R25E

This was a mission maintained by the Methodists for the instruction of Shawnee Indian children. There were emigrant campgrounds in its vicinity.

For those who approached the Oregon Trail from Westport, the Shawnee Mission, five miles southwest of that town and within the Indian Territory, marked the limit of civilization.

John Boardman, May 29, 1843. Mentions passing the mission. [37: 99]

Edith C. Ross, 1928. History of the Mission (not examined). [334: 28]

William J. Ghent, 1934. ". . . about a mile farther [the road] crossed the state boundary into the Indian country. Closer by was the Shawnee Mission, established near the present Turner, by the Rev. Thomas Johnson, a Methodist, in 1830, and moved to this location in 1838 . . . continued to be known as the Shawnee Mission, [but] it took the formal name of the Shawnee Indian Manual Labor School." [149: 122]

Merrill J. Mattes, 1969. ". . . going past the 1839 Shawnee Methodist Mission (three brick buildings still exist in Johnson County, as a Kansas state park)." [249: 137]

Gregory M. Franzwa, 1972. ". . . the Shawnee Mission (Mission Rd. at 51st St.). . . ." [141: 106-07]

USGS map, Kansas City, Mo-Kans., 1:250,000, 1956 ed.

CROSSING OF BLUE RIVER (RED BRIDGE)
Mile 15.2 — South of Metropolitan Kansas City
500 Ft. W. of Center, Sec. 4, T47N, R33W

The crossing of Blue River was near the present Red Bridge,

south of metropolitan Kansas City. This first stream crossing on the Santa Fe-Oregon-California Trail was a ford at least as late as 1846, and just when the "old Red Bridge" was built there has yet to be established.

Virgil Pringle, May 8, 1846. "Went 12 miles to the Blue [from a starting point four miles outside the town of Independence] and encamped, it being to high to cross. Another wagon capsized. . . ." May 9, Crossed the Blue soon in the morning. . . ." [275: I, 166]

Merrill J. Mattes, 1969. "The original Santa Fe-Oregon-California Trail dropped southward from Independence along Blue Ridge via present Raytown to the old Red Bridge crossing. . . ." [249: 136] Paul Henderson's Ms. map shows the Red Bridge as an Oregon Trail site.

USGS map, Grandview, Mo.-Kans. 1:24,000, 1964 ed.

FITZHUGH'S or WATTS MILL_p
Mile 16R2 — On Indian Creek at 103rd Street
Kansas City, Mo.
Jackson County — Near center Sec. 31, T48N, R33W

This water-powered flouring mill was built by John and George Fitzhugh in 1832 and passed through several ownerships before 1850, when it was purchased by Anthony B. Watts. The Watts family operated the mill until it was dismantled in 1942. This was the last place where emigrants could lay in a supply of flour, though flour could also be obtained at other mills near Independence—particularly at the Blue Mills on Little Blue River.

There was an emigrant campground west of the mill at "Fitzhugh's Grove," and it was there that the "Great Migration" of 1843—at least 845 emigrants—gathered before departing for Oregon. Jim Bridger, whose farm was immediately east of the mill, died in the Watts home in 1881 and he was buried nearby. His remains were removed to Mount Washington Cemetery in 1904. (Information from Ona Gieschen.)

James W. Nesmith, 1843. "Thursday, May 18, 1843—The Oregon Company met at the grove west of Fitzhugh's Mill. . . ." [290: 329]

Author's note: Only the foundations for the mill remain, badly in need of stabilization.

Reference. Ronald Becher, "Whatever Happened to Fitzhugh's

Mill?" in *Overland Journal*, 9/4 (Winter 1991), 2-14.
USGS map, Grandview, Mo.-Kans., 1:24,000, 1964 ed.

NEW SANTA FE
Mile 17.9 — near 123rd. St. and State Line Rd.
Kansas City, Mo.
Jackson County — S½ of Sec. 7, T47N, R33W

This settlement, which is also known as "Little Santa Fe," stood at the point where the Santa Fe Trail passed over the Missouri line into the Indian Territory. Its essential purpose was the sale of whiskey, which was prohibited farther west. The emigrant who left Missouri at this point also passed beyond the limits of law and order—other than that of his own making—when he went over the line.

Merrill J. Mattes, 1969. "On the Missouri side of The Line were Fitzhugh's Mill and Little Santa Fe, where wagon trains would camp to recruit and reorganize. In 1849 William Kelly says there was also a tavern called the House of Refuge, which straddled The Line where lawbreakers were safe from the Jackson County sheriff. Henry Shombre says he visited a 'dogery' on The Line near Westport to have one last spree. . . ." [249: 136-37]

Gregory M. Franzwa, 1972. "Back in the mid-19th century there was a little town south of Westport on the Missouri state line, then the western border of the United States, at about where 122nd St. is today. The land to the west was Indian Territory, and that little town of New Santa Fe was the last civilized settlement the emigrants would see until they hit the valley of the Willamette, and the last place the Santa Fe traders would see until they hit San Miguel. In Indian territory, booze officially was a no-no. Hence, a lively cluster of saloons sprang up and the town of New Santa Fe was born.

"The original land patents were dated in December 1844. A few years back there was nothing there but the old frame church, built about 1895, and the more ancient graveyard behind (north of) it. The church was razed in 1971 and a new one erected to the east of the site. Encroaching clusters of fine new homes are moving in . . ." [141: 108]

USGS map, Grandview, Mo.-Kans., 1:24,000, 1964 ed.

LONE ELM CAMPGROUND_P
Mile 32.0 — 167th and Lone Elm Rd.
South of Olathe, Kansas
Johnson County — NW¼ of NW¼, Sec. 23, T14S, R23E

The Lone Elm campground of about 40 acres, was on the head of Cedar Creek, where the Santa Fe-Oregon Trail crossed that stream. Two and one-fourth miles northwest, where the Olathe road crossed Cedar Creek, was another campground variously known as "Round Grove," then as "Elm Grove." "Lone Elm," often confused with its neighbor, was named for its single surviving tree.

The first campground in the Indian Territory for parties following the Santa Fe-Oregon route from Independence, Mo., Lone Elm was also conveniently located with regard to traffic from Westport, Mo.

Rufus B. Sage, fall, 1841. "About sundown we reached a small creek known as Elm Grove, and encamped. . . . Timber proved quite scarce in this vicinity, and it was with great difficulty we procured sufficient for cooking. . . ." [338: IV, 135-36]

Peter H. Burnett, May 22, 1843. ". . . we reached Elm Grove, about fifteen miles [from camp on Blue River] . . . This grove had but two trees, both elms, and a few dogwood bushes . . . The small elm was most beautiful in the wild and lonely prairie; and the large one had all its branches trimmed off for firewood." [55: 67]

Virgil Pringle, May 9, 1846. "Went 16 miles over prairie [from camp on Blue river] . . . encamped at the lone tree, no wood but green willows. . . ." [275: I, 166]

James A. Pritchard, May 3, 1849. "At 3 p.m. we reached the noted lone Elm, where we encamped for the night. This lone tree stands on the bank of a small stream, with no other tree in sight, all the branches have been cut from it by traders & Emegrans for the purpos of fuel . . . from Indipendance 34 miles." [317: 56]

William J. Ghent, 1934. ". . . Elm Grove (also known as Round Grove or Caravan Grove) . . . Wislizenus, in 1839, said that there then remained but, 'a venerable elm tree that must have seen many ages'; and this, with another which he must have overlooked, was cut down for fuel by the emigrants in 1843." [149: 123] [based on the statement of James W. Nesmith, May 22, 1843, to the effect that only "one old elm stump" remained; however, Pritchard witnesses the fact that the Lone Elm was standing as late as May 1849].

Merrill J. Mattes, 1969. "In 1852 Gilbert Cole reported that there was 'no Lone Tree to be found.'" [249: 137]

Gregory M. Franzwa, 1972. "On that corner [167th St. and Lone Elm Road], behind the marker, is the famous Lone Elm Campground, generally reached by the emigrants the first night out from Westport. The campground was a large one—it extended back along 167th for perhaps a quarter of a mile, and down Lone Elm for another quarter of a mile." [141: 131]

Reference. Melburn D. Thurman, "Lone Elm, Kansas: The History of a Trail Campground," in *Overland Journal*, 4/4 (Fall 1986), 42-53.

USGS map, Ocheltree, Kans., 1:24,000, 1956 ed., rev. 1970.

JUNCTION, SANTA FE & OREGON TRAILS_P
Mile 39.4 — 1.8 miles west of Gardner, Kans.
Johnson County — NW¼ of SW¼, Sec. 27 T14S, R22E

At this point the Oregon Trail branched to the right from the Santa Fe route. Once marked by a signpost indicating the "Road to Oregon," this site is now in a field used as a tree nursery in 1972. It marks the beginning of the Oregon Trail as a separate route.

Virgil Pringle, May 10, 1846. ". . . about 9 miles . . . Then left the Santa Fe road. . . ." [275: 1, 166]

James A. Pritchard, May 4, 1849. ". . . in 8 miles [from Lone Elm] came to where the Santa Fe road leaves the old Oregon trail." [317: 56]

House Committee on Roads, 1925. "There are two great trails in the history of America—the Santa Fe and the Oregon. Both of them left Independence, Mo., then followed the same track for 40 miles to where Gardner, Kans. is now located, where the Santa Fe veered to the southwest and the Oregon to the northwest. At the forks was a sign, 'Road to Oregon.'" [384: 23]

William J. Ghent, 1934. "Here, in the early days, some well-disposed person had set up a sign with the words, 'Road to Oregon.'" [149: 123]

Merrill J. Mattes, 1969. "In 1839, when he turned here for Fort Laramie, Dr. Wislizenus had found the Trail so indistinct that 'our leader at times lost it.' Now it was fast becoming a boulevard [1849]. . . ." [249: 138]

Gregory M. Franzwa, 1972. "There is a small roadside park on the other side of the highway [US 56, 2.3 miles west of Gardner, Kansas], with a marker describing the famous junction of the Oregon and Santa Fe Trails [distant 1,250 ft. from the monument on Az. 350 degrees true] . . . the ground now serves as a tree nursery . . . here, perhaps, stood the little sign, 'Road to Oregon'. . . ." [141: 133-34]

USGS map, Gardner, Kans., 1:24,000, 1957 ed., rev. 1970.

OBSERVATION BLUFF_p
Mile 47L1 — A ridge west of Captain Creek
Johnson County, Kansas
Sections 23, 26 & 35; T13S, R21E

The first height of land along the route, Observation Bluff was climbed frequently by emigrants seeking a commanding view.

Merrill J. Mattes, 1969. ". . . called Coon Point, or Observation Bluff. . . ." [249: 138]

Gregory M. Franzwa, 1972. "Many an emigrant succumbed to temptation there and climbed the hill to get a good close look at infinity." [141: 138]

USGS map, Eudora, Kans., 1:24,000, 1951 ed.

CROSSINGS OF WAKARUSA RIVER_p
Mile 54.3 — (Blue Jacket) 5.1 miles southeast of Lawrence, Kans.
Douglas County — NW¼ of NE¼, Sec. 13, T13S, R20E
Mile 57L3 — (Wakarusa) 3.0 miles due south of Lawrence, Kans.
Douglas County — NW¼ of NW¼, Sec. 19, T13S, R20E

The waters of the Wakarusa could spread from a sluggish flow within steep banks to a dangerous flood, overflowing the marsh on each side of the channel. The lower crossing, later the site of Blue Jacket's ferry, may not have been as popular with earlier emigrants as the upper crossing some four miles to the west. This was the first really difficult stream crossing on the Oregon Trail.

Rufus B. Sage, September 7, 1841. ". . . to the Wakarousha, a considerable tributary of the Kansas . . . The remainder of the day was occupied in crossing the creek—a task by no means easy, its banks being so precipitous we were compelled to lower our waggons by means of ropes. In so doing it required the utmost caution to prevent them from oversetting or becomming broken in the abrupt descent." [338: IV, 139-40]

Matthew C. Field, May 1843. "Encamped upon the *Wahkaroosi,* or Big Elk . . . only some sixty miles beyond Westport. . . ." [137: 30]

Virgil Pringle, May 11, 1846. ". . . the Wakarusa, a fine stream of clear water, between a creek and river in size . . . About half of the emigration missed the road and crossed about 4 miles above." [275: 1, 166]

Albert D. Richardson, 1867. ". . . first town in Kansas . . . Five miles south ran the little Waukarusa. Pleased with the name, they gave it to their nascent city. Their first *Herald of Freedom*—for a newspaper is mothers milk to an infant town—bears the date 'Wakarusa, Kansas Territory, October 21, 1854.' But the settlers soon learned this romantic legend of the origin and significance of the name: Many moons ago, before white men ever saw these prairies, there was a great freshet. While the waters were rising, an Indian girl on horseback came to the stream and began fording it. Her steed went in deeper and deeper, until as she sat upon him she was half immersed. Surprised and affrighted she ejaculated 'Wayka-ru-sa!' (hip deep). She finally crossed in safety, but after the invariable custom of the savages they commemorated her adventure by renaming both her and the stream, 'Waukarusa.' On reflection, the settlers decided not to perpetuate the story, and changed the name of their town to Lawrence, in honor of one of its most generous patrons, Amos Lawrence of Boston." [322: 36-37]

Irene D. Paden, 1943. The name, Wakarusa, "is said to indicate 'thigh-deep'. . . . The stream "lay some twenty feet below us at the bottom of precipitous banks. . . . Blue Jacket was a smart Indian . . . with an eye out for profit. He kept a roadhouse at the ford. . . ." P. 31: "Blue Jacket's roadhouse loomed ahead . . . old two-story house was a miracle of unattractiveness . . . had fallen, at last, into the hands of an insurance company . . . agent in charge. He looked at the paintless old building with extreme disfavor . . . 'probably it can be remodeled'. . . within a hundred yards we found the old wagon ruts and followed them . . . grass-grown . . . so old that a large tree grew midway of the sunken marks . . . Wakarusa . . . lay below us in a sequence of murkey, brown pools . . . had a slimy glisten as of water snakes and leeches. . . ." P. 34: ". . . ford. It was some fifteen or twenty feet below . . . approach was the next thing to perpendicular . . . plain that the channel carried a great deal of water in the spring flood . . . wagons had been let down with ropes . . ." [298: 29,

31, 34]

Merrill J. Mattes, 1969. "According to Thomas Eastin, Wakarusa meant black corn." [249: 139]

Gregory M. Franzwa, 1972. Locates the upper crossing and says: "In the spring of 1849 James Pratt noted that there was a Shawnee Indian nearby who was making a nice living pulling wagons out of the mud of the Wakarusa." [141: 140-41]

Reference. Ronald Becher, "Oregon Trail Fords of the Wakarusa River," in *Overland Journal,* 8/1 (1990), 2-10.

USGS map, "Lawrence East, Kans.," 1:24,000, 1950 ed.

BLUE MOUND[P]
Mile 54L2 — about 5 miles southeast of Lawrence, Kans.
Douglas County — NW¼ of SW¼, Sec. 22, T13S, R20E

This is an oval, tree-covered summit with an elevation of 1,052 feet, of which 150 feet stands cleanly above the surrounding terrain. The prominent upper portion is 2,200 by 3,000 feet, with its principal axis east-west. The landmark is visible for many miles.

John Minto, May 1844. Minto noted "the Blue Mound," and later, while at Fort Bridger, he referred back to it as "the famous Blue Mound." [266: 137]

Irene D. Paden, 1943. "Blue Mound is visible a long way in all directions. In fact, Fremont, starting his expedition of 1843, placed a prearranged signal on its summit to summon his Indian hunters." [298: 34]

Merrill J. Mattes, 1969. "The trail went west in Douglas County past the Blue Mound (mentioned by John C. Fremont) . . ." [249: 138]

Gregory M. Franzwa, 1972. ". . . the famed Blue Mound about a mile long and now used as a ski slope. This great bump on the plain was a favorite spot for skylarking emigrants, and many of them climbed to the top for the big view." [141: 139-40]

USGS map, "Lawrence East, Kans.," 1:24,000, 1950 ed.

COON POINT[P]
Mile 71.1 — 3.4 miles SW of Lecompton, Kansas
Douglas County — W½ of Sec. 16, T12S, R18E

Coon Point is actually a ridge, extending northward toward

Coon Creek. It is a landmark mentioned in several emigrant diaries.

James A. Pritchard, May 4, 1849. ". . . camp at what is called coons point, on a small ravine with some timber along its banks." [317: 56]

USGS map, Perry, Kans., 1:24,000, 1949 ed.

COON POINT CAMPGROUND,
Mile 71R3 — At the mouth of Coon Creek
West of Lecompton, Kansas
Douglas County — NW¼ of Sec. 34, T11S, R18E

The Coon Point Campground was used by emigrants traveling an alternate of the Oregon Trail which followed the south bank of the Kansas River in this vicinity.

Gregory M. Franzwa, 1972. "In that area [on Coon Point] is a marker stating that the Coon Point campground on the Old Oregon Trail was three miles north, and this is true. This was an early variant of the trail which passed along the south bank of the Kansas River. The campground was on the west edge of present Lecompton." [141: 142]

USGS map, Perry, Kans., 1:24,000, 1949 ed.

BIG SPRINGS (COON HOLLOW),
Mile 76.4 — Near Big Springs, Kansas
Douglas County — NE¼ of NE¼, Sec. 14, T12S, R17E

Big Springs was a campground at a junction in the Oregon Trail. The earlier route stayed to the left, away from the Kansas River, leading to the Union Ferry crossing higher upstream. The right track led directly down to the lower crossing, the Pappan Ferry.

William J. Ghent, 1934. "Big Springs . . . where the trail divided. The emigrant who meant to take an upper ford of the Kansas here turned to the left." P. 124 ". . . others reached it at the site of Topeka.

"The location of the main ford of the Kansas is disputed . . . the Kansas had . . . many crossing places . . . though many thousands crossed at Topeka, other thousands, especially when the river was high, kept moving up its south bank until they found what they deemed a safer ford. The upper fords would seem to have been more generally used in the earlier days; but after 1844, when a ferry was established at the Topeka site by two halfbreeds named Papin, this lower crossing seems to have become the favored one." [149: 123-24]

Irene D. Paden, 1943. ". . . passed Coon Hollow Camp—or Big Springs, as it is sometimes called. It was a favorite camping spot of the fifties. Here the trail split. The later-used fork went . . . to Topeka . . . an older fork wound prosaically across fields to the left . . . to the ford at old Unionville. . . ." [298: 36]

USGS map, Perry, Kans., 1:24,000, 1949 ed.

CROSSING OF SHUNGANUNGA CREEK
Mile 84.0 — At Lawrence St. bridge, Topeka, Kansas
Shawnee County — NW¼ of SW¼, Sec. 33, T11S, R16E

The little Shunganunga cut a deep trench, making the crossing difficult. It was a typical prairie stream.

James A. Pritchard, May 6, 1849. "At 2 p.m. we reached a fine large creek called Shunganung. We found a large number of wagons crossing. They had to take it by turns and let their wagons dow[n] the steep banks. . . ." [317: 56-57]

Gregory M. Franzwa, 1972. ". . . cross a little bridge at Lawrence St. This bridge is over Shunganunga Creek. As nearly as can be determined, the old emigrant road passed beneath this bridge too. . . ." [141: 143]

USGS map, Topeka, Kans., 1:24,000, 1950 ed., rev. 1970.

CROSSING OF KANSAS RIVER (PAPPAN FERRY)
Mile 87.7 — within Topeka City Limits
Shawnee County, Kansas

The Pappan Ferry consisted of two canoes bridged with poles, upon which wagons could be placed and transported across the river. It was operated by two half-breed brothers, Joseph and Lewis Pappan, or Papin, from 1844 into the fifties, at a point 1.5 miles above the Topeka Avenue Bridge (Henderson), or just below it (Franzwa).

The Kansas River was seldom fordable and time was lost (and sometimes lives and property) improvising a means of crossing. The public ferries operated by the Pappans and others were a great assistance in passing this dangerous stream.

Matthew C. Field, May 27, 1843. "We crossed the Kansas upon a *pirogue*, a species of water craft understood here as a raft constructed on two canoes . . . vehicles and their contents were floated over, where the stream was about two hundred yards wide, with a rapid, turbid and deep current, and then the animals were made to swim across. . . ." [137: 35]

Overton Johnston, May 1843. "Kanzas River . . . not being fordable . . . constructed two large canoes . . . platform of round poles . . . placed wagons by hand, and ferried . . . cattle and horses . . . made to swim." [208: 68]

John Boardman, June 3, 1843. "Passed Caw on a raft, half canoe and half raft . . ." [37: 99]

Virgil Pringle, May 15, 1846. ". . . remainder of the company crossed the ferry, which consisted of two flat boats owned by a Shawnee Indian whose name is Fish." (Charles Fish, who had been a government blacksmith for the Kansas Indians.) [275:1, 167]

James A. Pritchard, May 7, 1849. "We had to travel 16 miles to upper ferry or 3 to the lower ferry [Pappan's] . . . as nearly all the Emegrants were going to the lower ferry, we took the upper one." [317: 57]

William J. Ghent, 1934. ". . . but after 1844, when a ferry was established at the Topeka site by two half-breeds named Papin, this lower crossing seems to have become the favored one. The boats were crude, and in times of high water the overflow of the bottom land rendered approach to them difficult, while the raging current made the crossing hazardous. Not infrequently the passage [was] attended with disaster." [149: 124]

Irene D. Paden, 1943. "Papin's ferry (sometimes spelled Pappan's) came rather late . . . into the history of the Oregon Trail. . . ." [298: 38.] (This is on the authority of George A. Root, "Ferries in Kansas," 1933-34.)

Merrill J. Mattes, 1969. ". . . according to Wm. Johnston, who describes the operation [1849]: 'By means of a rope, one end of which was coiled around a tree, the wagons were let down the steep banks of the river, and placed in the boat. Two wagons and 12 mules were taken over at a time, the boat being propelled by poles. A Frenchman and his two sons, half-breed Kaws, own and work the ferry. Their charge is $4 for each wagon, 25¢ for a mule, and 10¢ each man. Double teams are required to haul the wagons up the northern bank, and through the deep sands extending ¼ mile back from the river.'" [249: 139-40]

Gregory M. Franzwa, 1972. "There is nothing at the site now

but a well-manicured levee. . . ." [141: 145] (This refers to the river bank immediately below the Topeka Avenue Bridge; Paul Henderson indicated it was opposite Auburndale Park—where the north shore is flatter and sandier, and thus more in keeping with Johnston's description.)

USGS map, Topeka, Kans., 1:24,000, 1950 ed., ref. 1970.

SMITH'S FERRY — 1853_p
Mile 92L½ — In Shawnee County, about 6 miles west of Topeka
NW¼ of SW¼, Section 30, T11S, R15E

This was a short-lived ferry crossing of the Kansas River, of importance only to the late Oregon Trail traffic.

The location is shown on a manuscript map by Paul C. Henderson.

JUNCTION WITH ROAD FROM UNION FERRY_p
Mile 101.8 — About ½ mile north of Rossville, Kansas.

Paul C. Henderson places the junction 2,100 feet due east of the common corner of Sections 27, 28, 33 and 34, T10S, R13E. Gregory M. Franzwa places it east of town 1,600 feet on the centerline of Section 34, T10S, R13E. The point is not precise.

At this junction, the road used by those emigrants crossing at the upper (Union) ferry crossing rejoined the route from Pappan's Ferry.

William J. Ghent, 1934. ". . . present Rossville, where they were joined by those that had crossed at Uniontown. . . ." [149: 124]

USGS map, Rossville, Kans., 1:24,000, ed. 1952.

UNION FERRY (CROSSING OF KANSAS RIVER)_p
Mile 106.2 — 0.4 mile northwest of Willard Station, Kansas
Shawnee County — NE¼ of NE¼, Section 15, T11S, R13E

This crossing was in general use by the fur traders, missionaries and early emigrants. The Kansas River could be forded here at low water, otherwise ferriage had to be devised. A commercial ferry was operating here as early as 1846. After 1849 the ferry was operated by Charles Beaubien and Lewis Ogee.

In its day, the Union was the most important crossing of the Kansas River. After the establishment of Pappan's ferry, use of the upper crossing declined.

Rufus B. Sage, September 9, 1841. "Early in the forenoon we came to the Kansas, and were employed till nearly night in effecting a ford. This proved rather difficult, as the water was deep and the bottom sandy;—the course, bearing directly across, till near midway of the river, follows the current for six or eight hundred yards, and then turns abruptly to the opposite shore. The Kansas, at the crossing, was not far from six hundred yards wide, with steep banks of clay and sand." [338:IV, 143-44]

Overton Johnson, late May, 1843. "Kansas River . . . not being fordable . . . constructed two large canoes . . . platform of round poles . . . placed wagons by hand, and ferried . . . cattle and horses . . . made to swim." [208: 68]

Samuel Penter, 1843. ". . . Kaw River . . . They [the party ahead] made two large dugouts of which they made a ferryboat to cross wagons. . . ." [31 1: 57]

James W. Nesmith, May 26, 1843. ". . . Kansas. Crossed the river on a platform made of two canoes . . ." [290: 330]

George McKinstry, May 20, 1846. ". . . we crossed the Kansas 110 miles from Independence using the missions [crossing] . . . with two flat boats owned by a half-breed Frenchman charging one dollar for each wagon the oxen & horses were swum over the river. . . ." [275:I, 204]

James A. Pritchard, May 7, 1849. ". . . to upper ferry . . . what we lost on this side by travelling to the upper ferry we gained on the other . . . one mile before strikeing the Kansas river is a mission and trading post called Potiwatimi . . . a hault of an hour or such a matter in the town and let the boys trade a little . . . crossed at 3 p.m. There was 2 ferryboats, one Kept by a half breed Indian (Michegan) & the other by a white man. This river is about 120 yards wide, with a strong bold current; the water is rather turbed." [317: 57]

William J. Ghent, 1934. "[emigrants] . . . especially when the river was high, kept moving up its south bank until they found what they deemed a safer ford. The upper fords would seem to have been more generally used in the earlier days." [149: 124]

George A. Root, 1933-1934. Provides information on "Ferries in Kansas." [333: 363-65]

Irene D. Paden, 1943. "The first crossing used by fur traders, hunters, travellers and the earliest emigrants was just north of what is now Rossville . . . at Coon Hollow those early wayfarers

remained south of the river . . . fording Otter and Mission creeks. Near the latter they found a Baptist Mission with a farm . . . It was a heavy stone structure and is now incorproated in a dairy barn on the Prairie Dell Farm five or six miles west of Topeka . . . told by old settlers that the bridge [at Rossville] is located at the site of the earliest crossing. The attendant settlement was situated on a hill some three-quarters of a mile south of the ford and was called Union Village. In '49 it consisted of a few log buildings . . . [at the] end of a dry season the ford offered no insurmountable problem as the bottom was gravelly and the current evenly spread and wide . . . spring when fording was not practical . . . ferry, belonging to two Indians . . . couple of fairly substantial scows. . . ." [298: 38]
USGS map, Willard, Kans., 1:24,000, 1952 ed.

ST. MARYS MISSION
Mile 109.6 — Immediately east of the town of St. Marys, Kansas, Pottawatomie County — SE¼ of Section 10, T10S, R12E

St. Marys was a Catholic mission established among the Potawatomie Indians by Belgian Jesuits from Florissant, Missouri, in 1848. Its establishment culminated many years of missionary work among these Indians, who were helpful to the emigrants as ferrymen and provisioners.

James A. Pritchard, May 8, 1849. ". . . a Catholic mission, surrounded with a number of Indian Wigwams." (Note 15, 146): "The site for the mission was selected in the summer of 1848 by Father Felix L. Verreydt, and it was given into the charge of a Swiss Jesuit, Father Maurice Gaillard. . . ." [317: 58, 146]

Irene D. Paden, 1943. "A Catholic college now occupies the site where, from the year 1848, stood the mission to the Pottawatomies. A kindly old priest let me examine and sketch the framed picture of the original building which hangs inconspicuously at the end of a long dark hall . . . a little L-shaped log structure with a sharply pointed cupola containing a bell at the east end . . . [it] was adjacent to the old overland road. . . ." [298: 42]

Merrill J. Mattes, 1969. "A few miles west of Cross Creek was the log and bark village of St. Marys. . . ." [249: 140]

Gregory M. Franzwa, 1972. "On the east edge of town [St. Marys, Kansas] along the north (right) side of the road, is the old St. Marys Catholic Mission, founded here by Belgian Jesuits from the Bishop's farm in Florissant, Mo., northwest of St. Louis . . . The original building of the U.S. Pottawatomie Agency still stands in the seminary grounds." [141: 149]

Additional information on the mission is available in the following: William E. Connelley, *The Prairie Band of Pottawatomie Indians* (1915-1918), and Fr. Maurice Gaillard, *Early Years at St. Mary's Pottawatomie Mission.* (1953).

USGS map, St. Marys, Kans., 1:24,000, 1953 ed.

VIEUX TOLL BRIDGE (SITE)
Mile 120.0 — 5 miles northeast of Wamego
Pottawatomie County, Kansas
North of center of Section 24, T9S, R10E

Louis Vieux built a toll bridge at the crossing of the Red, or Little Vermillion Creek in 1847 or 1848. It is said to have stood on the site of the present bridge. Vieux thus alleviated another vexing minor stream crossing of the Oregon Trail.

Irene D. Paden, 1943. ". . . perpendicular banks of the Red Vermillion just above the confluence of its tributary, Rock Creek . . . a perfect serpent of a river, narrow, dark, and opaque at the bottom of its deep-gorged ravine. . . ." [298: 42]

Gregory M. Franzwa, 1972. ". . . Louis Vieux Sr.—business agent, interpreter, and, finally, chief of the Potawatomie Indians. He was born Nov. 30, 1809, at the site of present Chicago, and was given an allotment of land on the Red Vermillion in 1847 or 1848. He raised his family there. Vieux built a bridge across the river and charged a toll of $1 an outfit; also, supplied the emigrants with hay and grain. [Louis Vieux is buried in a small cemetery near the bridge.]

"The area is the site of one of the great tragedies of the trail. Late in May 1849, a huge outfit camped around the ford on the east bank of the river. Asiatic cholera took over and before the week was over 50 were dead. They were buried to the west, toward the river." [141: 151-52]

Obvious channel changes, cutting off former meanders of the stream, indicate the campground may have been 1,200 feet to the west of the present stream—in the SE¼ of the NW¼, Sec. 24, T9S, R10E. As the stream runs now, there is not enough room for a wagon camp on the east side of the stream. The Vieux Cemetery is adjacent to the county road, east of the bridge, in the SW¼ of the NE¼, Sec. 24, T9S, R10E. There is a small cemetery on the east bank of the river, a short distance above the present bridge, containing graves of many forty niners. One marked and fenced grave has the stone of T. S. Prather, who died May 27, 1849.

The official second largest American Elm tree in the United States stands prominently in the field west of the bridge. It is 99' tall and 23'2" inches in circumference.

USGS map, LaClede, Kans., 1:24,000, 1964 ed.

SCOTT SPRING$_P$
Mile 132.2 — 0.7 mile south of Westmoreland, Kansas Pottawatomie County — NW¼ of SW¼, Sec. 3, T8S, R9E

Scott Spring is at the base of a rocky ridge, and is marked by a monument in a highway rest area 550 feet to the south. There appears to be an emigrant grave north of the spring.

Gregory M. Franzwa, 1972. ". . . historical marker . . . states that Scott Spring is '180 yards north' . . . across the road, climb the barbed wire fence and stay on the east side of the north-south fence. About 100 paces from the highway [State 99] is the spring, now just a gurgle eminating from the base of a steep rock hill. The mound a few yards to the north evidently is an emigrant grave. The marker says the stream still offers the 'delicious cold water' of the emigrants' day. Don't drink it. . . ." [141: 153]

USGS map, Westmoreland, Kans., 1:24,000, 1964 ed.

CROSSING OF BIG VERMILLION CREEK
Mile 152.5

The crossing is now under the waters of Tuttle Creek Reservoir. There was a trail junction on the east bank of the "Big" or Black Vermillion River, probably near the center of Sec. 2, T5S, R8E, where a later route much favored by gold rush traffic parted from the usual Oregon Trail in order to ferry the Big Blue River at Marysville.

Rufus B. Sage, Sept. 14, 1841. ". . . we passed the 14th encamped at Big Vermilion, for the purpose of procuring a quantity of hickory for gun sticks and bow-timbers. Hickory . . . this being the last place on the route affording it. . . ." [338:IV, 146]

John Minto, 1844. Party held up by high water. [266: 137]
George McKinstry, May 25, 1846 . . . crossed the 'big Virmillion'
a large creek with a steep bank on the east side. [275:I, 207]

William J. Ghent, 1934. ". . . the Big (or Black) Virmillion. . . . As [the Oregon Trail] approached the crossing of the
Big Blue it divided . . . Chittenden says that the main ford was
near the mouth of the Little Blue, but the journals indicate that
it was farther north, in the neighborhood of present Marysville,
174 miles from the start [the lower crossing was 160 miles—
Ghent] . . . Here, in 1851 . . . a settlement was started." [149:
125]

Irene D. Paden, 1943. "We found the second Vermillion to be
of the same general type as the first, oozy and malodorous, lying
incredibly far below its ancient, one-way bridge." [298: 47]

The junction of the later alternate route by way of Marysville
left the original Oregon Trail on the north bank of Big Vermillion
Creek. The alternate was a product of the gold rush traffic,
which often preferred the ferry at Marysville to the difficult
Independence Crossing of the Big Blue River.

USGS map, Frankfort, Kans., 1:24,000, 1969 ed.

ALCOVE SPRING$_P$
Mile 165.1 — 7 miles south of Marysville, Kans.
Marshall County — SE¼ of NE¼, Sec. 31, T3S, R7E

Alcove Spring originates in an unusual rock formation on the
east bank of the Big Blue River. It was used by early emigrants
who left a record of their presence on adjacent rocks. The area
is now owned by Mrs. Stella Hammett, of Blue Rapids, Kansas,
and was opened to the public in May 1993. The spring is 800 feet
east of the point where Alcove Spring Creek flows beneath the
River Road.

The idyllic setting was named by members of the ill-fated
Donner (Reed) party of 1846.

George McKinstry, May 30, 1846. ". . . about a half mile from
Camp up the spring branch on the right hand fork is a most
beautiful spring and a fall of water of 12 feet   Mr Bryant of our
party has named it the 'Alcove Spring'   the water is of the most
excellent kind   the spring is surrounded with Ash Cotton wood
& Cedar trees   it is an excellent place to camp for a day or two
to wash, recruit the cattle &c   I this day cut the name of the
spring in the rock on Table at the top of the falls. . . ." [275:1,

209]

Irene D. Paden, 1943. ". . . we sampled the water. It was cool and good . . . Edwin Bryant wrote: 'We named this the "Alcove Spring" and future travelers will find the name graven on the rocks' . . . We found it carved deeply and well in letters around eight inches high just above the brink of the fall . . . [We] found, among the manuscript diaries at the Bancroft library . . . a small notebook [McKinstry's] . . . A rock as large as the top of our car lay in the stream. . . . Firmly carved, in large letters showed upon the surface, 'J. F. Reed—26 May—1846'. . . ." [298: 50-52]

Merrill J. Mattes, 1969. The Alcove Spring is described. [249: 141-42]

Gregory M. Franzwa, 1972. "Turn into the gravel parking area and park. . . . there is a turnstile at the end of the path leading to the spring itself. Follow the path. It will cross a little creek now polluted and continue up a gentle incline. A sharp turn to the right and the path leads over a wood footbridge to the alcove itself. The alcove is sort of an amphitheater, with a large rock over the stage. In the spring, water trickles over the path and over the ledge, to splash down to the rocks 10 feet below.

"Walk down into the alcove. Cross a large boulder and, immediately to the right and directly beneath the wood footbridge is the spring itself. It gushes from a porous rock formation. It would not seem to be polluted; it definitely is clear and cold as the emigrants said it was." [141: 158-63]

USGS map, Blue Rapids, Kans., 1:24,000, 1968 ed.

SARAH KEYES MONUMENT_P
Mile 165.2 — Entrance to Alcove Spring Area
Marshall County, Kans. — SE¼ of NEVA, Sec. 31, T3S, R7E

There is an incribed stone placed by the Daughters of the American Revolution (DAR) to commemorate the burial of Mrs. Sarah Keyes on May 29, 1846. Mrs. Stella Hammett, owner of the Alcove Spring site, advises that the actual grave is beneath the east shoulder of the county road, about 300 feet north of the monument.

George McKinstry diary, May 29, 1846. "Mrs. Keyes the mother of the wife of Mr. Reed of Illinois died of consumption aged . . . 70 had been sick [p. 209] for a long time has been blind and deaf for some time past . . . [traveling] to meet an only son from

Oregon. The funeral took place this evening at 2 o'clock which was attended by every member of the company Mr. Cornwall one of our party and a Presbyterian clergiman conducted the burial and delivered a sensible sermon at the grave takeing his text from Thessilonians 'Trouble yourselves not about those that sleep' the grave is under an Oak tree beside the Oregon road about ¼ mile west [east] of Blue earth river." The Virginia Reed letter, p. 278, also describes the death and burial. [275:1, 208-09, 278]

Irene D. Paden, 1943. "It was called to our attention the next day that John Ellenbecker of Marysville has located her grave beyond much doubt, and that it lies in the open." [298: 49]

The monument placed by the DAR states: "God in his love / and charity has / called in this / beautiful valley / a pioneer mother / May 29, 1846."

USGS map, Blue Rapids, Kans., 1:24,000, 1968 ed.

INDEPENDENCE CROSSING[p]
Mile 165.4 — About 7 miles south of Marysville, Kans.
Marshall County — NW¼ of SE¼, Sec. 31, T3S, R7E

The Independence Crossing is a ford of the Big Blue River at the mouth of Alcove Spring Creek, and probably is flooded by backwater from the Tuttle Creek Reservoir. It was a particularly unpredictable crossing place, because of the sudden rises of the Big Blue River due to prairie storms.

Rufus B. Sage, 1841. "Leaving Big Vermillion, we travelled rapidly the two days subsequent, and arrived at the North Fork of the Blue [commonly called the Big Blue],—a large and deep stream, tributary to the Kansas. We were here detained till the 24th—the creek being impassable on account of high water." [338:1, 209]

John Minto, 1844. Describes his experience with high water. [266: 138]

George McKinstry diary, May 31, 1846. ". . . commenced crossing this morning immediately after breakfast in the canoes   the river fell but 7 inches last night   we crossed 5 wagons pr hour." [275:I, 209]

Virgil Pringle Diary, May 20, 1846. "Pushed ahead for Blue River, the foremost of the caravan reached in time to cross; found it rising fast . . . [May 23] Occupied this day crossing the Blue River by fording; raised our wagons by placing blocks between the beds and bolsters and went over dry." [275:1, 168]

James A. Pritchard, May 10, 1849. ". . . we came to the big Blue. This is a fine large Stream with a bold rapid current & gravelly bottom. We had here to lower our wagons down with ropes, which consumed the balance of the evening the bottoms are well timbered." [317: 59]

Irene D. Paden, 1943. "This ford was called Independence Crossing, in all likelihood to distinguish it from the crossing at Marysville, Kansas, used by those who did not come from Independence . . . [p. 49] The river carries a heavy current when it floods . . . a spell of high water recently, during which even Alcove Spring Creek had run ten feet deep . . . [p. 52] . . . we walked down to the Independence Crossing of the Big Blue, using for a pathway the bed of Alcove Spring Creek. We walked in dense and comforting shadow, for the belt of timber that lines the Big Blue . . . [is] extraordinary for the prairies." [298: 47, 49, 52]

Merrill J. Mattes, 1969. Description. [249: 141-42]

Gregory M. Franzwa 1972. Description. [141: 163-64]

USGS map, Blue Rapids, Kans., 1:24,000, 1968 ed.

"JUNCTION-OF-THE-WAYS",[P]
Mile 180.3 — 3 miles east of Hanover, Kans.
Washington County — near center of Sec. 13, T2S, R5E

This is the junction of the road from Independence with an alternate trail established in 1849 from St. Joseph, Missouri. The latter was an important feeder popularized by the forty niners.

James A. Pritchard, May 11, 1849. "By noone today we came to where the St. Joseph road & Indipendence road came together." [317: 59]

Irene D. Paden, 1943. "In '49 a new trail was blazed from the Black Vermillion up the east side of the Big Blue to Marysville so that travelers from Independence might, if they chose, short-cut to the St. Joe road and use its crossing . . . [p. 63] In one-half mile we bisected the old trail from Independence Crossing which was running northwest. In another mile we crossed the St. Jo Road going due west to meet it. The famous intersection occurs in a field within a hundred yards of the county line . . . not more than six miles in an air line from Marysville." [298: 47, 63]

USGS map, Hanover East, Kans., 1:24,000, 1966 ed.

HOLLENBERG RANCH HOUSE
Mile 181.9 — 1.8 miles northeast of Hanover, Kans.
Washington County — SE¼ of SE¼, Sec. 3, T2S, R5E

This old building is an original ranch house and Pony Express station, now preserved as a state park. It is less then two miles from the point where the St. Joe road joined the Oregon Trail from Independence.

Gregory M. Franzwa, 1972. ". . . the Hollenberg ranch house . . . was built about 1857 by Gerat H. Hollenberg, in order to capitalize on the Oregon-California trade which passed the doorway. Three years later it became a Pony Express home station. It is believed to be the only such station on the entire trail which is neither altered nor moved from its original location. It is much as it was in the beginning. . . ." [141: 167]

USGS map, Hanover East, Kans., 1:24,000, 1966 ed.

OREGON TRAIL MONUMENT
Mile 189.9 — between Washington County, Kans.,
and Gage County, Nebr.

Known as the "Tri-County Marker," this monument is on the Kansas-Nebraska state line 600 feet east of the line separating Jefferson and Gage, two Nebraska counties. It marks the place where the Oregon Trail passed from Kansas into Nebraska.

USGS map, Diller, Nebr.-Kans., 1:24,000, 1970 ed.

FREMONT SPRINGS$_P$
Mile 194L½ — 4.1 miles south of Diller, Nebr.
Jefferson County — NE¼ of Sec. 15, T1N, R4E

The "Pathfinder," John C. Fremont, is said to have camped at these springs in 1842; however, another spring at Quivera Park (NE¼ of NE¼, Sec. 34, T2N, R3E) has also been so called, on the basis of graffiti which once adorned a sandstone outcrop on the east side of Rock Creek. If the signatures reproduced on the D.A.R. monument at the spring in Quivera Park are truly facsimiles of those which formerly appeared on the nearby bluff, then there is reason to doubt the authenticity of this presumed evidence. In 1842 Fremont was only a second lieutenant of the Corps of Topographical Engineers, and he would not have signed himself "Col. John Fremont." The site is also an unlikely camping place, appearing too far removed from the emigrant route to be the campground of June 22, 1842.

Irene D. Paden, 1943. "On the bank of a microscopic streamlet, about a mile from the grave of [p. 71] David McCanles, rises a rocky cliff. At the top is a high, iron-spiked fence guarding a short section of the face of the cliff. We had come here to see the most illustrious names which are carved anywhere in the two thousand miles of the trail . . . scanned the marred surface of the sandstone . . . 'John Fremont and Kit Carson—1842' . . . Other signatures, partially obliterated, and other dates, old enough to be noteworthy in themselves . . . crowd the rock . . . names of later date were much more worn and illegible . . . [p. 72] . . . a book entitled 'Pioneer Tales of the Oregon Trail and Jefferson County' . . . published in 1912 by Charles Dawson, then a resident of the county for forty years . . . list of names carved on the rock in Quivera Park . . . Mr. Dawson was taking steps to prevent [fading of the names]. . . in the case of John Fremont and 'Chris' Carson by slightly deepening the carving." [298: 70-73]

Gregory M. Franzwa, 1972. ". . . a small spring branch crossing beneath the highway. The water is from Fremont Spring, which rises about 0.2 mile due north of there. Fremont, Kit Carson, Preuss and the other members of his company camped there in 1842. [141: 170]

USGS map, Diller, Nebr.-Kan., 1:24,000, 1970 ed.

CALDWELL STATION$_P$
Mile 194.4 — 3.6 miles south of Diller, Nebr.
Jefferson County — NE¼ of Sec. 15, T1N, R4E

This is the site of a Pony Express station.
Information from a manuscript map by Paul C. Henderson.

ROCK CREEK STATION (East Ranch)
Mile 201.3 — 3 miles northeast of Endicott, Nebr.
Jefferson County — SW¼ of NE¼, Sec. 26, T2N, R3E

This is the site of a Pony Express station and locale of the McCanles-Hickok fight. It is now included in a well-run Nebraska State Historical Park.

Irene D. Paden, 1943. ". . . two miles northeast of Endicott . . . came to Rock Creek and the site of the old Rock Creek Station . . . setting of the historic gun fight between David McCanles, owner of the log station building leased to the stage company, and handsome Wild Bill Hickok [James Butler Hickok] . . . 1861 . . . [p. 70] A small boy . . . asked questions until he had located the former position of the station and barn . . . we came to a large boulder bedded in weeds and partially shaded by a ragged tree . . . boy [said] . . . 'And there's McCanles' grave.' There are others buried in these quiet acres. . . ." [298: 69-70]

USGS map, Endicott, Nebr.-Kans., 1:24,000, 1970 ed.

VIRGINIA STATION_p
Mile 210.5 — 4.5 miles due north of Fairbury, Nebr.
Jefferson County — NE¼ of NE¼, Sec. 27, T3N, R2E

This is the site of a Pony Express station. A monument is on the west side of State Route 15, 4.0 miles north of its junction with U.S. 136.

GEORGE WINSLOW GRAVE_p
Mile 211L½ — 5 miles northwest of Fairbury, Nebr.
Jefferson County — SW¼ of SE¼, Sec. 21, T3N, R2E

This is a marked grave of a cholera victim of the gold rush period.

Gregory M. Franzwa, 1972. "There is a sign directing persons to the grave of George Winslow, who died June 8, 1849 . . . The granite obelisk is atop the gentle hill in the field. Winslow's sons found the original marker and imbedded it in the newer stone monument . . . In the west face of the monument is a bronze tablet in which is cast: 'IN MEMORY OF GEORGE WINSLOW who died on this great highway June 8, 1849 and was buried here by his comrades, of the Boston and Newton Joint Stock Association. This tablet is affectionately placed by his sons, George Edward and Orrin Henry Winslow' . . . The original marker, of extremely hard stone, evidently was cut right on the spot, probably on the date [p. 173] of Winslow's death . . . reads 'George Winslow. Newton, Ms. AE 25'." [141: 172-73]

This property has been in the possession of owner Ed Brody's family for 110 years. Three prominent rut swales cross the hill about 300 feet below the monument.

USGS map, Fairbury, Nebr., 1:24,000, 1960 ed.

LITTLE SANDY STATION_P
Mile 214.4 — 6.5 miles northwest of Fairbury, Nebr.
Jefferson County — NW¼ of NW¼, Sec. 19, T3N, R2E

This is the site of a stage station.
Information from a manuscript map by Paul C. Henderson.

BIG SANDY STATION_P
Mile 218.7 — 2.0 miles west of Powell, Nebr.
Jefferson County — NE¼ of SW¼, Sec. 16, T3N, R1E

This is the site of a Pony Express station.
Information from a manuscript map by Paul C. Henderson.

MILLERSVILLE STATION_P
Mile 226.7 — 2.2 miles southwest of Belvidere, Nebr.
Thayer County — NW¼ of SE¼, Sec. 22, T3N, R1W

This is the site of a Pony Express station. The information is from a manuscript map by Paul C. Henderson. This location is disputed, however, and other information indicates the station may have been in the SE¼ of Sec. 22, T3N, R2W.

KIOWA STATION_P
Mile 242.8 — 6 miles south of Davenport, Nebr.
Thayer County — SE¼ of NE¼, Sec. 16, T3N, R4W

This is the site of a Pony Express station.
Information from a manuscript map by Paul C. Henderson.

OAK GROVE STATION_P
Mile 248.9 — 1.7 miles east of Oak, Nebr.
Nuckolls County — NE¼ of NW¼, Sec. 15, T3N, R5W

This is the site of a Pony Express station. It is marked by a monument commemorating an Indian massacre in 1864.

Irene D. Paden, 1943. ". . . to the age-old trees at Oak Grove Ranch where we came to a monument commemorating the victims of the Indian massacre of '64 . . . once boasted a stage station." [298: 75]

The historical panel in Oak, Nebr., helps locate nearby trail sites.

USGS map, Ruskin, Nebr., 1:24,000, 1960 ed.

"THE NARROWS"ₚ
Mile 252.5 — 1½ miles northwest of Oak, Nebr.
Nuckolls County — SW¼ of Sec. 6, T3N, R5W

The emigrant trail was bottle-necked between the Little Blue River and the bluff on its east bank, at "The Narrows." There is no road within a half mile of the site. It is a minor landmark with a monument on top of the bluff.

Irene D. Paden, 1943. ". . . the Narrows crowded . . . wagons into a bottleneck between the river and encroaching bluffs." [298: 76]

Gregory M. Franzwa, 1972. ". . . past 'The Narrows,' where the space between the river bank and the bluff leaves only enough room for a single wagon. The traveler is unable to see this . . ." [141: 175]

Another emigrant landmark, "The Black Pool," was one-half mile down the Little Blue River, at the mouth of Elk Creek (NW¼, SE¼, Sec. 7).

USGS map, Edgar, Nebr., 1:24,000, 1960 ed.

LITTLE BLUE STATIONₚ
Mile 254.5 — 2.3 miles east of Angus, Nebr.
Nuckolls County — SW¼, Sec. 36, T4N, R6W

This is the site of a stage station.
Information from Reg P. Duffin.

LIBERTY FARMₚ
Mile 266.4 — 0.7 mile northwest of Deweese, Nebr.
Clay County — NW¼ of NE¼, Sec. 32, T5N, R7W

This is the site of an overland stage station destroyed by Indians in 1864. Mrs. Eubanks and Miss Roper were not captured here, as Ghent states, but near "The Narrows."

William J. Ghent, 1934. "At Liberty Farm, on the Little Blue, in southern Nebraska, the station and a wagon train were destroyed [by Cheyennes, in August 1864]; Joseph Eubanks, the stage driver and station keeper, and eight or nine others were killed and scalped, and Mrs. Eubanks, her two children and a Miss Roper were carried into captivity." [149: 223]

Irene D. Paden, 1943. ". . . white knoll at the site of old Liberty Farm Station . . . This station did not survive the terrible massacre in 1864 but was replaced by one known as Pawnee Station." [298: 77]

USGS map, Deweese, Nebr., 1:24,000, 1960 ed.

SPRING RANCH$_P$
Mile 272.1 — 5.7 miles east of Pauline, Nebr.
Clay County — SE¼, Sec. 8, T5N, R8W

This is the site of a stagecoach stop; a trading post stood nearby.

Irene D. Paden, 1943. "We crossed Pawnee Creek just above the trestle. A few hundred yards downstream, at its confluence with the Little Blue, stood in the old days Weston and Roper's trading post. From there we went to Spring Ranch. . . ." [298: 77]

Information from a manuscript map by Paul C. Henderson.

USGS map, Fairfield NW, Nebr., 1:24,000, 1969 ed.

LONE TREE STATION$_P$
Mile 274.9 — 10 miles south of Hastings, Nebr.
Adams County — SW¼ of SW¼ Sec. 28, T6N, R9W

This stage and Pony Express station took its name from a single giant cottonwood tree visible for many miles. The tree, which was blown down in 1865, was said to have been an Oregon Trail landmark.

The exact location of this station is in doubt; it may have stood north of the common corner of sections 28, 29, 32 and 33.

Irene D. Paden, 1943. ". . . Nine Mile Ridge, where in staging days stood Lone Tree Station. The solitary tree . . . used to be

visible for a long distance in each direction and helped to break the monotony of the bare, rolling prairie hills. . . ." [298: 77-78]
USGS map, Pauline, Nebr., 1:24,000, 1969 ed.

32-MILE STATION_p
Mile 288.1 — 32 miles southeast of Fort Kearny
Adams County, Nebr. — NE¼ of NE¼, Sec. 6, T6N, R1OW

This was a stage and Pony Express station.
Irene D. Paden, 1943. ". . . the long and low log cabin which served as Thirty-two Mile Station." [298: 78]
Information from a manuscript map by Paul C. Henderson.
USGS map, Hastings West, Nebr., 1:24,000, 1969 ed.

MUDDY STATION_p
Mile 294.4 — 4.1 miles west of Juniata, Nebr.,
on Thirty-Two Mile Creek
Adams County — NE¼ of NE¼, Sec. 17, T7N, R11W

This was a stage station.
Information from a manuscript map by Paul C. Henderson.

SUMMIT STATION_p
Mile 298.3 — 1.7 miles south of Kenesaw, Nebr.
Adams County — NE¼ of NE¼, Sec. 10, T7N, R1 2W

This was a stage and Pony Express station.
Irene D. Paden, 1943. ". . . Summit Station . . . 'stood' is not the best word, for the building was only three feet above ground and extended four feet below . . ." Story of the near-hanging of the station keeper by emigrants, who thought he had taken their horses for the reward. [298: 79-80]
Information from a manuscript map by Paul C. Henderson.
USGS map, Kenesaw, Nebr., 1:24,000, 1969 ed.

SUSAN HAIL GRAVE
Mile 304.0 — 4 miles northwest of Kenesaw, Nebr.
Adams County — 150' North of S¼ Corner,
Sec. 18, T8N, R12W

The grave of Susan Hail, with the woods of the Platte River in the distance.

This is the marked grave of a woman who died June 2, 1852, probably of cholera. The grave is protected by a pipe fence. There is a particularly intriguing story behind this trailside burial.

William Woodhams, 1854. "Wednesday, May 10 . . . Left Little Blue this morning for the Platte valley. Travelled all day over a high rolling prairie; no wood or water fit to use. Saw plenty of wolves, and passed many graves. One had a nice marble head stone with a woman's name on it. It stood on the top of a little sandhill, and strange enough was that sad evidence of civilization here in the wilderness, the more so as it bore a woman's name." [Diary excerpt supplied by Reg P. Duffin, Jan. 14, 1982.]

Irene D. Paden, 1843. "Somewhere among the labyrinth of dunes . . . [is] what is known locally as the Lone Grave. . . ." The story of the woman's death from "poisoned spring" water is told, with the husband returning to St. Joe for a tombstone. ". . . bought a wheelbarrow and trundled it before him . . . accomplished his purpose immortalized her resting place and disappeared from history . . . overlooking the great valley of the Platte, Susan Hail lies beneath a stone with her name upon it close to the Adams-Kearney county line." [298: 81]

Gregory M. Franzwa, 1972. ". . . a lonely little grave . . . the last resting place of Susan D. Hail, buried some 50 yards off to the right on one of the sand hills . . . Mrs. Hail, so the story goes, drank from a spring poisoned by Indians on June 2, 1852, and the 34-year-old woman died with shocking suddenness. It is much more probable that she died from polluted water, either from a well too close to the campground or too close to a buffalo wallow. Dysentery or cholera could kill a person in a matter of an hour or two.

"The griefstricken bridegroom had no intention of leaving
the grave unmarked. It is said that he moved quickly back to St.
Joseph after installing a temporary marker, had a good stone
engraved, and moved it back to this point in a
wheelbarrow . . . ironic that no one knows the location of her
husband's grave, or even his first name. The stone over the
grave . . . not the original." [141: 181-82]

There is a Nebraska State informational panel on the paved
road along the Adams-Kearney county line. The grave is 0.6 mile
due east of the panel, adjacent to an unimproved farm road.

USGS map, Denman, Nebr., 1:24,000, 1962 ed.

HOOK'S RANCH ("DOGTOWN")_p
Mile 31OR¼ — 9.5 miles east of Fort Kearny
Kearney County, Nebr. — Center of Sec. 18, T8N, R13W

This was a stage station and trading post at the junction of the
Oregon Trail and the Old Fort Kearny road, 1.4 miles east of the
later Fort Kearny Military Reservation.

James A. Pritchard, May 17, 1849. ". . . reached the Platte by
6 PM opposite or nearly at the head [downstream end] of Grand
Island where we encamped. . . ." [317: 63]

William J. Ghent, 1934. ". . . to the Platte, 316 miles from
Independence. 'About twenty miles above the head of Grand
Island,' says Chittenden . . . but the intersection was anywhere
the emigrants chose. Bryant's party reached the river eight miles
below the head of Grand Island, or nearly thirty miles to the
east. . . [here] came in another feeder from the east—the old
Fort Kearney (or Nebraska City) road. . . ." [149: 127-28]

WPA Writers' Project, 1939. "The several eastern feeders of
the emigrant route best known as the Oregon Trail
united—insofar as any trails united on the prairies—on the
south shore of the Platte near the head of Grand Island." [146:
69]

Irene D. Paden, 1943. "In trail days there was a utilitarian, if
ugly, settlement at the junction, bearing the vulgar title Dogtown.
As late as 1865, it was the first town west of Marysville . . . a
journey of nearly a hundred fifty miles . . . name [from] . . .
prairie dogs nearby . . . still eight or nine miles from old Fort
Kearney. . . ."

VALLEY STATION_p
Mile 310.5 — 9.0 miles east of Fort Kearny, Nebr.
Kearney County — SE¼ of NE¼, Sec. 18, T8N, R13W

This was a stage and mail station on the Oregon Trail.
Information from a manuscript map by Paul C. Henderson.
USGS map, Gibbon South, Nebr., 1:24,000, 1962 ed.

2

Fort Kearny to Robidoux Pass

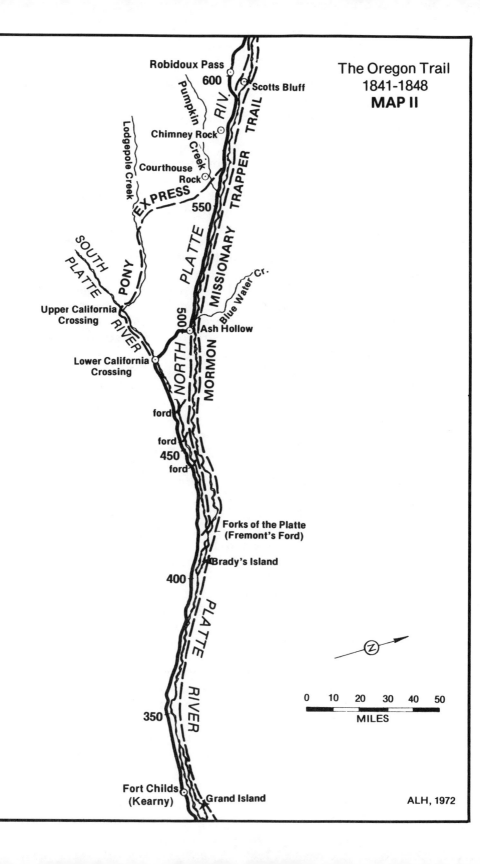

The Oregon Trail
1841-1848
MAP II

Robidoux Pass
600
Scotts Bluff

Pumpkin Creek

N. PLATTE RIV.

TRAPPER TRAIL

Lodgepole Creek

Chimney Rock

550

MISSIONARY

Courthouse Rock

EXPRESS

NORTH PLATTE

SOUTH PLATTE

PONY

500

RIVER

Blue Water Cr.

Ash Hollow

MORMON

Upper California Crossing

Lower California Crossing

ford

ford

450

ford

Forks of the Platte
(Fremont's Ford)

Brady's Island

400

PLATTE RIVER

350

Fort Childs
(Kearny)

Grand Island

0 10 20 30 40 50
MILES

ALH, 1972

FORT KEARNY ("FORT CHILDS")
Mile 319.4 — 5.5 miles southeast of Kearney, Nebr.
Kearney County — SW¼ of SW¼, Sec. 22, T8N, R15W

Fort Kearny was an open fort, composed mainly of sod and adobe buildings and was located on the bottomland south of the Platte River, near the upper end of Grand Island. It was a notoriously uncomfortable and unhealthy post, but also a busy and important one. It was the supply point for the garrisons and detachments guarding the eastern end of the Oregon Trail, and it was the base from which Gen. Albert Sidney Johnston's army moved against Utah during the brief Mormon War. The site is now a Nebraska State Historical Park.

James A. Pritchard, May 18, 1849. "At noon we reached Fort Kearney, passed through the place 1 mile and stoped to greaze & rest a couplet of hours. Here we found a Military post established and some 80 or 90 Dregoons posted here—also a kind of Post office establishment, which gave us an opportunity of sending back letters. The Fort is about 12 ms above the head of Grand Island, and the houses are built of adob[e]s or sun dried brick." [317: 64]

George Gibbs, May 29, 1849. "Fort Kearny, first called Fort Childs, was established under the act creating forts on the Oregon route in 1846-47 . . . first sent here were a battalion of mounted Missourians known as the Oregon battalion, who encamped at the place during the summer of 1847 and erected the walls of the long adobe building and the turf walls of a few others now used as officers quarters. The battalion was marched back in the fall and disbanded and the post occupied in October by two companies of Mounted Riflemen under Captain, now Brevet-major Ruff, who has since remained in command. The buildings, such as they are, were completed by the troops, and with a turf corral now constitute the 'fort' . . . on the low flat bottom, about a third of a mile from the Platte river, near the head of Grand island, and fifteen from where the trail enters the valley . . . a more unfortunate one . . . could hardly have been chosen . . . The original design was to form an inclosure of pickets, inclosing the building and an area of about four acres, with blockhouses on the diagonal comers containing each four guns. The number of these is however reduced to two each. The pickets and blockhouses are expected to be built of cottonwood . . . establishment, including the expenses of the Missouri battalion, cannot have cost less than half a million . . .

turf buildings are already . . . almost uninhabitable in wet weather. . . ." [101: 299]

J. Goldsborough Bruff, June 17, 1849. "I visited the Fort . . . This place is as yet merely the site of an intended fort; it has some adobe embankments, quarters—&c. of adobe & frame, and a number of tents & sheds. Is on the bank of the Platte, where Grand Island makes a narrow branch of the river between it and the shore." [52: 21]

William J. Ghent, 1934. "On the south side, near the head of Grand Island, in April 1848 a military post was established, the first of its kind along the trail. Shortly afterward it became the new Fort Kearney, its misspelled name given in honor of the famous General Stephen Watts Kearny, who died on October 31 of that year." P. 250: ". . . markers . . . Nebraska. The first one was dedicated on February 14, 1910, by the Fort Kearney Chapter of the Daughters of the American Revolution and marks the site of old Fort Kearney." [149: 128, 250]

WPA Writers' Project, 1939. "The park [Fort Kearny State Park] includes 80 acres . . . on the site of the famous frontier military post. Still visible on the grounds are rifle pits and other earthworks, one corner of the blockhouses, and a grass-covered mound that was the magazine in which munitions were stored for use along the trail between this point and Fort Laramie.

"The first Fort Kearny was a blockhouse on the Missouri River at what is now Nebraska City . . . 1846-1847. The post was transfered . . . to give emigrants protection. . . .

"Lt. Daniel P. Woodbury, who chose the site . . . in June 1848, with 175 men, who began the construction . . . first making adobe blocks; they also set up a sawmill and erected sod stables. Plans drawn in 1852 show that the fort included two two-story corner blockhouses of heavy timbers, powder and guard houses, a lookout accessible by ladder . . . and officers' quarters. Numerous barracks and other facilities were added in succeeding years.

"During the Civil War regular troops were withdrawn and the fort was manned by volunteers that included a number of former Confederate soldiers, called Galvanized Yankees. In 1965 Pawnee were enlisted to help hold the Sioux in check . . . abandoned in 1871, and a few years later the military reservation was thrown open to settlement." [146: 69-70]

Irene D. Paden, 1943. ". . . first called Fort Child in honor of Brigadier General Child . . . later . . . honoring Colonel Stephen Watts Kearny. . . ." [298: 84]

Lyle E. Mantor, 1948. History of the fort. [237: 175-207]

Robert W. Frazer, 1965. ". . . The site, chosen by First Lieutenant Daniel P. Woodbury, Corps of Engineers, in the fall of 1847, was purchased from the Pawnee Indians for $2,000 in trade goods. . . Constructed under the direction of Lieutenant Colonel Ludwell E. Powell, Missouri Mounted Volunteers. First called "Post at Grand Island," it was soon referred to, although never so designated officially, as Fort Childs, in honor of Major Thomas Childs, 1st U.S. Artillery. It was designated Fort Kearny on December 30, 1848. The post was frequently referred to as New Fort Kearny to distinguish it from its predecessor." [142: 87]

USGS map, Kearney, Nebr., 1:24,000, 1962 ed.

"DOBEYTOWN"ₚ

"DOBEYTOWN"~p~

Mile 322.4 — 1.9 miles west of Fort Kearny, Nebr.
Kearney County — NW¼ of NW¼, Sec. 30, T8N, R15W

"Dobytown" was an informal settlement two miles west of the Fort Kearny military reservation.

Irene D. Paden, 1943. "Two miles to the west . . . the hamlet called Dobytown, a squalid settlement of 'dobe huts whose very mention was next door to an indelicacy . . . type of hell-hole that clung to the fringes of any military reservation and, owing to the fact that Fort Kearney was far toward the western edge of its reserve, the group of mud buildings . . . We found Leo Nickel's Ranch on the spot . . . casual tourist may recognize it by a row of evergreens along the fence line instead of the more common cottonwoods . . . In staging days a large reserve stable for work stock was erected at Dobytown, and the name Kearney City was arbitrarily selected in a vain attempt to throw a veil of respectability over the community. The name never 'took' . . . [p. 89] The place was a grisly combination of delirium tremens, stale humanity, and dirt." [298: 88-89]

Gregory M. Franzwa, 1972. "Two miles west of the fort is the historical marker for 'Dobytown,' a cluster of up to 15 adobe buildings built to house the retinue of camp followers, male and female, that accompanies any military installation. Within two years after the fort was abandoned, in 1871, so was Dobytown." [141: 186]

Author's note, 1991. The historical marker for this site appears to have been misplaced, probably on the basis of Irene Paden's statement that the site was 'two miles to the west.' That would be correct only if she was referring to the west boundary of the military reserve, which was a mile from the fort proper on that side. Charles Martin, Sr., agrees that Dobytown was three miles west of the fort buildings.

USGS map, Kearney, Nebr., 1:24,000,1962 ed.

PLATTE STATION_p
Mile 326.4 — 7.3 miles west of Fort Kearny, Nebr.
Kearney County — 1,200 ft. S. of NW corner, Sec. 21, T8N, R16W

This was a Pony Express station, according to a manuscript map prepared by Paul C. Henderson.

USGS map, Alfalfa Center, Nebr., 1:24,000, 1962 ed.

17-MILE STATION_p
Mile 329.2 — 10.2 miles west of Fort Kearny, Nebr.
Phelps County — NE¼ of NE¼, Sec. 23, T8N, R17W

This is the location of a stage station.

Sir Richard Burton, 1860. "...we made 'Seventeen Mile Station,' and halted there to change mules." [56: 54]

USGS map, Alfalfa Center, Nebr., 1:24,000, 1962 ed.

CROSSING OF PLATTE RIVER_p
Mile 333R — About 14 miles west of Fort Kearny, Nebr.
Phelps County — Not a precise location.

This is the easternmost ford connecting the Council Bluffs road, north of the Platte River, with the Oregon Trail on the south bank.

Lodisa Frizzell, May 27, 1852. "Two horsemen were testing the route, setting willow poles deeply in the sand bars to mark the way . . . wagons . . . were two hours in crossing." [298: 100]

Irene D. Paden, 1943. "About fourteen miles west of Fort Kearney there was a wagon ford across the Great Platte. There was no pressing need to cross . . . [but] always some who for one reason or another . . . mile and a half of rushing water . . . a smug little sign board which announced unfeelingly that the ford was safe. . . ." [298: 100]

GARDEN STATION_p
Mile 336.5 — 4.6 miles southeast of Elm Creek, Nebr.
Phelps County — SE¼ of SW¼, Sec. 14, T8N, R18W

A stage station was located here, according to a manuscript map prepared by Paul C. Henderson.

USGS map, Elm Creek East, Nebr., 1:24,000, 1962 ed.

PLUM CREEK CEMETERY
Mile 351L¼ — 6 miles southwest of Overton, Nebr.
Phelps County — SE¼ of SE¼, Sec. 8, T8N, R20W

The Plum Creek Cemetery holds the graves of twelve to fourteen persons killed in an Indian attack on August 8, 1864. The Plum Creek Station site is 0.7 mile west of the cemetery (NW¼ of SW¼, Sec. 8). A sign outside the cemetery fence places the Plum Creek Military Post and second Freeman Store 600 yards northwest. Most of the victims of the attack were originally buried about 1½ miles to the east (near the SE corner of SW¼ of Sec. 10) where their wagon train was destroyed.

Sir Richard Burton, 1860. "... we dined at Plum Creek on buffalo, probably bull. ..." [56: 551]

LeRoy R. Hafen, 1938. "On August 8 an attack was made upon some trains at Plum Creek, thirty-five miles east [west] of Fort Kearney. Fourteen men were reported killed and some women and children taken prisoner. Three men were killed west of the fort." [156: 323]

Irene D. Paden, 1943. "... [Plum Creek was the] only station left undestroyed between Fort Kearney and Julesburg in the uprising of '64—a pleasant circumstance which was supremely unimportant to its dozen or so inhabitants, who were all scalped. Their nearby grave evidently is seldom visited, but in the center of the plot stands a massive stone monument inscribed, 'The Pioneer Men and Women Who Lost Their Lives by Hostile Indians in the Plum Creek Massacre, Aug. 7, 1864'." [298: 96]

Author's note, 1991. Irene Paden is mistaken in using August 7, 1864, as the date of the Plum Creek Massacre—it occurred on the 8th. The large sign on the cemetery fence describing this event is also in error.

USGS map, Overton, Nebr., 1:24,000, 1962 ed.

WILLOW ISLAND STATION$_p$
Mile 365.2 — 5.3 miles southwest of Lexington, Nebr.
Dawson County — Center of SE¼, Sec. 8, T9N, R22W

The Willow Island stage station was characterized as a "drinking shop." A building now in the Cozad, Nebr. town park may have been moved from this station.

Sir Richard Burton, 1860. ". . . we watered at 'Willow Island Ranch' . . ." [56: 55]

USGS map, Lexington West, Nebr., 1:24,000, 1962 ed.

MIDWAY STATION$_p$
Mile 383.2 — 4 miles south of Gothenburg, Nebr.
Dawson County, NW¼ of NW¼, Sec. 35, T11N, R25W

Midway Station is a log structure, 12'6" by 41'2", built of cedar and originally with a dirt floor and earth roof. (Now it has a concrete floor and a shingle roof.) The west two-thirds was probably built in 1855 and may have served as a trading post before being used as an Overland stage station and Pony Express station. It was midway between Forts Kearny and Laramie. It was a "home station" of the Pony Express, and is one of the few such stations which also served the Overland Stage. Oregon Trail ruts are visible nearby, and ox yokes and other items of trail equipment have been recovered from a nearby slough.

Sir Richard Burton, 1860. "Midway Station . . . whilst changing mules, we attempted . . . to persuade the landlady . . . into giving us supper . . . [but were] refused. . . ." [56: 56]

Joseph G. Masters, 1933. "Midway ('Pat Mullaly's' Ranch) . . . On June 8, 1860, Jim Moore rode from Midway to Julesburg and return distance of 240 miles in fourteen hours and forty-six minutes. Old building still standing and still used as a home on the 96 Ranch . . ." [240: 2]

WPA Writers' Project, 1939. "Lower 96 Ranch . . . A lean-to of the tree-shaded black and white ranch house is a former Pony Express station, a log cabin in good condition; the crevices between the logs have been cemented. This old house, was known as the Pat Mullaly station. . ." [146: 73]

[National Register, Nebraska] contains a detailed description and much additional historical information. There are references to Mark Twain, *Roughing It* (1872); Charles Dawson, *Pioneer Tales of the Oregon Trail* . . . (1912); and Mattes & Henderson, "The

The Old Midway Station, south of Gothenburg, Nebr. The ox yoke at right was found in a nearby slough, on the Oregon Trail.

Pony Express. . . . ." in *Nebraska History,* 41 (June 1960), 83-122. [287: 73]

Author's note, July 15, 1972. This ranch building stands on a ridge of slightly elevated ground extending northward to what was formerly the bank of the Platte River. Springs around the base of this bench provided water for the station which was directly on the Oregon Trail. Where the trail passes a slough about 500 feet west of the station, many artifacts associated with the emigrants—including two ox yokes—have been recovered. That portion of the trail has been preserved from cultivation and is quite apparent as a "swale" several hundred feet in length.

The construction of the ranch building, which was barely saved from destruction when the later ranch house it was adjacent to burned down, shows two types and stages of building. The west two-thirds is "Canadian" post-and-sill type—very probably built by French-Canadian axemen familiar with that style—while the remainder, an obvious addition, is conventional saddle-and-rider type of cabin log-work. Every effort should be made to preserve this magnificent example of early cedar log construction.

USGS map, Gothenburg, Nebr., 1:24,000, 1980 ed.

GILMAN'S STATION$_P$
Mile 401R¾ — 7 miles west of Gothenburg, Nebr.
Lincoln County, SE¼ of SW¼, Sec. 4, T11N, R26W

The building now in the town park at Gothenburg may have been part of the station house of Gilman's. (Doubt exists as to its authenticity as a Pony Express structure.) Robert M. Williams of Gothenburg, manager of the 96 Ranches, says it was originally a two-story structure with stables below, but that only the 15' x 34' upper portion was relocated. It was probably built no earlier than 1858. Being more easily defended because of its two-story construction, Gilman's Station survived the Indian troubles of the mid-1860s.

Eugene F. Ware, 1863. Notes that it was the ranch of J. K. and Jud Gilman. The elder of the two was with the Walker filibuster— Ware says, "to Cuba," but it was to Nicaragua in 1855-57; surviving that he started to California but stopped on the Platte River to trade with the Indians. "They now [1863] had a very fine and defensible ranch. They told us how they made their money . . . traded one well animal for two footsore animals,— even trade, two for one . . . They had a large stock of goods . . . J. K. Gilman . . . a very capable, intelligent man, as was also his brother, although the older was better informed . . ." P. 54, "October 11th, and passed Gilman's ranch, which was built of cedar. . . ." P. 60, "The Gilmans had two hundred cows, but never milked one. The ranch had a number of herders . . . some full-blood French of the Canadian variety. . . ." P. 320 [January 1865] "Indians had been seen around Gilman's ranch east of us, at which a company of Nebraska Cavalry had been stationed." [389: 51-54, 60, 320]

Joseph G. Masters, 1933. "Gilman's Ranch . . . Famous ranch

The blacksmith shop at Machette's Station, west of Gothenburg, Nebraska, still stands.

of the Gilman brothers. William Campbell, the last Pony Express rider married a sister of the two brothers. . . . Owned today by Harry L. Williams of Gothenburg. Mark Twain stopped at this ranch for a meal in crossing the plains in 1861." [240: 2]

WPA Writers' Project, 1939. Concerning the log building in the town park at Gothenburg, Nebraska, "in whose park stands a FUR TRADE POST HOUSE (*adm. free*) that was erected in 1854 on the Oregon Trail four miles east of Fort McPherson. In 1860-1 it was the Fred Machette Pony Express station; later an Overland Stage station, and after the coming of the railroads became a ranch building . . . Gilman Ranch House . . . Mark Twain stopped here on the trip across the plains described in *Roughing It.*" [146: 73]

USGS map, Jeffrey Reservoir NE, Nebr., 1:24,000, 1980 ed.

MACHETTE'S STATION
Mile 402.7 — 4½ miles SW of Brady, Nebr.
Lincoln County — SW¼ of SE¼, Sec. 19, T12N, R27W

The cedar log building remaining at this site is marked as

Pony Express related; however, that has been questioned. What remains is a 13' x 17' structure said to have been a blacksmith shop originally, but now used for the storage of oil and grease on the Upper 96 Ranch. There is an earthen floor and a puncheon roof, now covered by a shingle false roof. The overhang of logs, at the corners, is dressed in a manner similar to those on the building at the Dan Smith West Ranche. This suggests both may have been built by the same workmen.

USGS map, Brady SW, Nebr., 1:24,000.

COTTONWOOD SPRINGS_P
Mile 406.6 — 4.4 miles south of Maxwell, Nebr.
Lincoln County — Center of NW¼, Sec. 15, T12N, R28W

Cottonwood Springs was a fine spring used by emigrants on the Oregon Trail, and later as the water supply for Cottonwood Ranch station and Fort McPherson. It was the only good spring for a considerable distance each way along the Platte River. The claim that the first settlement in the Platte Valley was here appears unlikely.

Eugene F. Ware, Oct. 11, 1863. ". . . camped at a spring called Cottonwood Springs . . . merely a seep in a gulley which had been an old bed of the river, and which had curved up toward Cottonwood Canyon. The water-bed of the river being largely composed of gravel, the water came down . . . and seeped out at a place down in the bank where there had grown a large cottonwood tree. This spring had been dug out, and was the only spring as far as then known along the Platte for two hundred miles . . ." [389: 44-45]

The Fort McPherson marker, Cottonwood Springs.

"Charles McDonald had built a cedar ranch at the mouth of Cottonwood Canyon . . . [p. 46] a year or so before our arrival . . . The main building was about twenty feet front and forty feet deep, and was two stories high. A wing 50 feet extended to the west. The latter was, at the eaves, about eight feet high and fifteen feet deep in the clear. Around it in the rear was a large and defensible corral, which had been extended to the arroyo coming out of the canyon . . . There was a stage station there, and a blacksmith shop kept by a man named Hindman. In the stage station was a telegraph office. There was also on the other side of the road a place where canned goods and liquors were sold, kept by a man named Boyer, who had lost a leg, and whom the Indians called 'Hook-sah,' which meant 'cut-leg.' McDonald had dug, in front of his store, and cribbed up, an inexhaustible well, which was said to be forty-six feet deep; it was rigged with pulley, chain, and heavy oaken buckets. . . ." [389: 45, 46]

Sir Richard Burton, 1860. ". . . halt at Cotton Wood Station. Cramped with a four days' and four nights' ride in this narrow van, we entered the . . . tenement, threw ourselves upon the mattresses, averaging three to each, and ten to a small room, every door, window, and cranny being shut,—after the fashion of these western folk, who make up for a day in the open air by perspiring through the night in unventilated log-huts . . . [p. 59] breakfast composed of various abominations, especially cakes of flour and grease, molasses and dirt, disposed in pretty equal parts. After paying the usual $0.50. . . ." [56: 56, 59]

Irene D. Paden, 1943. "Eighty miles west of Fort Kearney the emigrants found a spring surrounded by cottonwoods. Near it the ravines were filled with scrub cedar. It was always a favorite stop and later became an important stage stop . . . The cedar wood was . . . [p. 101] freighted by ox train for a hundred miles in each direction to supply the stations . . ." [298: 100, 101]

Author's note, July 15, 1972. A monument, accompanied by a wooden signboard, is on the south side of the paved road (which here overlays the Oregon Trail) about 200 feet west of Cottonwood Creek. The monument is a tall slab of red sandstone (8" x 2' x 8') marking the site of the first settlement in the Platte Valley, established in January 1860.

USGS map, Maxwell, Nebr., 1:24,000, 1970 ed.

FORT McPHERSON
Mile 406.7L — 4.4 miles south of Maxwell, Nebr.
Lincoln County — Center of Sec. 16, T12N, R28W

Fort McPherson, a military post, was established to protect

the Platte River route during the turbulent 1860s. A monument portraying a soldier standing at parade rest has occupied the site of the fort's flagstaff since 1928; that and nearby Fort McPherson Military Cemetery (on the reservation of the former fort are all that remain. It was an important that during the Indian wars. The cemetery holds the soldier dead from many fights with the Indians.

Eugene F. Ware, 1863. "Our fort was called 'cantonment McKean,' but the War Department afterwards named it 'Fort McPherson,' after General McPherson, who was killed while with Sherman near Atlanta, Georgia; but the fort was popularly known as 'Fort Cottonwood.'" [389: 61] Details of establishment of a military camp for one troop, completed Nov. 28, 1863, are given. [46-51 and 53-54]

Memorial to Grattan Massacre dead in Fort McPherson cemetery.

Irene D. Paden, 1943. "One of the largest monuments commemorates the victims of the horribly unnecessary Grattan massacre— buried with Christian and military impartiality a few yards from the great monument, lies the body of the Indian, Spotted Horse." [298: 102]

Author's note, July 15, 1972. A monument of white marble in Sec. B, Fort McPherson National Cemetery, marks the reburial place of the remains of 28 enlisted men from the Grattan Massacre. This stone, which is 2 feet by 2 feet, by 3 feet high, states: "In Memory /of / Enlisted Men / Co. G, 6th Inf. / Killed in Action / Near / Ft. Laramie, Wyo. / (Grattan Massacre) / Aug. 18, 1854. "The names of 26 privates, a corporal and sergeant are listed.

USGS map, Maxwell, Nebr., 1:24,000, 1970 ed.

BRADY ISLAND
Mile 410R — just below the town of North Platte, Nebr.

Brady Island, in the Platte River, was a landmark even from the early days of the fur trade.

John C. Fremont, July 1, 1842. Mentions encamping "one mile and a half above the lower end of Brady's island . . ." [Note 14] ". . . fifteen miles long, lies just below North Platte, Nebr. . . . apparently named after . . . Brada or Brady . . . reported to have been killed in 1827 or 1833." [202: 188, 190]

FREMONT'S FORD
Mile 418R2 — 3 miles east of North Platte, Nebr., at the forks of the Platte River
Lincoln County — In Sec. 1 & 12, T13N, R30W

This crossing of the Platte River was popularized by John C. Fremont. Emigrants attempting to follow Fremont evidently crossed at many places immediately above the forks to get upon the tongue of land between the forks. This early ford was little used in later years.

John C. Fremont, July 2, 1842. "The stream is here divided by an island into two channels . . . southern is four hundred and fifty feet wide, having eighteen to twenty inches of water in the deepest . . . exception of a few dry bars, the bed of the river is generally quicksands, in which the carts begin to sink rapidly so soon as the mules halted . . . northern channel, 2,250 feet wide . . . deeper, having frequently three feet of water . . . bed coarse gravel. The whole breadth of the Nebraska [Platte River] . . . 5,350 feet . . . encamped at the point of land immediately at the junction of the North and South forks. . . ." [202: 189]

William J. Ghent, 1934. "Palmer's party in 1845, crossed about five or six miles above the forks. . . ." [149: 130]

Irene D. Paden, 1943. "We traced our steps from the ford at the Forks back to the trail proper . . . between us and the river (which was now the South Platte) lay Fremont's Slough . . . [p. 106] many crossed immediately above the forks, following Fremont's example. There were several little-used fords. . . ." [298: 105-06]

Author's note, July 16, 1972. The tongue of land between the forks is flat for 20 miles upward and the South Fork was probably fordable at many places. Overton Johnson crossed above the forks in 1843, and John Minto crossed four or five miles above in 1844.

USGS map, Maxwell SW, Nebr., 1:24,000, 1970 ed.

COLD SPRINGS_P
Mile 421.1 — 1.5 miles south
of North Platte interchange on I-80.
Lincoln County — SE¼ of SE¼ of Sec. 18, T13N, R30W

A Pony Express and stage station was established here, on the site of Cold Springs, known to the emigrants.

J. Goldsborough Bruff, June 24, 1849. "A delightful cool spring near us. Clay bluffs ahead [O'Fallon's Bluff) on the left, & half a mile below, on the right are the forks of the Platte." [52: 23]

Merrill J. Mattes, 1969. "Here, due south of present North Platte, was a Pony Express and stage station called Cold Springs . . . and Cold Springs Ranch and stage station, of cedar and adobe. [249: 277]

USGS map, Lake Maloney, Nebr., 1:24,000, 1970 ed.

FREMONT SPRINGS_P
Mile 433.0 — 2 miles southeast of Hershey, Nebr.
Lincoln County — NW¼ of NW¼ of Sec. 4, T13N, R32W

This name was given to a group of springs discovered by John C. Fremont in 1842. A Pony Express and stage station was later established here.

Sir Richard Burton, 1860. ". . . at Fremont Springs, so called from an excellent little water behind the station. The building is of a style peculiar to the south . . . two huts connected by a roof-work of thatched timber, which acts as the best and coolest of verandahs." [56: 59]

Irene D. Paden, 1943. "We passed the marker at the site of Bishop's Station. . . ." [298: 105]

Merrill J. Mattes, 1969. "Opposite Hershey and at the site of the Lower Crossing of the South Platte was Fremont Springs Pony Express and Stage Station, another home station . . . Clark calls it Buffalo Ranch. . . ." [244: 277]

USGS map, Hershey East, Nebr., 1:24,000, 1970 ed.

FORD NO. 1 (LOWER FORD)
Mile 443.7

The first ford cannot now be located at a precise point. Crossings were made between Fremont Springs and O'Fallon's Bluff as conditions dictated—that is, from 10 to 20 miles above the forks. The early Oregon emigrants tended to cross the South Platte at points lower than the later, California-bound traffic.

J. M. Harrison, 1846. "Traveled up South fork of Platte, 20 miles then crossed it, deep fording, raised wagon beds, bottom quicksand, all got over safely. Left south fork—struck up north fork of Platte to mouth of Ash Hollow. . . ." [165: letter]

George McKinstry, June 17, 1846. ". . . travelled 17 miles [from the forks] crossed the Platte . . . river about ¾ mile wide 2½ feet deep   distance by way of the crossing one mile   the bottom of the river is coarse sand and gravel all the wagons crossed safe, the river was riseing some 6 or 8 inches pr day would not been able to cross next morning." [275:I, 213]

Merrill J. Mattes, 1969. Prefers to place this ford 10 miles downstream, or in the vicinity of present Hershey, Nebr. [249: 265, 277]

USGS map, North Platte, Nebr., 1:250,000, 1954 ed.

O'FALLON'S BLUFF
Mile 444.5 — 2 miles southeast of Sutherland, Nebr.
Lincoln County — Sec. 33 & 34, T14N, R33W

O'Fallon's Bluff is a low, sandstone ridge one and a half miles in extent blockading the south bank of the river. The Oregon Trail bypassed this landmark of the fur trade by a swing to the left, or south. A stage station and military post was later established east of the bluff.

Osborne Cross, 1849. Described O'Fallon's Bluff. [101: 311]

Irene D. Paden, 1943. ". . . the first of the famous trail landmarks south of the river: O'Fallon's Bluffs . . . only remarkable in being the vanguard of the sandstone formations . . . [p. 106] We went up and over the flat top of the bluff just as the emigrants had been forced to do." [298: 105-06]

Merrill J. Mattes, 1969. ". . . O'Fallon's Bluff Station . . . or Military Post . . . east of the famous bluff itself, at the point where the upland detour began . . . [p. 264] Emigrant Starr places this seventeen miles above Brady's Island and says it was named after a man who made a fortune selling liquor to the Indians at this place. Meline thought it was named after a hunter killed there by Cheyennes. Birge understood that this unfortunate was Benjamin O'Fallon of St. Louis . . . since the bluff came nearly to the river, most travelers avoided any threat of Indian ambush here by taking a trail which detoured southward over the bluff, described in the Council Bluffs *Daily Telegraph* as a 'precipitous sand ridge.'" [249: 277, 264]

Author's note. O'Fallon's Bluffs were probably named for the early Indian agent, Benjamin O'Fallon, or for his fur-trading brother, John. Both were prominent in the trans-Mississippi region. [160:V, 255,281]

At the rest stop on the east-bound lane of I-80 (1.6 miles east of the Sutherland exit) the Oregon Trail rut swale may be seen as it passes over O'Fallon's Bluff. About 400 feet behind the rest area wagon tires have been set in the ruts to mark the line of the swale.

USGS map, Hershey West, Nebr., 1:24,000.

FORD NO. 2 (MIDDLE FORD)$_P$
Mile 453.0 — Paxton, Nebr.
Keith County — Sec. 8, T13N, R35W

This is among the lower fords of the South Platte River.
Claire W. Churchill, 1853. Identified this crossing. [72: 77]
William J. Ghent, 1934. ". . . Bryant's party, in 1846, [crossed] thirty-four miles above." [149: 130]
Author's note. Site identified by Paul C. Henderson.
USGS map, Paxton South, Nebr., 1:24,000.

ALKALI LAKE$_P$
Mile 460.6 — 7.5 miles west of Paxton, Nebr.
Keith County — NE¼ of SW¼, Sec. 12, T13N, R37W

This feature was of little interest to the emigrants, but important both as a Pony Express and stage station in later years.
Merrill J. Mattes, 1969. "There was a Pony Express and stage station here (a home station, according to R & C), about seven miles west of Paxton. In 1860 Clarke named it Pikes Peak Station, but it seems generally to be known as Alkali Lake . . . or

'Alkali Station, Telegraph Office and Military Post' . . . Young and Meline both describe the place as surrounded by the white incrustation of alkali. All agree it was 'a dreary, desolate location.'" [249: 278]

USGS map, Paxton SW, Nebr., 1:24,000.

FORD NO. 3 (MIDDLE OR NEW FORD)
Mile 463.4 — Near Roscoe, Nebr.
Keith County — Sec. 3, T13N, R37W

This crossing was first used by Capt. Benjamin Bonneville in 1832, but seldom used by emigrants until rediscovered during the gold rush.

John Ball, 1832. Identified the crossing by mileage. [314: 87]

Virgil Pringle, June 11, 1846. "Went on to the ford and found ourselves too late to cross . . . [June 12] Crossed the river in the morning. Found the water in no place over our forward axle, seldom that deep; the pulling hard through the sand; put double teams to our wagons; the difficulty nothing compared to the appearance. The distance with the angle we took being about one and a half miles. Traveled up the south fork to the place of leaving it for the N. fork, it being 12 miles." [275:1, 172]

George McKinstry, June 18, 1846. After crossing South Platte River, he states: "Travelled up the south fork some 13 miles to the upper crossing and camped." [275:1, 213] Since the next day's drive of 23 miles brought them to Ash Hollow, the camping place was the Lower California Crossing, and the place where they crossed was Ford No. 3.

Merrill J. Mattes, 1969. "Here were the adobe ruins of Omaha Ranch. Somewhere in this same area was the Middle Crossing of the California Gold Rush. . . . [p. 265] The Middle Ford was first used by Capt. Bonneville in 1832. It was not used much after that until the Gold Rush, when it was sometimes referred to as 'the new ford.'" [249: 278, 265]

USGS map, Ogallala SE, Nebr., 1:24,000.

GILL'S STATION[p]
Mile 472.9 — One mile due south of Ogallala, Nebr.
Keith County — NE¼ of SW¼, Sec. 7, T13N, R38W

This was a Pony Express station and a military post.

Merrill J. Mattes, 1969. "Across the river from Ogallala was a routine Pony Express and stage station variously called Gill's . . . Sand Hill . . . and Sand Hill Stage Station. Frank Young found it occupied by soldiers, and it looked 'as comfortless as a Siberian picture in a story book'." [249: 278]

USGS map, Ogallala SW, Nebr., 1:24,000.

DIAMOND SPRING STATION_P
Mile 482.3 — 1.5 miles southwest of Brule, Nebr.
Keith County — SE¼ of SW¼, Sec. 21, T13N, R40W

This was a Pony Express and stage station.

Merrill J. Mattes, 1969. "Opposite and less than a mile west of Brule is the identified site of the Pony Express and stage home station called Diamond Springs by everyone without argument. It was of cedar." [249: 278]

USGS map, Brule, Nebr., 1:24,000, 1961 ed.

BEAUVAIS TRADING POST (STARR RANCH)_P
Mile 484.3 — 3.3 miles southwest of Brule, Nebr.
Keith County — NW¼ of NW¼, Sec. 30, T13N, R40W

This trading post was established by Geminien P. Beauvais in 1859 to accommodate the emigrant traffic to Colorado, and abandoned in 1865 as a result of continual Indian harrassment.

Merrill J. Mattes, 1969. "Robidoux's several posts in the Scott's Bluffs vicinity and Beauvais' post at Old California Crossing were the only ones that had the semblance of permanent structures. [p. 279] . . . This point, four miles west of Brule, was the famous pre-1859 Upper Crossing or Old California Crossing and the identified site of Beauvais' Ranche. M.O. Morris and Sarah Herndon call it the Star Ranche. Young describes it as 'a famous old trading post. Beauvais is an old French trader who has been located here for the best part of a generation.' He found here, in addition to cedar houses, one big 'doby storehouse, with three or four small dobys alongside, and a barracks for a small garrison.' This was called Beauvais Ranche Military Post . . ., or Beauvais Station by Sitgreaves, whose map of the environs shows the South Platte Ford less than one half mile west of Beauvais Station." [249: 270, 279]

Author's note. For the dates of establishment and abandonment of this post, and for the circumstances of its use, see LeRoy R. Hafen. [160:VII, 39-41]

USGS map, Brule, Nebr., 1:24,000, 1961 ed.

LOWER (OLD) CALIFORNIA CROSSING_p
Mile 485.0 — 3.8 miles west of Brule, Nebr.
Keith County — SW¼ of SW¼, Sec. 19, T13N, R40W

This crossing of the South Platte River consisted of a ford requiring from three-quarters to one and a half miles of travel through shallow water covering a bottom of shifting sand.

Although known earlier, this crossing was popularized by the forty niners, and it was from their use that it came to be known as a "California" crossing—further differentiated from a later crossing used by California-bound emigrants by adding "Lower," or "Old," to the name. The later crossing was about 22 miles up the South Platte River (westward) at the mouth of Lodge Pole Creek and near where Julesburg, Colorado, appeared.

James A. Pritchard, May 26, 1849. ". . . by noon reached the ford, 15 ms distant. And by 3 PM were all safely landed across the river. . . here is about one mile wide, with a bottom composed of quick sand. The sand breaks under the wagon wheels and it jars worse than if it was passing over the roughest kind of frozen ground . . . compelled to put two teams to each wagon . . . If the wagon is permitted to stand for one minute they bury down in the sand. [p. 73] . . . difficult finding the road on account of the holes in the bed caused by the action of the current which was constantly shifting the sand. There was a Frenchman there who acted as pilott—his charge was a tin full of sugar and coffee to the wagon. . . ." [317: 72-73]

William J. Ghent, 1934. "What came to be known as the Lower California Crossing is a few miles west of Brule, Keith County, about sixty-three miles from the forks." [149: 130]

Irene D. Paden, 1943. ". . . the great bulk of the migration crossed four miles above Brule, Nebraska, at a spot called the Lower California Crossing, although in the late fifties and the sixties the Upper California Crossing at Julesburg, Colorado, became a rival. [p. 107] A farm road brought us to a long, one-way bridge—very old and very quaint . . . as nearly as possible at the site of the old ford . . . river is now quite-ordinary . . . pioneers estimated the South Platte at this point . . . [at more than] a half-mile . . . [p. 108] . . . width varied greatly from week to week and even from day to day . . . wagon trains never traveled straight across: they went down with the current to about the middle of the distance and then if able turned and came up diagonally against the current. One train which found the river about three-quarters of a mile wide, traveled a mile and a half in the water . . . the crossing at Brule was the greatest ford of the Overland trek . . . other large streams were ferried or bridged, but not the South Platte. Its great width, yielding quicksands and lack of large timber near at hand . . . shallows and sand bars prevented the operation of a ferry . . . [p. 109] Ten and fifteen yoke of oxen were sometimes hooked to a wagon . . ." [298: 106-09]

Merrill J. Mattes, 1969. "The one most heavily used was the Upper Crossing, otherwise known variously as Kearny's Ford (from 1845 expedition), Beauvais' Crossing (from the nearby trading post), Laramie Crossing, Ash Hollow Crossing, or California Crossing. After 1859, with a new California Crossing at Julesburg, this became the Old California Crossing." [249: 265, 266]

Author's note, July 16, 1962. The South Platte River was here found to be a very insignificant stream, due to withdrawal of irrigation water higher up. The growth of vegetation—cottonwood trees and willow brush—on the bottomlands has altered the open aspect of pioneer days to that of a brushy jungle where the river's course is more sensed than seen.

USGS map, Brule, Nebr., 1:24,000, 1961 ed.

CALIFORNIA HILL MONUMENT
Mile 486.0 — 4.3 miles west of Brule, Nebr.
Keith County — S¼ Cor., Sec. 13, T13N, R41W

The emigrants had to climb 240 feet in 1.7 miles, from the Beauvais (or Lower California) Crossing of the South Platte River, to reach the high plateau between the two forks. The Oregon Trail shows plainly the entire way up the hill, with some very imposing ruts in places. Undue notice was given this grade because the emigrants had not yet seen any really steep terrain. The name came naturally from its proximity to one of the two crossings most popular with gold rush travelers.

Irene D. Paden, 1943. ". . . left the South Platte . . . began to climb the rough, high land between the forks. They called the

Author Haines has lined up his roll of maps with the scar up California Hill.
The view from the hill is back toward the South Platte River.

first steep pull 'California Hill.' Deep ascending ruts still mar its
surface. A tiny school sits squatly on the rounded hillside like a
flea. [298: 112-13]

   Author's note, July 16, 1972. An Oregon Trail monument
located 100 feet north of Highway 30, at the approximate
crossing of the trail, states: "Oregon / Trail / marked by / the
State of / Nebraska 1912 / Old California / River Crossing /
South 14 Degrees / East. At a point 300 feet south of the Union
Pacific Railroad track, and also on the trail, is a rectangular
"entrenchment" (according to local residents). This 1½-foot-
deep trench, with spoil bank on the outside, encloses an area 54
by 99 feet. It is oriented with its long axis due north and is on
land which has never been cultivated. It is the property of the
Emil Ruser estate.

   From the northeast corner of the "entrenchment," a weathered
sign on the fence line is 543 feet distant, on azimuth 74 degrees
true. The sign, which has an arrow pointing south, states:
"Lower California / Crossing / of the Oregon Trail / Beauvais
Station / ¼ mile."

There is some local opinion that the "California Hill" was a small knoll north of the railroad track and almost exactly on the line between sections 19 and 24, but the plain evidence of the Oregon Trail track disproves that.

The land containing the major rut swales is now owned by the Oregon-California Trails Association.

USGS map, Brule, Nebr., 1:24,000, 1961 ed.

WINDLASS HILL
Mile 500.8 — Near the head of Ash Hollow
Garden County, Nebr. — NE¼ of NE¼, Sec. 22, T15N, R42W

This is a steep hill by which the main emigrant route descended into Ash Hollow, about three miles south of its mouth. Here wagons had to descend on a slope of 25 degrees for about 300 feet (a vertical drop of 150 feet), and subsequent erosion of the track worn by rough-locking the wheels has left visible evidence.

This was the first really steep grade encountered on the Oregon Trail, and the impression made upon emigrants was particularly vivid. There is no evidence to support the legend behind the name, "Windlass Hill," which is not contemporary.

James A. Pritchard, May 27, 1849. "The descent into the hollow is very steep and difficult to get down." [317: 74]

Osborne Cross, June 15, 1849. ". . . high level prairie until you approach near the Platte where you strike Ash Hollow, a deep ravine . . . about two miles long . . . were compelled to let the wagons down into it by ropes . . . are a few ash trees and dwarf cedars . . . lost more than three hours. . . ." [101: 89]

Howard Stansbury, July 3, 1852. "Here we were obliged, from the steepness of the road, to let the wagons down by ropes, but the labor of a dozen men for a few days would make a descent easy and safe. The bottom of Ash Creek is tolerably well wooded, principally with ash and some dwarf cedars . . . traces of the great tide of emigration . . . plainly visible in remains of camp fires, in blazed trees covered with innumerable names . . . total absence of all herbage." [361: 41]

Irene D. Paden, 1943. The "Windlass Hill" legend makes an appearance in this entirely improbable account of how the descent was accomplished—by staking down a wagon at the top of the hill with one set of wheels free, taking a turn of the lowering-line around the axle and having men hold back on the wheel spokes (an impossibility since a wagon axle does not

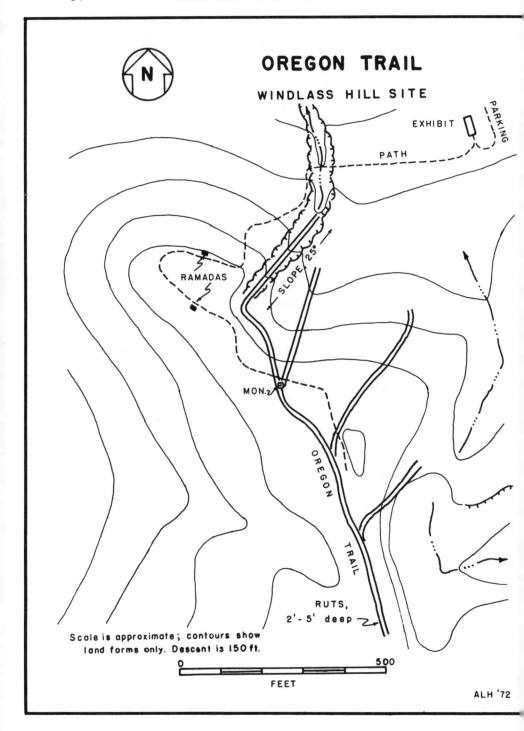

OREGON TRAIL

WINDLASS HILL SITE

N

EXHIBIT

PARKING

PATH

SLOPE 25°

RAMADAS

MON.?

OREGON

TRAIL

RUTS,
2'- 5' deep

Scale is approximate; contours show
land forms only. Descent is 150 ft.

0   500

FEET

ALH '72

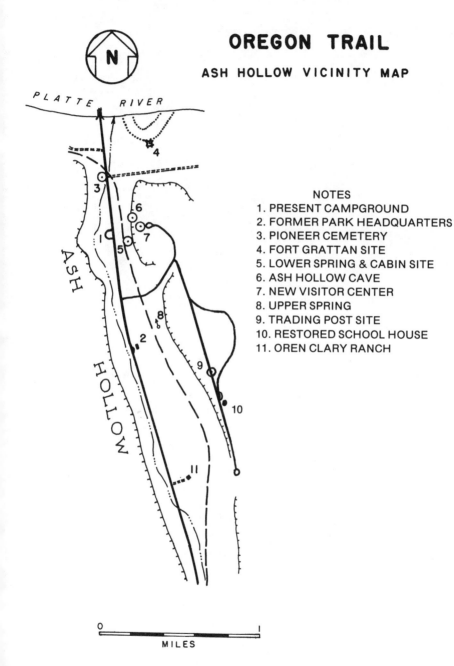

OREGON TRAIL

ASH HOLLOW VICINITY MAP

NOTES
1. PRESENT CAMPGROUND
2. FORMER PARK HEADQUARTERS
3. PIONEER CEMETERY
4. FORT GRATTAN SITE
5. LOWER SPRING & CABIN SITE
6. ASH HOLLOW CAVE
7. NEW VISITOR CENTER
8. UPPER SPRING
9. TRADING POST SITE
10. RESTORED SCHOOL HOUSE
11. OREN CLARY RANCH

PLATTE RIVER

ASH HOLLOW

0 1
MILES

ALH '72

Haines is shown here atop Windlass Hill, looking back toward the south.

rotate with the wheels, but is fixed in place). [298: 120-21]

Merrill J. Mattes, 1969. "Just how does the 'windlass' idea fit into this picture? No fixed contraption for lowering wagons is mentioned in any of several hundred researched emigrant journals during the period of our concern, 1830-1866. If there ever was a windlass, it had to be sometime after 1866—not during the migrations to Oregon and California. . . . Citing the hearsay evidence of old-timers, Mari Sandoz has described how an ingenious wagon boss, using ropes, chains, and an ash tree trunk, improvised a drum windlass to lower his wagons and that this device was used by freighters for several years . . . does not associate this legendary affair with the covered wagon emigrants." [249: 295] Pp. 293-95 provide more information on Windlass Hill.

Gregory M. Franzwa, 1972. "Look straight up the hill. . . . There is a faint set of ruts on the left, leading down from a stone monument atop the hill which is barely visible. To the right is an angry wash, coursing down this steep grade. This is the Oregon Trail. Wagon wheels cut into the turf, pulverizing it, and

The view from the brow of Windlass Hill—light area in the center is the visitor parking lot.

the rains took it from there. The jagged scar is getting deeper." [141: 200]

Author's note, July 11, 1972. A parking area under construction at the foot of Windlass Hill will have an exhibit shelter in the form of a Conestoga wagon (stone base, iron bows and canvas top) containing metal-photos; and a paved trail will provide access to the top of the hill. Three routes of wagon descent are visible (see special sketch map, "Windlass Hill"). The westernmost track was evidently the most used as its swale is two to four feet deep on the steep part (a 300-foot section on a slope of 25 degrees, where the vertical drop is about 150 feet); below that, erosion has created a gulley now 25 feet deep, and equally wide, across the same bench the exhibit structure stands on. The two tracks to the east are not prominent. At the top of Windlass Hill is a granite monument which states: "Oregon / Trail / Marked By / The State Of / Nebraska 1912 / Windlass Hill / Entrance To / Ash Hollow.

USGS map, Ruthton, Nebr., 1:24,000.

Wilma (Mrs. Aubrey L.) Haines is shown beside the jagged scar up Windlass Hill. Erosion attacked the soil pulverized a century earlier by the wagon wheels.

ASH HOLLOW TRADING POST (SITE)
Mile 503.1 — Near the Oren Clary Ranch, Ash Hollow
Garden County, Nebr. — NE¼ of SE¼, Sec. 10, T15N, R42W

Evidences of three buildings have been found on the east side of Ash Hollow, about two miles from its mouth. These have been tentatively identified as structures of a trading post. Test excavations have yielded musket balls, bottle glass, nails, char, and other artifacts from two of the building sites. These are believed to be the structures noted by emigrants from 1851 to 1853.

Merrill J. Mattes, 1969. ". . . in 1851 . . . William Lobenstine's testimony . . . of an actual trading post . . . 'we met a kind of trading post where several articles for the remainder of the journey for a reasonable price can be got' . . . So the unidentified trading post of 1851 was a new structure in a new location, not at the canyon mouth like the 1846-1850 'post office' version, but halfway up the hollow, between the canyon outlet and the Cedar Grove intersection . . ." There are several other references to a trading establishment, pp. 307-08, but Mattes concludes: "The Ash Hollow trader of 1851-1853 remains an enigma." [249: 307]

Author's note, July 13, 1972. Visited the site with Park Superintendent Dennis Shimmin. It is about 500 feet north of the school house now being reconstructed and 100 feet west of the access road. Preservation of the schoolhouse (one of the first in this part of Nebraska) was included in the agreement through which the state obtained three parcels of land in Ash Hollow for park purposes.

According to the Nebraska Game and Parks Commission, the name of Ash Hollow goes back at least to 1832 [see 289], and John C. Fremont, who reached the place July 4, 1842, translated the French name, *Coulée des Frénes*, as the "Draw of the Ash Trees." [202:I, 192]

USGS map, Ruthton, Nebr., 1:24,000.

ASH HOLLOW SPRING (LOWER)
Mile 504.5 — Near the mouth of Ash Hollow
Garden County, Nebr. — Approx. center of Sec. 3, T15N, R42W

Ash Hollow Spring is at the foot of the rocky bluff, on the east side, and now feeds an ice pond which is 20 feet wide at the head and 100 feet wide at the dam, about 400 feet below. A cabin which served as an emigrant post office was associated with the spring.

The springs in Ash Hollow provided the best water to be had for many miles either way along the valley of the Platte Rivers, and this lower spring was evidently the best of several in the vicinity.

Rufus B. Sage, Fall 1841. ". . . mouth of Ash Creek . . . The stream at this place is a broad bed of sand, entirely dry, except at the spring mouths. Higher up, however, it affords a generous supply of pure running water, sustained by the numerous feeders that force their way into it, from the high grounds dividing the two rivers [the two principal branches of the Platte River]." [338:IV, 189]

Virgil Pringle, June 13, 1846. "The road down Ash Creek bad for three or four miles . . . a fine spring . . . and a cabin called Ash Grove Hotel . . ." [275:I, 172]

George McKinstry, June 19, 1846. ". . . the hills verry steep at the mouth of the hollow next the river we found a small log building put up by some Mackinaw boat men last winter as they were caught by the ice it is called 'ash hollow Hotel' . . ." [275:I, 213]

James A. Pritchard, May 27, 1849. "The bed of branch is sandy and heavy pulling with several good springs of clear cold water breaking out of the ground." [317: 74]

Angelina Farley, July 25, 1850. ". . . camped between two rocky bluffs, near an excellent spring a luxury we do not often enjoy." [133: diary]

Irene D. Paden, 1943. "On the right of the highway [east] are rush-filled ponds, fed by the spring which made the mouth of Ash Hollow a famous camping ground . . . prowling around the little ruined hut. It is the successor to the original trapper's log cabin that stood there in the first days of the migrations and was used as a sort of emergency post office. Notices of lost cattle were posted, and messages to friends traveling a few days or weeks behind. Letters to families . . . were pinned to the wall with a coin and note begging that some east bound trader or straggler returning . . . would take them back to 'the States' and mail them there." [298: 121-22]

Merrill J. Mattes, 1969. "Here at long last was an abundant supply of firewood, and the most copious supply of pure water this side of the Missouri River. [p. 298] . . . Ash Creek was not a true creek but a series of springs, culminating in an oasis near the mouth of the canyon." [249: 282, 298] See pp. 306-07 for more information on the post office-cabin.

Gregory M. Franzwa, 1972. "The spring mentioned in so many diaries is a half mile south of the grave [of Rachel Pattison], in a grove of trees now used as a campground." [141: 204]

Author's note, July 14, 1972. Oren Clary, who formerly owned the land on which the lower spring is located, recalls that cabin debris (chimney stones) were shoved aside in the building of the ice pond. Another spring, now very much overgrown, remains about 500 feet northeast of the present park headquarters (see Ash Hollow Vicinity Map, Site No. 8).

At a later time the cabin-post office at Ash Hollow Spring was superceded by the U.S. Mail Station No. 21, on the route to Salt Lake City, Utah Territory.

USGS map, Ruthton, Nebr., 1:24,000.

An Oregon Trail marker stands beside the grave of Rachel Pattison, in the Ash Hollow cemetery. The original gravestone is preserved behind glass in the cavity below the plaque.

RACHEL PATTISON GRAVE
Mile 504.9 — 2.2 miles southeast of Lewellen, Nebr.
Garden County, Nebr. — NW¼ of NW¼, Sec. 3, T15N, R42W

A cemetery has developed around several emigrant burials the most noted of them the grave of Rachel Pattison—at the mouth of Ash Hollow, between the highway and the western bluff. It is the only marked grave of many made in this vicinity during the latter days of the Oregon Trail.

J. Goldsborough Bruff, July 1, 1849. "Grave on end of bluff terminating Ash Hollow. above—left of trail leavg hollow—'Rachel E. Pattison Aged 18, June 19, 49.'" [52: 27]

Irene D. Paden, 1943. "A local legend has grown up to the effect that it was in reprisal of an attempt to kill or capture her that the battle of Ash Hollow was fought. This is a contradiction of the fact that she had been dead for several years when the fight occurred." [298: 122]

Annals of Wyoming, 1949. Concerning the dedication of the

monument honoring Rachel E. Pattison, in June 1949, at Ash Hollow; students of the Lewellen High School provided the plaque, W. W. Morrison of Cheyenne designed the monument and residents of Lewellen provided materials and labor for its construction. [14: 223]

Merrill J. Mattes, 1969. ". . . Rachel Pattison, age eighteen, a bride of three months. Her train reached the Hollow on June 18 and paused for repairs. On the following day, according to Nathan Pattison, cholera struck her in its swift, terrible way: 'Rachel taken sick in the morning, died that night.'" [249: 301]

W. W. Morrison, July 10, 1972. His notes indicate: "d. of cholera—with child—18 yrs. old—Sanford Johnson grave nearby—d. smallpox—small stone." [279: Oral information]

Author's note, July 14, 1972. The monument is a stubby obelisk with a glass-covered niche containing the original headstone. A granite Oregon Trail monument is four feet to the right (north) and an unmarked limestone is 16 feet to the left (south), probably marking the grave of Sanford Johnson. Four other early graves are said to intervene. These are only a few of the many burials in and near Ash Hollow. Eli Griggery was buried June 19, 1846, at the foot of the bluff near the lower spring [Nicholas Carriger Diary—275:I, 152-53]. Theodore Potter noted "sixty fresh made graves" in 1852, and five of Gen. Hamey's soldiers—casualties in the Battle of Blue Water—were buried just west of Ash Hollow Cemetery, beside the emigrant road, in 1855. The exact situation of all these burials is now unknown. There was a grim reminder of the mortality at this place when a freshet washed out a skull last spring near the park headquarters.

Reference. Randy Brown, "Buried at Ash Hollow," in *Overland Journal*, 8/3 (1990), 18-25.

USGS map, Lewellen, Nebr., 1:24,000.

FORT GRATTEN$_p$
Mile 505R⅓ — At the mouth of Ash Hollow
Garden County, Nebr. — SE¼ of Sec. 34, T16N, R42W

Fort Grattan was a rectangular, sod-walled redoubt 20' x 40' in size with a roof and square loopholes. A low mound left by subsidence of the south wall is all that remains, the other walls having been swept away by a meander of the North Platte River.

This was a temporary supply depot which may also have been

used as a temporary mail station. The establishment of this defense point in September 1855 followed the Battle of Blue Water, which developed out of the Grattan Massacre. Its use by the army was limited to a few months.

LeRoy R. Hafen, 1938. "General Harney established a temporary post, called Fort Grattan, at the mouth of Ash Hollow, garrisoned it with a company of the Sixth Infantry and then continued up the Platte to Fort Laramie." [156: 243; 240-45 for a description of the Battle of Blue Water]

LeRoy R. Hafen, 1958. A description of the Battle of Blue Water ("Harney Massacre") as given by Captain Phelps in 1857. [158: 113-14]

Merrill J. Mattes, 1969. ". . . Fort Grattan . . . a sort of convalescent station and military supply depot . . . was apparently abandoned before the spring of 1856 and possibly earlier, had no official standing as a military post . . . viewed by Grant Shumway about forty years after the battle, 'the roof had been removed, and the sod walls with the square port holes were all that remained. It was about 20 feet north and south, 40 east and west.' In 1904 Robert Harvey found here 'ridges and depressions,' which were the only remains. . . ." [249: 329-30; The Battle of Blue Water is discussed at length, 311-38.]

Author's note, July 14, 1972. The remaining evidence of Fort Grattan is a low mound on the south bank of a meander of the North Platte River, about 1,500 feet east of the highway bridge by which U.S. 26 crosses to Lewellen. It is covered by a triangular patch of buckbrush about 20 by 30 feet in extent (the only such growth along the north edge of Oren Clary's hay meadow). The authenticity of the site is attested by Clary, who is 70 years old and can remember the ruin before the river swept most of it away.

USGS map, Ruthton, Nebr., 1:24,000.

LONE TREE$_p$
Mile 505R2 — About 2 miles east of the mouth of Ash Hollow
Garden County, Nebr. — SW¼ of Sec. 36, T16N, R42W

This particular "Lone Tree," a landmark of Oregon Trail days, stood on the north bank of the North Platte River, but it was visible to emigrants approaching Ash Hollow by the road on the south side of the river, as well as those following the Council Bluffs road on the north. Like most solitary trees along the emigration route, it was probably used for firewood.

Irene D. Paden, 1943. ". . . the Lone Tree, nearly opposite Ash Hollow, was the only specimen [north of the river] for two hundred miles." [298: 115]

Merrill J. Mattes, 1969. "Orson Pratt . . . 1847 . . . describes another notable landmark which was on the north bank and a short distance downstream from Ash Hollow—'Lone Tree.' . . . 'May 20 . . . halted for noon directly opposite the place where the Oregon Road strikes the North Fork . . . A short distance below our noon halt we passed a lonely cedar tree upon the north bank of the river, in the branches of which were deposited the remains of an Indian child.'" [249: 292]

USGS map, Ruthton, Nebr., 1:24,000.

A. KELLY GRAVE_p
Mile 506.8 — 0.2 miles southwest of Lewellen, Nebr.
Garden County — 700' N. of SE cor., Sec. 32, T16N, R43W

This is a trailside grave of the late Oregon Trail period; probably one of several burials at this place.

Author's note, July 16, 1972. This site is 1.4 miles west of the junction of US Highway 26 with the county road along the south side of the North Platte River, on a low ridge between the county road and the entry road to the Kate Taylor place. The Kelly grave is marked by a 1' x 2' x 5' granite slab, facing north, incised as follows: "Oregon / Trail / Marked By / The State Of / Nebraska / 1913 / Trail 300 Ft. No. / Following Copied From Original / Marker / A. Kelly /B._____ / Died July 14. 52"

Eight feet east and three feet south of the monument is a 4" x 10" limestone projecting eight inches out of the ground, with a depression behind it; and six feet west and two feet south of the monument is a 2" x 6" limestone projecting four inches out of the ground, with no evident depression.

The monument is 30 feet above the farm yard of the Taylor ranch, which is on the Oregon Trail alignment.

USGS map, Lewellen, Nebr., 1:24,000.

JOHN HOLLMAN GRAVE_P
Mile 519.5 — 2½ miles south of Oskkosh, Nebr.
Garden County — NW¼ of NE¼, Sec. 10, T16N, R44W

This trailside grave is from the late emigration period, and is marked by the original stone.

Author's note, July 17, 1972. The grave is 80 feet north of the county road, on the edge of a broad, sandy wash. It has been enclosed by concrete sills forming a 10-foot square supporting a hogwire fence topped with a strand of barbed wire. The original gravestone (a cracked sandstone), has been set into concrete, and this much of the inscription is readable: "JOHN _____LLMAN / JUNE 5 / AD 01" Both the concrete carrying the gravestone and the sill on the west side have slumped due to undercutting of the bank by high water in the wash.

There is another monument which formerly stood northeast of the grave. This granite slab of the type used by the state of Nebraska to mark the Oregon Trail sixty years ago, was 275 feet north of the county road, under a large tree, but it has been moved several hundred feet southeast to a position alongside an information panel facing Nebraska State Route 27. It is incised as follows: "Oregon / Trail / Marked By / The State of / Nebraska / 1914 / Grave of / John Hollman / Died June 5, 1852 / S. 72 degrees 21 minutes / W. 715 Feet" (The bearing and distance are no longer correct.)

USGS map, Oshkosh, Nebr., 1:24,000.

ANCIENT BLUFF RUINS_p
Mile 544R2 — 4 Miles east of Broadwater, Nebr.
Morrill County — Sec. 31 & 32, T19N, R47W

This is a landmark formation of eroded sandstone on the north bank of the North Platte River. It was of particular interest to emigrants on the Council Bluffs road as the first place from which Chimney Rock was visible.

George W. Fox describes this feature. [140: 580-601]

USGS map, Broadwater, Nebr., 1:24,000.

U.S. MAIL STATION NO. 22_p
Mile 544.3 — 4.5 miles southeast of Broadwater, Nebr.
Morrill County — SE¼ of NE¼, Sec. 12, T18N, R48W

This location was established on a manuscript map prepared by Paul C. Henderson.

USGS map, Broadwater, Nebr., 1:24,000, 1965 ed.

PUMPKIN CREEK
Mile 558.2 — 4 miles southeast of Bridgeport, Nebr.
Morrill County — SE¼ of SW¼, Sec. 12, T19N, R50W

Pumpkin Creek, with a lesser fork, drains the vicinity of Courthouse Rock. The emigrants knew it by various names, mostly of obscure origin; and modern cartography has solved the problem by settling upon Pumpkin Creek—a name which appeared first in 1859.

Rufus B. Sage, Oct. 24, 1841. "About noon we crossed Gonneville's creek, a large easterly affluent of the Platte. This stream also derives its name from a trapper, killed near it in an Indian fight, some eight years ago. [338:IV, 199]

Sir Richard Burton, 1860. "The principal [streams] are Omaha Creek, more generally known as 'Little Punkin,' and Lawrence Fork . . . a pretty bubbling stream, running over sand and stones washed down from the Courthouse Ridge. . . ." [56: 80]

Merrill J. Mattes, 1969. The confusion surrounding the name of this stream and its minor branch is considered in some detail. He says: "For purposes of convenience, and to preserve the reader's sanity, it will be referred to here as Pumpkin Creek, since that name (or its variants 'Punkin' or 'Pumpkinseed') has been in use for over 100 years." [249: 341-42]

USGS map, Bridgeport, Nebr., 1:24,000, 1965 ed.

COURTHOUSE ROCK
Mile 561L4 — 5 miles due south of Bridgeport, Nebr.
Morrill County — NW¼ of NW¼, Sec. 29, T19N, R50W

Courthouse Rock is a massive sandstone protuberance south of the Oregon Trail. It was variously likened to a courthouse or a castle. A smaller feature to the east was called the jail house (Jail Rock).

Rufus B. Sage, November 1841. "Upon the south bank of Gonneville's creek, ten or twelve miles from the river, is a singular natural formation, known as the Court House, or McFarlan's Castle, on account of its fancied resemblance to such a structure. It rises in an abrupt quadrilangular form, to a height of three or four hundred feet, and covers an area of two hundred yards in length by one hundred and fifty broad. Occupying a perfectly level site in an open prairie, it stands as the proud palace of Solitude, amid here boundless domains.

"Its position commands a view of the country for forty miles around, and meets the eye of the traveller for several successive days, in journeying up the Platte. . . ." [338:IV, 199]

Charles Preuss, July 8, 1842. "To several of these localities where the winds and rain have worked the bluff into curious shapes, the voyageurs have given names according to some fancied resemblance. One of these, called the Courthouse, we passed. . . ." Note 37: ". . . A study of trail landmarks by Dale L. Morgan indicates that the name of Courthouse Rock was unknown in the literature before JCF[remont]'s first Report was issued . . . one more indication of the impact of his Report. . . ."[202:I, 215] (Sage used the term prior to Fremont, as the preceding item shows.)

Virgil Pringle, June 18, 1846. "Visited Parker's Castle, a most beautiful location on the meadows of a tributary of Platte. The Castle bearing strong resemblance to a castle of ancient date." [275:I, 172]

William Taylor, June 5, 1846. "Came in sight of Castle Rock . . ." [275:1, 125]

James A. Pritchard, May 29, 1849. ". . . we came in sight of the Courthouse rock. It presents to the Eye the appearance of an artificial Superstructure. It has a round top with doams and Spires. This Court house rock is about 4 ms to the left of the road." [317: 75]

Angelina Farley, August 1, 1850. "Passed the Court house." [133: diary]

William J. Ghent, 1934. "Here the trail from the Upper California Crossing, by what was known as the Ridge Route, rejoined the parent trail." [149: 132]

Irene D. Paden, 1943. ". . . enormous rock . . . juts up from a large expanse of pasture land . . . able to drive within a few yards of the base . . . most of the names and dates were obliterated—'Marshall McAllister', sprawlingly inscribed, being far the best preserved." [298: 142-45]

USGS map, Courthouse Rock, Nebr., 1:24,000, 1965 ed.

WPA Writers' Project. Northport, Nebraska.

CAMP CLARKE BRIDGE
Mile 567R¾ — 5 miles west of Bridgeport, Nebr.
Morrill County — Sec. 22, T20N, R51W

The Camp Clark Bridge, the lowest over the North Platte River, was built in 1876 for the accommodation of stage traffic to the Black Hills of the Dakota Territory. It became the focal point of early settlement.

". . . is the site of Camp Clarke, as well as the site of Camp Clarke Bridge. In 1876 the first wagon bridge across the North Platte River was built here by Henry T. Clarke of Omaha, to accommodate stages traveling between Sidney and the Black Hills. For a time soldiers guarded both ends of the bridge; a toll of $1 for a team, 50 cents for a person was charged. The bridge was used until 1910.

"At the south end of the bridge were a post office, store, saloon, stage barn and other buildings destroyed by a prairie fire in 1910." [146: 166]

Author's note. This location is from a manuscript map drawn by Paul C. Henderson in 1972. There is an Oregon Trail monument at the junction of Routes 88 and 92, near the railroad station in Bridgeport. It was erected in 1939 of cemented quartz rock and provides a brief but helpful resume of Oregon Trail and local history.

USGS map, Bridgeport, Nebr., 1:24,000, 1965 ed.

CHIMNEY ROCK
Mile 575L1½ — 3½ miles southwest of Bayard, Nebr.
Morrill County — NW¼ of SW¼, Sec. 17, T20N, R52W

This prominent column of clay and sandstone resembled a tall factory chimney. From the bottom of its funnel-shaped base to the tip of the column is over 300 feet today. The name is a relic of early fur-trade days. It is a unique and memorable

landmark, mentioned by nearly all the diarists who passed along the Oregon Trail.

Merrill J. Mattes, 1955. This particularly thorough monograph contains 31 quotations from original sources between 1830 and 1863, and 14 early pictorial representations. There is also a tabulation (pp. 20-22) which shows Chimney Rock to be the most-often-noted landmark on the Oregon Trail, and it lists 97 accounts in which the feature is mentioned. [246: passim]

Author's note, July 17, 1972. Adjacent to State Route 92, northeast of Chimney Rock 1. 7 miles, is a monument set by the State of Nebraska in 1912 to mark the Oregon Trail at its nearest approach to the feature. Nearby is an informational panel and a Pony Express marker. Unimproved local roads give access to an early cemetery east of Chimney Rock (the oldest marked burial was made in 1891, but a local school teacher pointed out unmarked graves which he thought were those of Oregon Trail emigrants; there are similar unmarked graves near the town of Bayard, north of Chimney Rock.) From the cemetery parking area a rude trail leads to the base of Chimney Rock, about a quarter mile to the west. At that point, where the base pitches steeply upward, there is a tablet set in concrete which recognizes the generosity of the family of Rozel F. Dumal for the gift to the public of the land surrounding Chimney Rock (1940).

USGS map, South Bayard, Nebr., 1:24,000, 1965 ed.

REBECCA WINTERS GRAVE
**Mile 59IR2½ — 3.5 miles southeast of Scottsbluff, Nebr. Scotts
Bluff County — NW¼ of NE¼, Sec. 31, T22N, R54W**

Rebecca Winters succumbed to cholera on the so-called "Mormon Trail" in 1852. (The 1847 date cited below is at variance with the 1852 date incised in the grave marker stone. The 1847 date is highly unlikely because cholera was not a menace on the Oregon Trail until 1849.)

This is one of the best-maintained graves of the emigration period, and is of particular interest because of the story that the CB&Q railroad shifted its location to avoid disturbing this grave.

Addison T. Smith, Congressman from Idaho, 1925. (Information from Walter E. Meacham): "As the Burlington was building its line along the Platte, a crew of engineers stumbled upon a lonely little grave out in the sagebrush and across it was a wagon tire, rusted and crusted with time, and on it rudely carved was these words: 'Rebecca Winters, age 50 years'

'Boys, said the leader, we'll turn aside,
Here, close by the trail, her grave shall stay,
For she came first in this desert wide,
Rebecca Wright holds right of way.'

"A touching bit of sentiment in a hard-boiled world. And so the line of a great railroad was turned to the west that she might lie in peace in the little grave she had occupied these many years, for she was one who came with the Mormon migration in 1847." [384: 24] WPA Writers' Project, 1939. ". . . Rebecca Winters, the mother of Mrs. Augusta Winters Grant, wife of a President of the Mormon Church, was a victim of the cholera epidemic of 1852.

"A member of a Mormon train, she was one of many who developed cholera soon after leaving the Missouri; though she did not die of the disease it left her weak and wasted. For five hundred miles she lay on a bundle of quilts in a jolting wagon before succumbing. The Latter-Day Saints have erected a monument over her grave. When the Burlington Route right-of-way was surveyed, the grave was found to be in direct line with the proposed road. The route was changed to leave the grave undisturbed." [146: 167]

Author's note, July 17, 1972. The grave is 15 feet north of the centerline of the railroad tracks. It is marked by a modern gravestone in addition to the original wagon tire; both within a 6' x 15' plot fenced with iron pipe. A pump has been installed close by to provide water for the grass within the plot.

USGS map, Minatare, Nebr., 1:24,000, 1965 ed.

SCOTTS BLUFF
Mile 596R3½ — 2 miles northwest of Gering, Nebr.
Scotts Bluff County, Sec. 33, T22N, R55W

This massive bluff stands like a bastion on the south bank of the North Platte River. It is named for Hiram Scott, who is presumed to have died nearby after being abandoned by comrades who were taking the sick man down the river. It is now a National Monument.

It is a landmark generally noted by Oregon Trail diarists, both because of its imposing appearance and the intriguing story connected with its naming in the fur trade days.

Particularly good descriptions are found in the following:

Rufus B. Sage, October 26, 1841. [338:IV, 211]

Charles Preuss, July 11, 1842. [202:1, 217]

James A. Pritchard, June 1, 1849. [317: 78]

Merrill J. Mattes, 1945. An article which covers the man and the incident from which Scotts Bluff draws its name. [242: 127-

62] Merrill J. Mattes, 1958. A monograph which includes many quotations from original journal sources. [247: passim.]

USGS map, Scottsbluff South, Nebr., 1:24,000, 1963 ed.

MITCHELL PASS
Mile 597R2½ — 2½ miles west of Gering, Nebr.
Scotts Bluff County — SW¼ of Sec. 33, T22N, R55W

Mitchell Pass was used after 1850 to negotiate the prominent ridge which terminates against the North Platte River as Scotts Bluff.

The route made possible by the opening of a road through the Mitchell Pass was popular with emigrants of the gold rush period and later traffic on the Oregon Trail.

Sir Richard Burton, 1860. "The route lay between the right-hand fortress [Scotts Bluff] and the outwork, through a degraded bed of softer marl . . . sudden torrents which pour from the heights on both sides, and the draughty winds . . . have cut up

Swale of Oregon Trail through Mitchell Pass, Scotts Bluff.

the ground into labyrinths of jagged gulches steeply waned in. We dashed down the drains and pitch holes with a violence which shook the nave bands from our sturdy wheels." [56: 87-88]

Irene D. Paden, 1943. "Mitchell's Pass, used by the highway, is the best and shortest and lies nearest the river; but it was not passable to the early migrations. Probably it was obstructed by fallen rock. . . ." [298: 148].

Author's note, 1972. It seems more likely that it was the eroded badland lying between Mitchell Pass and the North Platte River which caused the early Oregon Trail migration to use Robidoux Pass farther south. The pass did not receive the name by which it is now known until after Camp Mitchell was established.

USGS map, Scottsbluff South, Nebr., 1:24,000, 1963 ed.

PIERRE D. PAPIN GRAVE
Mile 597L3, 6 miles south of Gering, Nebr.
Scotts Bluff County — SW¼ of SW¼, Sec. 5, T20N, R55W

Pierre Didier Papin was a well-known trader who died at nearby Fort John in May 1853. The cedar post which marks his grave is mostly decayed, but a small iron pipe now serves as the principal marker.

Irene D. Paden, 1943. ". . . grave of the notable French trader Papin, some six miles due south of the museum . . ." [298: 148] The reference is to the museum at Scotts Bluff National Monument.

William A. Goff, 1972. A biographical sketch of the life of Papin, with a likeness (p. 22) and photograph of his grave (p. 313). [160:IX, 305-20, 322]

Reference. See "Pierre D. Papin Gravesite Rediscovered," in *Overland Journal*, 1/2 (Fall, 1983), 36-37.

USGS map, Scottsbluff, Nebr.-Col., 1:250,000, 1954 ed.

FORT JOHN (1850-1856 SITE)
Mile 597L4 — 7 miles south of Gering, Nebr., in Helvas Canyon
Scotts Bluff County — NW¼ of SE¼, Sec. 6, T20N, R55W

This trading post was built to replace the earlier Fort John, near the mouth of the Laramie River, when that establishment was sold to the United States Army for use as a military post

(Fort Laramie).

Although constructed to tap the emigrant trade, it was probably too far off the migration route to have profited much from that source.

Merrill J. Mattes, 1958. The fort is mentioned and located. [247: 37]

Author's note, July 18, 1972. There is a concrete monument at the site bearing a tablet which states: "Site of / Fort John / American Fur Trading Post / Built by Major Andrew Dripps / In 1850 / Father DeSmet, Missionary to / the Indians was here in 1851 / Katahdin Chapter D.A.R. / July 1, 1947." The site is surrounded by horseshoe-shaped bluffs, open to the north, and directly under a power transmission line, about 200 feet west of the dirt road which is the only access to that basin. There were supposed to be some graves north of the fort site, close to the line of demarcation between the range land and the cultivated fields which extend toward Gering, but they were not found (see Pierre D. Papin grave).

USGS map, Scottsbluff, Nebr.-Col., 1:250,000, 1954 ed.

ROBIDOUX (ROUBADEAU) TRADING POST
Mile 600.9 — 9 miles west of Gering, Nebr.
Scotts Bluff County — SW¼ of NW¼, Sec. 9, T21N, R56W

This small log trading post was established by Joseph E. Robidoux 1.1 miles southeast of Roubidoux Pass, late in 1848 or early in 1849. Whiskey, some supplies and blacksmithing were available there. The post was removed to a location in Carter Canyon early in the summer of 1852. It was of some assistance to emigrants and forty-niners.

Osborne Cross, June 20, 1849. "There is also a spring of delightfully cold water which we should have reached last evening . . . Here was a blacksmith shop and trading-house, built in the true log-cabin style. . . ." P. 323, George Gibbs, noted ". . . the 'fort' of an Indian trader, who with his half-breed family had settled himself here, posted up a sign 'Tinware, by A. Rubidue,' and occupied himself by doing blacksmith work for the emigrants. . . ." [101: 93, 323]

J. Goldsborough Bruff, July 7, 1849. "This is a basin, among the singular and romantic bluffs, is a beautiful spot. It appears to extend E. & W. about 5 ms. and about 3 ms. wide. In a deep gulch lies a cool spring and brook.—Close by is a group of

Indian lodges & tents, surrounding a log cabin, where you can buy whiskey for $5 per gallon; and look at the beautiful squaws of the traders. Flour here sells for 10¢ per lb. "Bruff noted their camp as "about 1 mile from a trading-post of Robedeaux's." [52: 31]

Howard Stansbury, July 1849. ". . . Scott's Bluff . . . There is a temporary blacksmith's shop here, established for the benefit of the emigrants, but especially for that of its owner, who lives in an Indian lodge, and had erected a log shanty by the roadside, in one end of which was the blacksmith's forge, and in the other a grog-shop and sort of grocery. The stock of this establishment consisted principally of such articles as the owner had purchased from the emigrants at a great sacrifice and sold to others at as great a profit. Among other things, an excellent double wagon . . . which he had purchased for seventy-five cents. The blacksmith's shop was an equally profitable concern; as, when the smith was indisposed to work . . . rented the use of the shop and tools for the modest price of seventy-five cents an hour. . . ." [361: 52]

Angelina Farley, August 3, 1850. "Our road passed over the bluffs at the first trading post between the forts [Kearny and Laramie] at a deep ravine where was an excellent spring. There we saw three wagons and part of another left." [133: diary]

Orral M. Robidoux, 1924. Information on Joseph E. Robidoux. [328: 226-27]

Irene D. Paden, 1943. "In the canyon, by the big spring, those travelers who passed between 1848 and 1852 found a blacksmith shop. . . . On June 22, 1852, Mary Stuart Bailey . . . wrote: 'Passed a Frenchman's blacksmith shop . . .' Only a few days after . . . the little cabin was destroyed . . . the bronze plaque marking the site of the blacksmith shop." [298: 149]

Merrill J. Mattes, 1949. An article on the Robidoux post [245: 95-138]

Merrill J. Mattes, 1958. Information on Robidoux's trading post. [247: 33, 35-37]

Author's note, July 18, 1972. About 1,300 feet south of the trading post site (400 feet north of the Robidoux Pass road) is a fenced plot containing emigrant graves. There are no surface evidences of the trading post.

USGS map, Roubadeau Pass, Nebr., 1:24,000, 1963 ed.

EMIGRANT GRAVES
**Mile 601R¼ — 1 mile southeast of Robidoux Pass,
1,300 feet south of Robidoux's first trading post site.
Scotts Bluff Co., Nebr. — NW¼ of SW¼, Sec. 9, T21N, R56W**

Several unidentified graves are in a 12' x 24' fenced plot at the end of a 400-foot spur road. They are marked by a four-foot boulder of reddish chert, with a tablet which reads: "Honoring these, and / all the thousands / who lie in nameless graves / along the trail / Faith and courage / such as theirs / made America / May ours preserve it. / Katahdin Chapt. DAR AD 1942." Two burials are obvious.

J. Goldsborough Bruff, July 7, 1849. Noted, ". . . 3 graves near the spring:— 'Jesse Galen, Independence, Mo, F. Dunn, Aged 26, Joseph Blake.'" [52: 31]

Irene D. Paden, 1943. Mentions several burials in this vicinity (from emigrant journals). [298: 148-49]

USGS map, Roubadeau Pass, Nebr., 1: 24,000, 1963 ed.

ROBIDOUX'S 2ND TRADING POST
Mile 601L3 — 8.5 miles southwest of Gering, in Carter Canyon
Scotts Bluff County, Nebr. — Sec. 28, T21N, R56W

Joseph E. Robidoux's first trading post, on the emigrant road over Robidoux Pass, was destroyed by fire in 1852. Before then, however, he had built another at a protected site in the mouth of Carter Canyon. The decline in emigrant traffic over Robidoux Pass following the opening of a wagon route by way of Mitchell Pass probably influenced him in this move which put his new establishment over a mile south of the emigrant road upon which he was first located.

Irene D. Paden, 1943. 'a. Rubidue' simply moved one canyon south and built another shop and trading post." [298: 149] Merrill J. Mattes, 1958. The new post is described. [247: 3537]

Author's note, 1972. The site has yet to be positively identified, though the monument above the county road, south of the emigrant graves, is now known to be in the wrong place.

USGS map, Scottsbluff, Nebr. Col., 1:250,000, 1954 ed.

CAMP (FORT) MITCHELL
Mile 601R8 — 3.5 miles west of Scottsbluff, Nebr.,
and 3 miles west of Mitchell Pass.
Scotts Bluff County — Sec. 20, T22N, R55W

This military post was established in 1864 at or near the site of U.S. Mail Station 23 and an earlier American Fur Company post. The trading post was built in 1851 to replace Fort John in Helvas Canyon.

Camp Mitchell, named for Brig. Gen. Robert B. Mitchell, was abandoned after the 1867 season.

Merrill J. Mattes, 1969. The history of the post is adequately presented, pp. 473-79; but Mattes' entire Chapter XIV is pertinent to an understanding of the role of this locale. [249: 454-79]

Reference. Merrill J. Mattes, "Old Fort Mitchell, Nebraska, Revisited," in *Overland Journal*, 7/2 (1989), 2-11.

USGS map, Scottsbluff South, Nebr., 1: 24,000, 1963 ed.

ROBIDOUX (ROUBADEAU) PASS
Mile 603.8 — 10 miles west of Gering, Nebr.
Scotts Bluff County — SW¼ of SW¼, Sec. 5, T21N, R56W

This pass was used, with few exceptions, by Oregon Trail emigrants who passed Scotts Bluff prior to the California gold rush. It continued in use as an alternate to the Mitchell Pass route of later years, particularly when weather conditions rendered the latter passage difficult.

Irene D. Paden, 1943. "Robidoux Canyon or Pass . . . a large circular valley of loose sandy loam. . . ." [298: 148]

Merrill J. Mattes, 1958. The pass is described. [247: 26, 28, 32-33]

Merrill J. Mattes, 1971. The spelling of the name of this pass, which is inaccurate as used by the USGS on official maps, is discussed in a footnote. [160:VIII, 308]

USGS map, Roubadeau Pass, Nebr., 1:24,000, 1963 ed.

3

Robidoux Pass to South Pass

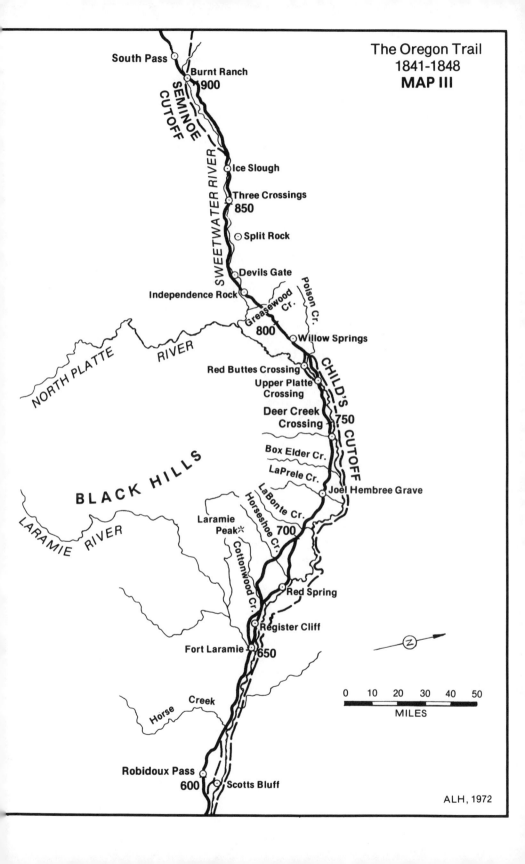

HORSE CREEK CROSSING
Mile 615.5 — 4 miles southwest of Morrill, Nebr.
Scotts Bluff County — Approx. center of Sec. 25, T23N, R58W

Horse Creek was a landmark of the Oregon Trail migration, with a name firmly fixed from fur trade days. Horse Creek was the site of an Indian treaty council in 1851, which had for its principal objective the security of the migration route.

Rufus B. Sage, Oct. 27, 1841. "The day being clear and pleasant, we travelled rapidly, and in the course of the afternoon reached Horse creek. This stream is a large affluent of the Platte, heading in the Black Hills, and, tracing its way in a northeasterly direction, through a timberless country (in many places mere barren wastes), makes its debouchment nearly fifteen miles above Scott's Bluff." Sage repeats a tale of the early discovery of gold on the headwaters of Horse Creek, and he notes, "a beautiful valley, shut in by two ridges of precipitous hills, known as Goche's Hole"—present Goshen Hole. [338:IV, 216-17]

Charles Preuss, July 12, 1842. ". . . we crossed Horse creek, a shallow stream of clear water, about seventy yards wide, falling into the Platte on the right bank. It was lightly timbered, and great quantities of drift wood were piled up on the banks." [202: 217]

Virgil Pringle, June 20, 1846. ". . . drove on to Horse Creek and encamped." [275:I, 173]

James A. Pritchard, June 3, 1849. "We reached Horse Creek, crossed. . . ." [317: 80]

J. Goldsborough Bruff, July 7, 1849. "Horse Creek is very shallow,—3 to 6 inches only, and sandy bottom. Scattered sage (Artemesia) in the plains." [52: 31]

William J. Ghent, 1934. ". . . mouth of Horse Creek (630 miles), where in 1851 was held the greatest Indian council in the history of the west." [149: 132]

Irene D. Paden, 1943. "Five years later, in 1851, the Sioux again congregated on Horse Creek . . . treaty . . . between the Sioux Nation and the United States . . . for the value of $50,000 in goods each year, the emigrants were given the right to travel unmolested . . . lasted about three years." [298: 157]

USGS map, Morrill, Nebr., 1:24,000, 1963 ed.

HORSE CREEK STATION$_p$
Mile 615.5 — 4¼ miles southwest of Morrill, Nebr.
Scotts Bluff County — NE¼ of NW¼, Sec. 25, T23N, R58W

This was a stage station on the west bank of Horse Creek. Sir Richard Burton, 1860. "... forded the Horse Creek ... entered at 8:30 p.m. the station in which we were to pass the night. It was tenanted by one Reynal, a French creole ... a companionable man, but an extortionate. ..." [56: 89]

The location is from a manuscript map by Paul C. Henderson, which places the station exactly on the meridian of 104 degrees west longitude.

USGS map, Morrill, Nebr., 1:24,000, 1963 ed.

OREGON TRAIL MONUMENT$_p$
Mile 618.1 — 2.7 miles south of Henry, Nebr.
Scotts Bluff County — 550 feet north of SW corner, Sec. 15, T23N, R58W

This monument, 50 feet west of the center line of State Route L79C, marks a crossing of the Oregon Trail. It is a granite slab l' x 2' x 4', incised "Oregon / Trail / Marked By / The State Of / Nebraska / 1912 / Nebraska/Wyoming / Monument / N. 57 degrees 40 minutes West 2086 Ft."

The Nebraska-Wyoming monument referred to is a large, red granite stone of somewhat oval shape located in a beet field nearly a half-mile to the west (approximately at the W¼ cor., Sec. 16, T23N, R58W). It is incised "Oregon Trail / Marked by / The Sons And Daughters / Of The / American Revolution / 1912."

William J. Ghent, 1934. "... the Sons and Daughters of the American Revolution of Nebraska and of Cheyenne joined hands in setting up a stone on the Wyoming-Nebraska boundary. The dedication was on April 4, 1913. The marker, a block of granite." [149: 250]

USGS map, Lyman, Wyo.-Nebr., 1:24,000, 1960 ed.

HENRY HILL GRAVE$_p$
Mile 620.4 — 2 Miles southwest of Henry, Nebr.
Goshen County, Wyo. — SE¼ of NW¼, Sec. 9, T23N, R60W

This grave is on an open knoll adjacent to the Oregon Trail. The information available is conflicting as to the age and date of death.

Author's note, July 9, 1972. The grave is covered with cobblestones and has a cement monument (9" x 16", standing 14" above the base). The top is marked "Henry Hill born June 8 / 1820 age 59", and on the east face, "Re-engraved August 28 / 1930 / by M. H. Stewart / A. H. and C. G. Jones." The original gravestone, a sandstone slab roughly 13" x 20" and 5" thick, is marked: "HENRV HILL / UNE 8 / 59 / M"

According to Paul Henderson, Henry Hill was born June 2, 1801, and died July 2, 1850. The cement monument was the work of the Historical Landmark Commission in 1931. The fencing of wood posts and iron pipe railings placed at that time is entirely gone.

The birthdate and age cast on the monument would make the year of death 1879, while the information provided by Paul Henderson makes the age forty-nine rather than fifty-nine. Reg P. Duffin presents facts in his article, "The Nancy Hill Story: The Final Chapter," *Overland Journal*, Fall 1986, which indicate that the inscription on the stone described above could be interpreted as, "Henry Hill [d.] June 8 [18]52 M[.]." See p. 61. It is unfortunate that so many conflicting records exist concerning this burial.

USGS map, Lyman, Wyo.-Nebr., 1:24,000, 1960 ed.

CHARLES BISHOP GRAVE_p
Mile 621R¼ — 1.8 miles southwest of Henry, Nebr.
Goshen County, Wyo. — NE¼ of Sec. 9, T23N, R60W

This grave is on the brow of a bluff adjacent to the Oregon Trail. It is of a member of the "Washington City and California Mining Association," who died of cholera on July 8, 1849.

J. Goldsborough Bruff, July 8, 1849. "At 1 p.m. poor Bishop died, of cholera—The first casualty in the Company, sudden and astounding . . . laid him out, sewed him up in his blue blanket, and prepared a bier, formed of his tent-poles. I had a grave dug in a neighboring ridge, on the left of the trail, about 400 yards from it. Dry clay and gravel, and coarse white sand-stone on the next hill, afforded slabs to line it with, making a perfect vault. I sat 3 hours in the hot sun, and sculptured a head and foot stone; and filled the letters with blacking from the hub of a wheel.

"I then organized a funeral procession, men all in clean clothes and uniforms, with music, (a key-bugle, flute, violin and accordian) and two by two, with stars and stripes over the body, we marched to the measured time of the dirge, deposited the body of our comrade in the grave, an elderly man read the burial service, and we filled up the grave, erected the stones, and returned to camp." [52: 32-33]

Author's note. Paul C. Henderson provided the following as the inscription on the gravestone: "Charles Bishop, d. July 8, 1849." The location, which is in a private pasture, is from his manuscript map.

USGS map, Lyman, Wyo.-Nebr., 1:24,000,1960 ed.

RED CLOUD INDIAN AGENCY$_p$
Mile 621R1¼ — 0.9 mile southwest of Henry, Nebr.
and north of Little Moon Lake
Goshen County, Wyo. — S½ of Sec. 3, T23N, R60W

This is the first site of the Sioux Indian Reservation established in 1871 and abandoned in 1873, when the agency was removed to a new location four miles west of Crawford, Nebr.

Author's note. According to Paul C. Henderson: "Red Cloud or Woc-co-pom-any Indian Agency—1871 to 1873. No marker or identification sign at present. The Wyoming State Parks Commission (WSPC) will be asked for one in the future. The agency covered most of the northern halves of the SE and SW¼, Sec. 3, T23N, R60W. This is private property but the owner will give a deed or lease the land for the site of a monument. A county road borders the east side of these grounds."

USGS map, Torrington SE, Wyo.-Nebr., 1:24,000, 1960 ed.

UNIDENTIFIED GRAVE$_p$
Mile 624R¾ — 1.0 mile northwest of Hunton Meadows
on Jamieson's Bluffs
Goshen County, Wyo. — SE¼ of SE¼, Sec. 30, T24N, R60W

This is a trailside burial on the Hunton Meadows branch of the Oregon Trail.

Author's note. The following information was obtained from Paul C. Henderson: "Pioneer Grave—Native sandstone marker.

Private property. On crest of Jamison's Bluff. Located near the center of the SE¼, Sec. 30, T24N, R60W."

It is possible that this is the grave of one of the men killed when Spotted Tail's Sioux attacked the Salt Lake mail stage at this place following the Grattan fight in 1854. Three or four were "buried by the roadside where they fell," and the bluff takes its name from one of them—a man named Jamieson. [see 249: 518-19]

USGS map, Torrington SE, Wyo.-Nebr., 1:24,000, 1963 ed.

UNIDENTIFIED GRAVE_P
Mile 624R¾ — 1.2 miles northwest of Hunton Meadows on Jamieson's Bluffs
Goshen County, Wyo. — NW¼ of SE¼, Sec. 30, T24N, R60W

This is another trailside burial on the Hunton Meadows branch of the Oregon Trail

Author's note. The following information was obtained from Paul C. Henderson: "Pioneer Grave—Native sandstone marker. One mile [500 feet according to the map] northwest of the above grave. Both on the Hunton Meadows detour of the Oregon Trail. Identification later."

See the preceding site for remarks on the possible circumstances of this burial.

USGS map, Torrington SE, Wyo.-Nebr., 1:24,000, 1963 ed.

WILLIAM CLARY GRAVE_P
Mile 625.0 — 4 miles southeast of Torrington, Wyo.
Goshen County — SE¼ of SE¼, Sec. 25, T24N, R61W

The Clary grave is on an open ridge north of the Oregon Trail. The headstone has been overturned and the fencing is down and scattered by cattle, but the footstone remains in place.

Author's note, July 19, 1972. The grave site is in open pasture on a ridge. The headstone, a 15" by 32" sandstone slab, is marked: "Wm. CLARY / 18". There is also a footstone (2" x 10" x 8"), yet in place, and scattered pieces of pipe fencing. (The grave has since been restored and fenced by OCTA.)

According to Paul Henderson, a concrete marker was set by the Historical Landmarks Commission in 1930, but no evidence of it was found. He has identified the burial as "Wm. D. Clary,

d. June 21, 1850."
USGS map, Torrington, Wyo., 1:24,000, 1963 ed.

UNIDENTIFIED GRAVE_p
Mile 625R⅓ — 1,900 feet due north of the
Wm. Clary grave
Goshen County, Wyo. — SE¼ of NE¼, Sec. 25, T24N, R61W

This is a mapped burial on the open ridge north of the
Oregon Trail.
Author's note, 1972. No evidence of the grave was found
during a limited search, but it is shown on the topographic map,
dated 1963. The area is a cattle pasture.
USGS map, Torrington, Wyo., 1:24,000, 1963 ed.

UNIDENTIFIED GRAVE_p
Mile 625R½ — 2,200 feet due north of the Wm. Clary grave
Goshen County, Wyo. — SE¼ of NE¼, Sec. 25, T24N, R61W

This mapped burial is on the open ridge north of the Oregon
Trail.
Author's note. The following information was obtained from
Paul C. Henderson: "Pioneer Grave—Unknown. Marked by a
native sandstone slab. No fence. 0.4 mile due north of Clary
grave. Private property."
This grave is shown on the 1963 topographic map, but it was
not found in 1972. Summer vegetation may have covered the
marker.
USGS map, Torrington, Wyo., 1:24,000, 1963 ed.

COLD SPRINGS STATION_p
Mile 626R¼ — 2.1 miles southeast of Torrington, Wyo.
Goshen County — NE¼ of SE¼, Sec. 22, T24N, R61W

This is the site of an Overland Stage station (1859-1862) and
a Pony Express relay stop (1860-61).
Author's note, July 19, 1972. The following information was
obtained from Paul C. Henderson: "Cold Springs Stage and
Pony Express Station—Marked by a steel post, engraved 'Cold
Springs Station,' set by the National Pony Express Assoc. 1959.

Private Property. Located in the southwest corner of Sec. 23, T24N, R61W." There is a reference to this station on the Cold Springs monument.

USGS map, Torrington, Wyo., 1:24,000, 1963 ed.

COLD SPRINGS$_p$
Mile 626.6 — 1.9 miles southeast of Torrington, Wyo.
Goshen County, SE¼ of Sec. 23, T24N, R61W

This spring caused the establishment of an emigrant campground here.

Author's note, July 19, 1972. There is a reference to the spring and its use by emigrants on the Cold Springs monument.

USGS map, Torrington, Wyo., 1:24,000, 1963 ed.

COLD SPRINGS MONUMENT
Mile 627L¼ — 1.5 Miles south of Torrington, Wyo.
Goshen County — Center of NW¼, Sec. 23, T24N, R61W

This marker was erected in 1914 at the approximate point where the Oregon Trail crossed the road running south from the Torrington Bridge (now U.S. Highway 85). The marker is accompanied by an informational panel.

William J. Ghent, 1934. "In Goshen County, on June 17, 1915, a stone was set up across the river from Torrington." [149: 250]

Author's note, July 19, 1972. The monument is granite, 1' x 1½' x 3½', with a tablet which states: "Oregon Trail / Marked By The / State Of Wyoming / 1914."

An informational panel to the left of the monument adds: "Cold Springs / ¾ mile east from this point. / A camping ground on the old Emigrant Trail to / Oregon-California-Utah. / A stage station for the Overland Route 1859-1862. / A Pony Express relay stop 1860-1861. / Station tender was M. Reynal."

The monument is on the east shoulder of U.S. Highway 85.

USGS map, Torrington, Wyo., 1:24,000, 1963 ed.

OREGON TRAIL MONUMENT
Mile 629R1½ — At Burlington Route station, Torrington, Wyo.
Goshen County — SW¼ of SW¼, Sec. 10, T24N, R61W

This marker was placed in the town of Torrington, mainly for the benefit of railroad passengers and travelers on U.S. Highway 26, which parallels the Oregon Trail on the opposite side of the North Platte River.

Author's note. Paul C. Henderson provided this information: "Oregon Trail Monument—Granite, cement base. Located at CB&Q RR station grounds in Torrington. Placed by the H[istoric] L[andmarks] Comm[ission]."

USGS map, Torrington, Wyo., 1:24,000, 1963 ed.

OLD ROCK RANCH₍ₚ₎
Mile 632R¼ — 3.5 miles west of Torrington, Wyo.
Goshen County — SE¼ of NE¼, Sec. 12, T24N, R62W

The two very old buildings here may be relics of a trading post from the emigration period.

Author's note, July 19, 1972. The following information was obtained from Paul C. Henderson: "Old Rock Ranch—no monument. Two old buildings remaining of the early P. F. Cattle Ranch. Reputed to have been a Pony Express and stage station at one time. Pony Express records do not bear out this fact. However, the two existing buildings were reconstructed from ruins by Capt. O'Brien in 1864, which points to the then ruins being those of an early fur trader's post. Investigations as to this are being made. Early names and dates on rocks south of the buildings. Old Oregon Trail passed 0.15 mile south of the site."

The buildings of interest were both very old—one of large cedar logs, 15' x 30', with stucco on the outside, is now used as a repair shop, and the other of rough masonry on a concrete foundation, 16' x 21', is now empty. An old fireplace on the south wall of the stone building, and a window on the north wall, had been closed up; the roof was new, although the structure may have gone without a roof for a considerable period. A frame building stands between the historic structures, and all three are aligned on a north-south axis with the stone building at the north. They now belong to the Andrews Cattle Company.

Cold springs break out of the bluff a quarter-mile southeast of the buildings.
USGS map, Cottier, Wyo., 1:24,000, 1960 ed.

OREGON TRAIL MONUMENT
Mile 637.4 — 2.4 miles south of Lingle, Wyo.
Goshen County — NW¼ of NE¼, Sec. 31, T25N, R62W

This marker is at the intersection of the Oregon Trail with the county road running south from the town of Lingle.
William J. Ghent, 1934. ". . . on June 17, 1915, a stone . . . across the river from Lingle. . . ." [149: 250]
Author's note. Paul C. Henderson supplied the following information: "Oregon Trail Monument—Granite, on cement base. 1.75 miles south of Lingle on the west side of oiled county road. Located on the old Oregon Trail that ascends the table land at this point. H. L. Comm. Mon. State property."
USGS map, Cottier, Wyo., 1:24,000, 1960 ed.

TEXAS CATTLE TRAIL MONUMENT
Mile 637R2 — 1.2 miles southeast of Lingle, Wyo.,
on U.S. Highways 26 & 85
Goshen County — SW¼ of NW¼, Sec. 21, T25N, R62W

This marker commemorates the Goodnight-Loving trail, used to move herds from Texas to northern ranges, particularly Montana, from 1868 to 1886.
Author's note. The following information is from Paul C. Henderson: "Texas Cattle Trail Monument. Large granite, cement foundation, bearing outline map of Texas Trail on front side. Brands of early cattle ranches on opposite side. Fenced with iron fence. Located on east bank of Rawhide Creek 1¼ mile east of Lingle. Now a safety rest stop under supervision of the Wyoming Highway Dept. H. L. C. placement."
The monument was dedicated Aug. 1, 1948.
USGS map, Cottier, Wyo., 1:24,000, 1960 ed.

OREGON TRAIL MONUMENT
Mile 638R2 — At Burlington RR station, Lingle, Wyo.
Goshen County — SE¼ of SE¼, Sec. 18, T25N, R62W

This marker was placed in the town of Lingle mainly for the benefit of railroad passengers and travelers on U.S. Highway 26, which parallels the Oregon Trail on the north side of the North Platte River.

Author's note. The following information is from Paul C. Henderson: "Oregon Trail Monument—Granite, cement base. H. L. Comm. Located at junction of U.S. No.'s 26/85 with oiled county road running south. On west side of junction next to CB&Q RR station grounds. This monument is on opposite side of North Platte River, 1.7 miles north of the Oregon Trail." USGS map, Lingle, Wyo.," 1:24,000, 1963 ed.

GRATTAN "MASSACRE" SITE_p
Mile 641R½ — 7.5 miles southeast of Fort Laramie
Goshen County, Wyo. — NW¼ of SE¼, Sec. 15, T25N, R63W

On August 19, 1854, Second Lt. John L. Grattan, with 28 soldiers, an interpreter and a fieldpiece, attempted to arrest several Sioux Indians who had killed and eaten the strayed cow of a Mormon emigrant. In the ensuing confrontation, all members of the arresting party and the Brule chief, "The Bear," were killed. The enlisted men, except for one who reached Fort Laramie mortally wounded, were buried on the battlefield (later removed to the Fort McPherson National Cemetery).

This unfortunate confrontation, which arose out of misunderstanding on the part of the Indians and the rashness of the officer, began many years of intermittent hostility along the Oregon Trail.

Sir Richard Burton, 1860. "Close to the station [Bordeaux's], and a little to the right of the road, we passed the barrow which contains the remains of Lieut. Gratton and his thirty men. A young second lieutenant of Irish origin and fiery temper . . . The whites in the neighborhood narrowly preserved their own scalps,— M. Badeau owned that he owed his to his Sioux squaw." [56: 98-99]

LeRoy R. Hafen, 1938. An account of the fight. [156: 221-32]

Irene D. Paden, 1943. ". . . we later made an intensive search for accurate data, and finally laid hands on the annual reports of the Commissioner of Indian Affairs. In the volume for 1854 we found the statement of the trader, Bordeaux, who was an eyewitness. Bordeaux was no scholar, and the tedious business of writing his statement had to be relegated to one Samuel Smith

View from the Grattan Battlefield monument toward the place where the soldier dead were buried (2,000 feet distant, in the field).

who, with six others, witnessed the laborious document." Excerpts from it show that the soldiers fired first, and that Grattan and five men were killed at the cannon, the others within a mile. [298: 159-60]

Miles Cannon, 1953. The story of the fight as heard from John Hunton, of Torrington, Wyoming, associated with Fort Laramie from 1858 until its abandonment in 1890, first as clerk, and from 1872 on, as post trader. Cannon notes: "The ground where the massacre took place was unmarked when John Hunton and I visited the place in 1923, save for the open grave of the enlisted men that was left when their bodies were removed." He was informed that only the enlisted men were buried on the battlefield, "in a common grave, covered by a pile of stone. . . ."; the body of Grattan was brought to Fort Laramie by Sergeant Snyder's burial detail and later sent to his home in Connecticut, where his grave is marked by a monument. [59: 106-07]

Wallace Stegner, 1964. Referring to the animal which was the cause of the confrontation: "it was the lame cow of a Danish Mormon convert. . . ." [363: 307]

Author's note, July 19, 1972. The burial site, which is now in a cultivated field, is marked by a rose granite monument, incised: "Grattan / Massacre / 1854 / Burials were / 40 ft. south / Erected by the/ Historical Landmark / Commission / of Wyoming / 1953." From the burial site monument, it is 2,200 feet on azimuth 160 degrees true to the monument on the north side of the paved road on the section line between 15 and 22, T25N, R63W. This more accessible monument commemorates the fight of August 19, 1854, stating: "An Indian killed a cow from a Mormon caravan. The detachment / of soldiers was sent to receive the offender. In the ensuing fight / all soldiers and the Sioux chief of the Brule's Sioux, Martoh-loway, / were killed." The monument is in the SE¼, SE¼, Sec. 15. The remains of the enlisted men—a sergeant, a corporal and 26 privates—were reburied in the Fort McPherson National Cemetery under a white marble stone marked: "In memory / of / Enlisted Men / Co. G. 6th Inf. / killed in action / near / Ft. Laramie, Wyo. (Grattan Massacre) / Aug. 19, 1854." It is in Section B.

The site was being farmed by Wayne Grosskoff.

USGS map Barnes, Wyo., 1:24,000, 1960 ed.

OREGON TRAIL MONUMENT
Mile 641.1 — 3 miles west of Lingle, Wyo.
Goshen County — NW¼ of NE¼, Sec. 22, T25N, R63W

This marker is placed on the south side of the county road, which is south of the Oregon Trail at this point.

Author's note, July 19, 1972. The following information was received from Paul C. Henderson: "Oregon Trail Monument— Granite, cement base, fenced with iron pipe. H. L. Comm. Mon. Located on south side of the above mentioned county road. 600 feet west of the above mentioned monument [Grattan], and directly south (approx. 2,000 feet) of the Grattan soldier's burial ground, from which the remains were removed to Fort McPherson National Cem. in about 1890. Highway property."

The monument is 9" x 20" x 42", with a tablet which states: "Oregon Trail / Marked By The / State of Wyoming / 1914." However, Thomas Sutherland's statement (1854) that the soldier's graves were "close by the road" would place the Oregon Trail at least 2,000 feet to the north.

USGS map, Barnes, Wyo., 1:24,000, 1960 ed.

BORDEAUX STATION_P
Mile 641R¾ — 2.5 miles west of Lingle, Wyo.
Goshen County — Center of Sec. 14, T25N, R63W

James Bordeaux built a trading post here in 1849. It was used more or less continuously through 1868 as a place of trade with the Sioux Indians and emigrants on the Oregon Trail, and also as a stage station.

Robert Campbell, Sept. 14, 1854. "We traveled 8 miles to Bordeau's station. There are mountaineers settled here and they do blacksmithing and trade oxen and horses. It was at this place that the Indians killed the 29 soldiers with their officer." [156: 216]

Sir Richard Burton, 1860. ". . . halt to change mules at Badeau's Ranch, or . . . 'Laramie City.' The 'city' . . . still appertains to the category of things to be . . . a single large 'store,' with outhouses full of small half-breeds . . . articles of traffic are liquors and groceries for the whites, and ornaments for the Indians, which are bartered for stock (i.e., animals) and peltries." [56: 97-98]

John D. McDermott, 1968. A biographical sketch of James Bordeaux provides glimpses of his business affairs at this place (see 71-79). [160:V, 65-80]

USGS map, Barnes, Wyo., 1:24,000, 1960 ed.

FORT BERNARD_P
Mile 644R½ — 5.5 miles southeast of Fort Laramie, Wyo.
Goshen County — SW¼ of SW¼, Sec. 5, T25N, R63W

This trading post was established in opposition to the American Fur Company's Fort John (Laramie) by Joseph Bissonette in the summer of 1845. The post was operated by John Baptiste Richard until it burned during his absence during the winter of 1846-1847. There appears to have been some use of this site as late as 1850.

George McKinstry, June 23, 1846. ". . . arrived at Fort John or Bernard . . . went 7 or 8 miles to Ft. Laramie stopped for a few minutes. . . ." [275:I, 214]

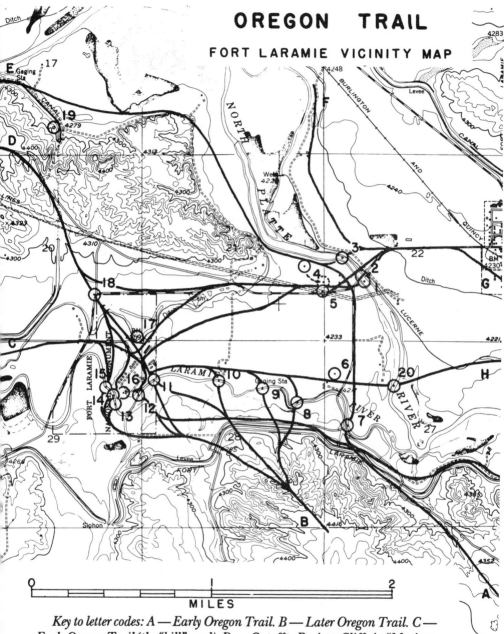

OREGON TRAIL

FORT LARAMIE VICINITY MAP

Key to letter codes: A — Early Oregon Trail. B — Later Oregon Trail. C — Early Oregon Trail (the "hill" road). D — Cutoff to Register Cliff via "Mexican Hill. "E — The River Road, opened by the Mormons in 1847. F — Child's Cutoff, opened by Argonauts in 1850. G — The Mormon Trail. H — Early trapper-missionary route. (See text for key to numbered sites.)

William J. Ghent, 1934. "Thirty miles farther [from Horse Creek] they came to a small trading post, known as Fort Bernard. . . ." [149: 132]

Irene D. Paden, 1943. ". . . Fort Bernard, eight miles down the North Platte [from Laramie River]. Francis Parkman visited Fort Bernard in '46 on his way to Laramie Fork and wrote that it was 'a rough structure of logs . . . a little trading fort, belonging to two private traders; and originally intended like all the forts of the country, to form a hollow square, with rooms for lodging and storage opening upon the area within. Only two sides of it had been completed.' In charge was the hair-trigger, whiskey-running Richard, a little, swarthy Frenchman more or less in bad odor with the American Fur Company. . . . [The post is] said to have burned sometime during the fall and winter of 1846-47; if so, it was evidently rebuilt, for E. A. Tompkins, who saw it in the summer of '50, said that it was an assemblage of log huts surrounded by great piles of buffalo hides, the size and shape of eastern haystacks." [298: 154-55]

Author's note, July 19, 1972. George Hill, of Fort Laramie, Wyo., informed me that the site of Fort Bernard is close to the bank of the North Platte River, on land owned by a Mr. Parrish, and that there is a prominent burned area showing glass, nails, etc.

USGS map, Barnes, Wyo., 1:24,000, 1960 ed.

GRATIOT HOUSES$_P$
Mile 645 — 3.5 miles southeast of Fort Laramie, Wyo.
Goshen County — NW¼ of SW¼, Sec. 5, T25N, R63W

This little-known trading post adjacent to the Oregon-California trail is remembered mainly because it was plundered by Sioux Indians as a direct consequence of the Grattan fight.

Author's note. This location is taken from a manuscript map prepared by Paul C. Henderson. He placed the site on the bank of the North Platte River, about a quarter mile east of the headgate of the Gratiot Irrigation Ditch.

USGS map, Barnes, Wyo., 1:24,000, 1960 ed.

OREGON TRAIL MONUMENT
Mile 648R1¼ — in the town of Fort Laramie, Wyo.
Junction of US Highway 26 &
the road to Fort Laramie National Historic Site
Goshen County — Sec. 23, T26N, R64W

This granite monument rests on a concrete foundation on town property. It is on the Council Bluffs Road (the fur trapper-missionary-Mormon route on the north bank of the North Plate River), and not the Oregon Trail. Travelers on that side crossed the river nearby—at the second or fourth crossings listed on succeeding pages—until the year 1850.

In that year "Child's Cutoff" was put into use, allowing travelers to remain north of the river. It became an alternate to the Oregon-California trail and saw some use during the gold rush period.

Joseph Price, 1850. Was discouraged from attempting the new route. [238: 251-52]

James A. Pritchard, 1849. "Next year a wagon road was worked out on the north side of the Platte above Fort Laramie, an especial convenience to emigrants from Council Bluffs who previously had had to cross the North Platte at or below Fort Laramie, and follow . . . south bank trails." [317: 152, note]

Irene D. Paden, 1943. "In 1850 . . . one or two daring companies refused to ferry and continued their journey north of the river. In a few days, when it was apparent they had not been forced to return, they were followed by Franklin Langworthy's train and others. The north bank road was open." [298: 155]

USGS map, Fort Laramie, Wyo., 1:24,000, 1950 ed.

FIRST CROSSING OF LARAMIE RIVER$_p$
(Site 7, Fort Laramie Vicinity Map)
Mile 648.8R — Goshen County
SW¼ of NW¼, Sec. 27, T26N, R64W

This crossing is about 2,000 feet above the confluence of the Laramie and the North Platte rivers. It often was a dangerous crossing but it could be forded at low water. It had to be ferried at flood stage. The crossing gave direct access to Fort William (1834-1841), and Fort Platte (1841-1845). Toll bridges were later established here; the first, built in 1852, washed out the following spring but another, built in 1859, was used until 1868.

This earliest crossing of the Laramie River was the principal one until 1841, when Fort John was built a mile upstream. Thereafter, it served Fort Platte until its abandonment. The forty-niners revived the use of the first crossing and restrictions on crossing near Fort Laramie in 1851 briefly re-established this as the most important one, particularly during the brief life of the early toll bridge.

Nathaniel J. Wyeth, June 13, 1832. ". . . crossed Larrimee fork . . . in getting over one of my rafts broke a tow line . . . went down stream lodged on a snag and upset wetting most of the goods on it and losing two Horse loads as it lodged in the middle of the river and the stream [being] very rappid the goods were with difficulty passed ashore. . . ." [406:I, 156] June 1, 1834. ". . . to Laramies fork . . . forded this fork with ease. . . ." [406:I, 223]

Washington Irving, 1843. "On the 26th of May [1832], the travelers [Capt. Bonneville's party] encamped at Laramie's Fork, a clear and beautiful stream, rising in the west-southwest, maintaining an average width of twenty yards, and winding through broad meadows. . . ." [200:III, 279]

Frederick A. Wislizenus, 1839. After locating Fort William, he says, "We crossed the Laramie toward noon, and encamped outside the fort." [405: 67]

James A. Pritchard, June 3, 1849. ". . . came to Laramie's fork about one and a half miles this side of the Fort. After a few minutes examination we commenced crossing and succeded without difficulty. The water just struck the fore part of the beds of the wagons." [317: 80]

J. Goldsborough Bruff, July 9, 1849. ". . . to the Ford of Laramie river, by 6 P.M. there we had to block some of the wagon-beds up, to keep the contents dry, as there was a deep place in the ford. . . . The bar on which we drove over—extended nearly across, and was composed of coarse pebbles and stones: Current—rapid—About 100 yds. over." [52: 35]

James Abbey, June 1, 1850. ". . . came to a running stream of muddy water called Laramie River, about 100 yards wide, which we crossed with our teams. The water being up to the after axle." [1: 25]

Capt. Howard Stansbury, July 12, 1852. "Cross the Laramie Fork below the fort about one mile." [361: 273]

O. Allen, 1859. "Fort is situated on the Laramie river one mile above its mouth, if too high to ford cross on the bridge one mile east of the fort. . . ." [8: 62]

Merrill J. Mattes, 1947. Information obtained by investigation of the site is included; also an 1868 photograph of the toll bridge. [244: 12-15, 17, 23-24]

Dale L. Morgan, 1959. Information on this crossing is included in a discussion of those in use in 1849. [274: Apr., 6-12] Merrill J. Mattes, 1969. [249: 505-06]

USGS map, Fort Laramie, Wyo., 1:24,000, 1950 ed.

FIRST CROSSING OF NORTH PLATTE RIVER$_p$
(Site 20, Fort Laramie Vicinity Map)
Mile 649R⅓ — Goshen County
NE¼ of NW¼, Sec. 27, T26N, R64W

Fur traders and missionaries following the north bank of the North Platte River crossed here to reach Fort William. They forded during times of low water, and ferried, by bullboat or raft, during high water.

This crossing was of no particular importance after the abandonment of Fort William in 1841. Thereafter, emigrants who needed to cross did so near Fort Platte, although the army made some use of this place as a ford for cavalry and pack trains during low water.

Merrill J. Mattes, 1969. Cites an instance of fur trade use of this crossing (Warren A. Ferris, in 1830). [249: 481]

USGS map, Fort Laramie, Wyo., 1:24,000, 1950 ed.

SECOND CROSSING OF NORTH PLATTE RIVER$_p$
(Site 1, Fort Laramie Vicinity Map)
Mile 639R¾ — Goshen County
NW¼ of SW¼, Sec. 22, T26N, R64W

A privately operated ferry was in existence in 1849 and later was operated by the army. The site is at the North Platte River about 400 feet below the present (new) highway bridge.

The craft was a barge, probably poled or rowed at first, but later rigged on a line for operation by the current. It remained in use until the steel bridge was built in 1876.

This crossing was necessary for emigrants traveling by the Mormon or Council Bluffs road prior to 1850; thereafter, it served those who did not wish to continue on the north side of the river (Child's Cutoff) and also was the crossing for traffic on north-south routes.

Joseph Price, June 11, 1859. ". . . when we crossed the Platt down at Fort cearny we under Stood that we was clear of the Platt but the further we came up the more we became convinced that we was under a great mistake   it is said that a mountain goat cant go up this side of the river and consequently we had to cross at this point. . . ." He tells of the loss of the ferry boat by overloading the evening of their arrival (Sunday)—writing on Tuesday, June 11. [238: Sept., 251-52]

George W. Fox, July 18, 1866. "Crossed the Platte on a ferry which runs itself by the current . . ." [140: 589]

LeRoy R. Hafen and Francis M. Young, 1938. "On June 15 [1853] the Miniconjou Sioux captured the boat at the North Platte ferry near the fort. Sergeant Raymond recovered it, but while he was crossing the river one of the Indians fired at him and the shot struck near the boat . . ." (Lieut. Hugh B. Fleming attempted to arrest the culprit, precipitating a fight in which three Sioux were killed, three wounded and two taken prisoner.) [156: 209-10]

Irene D. Paden, 1943. ". . . the soldiers maintained boats for ferrying. . . ." P. 161: ". . . no necessity . . . for any man to risk (and sometimes lose) his life. . . . The officers were suspected of giving out misleading information to induce the emigrants to cross—at first, on account of the profit they could make from selling supplies . . . later because they ran a government ferry at five dollars per wagon. . . . The ferry later run by the soldiers was just down stream from the steel bridge." [298: 156]

Merrill J. Mattes, 1947. This is the authority for the location of the ferry site. [244: map]

David L. Hieb, 1954. Illustration—"Indians at the North Platte Ferry in 1868. From a photograph by Alexander Gardner in the Newberry Library." [177: 22]

Dale L. Morgan, 1959. ". . . during the height of the emigrating season, the North Platte 2 miles away [from Fort Laramie] consistently had to be ferried. . . ." The ferries at Fort Laramie are covered on pp. 6-12. [274: Apr., 6]

Merrill J. Mattes, 1969. A quotation from an emigrant named Isaac Foster indicates the ferry was in operation on June 16, 1849, the day before the army took over Fort Laramie. Excerpts from diaries kept in 1850 indicate those crossing had to do the work. "From 1859 to 1868 no mention is made of the ferry as such, but only skiffs and canoes, sometimes operated by Indians

for a fee." [249: 491, 506-07]
USGS map, Fort Laramie, Wyo., 1:24,000, 1950 ed.

THIRD CROSSING OF NORTH PLATTE RIVER$_p$
(Site 2, Fort Laramie Vicinity Map)
Mile 649R¾ — Goshen County
NW¼ of SW¼, Sec. 22, T26N, R64W

A three-span, bow-string girder steel bridge was erected in 1876 to provide a reliable crossing of the North Platte River about 1.4 miles easterly from Fort Laramie. It served the north-south traffic, which became dominant through the Fort Laramie area after 1868.

The bridge still stands. A monument at the eastern end commemorates the fact that it was the fourth structure to span the river. (It is also Wyoming's oldest bridge.)

Merrill J. Mattes, 1947. "The steel bridge . . . over the North Platte, one of the earliest steel bridges west of the Missouri River, was built just in time to serve as a key point on the new migration route [Cheyenne-Deadwood Trail] . . . A Congressional Act of June 12, 1874, appropriated $15,000 for the building. . . . Construction was authorized by the Secretary of War on August 28, 1874. Soldiers from the fort quarried the stone for the substructure. The King Bridge Company of Cleveland, Ohio, had the construction contract. The spans and girders went by rail to Cheyenne, and from there were hauled by mule team to the fort. Construction began in October 1875, with John Shaw as foreman. Many difficulties were encountered in constructing the bridge under rather primitive conditions. One span broke loose and had to be raised from the waters of the Platte. . . . The bridge was completed or at least available for crossing by March 1, 1876, when General Crook's cavalrymen rode north to battle the hostiles in the Powder River country." [244: 50]

Paul Henderson, Personal Notes (undated), made available July 10, 1972: "Old U.S. Government Bridge monument—white cement with plaque, cement base, fenced with iron fence. State Property. Commemorates the fourth wagon bridge constructed across the North Platte River in Wyoming. . . . Placed by H. L. Comm. 1952."

USGS map, Fort Laramie, Wyo., 1:24,000, 1950 ed.

FOURTH CROSSING OF NORTH PLATTE RIVER$_p$
(Site 3, Fort Laramie Vicinity Map)
Mile 649R¾ — Goshen County, Wyo.
NW¼ of SW¼, Sec. 22, T26N, R64W

In 1847 the Mormon pioneers established a ferry here, approximately 600 feet above the present (new) highway bridge over the North Platte River. It was nearly opposite the site of Fort Platte.

This "Mormon ferry" was of importance only briefly, because the crossing stabilized after 1849 at a point approximately 400 feet below the present highway bridge, where the army established a ferry.

U.S. Congress, 1925. The daily account of the Mormon pioneer band, prepared from the diaries of Apostle Orson Pratt and Elder William Clayton, states: "Wednesday, June 2. [1847]—Quite early in the morning several of the Apostles and other brethern crossed the North Fork in their skiff of sole leather and walked up to Fort Laramie, where they were kindly received by James Bordeaux. . . . they walked down to see his flatboat, which the brethern engaged at the reasonable price of $15 to ferry the wagons of the pioneer company across, as they had learned that traveling farther upon the left bank of the North Fork, would, if not altogether impracticable, be attended with much difficulty. Thursday, June 3 . . . Early in the morning the pioneers commenced ferrying across the North Fork, which at that point was 108 yards wide, being deeper than usual. They averaged about four wagons an hour. . . . Friday, June 4—The pioneers resumed their labor of ferrying their wagons across before 5 o'clock in the morning, and by 8 o'clock the last wagon was over!

"Elder Clayton put up a guide board on the north side of the river at the ferry with the following inscription on it: 'Winter Quarters 543¼ miles; junction of the forks, 227½ miles; Ash Hollow, 142½ miles; Chimmey Rock, 70¼ miles; Scott's Bluff, 50½ miles. William Clayton, June 4, 1847.'" [384: 108]

William Clayton, 1848. Calls this "'Fort John' or Laramie ford," adding, "The fort lays about one and a half miles west from the river. The ford is good in low water. River 108 yards wide." [78: 12]

LeRoy R. Hafen and Francis Young, 1938. Mentions the competitive spirit of the Mormons in ferrying at this point. [156: 126]

Irene D. Paden, 1943. "In 1847 the Mormons opened their

road on the north bank of the Platte but, through some misapprehension of the route ahead, felt that it was the lesser of two evils to ferry the river at this point. . . . the Forty-niners using the Mormon road did the same." P. 161: "The original crossing . . . made famous by the Mormon migration of '47 and perpetuated by their popular guidebook, was a few yards upstream. . . ." from the iron bridge [298: 155, 161]

Merrill J. Mattes, 1947. This is the source of the position given for the ferry site. [244: map]

David L. Hieb, 1954. "That spring [1847] the pioneer band of Mormons . . . passed up the north bank of the Platte to its confluence with the Laramie, and crossed near the ruins of Fort Platte." [177: 6]

Wallace Stegner, 1964. ". . . he [James Bordeaux] would ferry them for twenty-five cents a wagon, or rent his flatboat for fifteen dollars." [363: 143]

Merrill J. Mattes, 1969. "In 1847 the Mormon Pioneers, who had been traveling the north bank (the Mormon Trail, or Council Bluffs Road), crossed here en route to the Promised Land. They investigated the place thoroughly, making detailed measurements of Fort Laramie and the abandoned Fort Platte." [249: 485]

USGS map, Fort Laramie, Wyo., 1:24,000, 1950 ed.

FORT PLATTE ("RICHARD'S FORT")ₚ
(Site 4, Fort Laramie Vicinity Map)
Mile 649R¾ — Goshen County, Wyo.
NE¼ of SW¼, Sec. 21, T26N, R64W

Fort Platte was an adobe-walled post built by Lancaster P. Lupton to compete with Fort William. It was begun as early as 1839 but was still unfinished in 1841, when it was sold to Sybille, Adams & Co. The structure passed into the hands of Pratte & Cabanne in 1843 and was abandoned in 1845. It was probably never more than a small, shabby post of traders whose principal stock was whiskey.

The emigrants appear to have received very little assistance at Fort Platte, although some went there for entertainment.

Rufus B. Sage, 1841. ". . . occupies the left bank [ascending] of the North Fork of Platte river, three fourths of a mile above the mouth of Larramie . . . and stands upon the direct waggon road to Oregon. . . . It's walls are 'adobies' (sun-baked brick) four feet thick, by twenty high—enclosing an area of two hundred and fifty feet in length, by two hundred broad. At the northwest and southwest corners are bastions which command its approaches in all directions.

"Within the walls are some twelve buildings in all, consisting as follows: office, store, warehouse, Smith's shop, carpenter shop, kitchen and five dwellings,—so arranged as to form a yard and corel, sufficiently large for the accomodation of more than two hundred head of animals. The number of men usually employed about the establishment is thirty. . . ." [338:IV, 219-20]

John C. Fremont, July 15, 1842. ". . . it was built of earth, and still unfinished, being enclosed with walls, or rather houses, on three of the sides, and open on the fourth to the river." [202:I, 210]

John Boardman, July 14, 1843. ". . . At night to Fort Platte to a dance, where some of the company got gay. Pleasant." [37: 103]

Matthew C. Field, 1843. ". . . encamped upon Laramee's Fork, opposite Richard's fort. . . ." A footnote adds that the post ". . . was sometimes called Richard's because it had been built by the three Richard brothers, Jean, Noel and Pierre, of St. Charles. . . ." [137: 74]

Francis Parkman, 1846. Noted, "beyond was green meadow, dotted with bushes, and in the midst of these, at the point where the two rivers joined, were the low clay walls of a fort. This was not Fort Laramie, but another post of less recent date, which having sunk before its successful competitor, was now deserted and ruinous." [304: 83]

J. Goldsborough Bruff, July 9, 1849. Noted, "Several hundred yards back from the river's bank, on the right, stood the old adobe walls of Fort Platte . . . now in ruins; and looks like an old Castle. —It is rectangular." [52: 35]

Merrill J. Mattes, 1947. The position given here for Fort Platte is from the large-scale map which was compiled by field work in the summer of 1946; however, that does not agree with Bruff's "several hundred yards back from the river's bank." Evidences near the Fort Platte monument indicate the site might be adjacent to it. [244: 15-16, 18, map]

Merrill J. Mattes, 1969. "In the fall of that year [1840] or the spring of the following, a rival establishment appeared on the nearby banks of the North Platte." There is information on the whiskey trade at that post. [249: 482-83]

LeRoy R. Hafen, 1938. Provides a ground plan and description of Fort Platte, as measured by Seth Bullock of the Mormon pioneers in 1847. (He found the dimensions were 103 by 144 feet.) [156: 125-27]

Author's note. See next site description, Fort Platte Monument, Fort Laramie Vicinity Map, Site 5.

USGS map, Fort Laramie, Wyo., 1:24,000, 1950 ed.

FORT PLATTE MONUMENT
(Site 5, Fort Laramie Vicinity Map)
Mile 649¾ — Goshen County, Wyo.
NE¼ of SE¼, Sec. 21, T26N, R64W

Paul C. Henderson's notes are as follows: "Fort Platte monument—white cement, set on cement base, fenced with iron pipe. State property. On south [north] side of road leading to old Fort Laramie, 1,500 feet west of the Government Bridge monument. Commemorates and directs to Fort Platte. . . . H. L. Comm. Mon., 1952."

This appears to correctly mark the site of Fort Platte (1839-1845). See preceding site, Fort Platte ("Richard's Fort").

Author's note, July 19, 1972. The plaque on the monument states: "Fort Platte / A Trading Post Built By / Lancaster P. Lupton / in 1841 / Stood Fifty Yards to the / North / Placed by / The Historical Landmark Commission of Wyoming / July 1951." Occupational debris (rusted square nails and fragments of glass exposed on the right-of-way) indicates that pipeline and road construction at this point disturbed a pre-1895 site. If these evidences are from Fort Platte, it must have been located close to the present position of the monument. The area between the monument and the North Platte River is now a cornfield.

USGS map, Fort Laramie, Wyo., 1:24,000, 1950 ed.

FORT WILLIAM
(Site 6, Fort Laramie Vicinity Map)
Mile 649R½ — Goshen County, Wyo.
SW¼ of SW¼, Sec. 22, T26N, R64W

In 1834 Robert Campbell built a trading post here, on the north bank of the Laramie River above its mouth. It was rectangular, enclosing an area 80' x 100,' and was constructed entirely of hewn cottonwood logs. Its 15-foot walls were bastioned at opposite angles and supported a blockhouse over the main gate. Several buildings were ranged inside the walls.

As the precursor of Fort John, this post was an important point on the pre-Oregon Trail route across the Rocky Mountains. It served fur trade purposes mainly, but also sheltered missionaries, scientists and persons traveling for pleasure to the Far West.

William Anderson, June 1, 1834. "This day laid the foundation log of a fort on Laramee's Fork. A friendly dispute arose . . . as to the name . . . William Patton offered a compromise which was accepted, and the foam flew, in honor of Fort William, which contained the triad prenames of clerk, leader and friend. Leaving Patton and fourteen men to finish the job we started upwards." [308: 4-5]

Nathaniel J. Wyeth, June 1, 1834. ". . . to Laramies fork . . . At the crossing we found 13 of Sublettes men camped for the purpose of building a fort he having gone ahead with his best animals and the residue of his goods he left about 14 loads." [406:I, 223]

Osborne Russell, Nov. 1837. Contains details of arrangements and operation of the fort. [337: 76-80]

F. A. Wislizenus, 1839. "It is on a slight elevation, and is built in a rectangle of about eighty by a hundred feet. The outside is made of cottonwood logs, about fifteen feet high, hewed off, and wedged closely together. On three sides there are little towers on the walls that seem designed for watch and defense. In the middle a strong gate, built of blocks, constitutes the entrance. Within, little buildings with flat roofs are plastered all around against the wall, like swallows nests. One is a storehouse; another the smithy; the others are dwellings not unlike monks cells. A special portion of the courtyard is occupied by the so-called horsepen, in which the horses are confined at night. The middle space is free, with a tall tree in it, on which the flag is raised on occasions of state." [405: 67]

William J. Ghent, 1934. ". . . Fort William. A year later [1835] it was sold to Fitzpatrick, Milton G. Sublette and Bridger . . . [as they] had reached an understanding . . . [with] the American Fur Company, it thus became virtually a company post, and in the following year [1836] the transfer was formally made. . . . Fort William was erected on the east (north) bank of the Laramie, about three-quarters of a mile from the junction with the Platte. Later (possibly in 1841), the company built another and larger fort on the same side of the river, about a mile upstream, and thereupon abandoned . . . the first building." [149: 133-34]

LeRoy R. Hafen, 1938. Provides a thorough coverage of events at Fort William, but is inadequate in regard to the location of the post. [156: 27-70]

Merrill J. Mattes, 1947. ". . . Fort William . . . probably [was] about one-half mile above the present mouth of the Laramie, perhaps 200 yards back from the left bank, within the vicinity of the F. E. Bay farm buildings. . . . John Hunton, one-time post sutler, told . . . [that] remains of the palisades could once be found in this vicinity . . . [and] journals bear this out. . . ." [244: 11]

David L. Hieb, 1954. "To an artist, A. J. Miller, who traveled with Sir William Drummond Stewart, we are indebted for the only known pictures of Fort William. Made during his visit to the fort in 1837 [interior and exterior views]. . . ." [177: 3-4]

Merrill J. Mattes, 1969. "In 1835 the enterprising partners sold their interest in Fort William to James Bridger, Thomas Fitzpatrick, and others, who in turn released it to the western department of the American Fur Company (after 1838, Pierre Chouteau Jr. & Company) . . . There are no maps of the Fort William period, and archaeology has failed to reveal the exact site of Fort William. Some scholars have supposed that it was at or quite near Fort John, but the writer believes that this original establishment was literally 'at the mouth of Laramie's Fork,' as stated by William Anderson, and on low ground as suggested by the A. J. Miller sketches. . . ." [249: 481-83].

Gregory M. Franzwa, 1990. "People have been looking for the old fort since early in this century. . . . those guys didn't have ground penetrating radar (GPR) . . . but some resourceful and innovative volunteers do, and they used GPR with great success [reporting], 'A subsurface anomaly, exhibiting the historically reported dimension, approximate locations and susequent expected depth of burial of Fort William was detected' . . . 208 degrees from the southwest abutment of the old iron bridge, about 580 feet away. See *folio* 3/1 (1990), 2.

USGS map, Fort Laramie, Wyo., 1:24,000, 1950 ed.

SECOND CROSSING OF LARAMIE RIVER$_p$
(Site 8, Fort Laramie Vicinity Map)
Mile 649.1R — Goshen County,
Wyo. SE¼ of NE¼, Sec. 28, T26N, R64W

This ford is 0.3 mile above the original crossing of the Laramie River.

After the army began to discourage crossing the river opposite Fort Laramie, several new fording places were found lower down the river. This one appears to have been used mostly by gold rush traffic.

Merrill J. Mattes, 1947. Quotes parties which appear to have forded here in 1849 (William G. Johnston, Alonzo Delano, E. B. Farnham, David DeWolf, Kimball Webster and Capt. Howard Stansbury). C. W. Smith crossed here the following year. Mattes' map in this work is the authority for location of this site. [244: 20-24, map]

USGS map, Fort Laramie, Wyo., 1:24,000, 1950 ed.

THIRD CROSSING OF LARAMIE RIVER$_p$
(Site 9, Fort Laramie Vicinity Map)
Mile 639.3R — Goehen County, Wyo.
SW¼ of NW¼, Sec. 28, T26N, R64W

This ford is 0.5 mile above the original crossing of the Laramie River. It is another of the altemate crossings used during the gold rush period.

Merrill J. Mattes, 1947. The map in this work, based on field work by the author and Thor Borreson, is the authority for location of this site. [244: map]

USGS map, Fort Laramie, Wyo., 1:24,000, 1950 ed.

FOURTH CROSSING OF LARAMIE RIVER$_p$
(Site 10, Fort Laramie Vicinity Map)
Mile 649.5R — Goshen County, Wyo.
NE¼ of NW¼, Sec. 28, T26N, R64W

This ford is ¾-mile above the original crossing of the Laramie River. It is another of the alternate crossings used during the gold rush period.

Merrill J. Mattes, 1947. The map in this work was prepared from field work by Mattes and Thor Borreson, and is the authority for the location of this site. [244: map]

USGS map, Fort Laramie, Wyo., 1:24,000, 1950 ed.

FIFTH CROSSING OF LARAMIE RIVER
(Site 11, Fort Laramie Vicinity Map)
Mile 649.9 — Goshen County, Wyo.
NW¼ of NW¼, Sec. 28, T26N, R64W

This ford is directly east of the Fort Laramie parade ground. A wagon bridge occupied the site (1873-84), and there was an adjacent foot bridge (1869-90).

The extent of early use of this crossing is uncertain, but it may have been less important than later use as an access to military facilities on the south bank of the Laramie River.

Merrill J. Mattes, 1947. The map included in this work, prepared from field work by the author and Thor Borreson, is the authority for the location of this site. [244: map]

Author's note, July 20, 1972. A comparison of the site with the map of Lt. A. J. Dowlson (1851) indicates no essential channel change at this point.

USGS map, Fort Laramie, Wyo., 1: 24,000, 1950 ed.

SIXTH CROSSING OF LARAMIE RIVER
(Site 12, Fort Laramie Vicinity Map)
Mile 650.0 — Goshen County, Wyo.
SE¼ of NE¼, Sec. 29, T26N, R64W

This crossing of the Laramie River is opposite the site of Fort John. Ferry service was available, with boats belonging to that establishment. Emigrants were discouraged from crossing here after 1849, to prevent them from crossing the parade ground. The Army had a footbridge at this location from 1854 to 1862.

After the establishment of Fort John, this crossing was most convenient for traffic to that post.

Matthew C. Field, July 6-7, 1843. "Laramee Fork 30 yards wide, very swift, and 7 feet deep at the crossing—Camp moved to this crossing. Unloaded, and packed over in two skiffs—all over by noon." [137: 80]

Overton Johnson, July 13, 1843. ". . . came to Lauramie Fork, opposite Fort Lauramie . . . obliged to ferry . . . two small boats from the Forts, lashed . . . platform made of wagon beds . . . placed the loaded wagons by hand. . . ." [208: 77]

Merrill J. Mattes, 1947. Lists the Johnston-Winter party (July 12-13) and the Nesmith party as ferrying here in 1843. Francis Parkman's party tried unsuccessfully to ford here in 1846 (Indians were successful the following day), and William Clayton of the Mormon pioneer band described this crossing in 1847. [244: 16-18]

USGS map, Fort Laramie, Wyo., 1:24,000, 1950 ed.

SEVENTH CROSSING OF LARAMIE RIVER
(Site 13, Fort Laramie Vicinity Map)
Mile 650.0L — Goshen County, Wyo.
SE¼ of NE¼, Sec. 29, T26N, R64W

This crossing of the Laramie River, of uncertain importance, is southwest of the Fort Laramie parade ground.

Merrill J. Mattes, 1947. The map in this work, based upon field studies by the author and Thor Borreson, is the authority for the location of this site. The ford was on a firm ledge. [244: map]

Author's note, July 20, 1972. A comparison of the site with the map of Lt. A. J. Dowlson (1851) indicates very extensive channel changes at this point. The old channel is now heavily wooded.

USGS map, Fort Laramie, Wyo., 1:24,000, 1950 ed.

EIGHTH CROSSING OF LARAMIE RIVER
(Site 14, Fort Laramie Vicinity Map)
Mile 650.0L — Goshen County, Wyo.
SE¼ of NE¼, Sec. 29, T26N, R64W

This crossing of the Laramie River is southwest of the Fort Laramie parade ground. It is of uncertain importance.

Merrill J. Mattes, 1947. The map in this work, based on field work by the author and Thor Borreson, is the authority for the location of this site. [244: map]

Author's note, July 20, 1972. A comparison of the site with the map of Lt. A. J. Dowlson (1851) indicates very extensive channel changes here. The old channel is now heavily wooded.

USGS map, Fort Laramie, Wyo., 1:24,000, 1950 ed.

NINTH CROSSING OF LARAMIE RIVER
(Site 15, Fort Laramie Vicinity Map)
Mile 650.0L — Goshen County, Wyo.
NE¼ of NE¼, Sec. 29, T26N, R64W

A contemporary sketch of Fort John, in 1853.

This crossing of the Laramie River is west of the Fort Laramie parade ground. The extent of its early use is uncertain. Francis Parkman's experience would indicate that it was a useable alternative ford when high water prevented fording on the direct approach to Fort John (sixth crossing).

Francis Parkman, 1846. "We tried to ford Laramie Creek at a point nearly opposite the fort, but the stream, swollen with rains, was too rapid. We passed up along its bank to find a better place. . . . soon found a ford . . . the water boiled against our saddles, but our horses bore us easily through. The unfortunate little mules were near going down with the current, cart and all; and we watched them with some solicitude scrambling over the loose round stones at the bottom. . . . All landed safely at last; we crossed a little plain, descended a hollow, and, riding up a steep bank, found ourselves before the gateway of Fort Laramie. . . ." [304: 83]

Merrill J. Mattes, 1947. The map in this work is based upon field studies by Merrill J. Mattes and Thor Borreson. It is the authority for the location of this site. [244: map]

USGS map, Fort Laramie, Wyo., 1:24,000, 1950 ed.

FORT JOHN ("Fort Laramie")
(Site 16, Fort Laramie Vicinity Map)
Mile 650.0 — Goshen County, Wyo.
SE¼ of NE¼, Sec. 29, T26N, R64W

Fort John is the name given a trading post built by the American Fur Company in 1841, on the point of high ground 1.6 miles above the mouth of the Laramie River (at the southwest end of the Fort Laramie parade ground). Its adobe walls were 15 feet high and topped with a wooden palisade. They enclosed an area of 123' x 168'. Tower-like bastions stood at the south and north corners and there was a blockhouse over the main gate. The buildings were ranged against the inside of the wall.

As ". . . an island of civilization in the western wilderness. . . ." (Mattes, 1947), this post could usually provide essential supplies, blacksmithing and wagon repairs, and postal service. Assistance in ferrying the North Platte or Laramie rivers was sometimes available and information concerning trail conditions could usually be gotten from personnel of the post.

Rufus B. Sage, Fall 1841. "One mile south of it [Fort Platte], upon the Larramie, is Fort John, a station of the American Fur Company. Between these two posts a strong opposition is maintained." [338:IV, 221]

John C. Fremont, July 15, 1842. "A few hundred yards [from Fort Platte] brought us in view of the post of the American Fur Company, called Fort John, or Laramie. . . . It is on the left bank, on a rising ground some twenty-five feet above the water; and its lofty walls, whitewashed and picketed, with the large bastions at the angles, gave it quite an imposing appearance. . . ." P. 218: ". . . the fort, which is a quadrangular structure, built of clay, after the fashion of the Mexicans. . . . walls are about fifteen feet high, surmounted with a wooden palisade, and form a portion of ranges of houses, which entirely surround a yard of about one hundred and thirty feet square. Every apartment has its door and window, all, of course, opening on the inside. There are two entrances opposite each other and midway of the wall, one of which is a large and public entrance, the other smaller and more private; a sort of postern gate. Over the great entrance is a square tower, with loopholes; and, like the rest of the work, built of earth. At two of the angles, and diagonally opposite each other, are large square bastions, so arranged as to sweep four faces of the walls. . . ." [202:I, 210-11, 218]

Matthew C. Field, July 5, 1843. ". . . visited Fort Laramee, a large square structure of mud, strongly knitted with wood timber painted palisades around the parapets—towers—large cavayard—comfortable dwellings—like old low Spanish structures in New Orleans—Dimensions 150 by 125 feet—about 7 years old." P. 80: [July 6-7, 1843] ". . . fort situated on a high point, the water protecting two sides." [137: 74]

Overton Johnson, July 13, 1843. ". . . belongs to the American Fur Company . . . is built of Dobies (unburnt bricks). A wall of six feet in thickness and fifteen in height encloses an area of one hundred and fifty feet square. . . ." P. 78: "About one mile below Fort Lauramie is Fort Platte. . . ." [208: 77-78]

Samuel Parker, June 20-22, 1845. "Stayed at Fort Laramey, plenty of Indians." [302: diary]

Heinrich Lienhard, 1846. "The fort is a rectangle with 16 to 20 foot walls of dried brick. The interior was divided into various rooms . . . As far as I recall there was but one door, which was a large one. Various frontier Indians camped in the vicinity of the fort." [229: 67]

Francis Parkman, 1846. ". . . found ourselves before the gateway of Fort Laramie, under the impending blockhouse erected above it to defend the entrance." Pp. 84-85: Parkman's reception and assignment of quarters is described. P. 86: "The little fort is built of bricks dried in the sun, and externally is of an oblong form, with bastions of clay, in the form of ordinary blockhouses, at two of the corners. The walls are about fifteen feet high, and surmounted by a slender palisade. The roofs of the apartments within, which are built close against the walls, serve the purpose of a banquette. Within, the fort is divided by a partition: on one side is the square area, surrounded by the storerooms, offices, and apartments of the inmates; on the other is the *corral*, a narrow place, encompassed by the high clay walls, where at night, or in the presence of dangerous Indians, the horses and mules of the fort are crowded for safe keeping. The main entrance has two gates, with an arched passage intervening. A little square window, high above the ground, opens laterally from an adjoining chamber into this passage; so that when the inner gate is closed and barred, a person without may still hold communication with those within, through this narrow aperture. . . ." Pp. 88-89: Parkman describes mealtime at the fort. Pp. 91-92: The arrival of emigrants is described—"The men occupied themselves in procuring supplies for their onward journey; either buying them, or giving in exchange superfluous articles of their own." [304: 83-86, 88-92]

W. Clayton, 1848. "Fort 'John, or Laramie,' lays about one and a half miles from the river, in near a south-west course, and is composed of a trading establishment, and about twelve houses, enclosed by a wall eleven feet high. The wall and houses are built of *adobes,* or Spanish brick. It is situated on the Laramie Fork, and is a pleasant location." [78: 23]

Osborne Cross, June 22, 1849. "This fort is built in the form of a quadrangular figure and of unbaked clay or adobes. The wall is about twenty feet high, with a small palisading on a part of it. There are two blockhouses at the corners, diagonally from each other. Over the main entrance, which faces the river, there is also another small blockhouse. The buildings are inside, the wall forming a part of them. They are very small, and have but few comforts . . . no trees about the fort . . . two companies of the rifle regiment are stationed. . . ." [101: 98]

J. Goldsborough Bruff, July 9-10, 1849. ". . . the Fort . . . purchased by our Government . . . is an extensive rectangular structure of adobe. It forms an open area within—houses and balconies against the walls. Heavy portals and watch tower, and square bastions at 2 angles, infilading the faces of the main walls. It has suffered much from time and neglect. . . ." [52: 37]

Capt. Howard Stansbury, July 12, 1849. "Fort Laramie, formerly known as Fort John . . . The company sold it to the United States . . . and their people . . . temporarily encamped near the ford of the creek, having recently surrendered possession." [361: 53]

O. Allen, 1859. Notes, ". . . sutler's store, blacksmith shop and post office, at the fort." [8: 62]

H. S. Schell, December 8, 1870. "A portion of the old adobe fort was standing until 1862, when it was entirely demolished and the adobes used in the construction of the front portion of the magazine." [343: 347]

William J. Ghent, 1934. "Later (possibly in 1841), the company built another and larger fort on the same side of the river, about a mile upstream [from Fort William], and thereupon abandoned, leased or sold the first building. It was the new post that became the famous Fort Laramie, so named by the owners. Possibly its proper name for a time was Fort John, but . . . the real Fort Laramie was bought by the Government on June 26, 1849, after having been occupied by a garrison a month or so earlier. . . ." Pp. 250-51: Notes the Fort Laramie monument, ". . . a truncated pyramid of concrete, fourteen feet high," placed by the Wyoming Historical Landmarks Commission near the sutler's store in

1915. [149: 134, 250-51]

LeRoy R. Hafen, 1938. A comprehensive account of Fort John and its importance, including a ground plan (p. 127); however, this work does not clearly distinguish between Fort John and its predecessor, Fort William. A wide range of documentary materials is presented. [156: 67-134]

Irene D. Paden, 1943. "At the north end of officer's row is a timeworn adobe building containing (according to old-timers of the vicinity) a fragment of the trading post erected on this site in 1836. It is a section of adobe wall forty inches thick including one doorway, and is still stout enough to justify the workman who hauled it a hundred yards or so for use in the new post office and sutler's building. This was in 1852. . . ." [298: 167] (Concerning this tradition, see 343: 347; and 244: 95-96.)

Merrill J. Mattes, 1946. Concerning the tradition that a fragment of Fort John construction was incorporated into the sutler's store, "There is a secondary error implied in both statements, since 1836 could not have been the date of the adobe bricks, even if their connection with Fort John could be proved. Adobe-walled Fort John did not replace its log-walled predecessor, Fort William, until 1841. However, there seems to be no solid evidence to support the belief that the adobe section of the sutler's store was in any way a carryover from the fur trade era which ended in June 1849. [243: 95]

Wallace Stegner, 1964. A drawing of Fort Laramie by Frederick H. Piercy, as he saw it in 1853, shows the Fort John structure in relation to "Old Bedlam." This drawing appeared first as an illustration in Linforth's book, *Route from Liverpool to Great Salt Lake Valley* (1855). [363: 149f]

Robert W. Frazer, 1965. Confuses Fort William with Fort John. [142: 181-82]

Merrill J. Mattes, 1969. Covers Fort John to its sale to the United States. [249: 483-87]

USGS map, Fort Laramie, Wyo., 1:24,000, 1950 ed.

FORT JOHN CEMETERY
(Site 17, Fort Laramie Vicinity Map)
Mile 650.3 — Goshen County, Wyo.
SE¼ of SE¼, Sec. 20, T26N, R64W

A burial ground of unknown dimensions occupies the rise where the post hospital was built in 1873. Milton Sublette,

Ruin of an army hospital building at Fort Laramie. The hospital was built over an old fur trade cemetery.

brother of William (the founder of Fort William), is among those lying in unmarked graves there. This was the cemetery for the fur traders and the military personnel prior to 1868, and probably contains some emigrant burials also.

Matthew C. Field, July 6, 1843. *"Milton Sublette's grave!* . . . *Laramee fort viewed from the grave yard at sun set."* [137: 80]

J. Goldsborough Bruff, July 10, 1849. "A few hundred yards from the fort, after rising a sand hill, the trail passes through a burial ground of the Traders, and mountaineers. Several picketed rectangular enclosures contain one or more graves: several had crosses erected on them. . . ." [52: 37]

David L. Hieb, 1954. "On the hill to the north stands the ruins of the post hospital erected in 1873. . . . There is good evidence that this building stands in the midst of the cemetery used by the furtraders before 1849 and by the Army before 1868. These early burials, probably including that of Milton Sublette in 1836, remain undisturbed." [177: 40]

LeRoy R. Hafen, 1965. "Milton [Sublette] was suffering with his diseased leg; it worsened, and on April 1, 1837, he died at the Fort." [160:I, 157]

Merrill J. Mattes, 1969. ". . . post cemetery. Before 1868, when this adjunct of all civilized communities was moved farther away, the cemetery was on the hilltop now occupied by the ruins of the

1883 hospital. In 1852 Caroline Richardson 'saw a person entered into the graveyard.' This plot of ground was well filled, not only by earlier fur traders and many soldier victims of scurvy and Sioux arrows, but by the considerable number of civilian employees and emigrants who, according to the journals, died here from 'colery' or other diseases, accident, murder or old age (including Harlow Thompson's little old lady who brought along her own coffin)." [249: 513]

USGS map, Fort Laramie, Wyo., 1:24,000, 1950 ed.

PORTUGEE PHILLIPS HORSE MONUMENT
(Site 18, Fort Laramie Vicinity Map)
Mile 650.5 — Goshen County, Wyo.
NW¼ of SE¼, Sec. 20, T26N, R64W

This monument has been placed on the right-of-way of the county road which gives access to Fort Laramie National Historic Site. It is located about ½ mile northwesterly from the parade ground.

It commemorates a relatively minor event of the Sioux War of 1866-1868 (a winter ride by "Portugee" John Phillips to obtain relief for the beleaguered Fort Phil Kearny, following the disastrous Fetterman fight). The plaque calls it "The Greatest Ride in History."

Herbert M. Hart, 1963. "The disaster threw the fort into near panic. Portugee Phillips, a trapper, rode 236 miles through sub-zero weather to Fort Laramie for reinforcements." The caption for a photograph of the monument states, "Phillips never recovered from his freezing journey and was crippled the rest of his life." [167: 45]

Author's note, July 10, 1972. Personal note from Paul C. Henderson: "Portugee Phillips Horse Marker—A concrete mono-lith, concrete base. At the northwest fence and county road corner (Ft. Laramie National Historic Site road). Placed by the H. L. Comm., 1952. The plaque on the monument states erroneous information in regard to dates and facts and must be changed. On county road property. Iron fence."

USGS map, Fort Laramie, Wyo., 1:24,000, 1950 ed.

MARY E. HOMSLEY GRAVESITE_p
(Site 19, Fort Laramie Vicinity Map)
Mile 651.2R¼ — Goshen County, Wyo.
SW¼ of SE¼, Sec. 17, T26N, R64W

This is a wayside burial of the late Oregon Trail period, which has been preserved through local generosity.

Statement from Paul C. Henderson: "Grave of Mary E. Homsley, died June 10, 1852. Concrete pyramidal marker, 6' high, cement base, iron fence. Original native sandstone marker set in a niche on the marker and covered with glass. . . ." Located on Bureau of Reclamation property near the north end of the Fort Laramie Irrigation Canal Tunnel No. 1. Marker placed by the H. L. Comm., 1952."

William J. Ghent, 1934. "In November 1925, three men walking across a hillside near Fort Laramie found a faintly inscribed fragment of sandstone that had evidently been broken from a stone still imbedded in the earth. . . . 'Mary E. Homsley Died June 25, 1852 Age 29.' A news article on the discovery, published in the *Fort Laramie Scout*, was followed by an editorial in the *Portland Oregonian*, which asked the question, 'Who was Mary Homsley?' . . . answered by a daughter . . . Mrs. Laura Gibson, of Portland, who seventy-three years before, at the age of three, had witnessed her mother's burial. . . . Father Benjamin Homsley, a blacksmith, with his two young daughters, had reached Oregon and had settled on a homestead. . . . reticent, undemonstrative man, he had never talked of the tragic loss, and only through the newspaper article did Mrs. Gibson learn the place of her mother's death. From contributions by citizens of Wyoming a cement monument, in which the old stone is imbedded, was erected at the grave, and on Memorial Day, 1926, it was dedicated by Professor [Grace R.] Hebard." [149: 253]

USGS map, Fort Laramie, Wyo., 1: 24,000, 1950 ed.

MEXICAN HILL_p
Mile 656.4 — 6.5 miles west of Fort Laramie
Platte County, Wyo. — SE¼ of Sec. 8, T26N, R65W

This is a steep descent from the benchland to the river bottom along the North Platte. The origin of the name is obscure.

Irene D. Paden, 1943. ". . . the descent, which is merely a steeply washed break in the bluffs. But it bore evidence that the wagons had descended at this point and is called . . . Mexican Hill. . . ." [298: 171]

USGS map, Register Cliff, Wyo., 1:24,000, 1952 ed.

REGISTER CLIFF
Mile 658.7 — 2.8 miles southeast of Guernsey, Wyo.
Platte County — NW¼ of NW¼, Sec. 7, T26N, R65W

This mile-long cliff of soft sandstone was used as a name register by emigrants from 1847 on. A portion of the inscribed cliff face has been enclosed behind protective fencing, but all has been vandalized by recent name-carving.

Register Cliff now displays few really early names, but it is important as a unit in a complex of interesting sites. (Refer to Register Cliff Vicinity Map.)

Irene D. Paden, 1943. ". . . a length of ancient chicken wire pegged to the ground in front of the bluff to keep people away. It was doing a good job, too. There are few things more insurmountable than a wobbling, eight-foot chicken-wire fence. . . . investigation proved that the jutting points of the bluffs all had initials, and sometimes full name and address and date, carved upon the soft stone . . . called Register Cliffs . . . among the best of the 'guestbook' rocks. . . ." [298: 172-73]

Wallace Stegner, 1964. Notes of the Mormons of 1847 that "Their first night's camp was . . . near what later came to be called Register Cliff. . . . Since no diarist mentions the cliff, it had evidently not yet achieved fame." The earlier route from Fort Laramie westward was the "hill" road, which stayed back

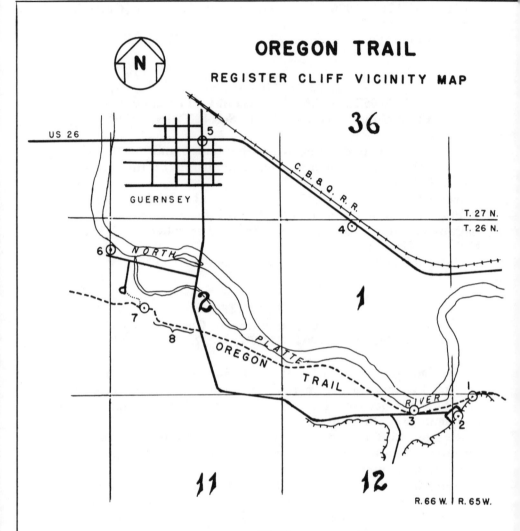

OREGON TRAIL

REGISTER CLIFF VICINITY MAP

36

US 26

C.B.&Q.R.R.

GUERNSEY

T. 27 N.
T. 26 N.

5

4

1

6

NORTH

2

7

8

PLATTE

OREGON

TRAIL

RIVER

1

3

2

11

12

R.66 W. | R.65W.

NOTES

1. REGISTER CLIFF MONUMENT   5. OREGON TRAIL MONUMENT
2. UNKNOWN PIONEER GRAVES   6. LUCINDA ROLLINS GRAVE
3. WARD & GUERRIER POST   7. OREGON TRAIL RUTS
4. ROADSIDE INFORMATION PANEL   8. DAMAGED TRAIL RUTS

0   1   2

MILES

ALH '72

from the North Platte River on the dry bench to the south. [363: 145]

Gregory M. Franzwa, 1972. "Thirty more yards [beyond the Register Cliff monument], look in the fenced area about two feet above grade. There, among hundreds of names carved in trail days, are three names, now badly deteriorating. The top one is A. H. Unthank 1850. The center one, O. N. Unthank 1869. The bottom one, O. B. Unthank, 1931. The first is significant in that his grave is only a week away, near Glenrock. Alva Unthank is said to have died of cholera. . . . O. B. Unthank was his great-grandson; O. N. Unthank, a nephew." [141: 240]

Author's note, July 20, 1972. The plaque on the Register Cliff monument reads: "Dedicated to the / Pioneers of Wyoming / Register Cliff / Acquired by the / State of Wyoming / Through the Gift of / Henry Frederick / Family / 1932." The face of the cliff is now protected by chain-link fencing for 200 feet east and 150 feet west of the monument (the fencing begins 150 feet east of the parking area).

An information panel concerning Register Cliff is located approximately one mile east of Guernsey, Wyoming, on U.S. Highway 26 (0.7 mile north of the actual site).

USGS map, Register Cliff, Wyo., 1:24,000, 1952 ed.

UNKNOWN PIONEER GRAVES
Mile 658.8 — 2.8 miles southeast of Guernsey, Wyo.
Platte County — NW¼ of NW¼, Sec. 7, T26N, R65W

A stone incised "Unknown Pioneer Graves" stands in a fenced plot, 30' x 10', located against the base of Register Cliff at the west side of the parking area. No contemporary information has been found concerning these burials and it is not known for certain if they are Oregon Trail related or connected with the nearby trading post-stage station-Pony Express station. Refer to Register Cliff Vicinity Map, Site No. 3.

Irene D. Paden, 1943. "Near one of the great rounded points of the cliff a group of forgotten pioneers sleep in unmarked graves. We passed them on our way to the ranch house [Frederick's Ranch] for information." [298: 174]

Gregory M. Franzwa, 1972. "Just below the cliff is an iron fenced area, protecting the graves of three emigrants, now unknown." [141: 239]

Author's note, July 20, 1972. This heavily overgrown plot is

retained by a low concrete wall with wrought-iron fencing set on it.
USGS map, Register Cliff, Wyo., 1: 24,000, 1952 ed.

WARD & GUERRIER'S TRADING POST (Site)
Mile 659.0 — 2.7 miles southeast of Guernsey, Wyo.
Platte County — NE¼ of NE¼, Sec. 12, T26N, R66W

This was the site of a Ward & Guerrier trading post (1841), a stage station (1859) and a Pony Express station (1860). Later, headquarters for a cattle ranch stood on the site. The monument is 1,300 feet west of the Register Cliff parking area, adjacent to the road. No direct connection with Oregon Trail events is apparent in the available sources.

LeRoy R. Hafen, 1938. August 29, 1855. ". . . Oglalas [Sioux] had a council with him [Indian Agent Thomas S. Twiss] at Ward and Guerrier's, seven or eight miles above the fort. . . ." [156: 240] Irene D. Paden, 1943. "Farther along [from Register Cliff], and out in the open, is a large Pony Express marker. No name is given on the plaque, but it commemorates the old Point of Rocks Station." Note, p. 157: "At the Torrington depot . . . the grave of William Guerrier, 'Indian Trader and Noble Gentleman . . .'" [298: 174]

Author's note. Information made available by Paul C. Henderson on July 13, 1972: "Monument, White cement on cement base PE medallion; placed . . . by Wyo. H. L. C. (1932), on land secured by easement."
USGS map, Register Cliff, Wyo., 1:24,000, 1952 ed.

LUCINDA ROLLINS GRAVE
Mile 661R¼ — 1.3 miles southwest of Guernsey, Wyo.
Platte County — NW¼ of NW¼, Sec. 2, T26N, R66W

This is the improved grave of Lucinda Rollins, who died here in June 1849. A white cement monument on the bank of the North Platte River has been vandalized by removal of the original headstone (said to have been thrown into the river). The marker commemorates a trail death of the gold rush period.

Irene D. Paden, 1943. "A knoll . . . On the summit was a conspicuous new monument, and we went up to look at it. The

The empty niche in this monument once held the original headstone for the Lucinda Rollins grave.

cement gravestone was just completed. . . . Sunk into a glass-fronted recess was an ordinary irregular rock. Its still legible inscription read: 'Lucinda Rollins—Died June '49'." [298: 175-76]

Author's note, July 20, 1972. The plaque reads as follows: "Grave of / Lucinda Rollins / 1849-1934 / Dedicated to the Pioneer Women of Wyoming / Erected by the Historical Landmark Commission of Wyoming." Recent concrete work at the gravesite is marked: at west end, "891st Engineers Kans. N.G. 1960," and at east end, "Restored by 419th C. A. Winona Minn. 1965."

Notes made available by Paul C. Henderson on July 13, 1972: "White cement on cement base—plaque (W), recess for original headstone (E); placed in improved plot by Wyo HLC (1934), on Guernsey City property."

USGS map, Guernsey Reservoir, Wyo., 1: 24,000, 1951 ed

OREGON TRAIL RUTS
Mile 660.7 — 1.3 miles south of Guernsey, Wyo.
Platte County — SW¼ of NW¼, Sec. 2, T26N, R66W

At this point, where the Oregon Trail crossed a ridge of soft sandstone, the track is worn to a depth of five feet, creating what is probably the most spectacular evidence of the importance of the Oregon Trail route.

The amount of traffic which passed over this route is evident from the erosion of the track; however, not all of it was emigrant vehicles. Military and other freighting probably contributed much of the visible wear.

Irene D. Paden, 1943. ". . . the most amazing cut on the whole overland road. It was at least shoulder-deep in solid sandstone and barely wide enough for a wagon. The bull-whackers and muleteers, who walked beside their teams, had kept to the right and left. They themselves, through the years, had worn footpaths deep. . . ." [298: 175]

Gregory M. Franzwa, 1972. "Park in another parking area and hike 100 yards or so to the top of Deep Rut Hill. There are ruts carved six feet deep in solid sandstone. They were made as countless wagons coursed over the knob." [141: 240]

Author's note, July 20, 1972. The ruts are approached from the parking area by a 400-foot improved trail on an easy grade. At the top, there is an information panel and a plaque designating the area a Registered National Historic Landmark.

Between this site and Register Cliff, two pipelines were constructed along 1,500 feet of Oregon Trail ruts, seriously damaging them.

USGS map, Guernsey, Wyo., 1:24,000, 1950 ed.

WARM SPRINGS ("Big Spring")$_P$
Mile 662.2 — About 2½ miles west of Guernsey, Wyo.
Platte County — SE¼ of SW¼, Sec. 4, T26N, R66W

These are two free-flowing springs—one gushing from a ledge of rock and the other bubbling up in a large pool. They are not as warm as might be expected. They are in a sandy draw about one-half mile below the place where the "hill road" from Fort Laramie crosses.

This was a particularly popular camping place, available to travelers on both the "hill" and "river" roads west from Fort Laramie. Several cross-connections between the routes existed in the vicinity.

Rufus B. Sage, Spring 1842. ". . . upon an Indian trail, we bore leftward from the river, and, in a short ride, came to a sand creek. . . . A transparent spring gushes from the right bank with considerable noise, furnishing a beautiful streamlet to its hitherto dry bed, which is known as the 'Warm Springs.'" [338:IV, 294]

John C. Fremont, July 21, 1842 ". . . ten miles from the fort we entered the sandy bed of a creek [from the hill road], a kind of defile, shaded by precipitous rocks, down which we wound our way for several hundred yards to a place where, on the left bank, a very large spring gushes with considerable noise and force out of the limestone rock. It is called 'the Warm Spring,' and furnishes to the hitherto dry bed of the creek a considerable rivulet." [202:I, 231]

James W. Nesmith, July 16, 1843. ". . . to the big spring on Sand Creek, about eight miles [from Fort Laramie]." [290: 341]

Virgil Pringle, June 24, 1846. ". . . the spring is very bold and rather warm." P. 215, June 29: ". . . travelled 20 miles [from Fort Bernard] and Camped at a large spring." [275:I, 174]

William Clayton, 1848. "'Warm Springs,' . . . This is a very strong spring of clear water, but it is warmer than river water, at all seasons of the year." [78: 12]

Osborne Cross, June 25, 1849. ". . . probably eight miles from the fort. On the right side of the road and about three hundred yards below where it crosses the ravine there is a fine spring that breaks from the side of the hill . . . affords an abundance of water. The men made an excavation that collected a sufficient quantity in a few minutes for the whole command. . . . by no means warm, although [it was] not as cold as springs generally are among the hills. [101: 102-03]

O. Allen, 1858. "Lime Kiln Springs." [8: 62]

William J. Ghent, 1934. "Leaving Fort Laramie . . . At thirteen miles they reached Big Spring (called also Warm Spring, because its water was not icy cold) . . ." [149: 135]

Irene D. Paden, 1943. ". . . it had its source in a most satisfying spring that gushed from the hillside. The Mormons camped here in 1847, and Apostle Orson Pratt wrote on June 5th: 'The name is Warm Spring; the water is not so cold as one would expect. The quantity is nearly sufficient to carry a common flour mill, being very clear. . . .' Beyond the spring was a lime kiln established and used by the soldiers from Fort Laramie. The evidences are still visible." [298: 177]

Gregory M. Franzwa, 1972. "The warm spring, known as the Emigrants' Laundry Tub, is 250 yards down the ruts, which gradually deteriorate into a cattle path . . . It would seem to have a temperature of about 70 degrees; not warm at all. [141: 241-42]

Author's note, July 21, 1972. The lower spring breaks out of a fissure in a 6-foot-high rim of rock which is topped by a 12-foot bank of clay. The flow of water is about that of a 4-inch pipe. The upper spring, 150 feet farther up the draw, is a shallow pool with a diameter of 40 feet where water bubbles up through a sandy bottom. The bottom of the pool is about on a level with the fissure from which the lower spring gushes, and its flow is twice as great. The runoff of these springs, which are close against the north side of a broad, sandy draw, flows away as a spreading, algae-filled wallow which sinks entirely within a half-mile. The water is not noticeably warm.

About a half-mile up the draw, on its north bank, is a 40-foot diameter knob which has the appearance of a hot spring cone but is made up of a soft sedimentary material. It is probably the site of the Army's limekiln.

USGS map, Wheatland NE, Wyo., 1:24,000,1951 ed.

MARKED GRAVE_p
Mile 663R1½ — 1.6 miles west of U. S. Highway 26 bridge over
North Platte River, Guernsey, Wyo., and
800 feet north of the highway at the foot of a ridge
Platte County — 1900 ft. north of S¼ cor., Sec. 33, T27N, R66W

This is a marked burial which has been identified by Reg P. Duffin as that of Solomon Dill of St. Joseph, Mo. He died June 20, 1850.

Author's note, July 23, 1972. The grave is covered with stones and has an iron drive-stake at each end. The one at the west has a VFW marker attached, and behind it is a bronze survey marker, set in concrete, and stamped, "No 21 / SDILL / R ROG". From the grave, the Cold Springs Rifle Pits are about ½ mile distant on Az. 279 degrees true.

USGS map, Guernsey Reservoir, Wyo., 1:24,000, 1950 ed.

COLD SPRINGS RIFLE PITS_p
Mile 664R1½ — 2.5 miles west of Guernsey, Wyo.
Platte County — NW¼ of SW¼, Sec. 33, T27N, R66W

At this spot five rifle pits form a well-arranged defense perimeter enclosing an area of roughly 100' x 150', on the military crest of a ridge 920 feet east of Cold Springs. The pits are from 18" to 24" deep, protected by piled-up rocks on the outer face.

The purpose this fortified position was intended to serve is not clear. Personnel at Fort Laramie National Historic Site thought it protected workers at the limekiln near the Warm Springs, but that place was more than a mile distant. More likely, it was related to the Oregon Trail alternate route which passed 500 feet north of Cold Springs—the track is still visible.

Author's note, July 22, 1972. The free-flowing Cold Springs are boxed and fenced. They are near the head of a draw on the Frederick Ranch—920 feet from the rifle pits on Az. 287 degrees true. There is a granite monument at a parking area on the north side of U.S. Highway 26—600 feet from the rifle pits on Az. 255 degrees true. It is incised, "The Oregon Trail / 1841 / Cold Springs Camping / Ground. Rifle Pits on / Brow of Hill 500 Feet / North. / Erected by The / Historical Landmark / Commission of Wyoming / 1943." The monument is protected by an iron pipe fence.

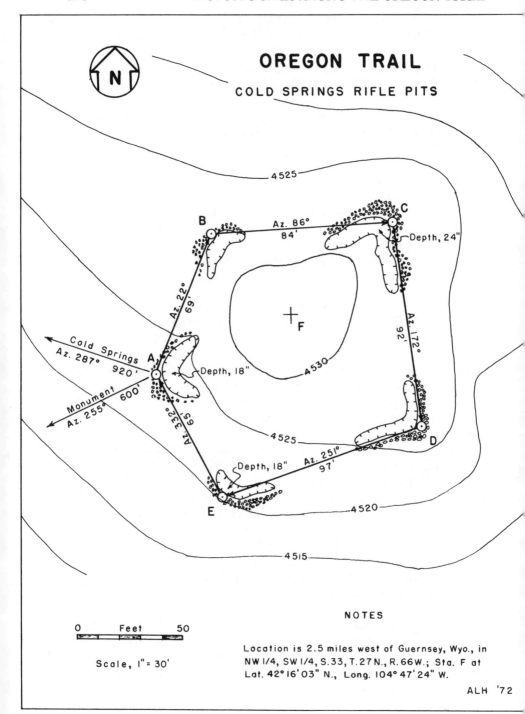

OREGON TRAIL

COLD SPRINGS RIFLE PITS

NOTES

Location is 2.5 miles west of Guernsey, Wyo., in NW 1/4, SW 1/4, S.33, T.27N., R.66W.; Sta. F at Lat. 42°16'03" N., Long. 104°47'24" W.

ALH '72

Above: The view to the southwest across rifle pit "D" at Cold Springs. U.S. Highway 26 is in the middle background. Below: the view of Laramie Peak is striking from the monument at mile 667.5. The ruts of the Oregon Trail are in the light areas in the foreground.

USGS map, Guernsey, Wyo., 1: 24,000, 1950 ed.

OREGON TRAIL MONUMENT$_P$
**Mile 667.5 — On a county road, 3.8 miles NW of its junction
with US Highway 26 near Cold Springs
Platte County, Wyo. — NW¼ of SW¼, Sec. 24, T27N, R67W**

This monument of red sandstone from the Deer Creek quarry
is 14" x 18" x 42", incised "Oregon Trail / Marked By The / State
Of / Wyoming / 1913." It is typical of a type of marker used
frequently in the vicinity of the Black Hills.

Author's note, July 23, 1972. The view of Laramie Peak, which
dominates the Laramie Range, or "Black Hills" of an earlier day,
is particularly good from this point. The name—Black Hills—is
a relic of the fur trade, and was first applied to all outliers of the
Rocky Mountains because of their somber appearance as approached from the plains. The cover of pine trees gave a dark
coloration first noticed by travelers on the Oregon Trail upon
reaching Robidoux Pass (mile 604).

Except in the historical sense noted here, the term Black Hills
now designates a hilly region of western South Dakota.

USGS map, Guernsey Reservoir, 1:24,000, 1950 ed.

PORTER'S ROCK$_P$
**Mile 668.6 — 7 miles west of Guernsey, Wyo.
Platte County — SE¼ of SW¼, Sec. 27, T27N, R67W**

This is an elliptical exposure of rock about 40 feet high.
Travelers along the Oregon Trail passed on either side. It is a
landmark reminiscent of the Mormon trek westward in 1847.

William Clayton, 1848. At 20½ miles from Fort Laramie, he
notes: "'Porter's Rock,' left of the road—a mile beyond this, you
descend to the lower land again. The descent is steep, lengthy
and sandy." [78: 12]

Claude Adams, 1970. He states the name derives from Porter
Rockwell (one of Brigham Young's enforcers) who put his name
there in 1847. [3: 254]

USGS map, Herman Ranch, Wyo., 1:24,000, 1951 ed.

OREGON TRAIL MONUMENT_P
Mile 670.3 — 1.5 miles SW of Wendover Station on Colorado-Southern Railroad
Platte County, Wyo. — At ¼ Cor. between Secs. 15 & 16, T27N, R67W

This concrete marker, 8" x 14" x 67", is placed on the railroad right-of-way adjacent to the county road. The bronze tablet states: "At this point / the Oregon Trail / crossed / Erected by Robt Rice / V.P. & G.M., C & S Ry., Jan 1, 1921." The monument faces the tracks.

Irene D. Paden, 1943. ". . . in 1937 . . . we found . . . an automobile highway laid out by CCC boys which follows the trail very closely from Guernsey to Wendover . . . at the hill's foot, ran the railroad tracks. Beside them stood a trail marker. It was little and old. The usual group of railway buildings surrounded the depot. . . ." [298: 178]

USGS map, Herman Ranch, Wyo., 1:24,000, 1951 ed.

CROSSING OF COTTONWOOD CREEK_P
Mile 672.0 — At the Herman Ranch, behind present barn
Platte County, Wyo. — NE¼ of SE¼, Sec. 24, T27N, R68W

Cottonwood Creek is a small stream where the emigrants found groves of bitter cottonwood trees—a welcome relief in a relatively treeless journey. There was a campground here. The stream is now known as Cottonwood Creek.

Rufus B. Sage, spring, 1842. "Towards night we arrived at a large creek, bearing the name of Bitter Cottonwood Creek—so called from the abundance of that species of poplar in its valley.

"These trees grow very tall and straight with expansive tops, averaging from twenty-five to one hundred and fifty feet in height.

"The creek occupies a wide, sandy bed, over which the water is dispersed in several shallow streams. The valley is broad and of a jetty, vegetable mould, variegated, at intervals, with layers of gravel deposited by aqueous currents, and is bounded on both sides by abrupt acclivities. . . ." [338:IV, 295]

John C. Fremont, July 22, 1842. "We halted at noon on the *Fourche Amére*, so called from being timbered principally with the *liard amére* (a species of poplar) . . . The bed of the creek is sand and gravel, the water dispersed over the broad bed in several shallow streams. . . ." [202:I, 234]

William Taylor, June 12, 1846. ". . . Camped on the Bitter Cotton Wood a Smal Stream." [275:1, 126]

O. Allen, 1858. "Bitter Cotton Wood Creek. . . ." [8: 63]

USGS map, Herman Ranch, Wyo., 1:24,000, 1951 ed.

JOHN F. MILLER GRAVE$_P$
Mile 672.1L — 1,200 feet northwest of Herman ranchhouse
Platte County, Wyo. — NW¼ of SE¼, Sec. 24, T27N, R68W

This grave, on the edge of a dry bench behind the Herman Ranch house (now owned by Jerry Cundall), was formerly thought to be Oregon Trail related, but a recent clean-up of the site revealed the dates 1852-1894 on the headstone, and information supplied Randy Brown by a relative indicated that Miller—the original settler in that area—died of tuberculosis in the latter year. Two of his children are buried nearby in unmarked graves.

In the hay meadow east of the Cundall house is a pile of stones which has been worked around for years. In the course of an examination during the summer of 1991, head and foot stones were found in place, along with an iron-pipe marker.

South of the Herman Ranch, close to the bluff on that side of Cottonwood Creek, there is a remnant of the old "Yellowstone Highway"—the early tourist route to Yellowstone Park.

USGS map, Herman Ranch, Wyo., 1:24,000, 1951 ed.

OREGON TRAIL MONUMENT$_P$
Mile 674.8 — 4.5 miles NW of Wendover, Wyo.
Platte County — SW¼ of SW¼, Sec. 30, T28N, R67W

This red sandstone monument is placed on the divide between Little Cottonwood Creek and the North Platte River, marking the river road" of the Oregon Trail.

William J. Ghent, 1934. ". . . in October 1913, stones were erected . . . on the divide between Little Cottonwood Creek and the Platte. . . ." [149: 251]

Author's note. The location has been determined from a manuscript map prepared by Paul C. Henderson.

USGS map, Herman Ranch, Wyo., 1:24,000, 1951 ed.

COTTONWOOD STATION SITE (Upper)
Mile 677.5 — ½ mile northwest of Coleman Butte
Platte County, Wyo. — SW¼ of NE¼, Sec. 30, T27N, R68W

This Pony Express Station was adjacent to the "hill road." The
site was marked with a steel post, stenciled "Cottonwood Pony
Express Station," placed by L. C. Bishop. The location is from
a manuscript map by Paul C. Henderson.
USGS map, Coleman Butte, Wyo., 1:24,000, 1950 ed.

RED (TWIN) SPRINGS$_P$
Mile 680.8 — 5 miles south of Glendo, Wyo.
Platte County — NW¼ of SW¼, Sec. 35, T29N, R68W

These springs were used by emigrants; later this was the site
of a roadhouse kept by M.A. Mouseau. It was destroyed in 1868
to keep liquor and supplies from the Indians. It is on the "river
road."
Red Springs was a camping place for emigrants and a stop-
over place for later travelers.
Irene D. Paden, 1943. Notes that the Oregon Trail passed by
these springs. [298: 181]
Virginia C. Trenholm, 1970. Describes the burning of
Mouseau's roadhouse as an aftermath of the "Battle of Horseshoe
Creek," March 19-21, 1868. [380: 256-57]
Author's note, July 23, 1972. The springs are now fenced and
appear to be part of a sheep ranch.
USGS map, Cassa, Wyo., 1:24,000, 1961 ed.

HORSESHOE STATION (Lower)$_P$
Mile 682.9 — 2 miles south of Glendo, Wyo.
Platte County — SW¼ of NW¼, Sec. 21, T29N, R68W

This is the site of the Old Bellwood Stage Station, burned by
Indians in 1857, and a later stage and Pony Express station. The
field surrounding the station was an early emigrant campground
on the "river road." The station has a particularly colorful
history from the late period of Oregon Trail use.
Sir Richard Burton, 1860. ". . . to Horse-shoe Station,—the
old *Fer à Cheval*,—where one of the road agents, Mr. Slade, lived,
and where we anticipated superior comfort . . . buildings were

on an extensive scale . . . regardless of expense . . . admitted into a house with a Floridia style of verandah. . . ." There is much more about the food and accommodation—both poor. [56: 101]

Irene D. Paden, 1943. ". . . a stack-studded hayfield belonging to an English gentleman, Mr. Foxton . . . fifty years of residence . . . In a field just outside his garden was the site of the famous Horseshoe Station, used by Jack Slade as a headquarters from which to operate the adjoining division of the stage line. The spot had been identified for Mr. Foxton by one of the two men who survived its burning by the Indians [brief story of that event]. Mr. Foxton took us to see the place. We found an irregular pit overgrown with scraggly sage and tussocks of grass. Half imbedded in the ground are segments of old and rotting timbers, all that remains of beautifully situated Horseshoe Station. . . ." [298: 182]

Author's note, July 23, 1972. There is a monument of granite, 10" x 24" x 46", set beside U.S. Highway 26/87 at a point 200 feet south of the bridge over Horseshoe Creek. It was placed by the Historic Landmarks Commission of Wyoming in 1937, and states: "530 yards southeast of / this monument on the / Oregon Trail was the site of / Horseshoe Creek Pony Express / and U.S. Military Telegraph / and Stage Station built in 1860." The site of the station is now a weedy flat in front of a farm house, and the steel post stenciled "Horseshoe Pony Express Station," placed by L. C. Bishop at the site of the building in 1959 could not be found. The emigrant campground is now a farm field.

USGS map, Sibley Peak, Wyo., 1:24,000, 1950 ed., rev. 1961.

HORSESHOE STATION (Upper)p
Mile 690.1 — 9 miles southwest of Glendo, Wyo.
Platte County — SE¼ of NW¼, Sec. 1, T28N, R70W

This station was at the crossing of Horseshoe Creek by the old, or "hill" road. Paul Henderson says this station served the stage, Pony Express and telegraph. The site is west of the Horseshoe Creek Road and south of the stream, according to Henderson. It probably is not as important as the station at the lower crossing.

Author's note, July 23, 1972. Larry Cundall, a rancher, stated that a monument had been placed about eight miles up Horseshoe Creek from Glendo by a Mr. Foy (who was 94 years old and in a rest home at Wheatland, Colorado, in 1972.) This monument is described as concrete, but there is doubt locally that it is really on the Oregon Trail.

According to local information, the site is best reached by ascending the Horseshoe Creek Road to its crossing of that stream. It is left of the road and south of the creek.

USGS map, Spring Creek, Wyo., 1:24,000, 1949 ed.

OREGON TRAIL MONUMENT_P
Mile 690.7 — 7 miles west of Glendo, Wyo.
Platte County — SE¼ of NW¼, Sec. 8, T29N, R69W

This red sandstone marker is adjacent to the Horseshoe Creek Road, marking the crossing of the "river road."

Author's note. This location is from a manuscript map prepared by Paul C. Henderson.

USGS map, Cedar Hill, Wyo., 1:24,000, 1949 ed.

ELKHORN STATION SITE_P
Mile 693.3 — 9 miles west of Glendo, Wyo.
Platte County — SW¼ of NW¼, Sec. 1, T29N, R70W

A Pony Express station was located here, on the crossing of Elkhorn Creek by the "river road." The site is marked by a steel post stenciled "Elkhorn Pony Express Station," placed by L. C. Bishop in 1959.

Author's note. The location has been determined from a manuscript map prepared by Paul C. Henderson.

USGS map, Cedar Hill, Wyo., 1:24,000, 1949 ed.

A. H. REEL WAGON TRAIN FIGHT (Site)_P
Mile 695.0 — 11 miles west of Glendo, Wyo.
Platte County — NE¼ of SE¼, Sec. 34, T30N, R70W

This is an extended site, 0.4 mile along the Oregon Trail, on the divide between Coffee Creek and North Elkhorn Creek. The A. H. Reel wagon train was attacked here by Indians on August 1, 1876. Included is the George Throstle monument, a stone marking the position of the corraled wagons (the position cited above), and a barrel hoop marker.

This was a minor incident of the period of Indian unrest which included the Custer disaster. This was a freight train, not an emigrant train.

Irene D. Paden, 1943. ". . . Elkhorn, and it was here that Heck Reel's freight outfit loaded with beer and flour was attacked by Indians and the wagons burned, adding a bizarre touch of beerkeg hoops to the grim austerities of the Black Hills." [298: 183]

Margaret Wilson, 1970. This event is described thus: Wagon-boss Throstle was out ahead of the train when Indians appeared out of a draw and fired on them, killing Throstle at the point marked by his monument. The forward 5 wagons were able to corral, but the last 3 wagons could not get up in time and were abandoned about 100 yards in rear at the point marked by the iron hoop, where they were burned. The defense of the corraled wagons was successful and there was no further loss of life. [402: 263-65]

Information from Paul D. Henderson, July 12, 1972. The stone 410 yards southeast of the George Throstle monument "marks the place where the wagons of the Heck Reel Wagon Train corraled to ward off an Indian attack. 50 to 100 yds SE [is] where 3 wagons were burned." The Throstle monument is described as "Native stone, incised, 'Geo. Throstle killed here Aug. 1, 1876.'" The third marker is an iron barrel hoop partially buried in the center of the Oregon Trail.

USGS map, Cedar Hill, Wyo., 1:24,000,1949 ed.

OREGON TRAIL MONUMENT$_P$
Mile 700.9 — 14 miles south of Douglas, Wyo.
Converse County — NW¼ of SW¼, Sec. 19, T30N, R70W

This Oregon Trail monument is on the ridge between Indian and Canyon creeks, in a particularly isolated situation. It is at the point where the "hill" and "river" roads rejoined.

Author's note. The location, not visited, is known only from map references—it is shown on the map below and on the General Highway Map of Converse County, Wyo.

USGS map, Dilt's Ranch, Wyo., 1:24,000, 1950 ed.

JAMES BRIDGER'S FERRY_P
Mile 702R10 — 13 miles southeast of Douglas, Wyo.
Converse County — NE¼ of NE¼, Sec. 19, T31N, R69W

This ferry was established to ferry Bozeman Road traffic over the North Platte River. The site is 1,500 feet above (west) of the present bridge by which U.S. Highway 26/87 crosses the river near Orin, Wyoming. It was of brief importance to traffic over the short-lived Bozeman Road to Montana Territory. It probably was in use only from 1864 to 1866.

George W. Fox, July 25, 1866. "Passed a ferry on the Platte. Bridgers, as usual, the proprietor has some Indians around him. . . . [140: 590]

Author's note, July 23, 1972. A granite monument on the southwest side of U.S. Highway 26/87, at a point 300 feet east of the center of the bridge, is incised: "James Bridger's Ferry / established in 1864, was / located 1500 feet up the / river from this monument / erected by the Historical Landmarks / Commission of Wyoming / 1937." The monument is in the NW¼ of the NW¼, Sec. 20, T3 1N, R69W, on the highway right-of-way.

USGS map, Orin, Wyo., 1:24,000, 1950 ed.

CROSSING OF LABONTE CREEK_P
Mile 706.0 — 10 miles south of Douglas, Wyo.
Converse County — SW¼ of NW¼, Sec. 3, T30N, R71W

The Oregon Trail crossed LaBonte Creek here, where there was an emigrant campground.

James A. Pritchard, 1849. ". . . came to LaBonte River (called by some Beaver creek). . . ." [317: 86]

J. Goldsborough Bruff, July 14, 1849. ". . . to 'La Bonte Creek,' good water, but rather low. Plenty of timber and brush in the bottom. Close by the Camp lay a large trunk of a Cottonwood tree; inscribed all over with names, initials, dates, & as usual." [52: 43]

Thomas Christy, 1850. "La Bonte River." [71: 32]

O. Allen, 1858. "La Bonte's Creek, U.S. Mail Station No. 26. . . ." [8: 63]

William J. Ghent, 1934. "The emigrants crossed at La Bonte Creek (733 miles). . . ." [149: 135]

Irene D. Paden, 1943. ". . . La Bonte (sometimes called Big Timber Creek). . . ." [298: 183]

USGS map, Poison Lake, Wyo., 1:24,000, 1949 ed.

OLD CAMP MARSHALL[p]
Mile 706L½ — 10½ miles south of Douglas, Wyo.
Converse County — NE¼ of NE¼, Sec. 5, T30N, R71W

Camp Marshall was a temporary military post on the west side of LaBonte Creek. Evidently it was abandoned prior to 1866.

William H. Jackson, Aug. 10, 1866. ". . . past ruins of old Fort LaBonte." [201: 125]

Author's note. According to Paul C. Henderson, a steel post stenciled "Camp Marshall" was placed at the site by L. C. Bishop in 1959. He also said the marked site is S. 64 degrees W., 2,600 feet from the location shown on the USGS map. The site was not recovered—the location given is from the USGS map.

USGS map, Poison Lake, Wyo., 1: 24,000, 1949 ed.

BILL HOOKER'S CABIN[p]
Mile 706R¼ — 10 miles south of Douglas, Wyo.
Converse County — SE¼ of NE¼, Sec. 33, T31N, R71W

This is the homesite of an early LaBonte Creek resident.

Author's note. The following information was obtained from Paul C. Henderson: "Slab of limestone from the ruin of La Bonte Stage Station, incised 'Bill Hooker 1874,' was placed by Hooker & J. M. Abney on private land in 1929."

Another monument, adjacent to U.S.Highway 20/87 (SW¼ of SW¼, Sec. 3, T32N, R72W) refers to this site. It was erected by F. W. LaFrentz, a "pioneer of Wyoming," in 1931, and states: "Commemorative Of / Bill Hooker / Bullwhacker / Who Built And Lived In A Cabin / On LaBonte Creek / Ten Miles From This Point / On The Bozeman Trail In / 1874." The cabin was on the Oregon Trail, not the Bozeman Trail.

USGS map, Dilts Ranch, Wyo., 1:24,000, 1949 ed.

LABONTE STATION SITE[p]
Mile 706.2 — 10 miles south of Douglas, Wyo.
Converse County — NE¼ of SW¼, Sec. 33, T31N, R71W

This is the site of a stage and Pony Express station on the west bank of LaBonte Creek, at the crossing of the Oregon Trail.

Irene D. Paden, 1943. ". . . on the west bank of LaBonte. He [E. B. Schaffner] showed us where had stood, in staging days, LaBonte Station. Showed us the two fords of the creek, one circling somewhat in order to pass by the station, and the other bearing straight across in the shortest possible way. Showed us where the two fords came together on the near side of the creek. [298: 184]

Lyle Hildebrand, 1970. An article on LaBonte Station. [178: 266-67]

Author's note. According to Paul C. Henderson, a steel post stenciled "La Bonte Pony Express Station" was placed at the site by L. C. Bishop in 1959. He also said the marked site is 3,300 feet south of the location shown on the USGS map. The site was not recovered—the location given is from the USGS, which appears to place the station correctly when the road system is considered.

USGS map, Poison Lake, Wyo., 1:24,000, 1949 ed.

LABONTE CABIN (Probable Site)ₚ
Mile 708R3 — At the mouth of LaBonte Creek
Converse County, Wyo. — SE¼ of Sec. 15, T31N, R71W

Rufus B. Sage, spring, 1842. "At night we encamped at the forks of a small stream called La Bonte's creek. Near the confluence of its waters with the Platte are the remains of a log cabin, occupied by a trading party several years since. [338:IV, 308]

John C. Fremont, July 24, 1842. ". . . encamped on the right bank of the Platte, where a handsome meadow afforded tolerably good grass. There were the remains of an old fort here . . . and on the opposite side was a picturesque bluff of ferruginous sandstone . . . latitude of the camp, 42 degrees, 47 minutes, 40 seconds." [202:I, 237]

Sir Richard Burton, 1860. ". . . below us the creek La Bonte,—so called from a French Voyageur . . ." [56: 149]

USGS map, Chalk Buttes, Wyo., 1:24,000, 1950 ed.

OREGON TRAIL MONUMENT
Mile 708.3 — 8.8 miles south of Douglas, Wyo.
Converse County — Center of Sec. 29, T31N, R71W

This red sandstone monument is on the east side of county road 0503, at the top of a prominent ridge. On the side facing the road it is incised, "Oregon / Trail / Marked by the / State of / Wyoming / 1913."

The Oregon Trail here entered "The Red Earth Country."

James W. Nesmith, 1843. Noted ". . . red pulverized earth, resembling vermillion. . . ." [290: 341]

Sir Richard Burton, 1860. "The land was a red waste . . . which after rains sheds streams like blood . . . presently we emerged from the red region. . . ." [56: 150]

W. W. Morrison, 1970. Provides quotes concerning the Red Earth Country, 1842-1852. [277: 268-69]

USGS map, Chalk Buttes, Wyo., 1:24,000, 1950 ed.

CROSSING OF WAGON HOUND CREEK$_p$
Mile 709.2 — 7.6 miles south of Douglas, Wyo.
Converse County — NE¼ of Sec. 20, T31N, R71W

This name is evidently a late development. The hounds are part of the front running gear of a wagon.

O. Allen, 1858. "Wagon Hound Creek. . . ." [8: 63]

William J. Ghent, 1934. "Wagon Hound Creek (sometimes spelled *Mound*), three miles farther. . . ." [149: 135]

Irene D. Paden, 1943. ". . . Wagonhound. Few knew the name, but none ever forgot the creek . . . always be identified . . . for it was red. The soil and the rock were almost audibly red, from the burnt hue of Mexican pottery to the clear vivid tone of a Madrone trunk . . . appeared to be brick dust. . . ." [298: 185]

USGS map, Chalk Buttes, Wyo., 1:24,000, 1950 ed.

KNOB HILL$_p$
Mile 711L½ — 7 miles south of Douglas, Wyo.
Converse County — NW¼ of NE¼, Sec. 13, T31N, R72W

This pyramidal mound of grey sandstone or limestone is outstanding in an essentially brick-red landscape. It has the appearance of piled-up boulders, as was a prominent landmark in the Red Earth Country.

James A. Pritchard, June 8, 1849. ". . . this morning we passed the red hills." [317: 87]

Sir Richard Burton, 1860. ". . . we saw on the left of the path a huge natural pile or barrow of primitive boulders, about 200 feet high and called 'Brigham's Peak,' because, according to Jehu's* whiskeyfied story, the prophet, revelator, and seer of the LatterDay Saints had there, in 1857[!], pronounced a 4th of July oration. . . ." [56: 150]

Irene D. Paden, 1943. "Within sight of the trail Grindstone Butte juts up from the rolling uplands—an isolated stony bulk where a few diarists mention gathering rock for whetstones." P. 186: "A stream just beyond Grindstone Butte, modernly entitled Bed Tick Creek. . . ." [298: 185]

Author's note, July 24, 1972. A wooden sign-frame which may once have held an information panel stands beside a gravel road one-half mile south of "Knob Hill." References to the striking coloration of this region have been assembled by W.W. Morrison, i.e., [277: 268-169]. James W. Nesmith spoke of the ". . . red pulverized earth, resembling vermillion. . ." (1943).

Paul C. Henderson indicates the emigrant route passed close to the eastern base. The name "Knob Hill" is used on his authority. A large limestone boulder 100 feet west of the Oregon Trail at this point was marked by L. C. Bishop in 1956. He chiseled on it, "Oregon Trail." This monument was in the SE¼ of the NE¼, Sec. 13. It could not be found.

USGS map, Chalk Buttes, Wyo., 1:24,000, 1950 ed.

BED TICK STATION (Site)_P
Mile 714.5 — 5 miles southwest of Douglas, Wyo.
Converse County — near W¼ Cor., Sec. 35, T32N, R72W

This is the site of a stage and Pony Express station. In 1959 it was marked by L. C. Bishop and Paul C. Henderson with a steel post stenciled "Bed Tick Station."

Irene D. Paden, 1943. ". . . modernly entitled Bed Tick Creek, was apparently nameless to the emigrants. . . ." [298: 186]

Author's note, July 24, 1972. To reach this site, turn south from U.S. Highway 20/87 about four miles west of Douglas and proceed 3.3 miles to an improved dirt road leading south. Follow it for 1.2 miles to a set of ranch buildings and turn east for 0.2 mile to a junction with an unimproved road. Proceed south 0.4 mile to another set of ranch buildings. The site is due

*The mad charioteer of the Bible. Stage drivers didn't like to be called that; it hurt their professional pride!

east 0.2 mile across a branch of Bed Tick Creek.
USGS map, Chalk Buttes, Wyo., 1:24,000, 1950 ed.

OREGON-BOZEMAN TRAIL JUNCTION$_P$
Mile 716.3 — 5 miles west of Douglas, Wyo.
Converse County — NW Cor., NE¼ of NE¼, Sec. 28, T32N, R72W

A red sandstone monument six feet high marks the point of
departure of the Bozeman Trail (1866). The monument is on
the right-of-way of the Box Elder Road, on the south side.

Author's note, July 24, 1972. There is another marker, placed
by the Historic Landmarks Commission in 1943, 3.1 miles north
on U.S. Highway 20/87. It wrongly states: "The Oregon Trail /
Four Miles South / Ft. Fetterman 1867 / Seven Miles North /
Highway Crosses Fetterman / Trail Route Here." The Fort
Fetterman site is 5.5 miles due north, and there is a "Bozeman
Trail" monument at 4.8 miles, in the N½ of the NW¼, Sec. 15,
T33N, R72W.

The Fort Fetterman site is now a Wyoming State Historical
Park, established in 1962. Today the visible remnants of the fort
are two buildings—a former officer's quarters (now a museum
and quarters for the caretaker) and the ordnance storehouse.
The cemetery and some foundations also are in evidence.

USGS map, Chalk Buttes, Wyo., 1:24,000, 1950 ed., and
Douglas, Wyo., 1:24,000, 1949 ed.

LAPRELE STATION$_P$
Mile 722.0 — 10 miles west of Douglas, Wyo.
Converse County — SW¼ of SW¼, Sec. 10, T32N, R73W

A stage and Pony Express station stood at this crossing of
LaPrele Creek. Well-preserved evidences indicate a single building, a well, and probably a cellar were here.

Thomas Christy, 1850. "La Prele River. . . ." [71: 33]

O. Allen, 1859. "LaPrale Creek—Wood, water and grass in
abundance." [8: 63]

L. C. Bishop, 1960. Lists "Lapierella (LaPrele)" as a station of
the Pony Express route, under the modified contract of July 1,
1861. [36: map]

Author's note, July 24, 1972. The station site on the Glen
Edwards Ranch is marked by an iron fence stake set by L. C.

Bishop. The stake stands beside the well (filled with ranch debris), and the station building was 50 feet to the north. It was a 24' x 42' structure with its long axis on Az. 54 degrees true. A hole, which may have been a cellar of 8' x 12', is ten feet outside the northwest corner of the station foundation. The ground on which the station stood is elevated about six feet above the meadow which borders LaPrele Creek on the east side. The Hembree-Baker graves are 300 feet from the stake at the well on azimuth 215 degrees true.

The creek takes its name from the French word for the horsetail plant (genus *Equisetum*) which was useful as fodder.

USGS map, Orpha, Wyo., 1:24,000, 1949 ed.

HEMBREE-BAKER GRAVESₚ
Mile 722.0 — 10 miles west of Douglas, Wyo.
Converse County — SW¼ of SW¼, Sec. 10, T32N, R73W

Two graves are near the old LaPrele Creek Station site. One is of a six-year-old boy, Joel Hembree, who fell under a wagon July 18, 1843, and was killed. The other is that of Pvt. Ralston Baker, Co. E, 2nd U.S. Cavalry, who died May 1, 1867. The Hembree grave is a re-burial, although marked by the original stone. The boy was the first casualty on the "Great Migration" of 1843, and his grave is the oldest marked burial related to the Oregon Trail emigration.

William T. Newby, 1843. Gives the date of the accident as July 18, and the name of the boy's father as Joel Jordan Hembree. [291: 28-29]

John Boardman, July 20, 1843. ". . . nooned on a creek where Applegate's Company had buried a boy that got killed by a wagon. . . ." [37: 103]

James W. Nesmith, July 20, 1843. ". . . at noon came up to a fresh grave with stones piled over it, and a note tied on a stick, informing us that it was the grave of Joel J. Hembree, aged six years, who was killed by a wagon running over its body. At the head of the grave stood a stone containing the name of the child, the first death on the expedition. The grave is on the left hand side of the trail close to Squaw Butte Creek." (LaPrele Creek.) [290: 341]

Matthew C. Field, 1843. "But one death seemed to have occurred among them, and this was far from the mountains. Here the loose riders of our moving camp gathered one morning to examine a rude pyramid of stones by the roadside. The stones had been planted firmly in the earth, and those on top were substantially placed, so that the wolves, whose marks were evident about the pile, had not been able to disinter the dead. On one stone, larger than the rest, and with a flat side, was rudely engraved: *Joel Hembree* and we place it here, as perhaps the only memento those who knew him in the States may ever receive of him. How he died we cannot of course surmise, but there he sleeps among the rocks of the West, as soundly as though chiseled marble was built above his bones."* [137: 28-29]

Gregory M. Franzwa, 1972. "In December 1961, the owner of that ranch started collecting rocks for a dam he was about to build. He came across one pile on the north bank of LaPrele Creek, and on turning over the largest of the dolomite boulders he noticed it had a flat face. Into that face had been chiseled '1843. J. Hembree.' The '4' was reversed.

"An article in a local newspaper about the find, and seeking information . . . to Paul Henderson in Bridgeport [Nebraska], who identified Hembree as a 9-year-old boy who became the first fatality of the Applegate migration. 'He fell off waggon tung & both wheels run over him,' reads the diary of one eyewitness. . . . [probably] riding on the tongue between the animals, with a hand on the back of each.

"The accident happened on July 18, and the company continued on into camp on LaPrele Creek with the unconscious boy. Joel died at 2 p.m. the next day, as the great company laid by. He was buried on the 20th and the company then continued the journey.

"Henderson hurried to the site with a team of experts. The grave had to be moved. Machines removed the first three feet of earth. Hand tools continued the job until some decayed wood was reached. This turned out to be an old oak dresser drawer, covering the top part of the body. Branches had covered the lower part. They rested on ledges on either side of the excavation. The deepest part contained the perfectly preserved skeletal remains of Joel. . . . The bones were moved 1,625 feet due west

---

*Dr. Marcus Whitman, writing on July 20, 1843, from Big Butte Creek, to the Rev. David Greene, Mission House, Boston, reported: "We buried a small boy this morning that died from a wagon having passed over the abdomen." (Transcript of Missionary Letters, American Board of Commissioners of Foreign Missions, Vol. 138, Letters 101, Newberry Library, Chicago.)

to higher ground, placed in a new pine box, and reburied."
[141: 245-46]

Author's note, July 24, 1972. From the Joel Hembree grave, the iron stake marking the site of LaPrele Station is 300 feet distant on Az. 30 degrees true. Five feet south of the Hembree headstone is another—of white marble, cut in the pattern formerly used for military burials—marked "Ralston / Baker Pennsylvania / Pvt Co E / 2 Regt Cavalry / Civil & Indian Wars / May 1, 1867." No further information has been found concerning this soldier who now lies beside Joel Hembree.

Reference. Reg P. Duffin, "The Grave of Joel Hembree" in *Overland Journal* 3/2 (Spring 1985), 6-16.

USGS map, Orpha, Wyo., 1:24,000, 1949 ed.

OREGON TRAIL MONUMENT
Mile 723.6 — 11½ miles west of Douglas, Wyo.
Converse County — Center of Sec. 9, T32N, R73W

This red sandstone monument is on the east shoulder of the Natural Bridge Road, on the ridge west of LaPrele Creek. The marker, which faces north, with one side toward the road, is incised: "Oregon / Trail / Marked By The / State Of / Wyoming / 1913."

Author's note, July 24, 1972. The stone has been defaced with scratched-on names, and the foundation is in need of shoring-up.

USGS map, Orpha, Wyo., 1:24,000, 1949 ed.

AYRES NATURAL BRIDGE
Mile 724L 1½ — 12 miles west of Douglas, Wyo.
Converse County — NW¼ of NE¼, Sec. 21, T32N, R73W

This bridge is in a beautiful red rock canyon coursed by the spring-fed LaPrele Creek. The stream is named for the horsetail plant which was used as forage—it is found in quantity on the lower reaches of the LaPrele.

Matthew C. Field, July 12-14, 1843. ". . . to visit a remarkable mountain gorge—a *natural bridge* of solid rock, over a rapid torrent, the arch being regular as tho' shaped by art—30 feet from base to ceiling, and 50 to the top of the bridge—wild cliffs, 300 feet perpendicular beetled above us, and the noisy current

The Ayres Natural Bridge spans LaPrele Creek. It is an unusual feature in an idyllic setting, which caused much comment by the emigrants.

swept along among huge fragments of rock at our feet. We had a dangerous descent, and forced our way through an almost impervious thicket, being compelled to take the bed of the stream in gaining a position below. We called the water 'Bridge Creek!'" [137: 95-96]

Miller-Reed diary, July 3, 1846. ". . . Camped on Beaver Creek [LaPrele] here is a natural bridge 1½ miles above camp." [275:I, 259]

Author's note, July 24, 1972. A small picnic area has been developed at the end of a difficult gravel access road. There is an Oregon Trail monument of mortared stream cobbles inlaid with relics (ox shoes, lynch pins, etc.) and marked "1850-1920." The area remains a beauty spot, although the ruin of a power plant 100 yards upstream from the arch is an intrusion on the scene.

USGS map, LaPrele Reservoir, Wyo., 1:24,000.

MARY KELLY, ET. AL., GRAVES_P
Mile 728.0 — 11 miles southeast of Glenrock, Wyo.
Converse County — SW¼ of SE¼, Sec. 35, T33N, R74W

This fenced plot contains the reburied (May 15, 1950) remains of "Little Mary Kelly," Sharp, Taylor, Franklin (colored) and another killed during and subsequent to an attack on a small wagon train July 12, 1864. It is adjacent to the Oregon Trail, the ruts of which are visible in this area.

The attack typified the harrassment of Oregon Trail traffic during the mid-1860s.

Irene D. Paden, 1943. Briefly retells the story of the attack and the death of Mary Kelly, as presented by her mother, Fanny Kelly, in *My Captivity Among the Sioux Indians.* [298: 186-89]

W. W. Morrison, 1971. This account is similar to his earlier article in *Annals of Wyoming*, Vol. 28 (October 1956), 168-72; this is also based on Mrs. Kelly's account. [278: 272-75]

Author's note, July 24, 1972. The attack on the wagon train took place 2,800 feet distant on Az. 66 degrees true, where the Oregon Trail climbed out of Little Box Elder Creek. The four men were originally buried there, but the need to construct a reservoir nearby led to removal of their remains to the Kelly gravesite. Mary Kelly was killed on a low ridge about 500 feet distant on Az. 95 degrees true, when she was spotted while attempting to reach a small party of soldiers the day following the attack.

The grave enclosure of chain-link fencing bears a bronze tablet stating: "This enclosure provided / by / John H. Wiggins / in memory of his cousin / Little Mary Kelly / Wyoming Historical / Society / 1966." It is on property of the Bill Barber Ranch (1.5 miles south of the ranch house).

The site of the attack on the wagon train was at mile 727.6 (NW¼ of SW¼, Sec. 36, T33N, R74W), in an area now devoted to the impoundment of seasonal runoff water. The Oregon Trail ruts in this vicinity are particularly good—a track three feet deep and 30 feet wide is on the slope down to the reservoir.

Reference. Randy Brown, "Attack on the Kelly-Larimer Wagon Train" in *Overland Journal*, 5/1 (Winter 1987), 16-38.

USGS map, Careyhurst, Wyo., 1:24,000, 1949 ed.

BOXELDER STATION$_p$
Mile 729.9 — 9 miles east of Glenrock, Wyo.
Converse County — NW¼ of NE¼, Sec. 27, T33N, R74W

A physical description of the Boxelder Station has not been found but there is evidence indicating the site was on the east side of Boxelder Creek, in a low meadow. The nearby Careyhurst Ranch building (of stone, built in 1890) is a handsome structure.

John C. Fremont, July 26, 1842. ". . . crossed a handsome stream, called *La Fourche Boisée*. It is well timbered." [202:I, 238]

James A. Pritchard, 1849. ". . . a fine bold running stream 4 miles this side of the North fork of the Platte. The Stream is called Foarche Bois River." [317: 87]

O. Allen, 1859. "Box Elder Creek—Wood, water and grass in abundance, U.S. Mail Station No. 27." [8: 63]

Sir Richard Burton, 1860. "The master, Mr. Wheeler, was exceptionally civil and communicative, he lent us buffalo robes for the night, and sent us to bed after the best supper the house could afford. . . ." [56: 150-51]

Author's note, July 24, 1972. The Oregon Trail crossing was exactly at the present bridge crossing Boxelder Creek, at the buildings of the old Careyhurst Ranch, which dates from 1878. A Mr. Foltzer, the foreman for the Bixby-Hereford Company, the present owners of the ranch, has been there 20 years. He pointed out the site of a blacksmith shop in the meadow across the bridge. This site, which is referred to there as "Blacksmith Meadow," has yielded many artifacts and is the probable site of Boxelder Station. A very fine ox yoke is displayed on the wall of a barn.

USGS map, Careyhurst, Wyo., 1:24,000, 1949 ed.

EMIGRANT NAMES[P]
Mile 732L¼ — 6.4 miles east of Glenrock, Wyo.
Converse County — SW¼ of SE¼, Sec. 17, T33N, R74W

A few emigrant names are carved in a low sandstone outcrop 2,800 feet south of old U.S. Highway 20/87, according to Paul C. Henderson.

USGS map, Glenrock, Wyo., 1:24,000, 1949 ed.

OREGON TRAIL MONUMENT
Mile 733.3 — 5.4 miles east of Glenrock, Wyo.
Converse County — NE¼ of SW¼, Sec. 18, T33N, R74W

This red sandstone monument was set by the Wyoming Oregon Trail Commission in 1913 to mark the route. It is 160 feet south of old U.S. Highway 20/87, on land owned by the Bixby Cattle

Company.

Author's note, July 25, 1972. The marker was found broken off near the ground and lying in the grass with this lettering up: "Oregon / Trail / Marked By The / State Of / Wyoming / 1913." The stone has since been reset.

USGS map, Glenrock, Wyo., 1:24,000, 1949 ed.

A. H. UNTHANK GRAVE₍ₚ₎
A. H. UNTHANK GRAVE_p

Mile 733.6 — 5.0 miles east of Glenrock, Wyo.
Converse County — SW¼ of SW¼, Sec. 18, T33N, R74W

This grave is marked by a brown sandstone slab incised, "A. H. Unthank Wayne Co. Ind. Died Jul. 2, 1850," and enclosed within a welded iron pipe fence. A footstone is marked, "A.H.U."

Unthank was one of many who died on the Oregon Trail in the late period of its use. He had cut his name in the soft sandstone of Register Cliff as he passed that point, and it can still be seen there with the names of two relatives.

Irene D. Paden, 1943. ". . . his is one of the most legible carvings on Register Cliffs. . . ." [298: 194]

Leroy Moore, 1971. Gives the spelling of the first name as "Alvah." [269: 276-77]

Gregory M. Franzwa, 1972. ". . . three names, now badly deteriorating. The top one is A. H. Unthank 1850. The center one, O. N. Unthank 1869 [a nephew]. The bottom one, O. B. Unthank, 1931 [a great-grandson] . . . Alva Unthank is said to have died of cholera. . . ." [141: 240]

W. W. Morrison, July 10, 1972. Stated that the "AT REST BDE" on the headstone is a latter-day addition. [269: interview]

Author's note, July 25, 1972. This grave is now 200 feet from the highway due to realignment of the route (U.S. 20/87). The surname is misspelled on the USGS map.

USGS map, Glenrock, Wyo., 1:24,000, 1949 ed.

EMIGRANT FORD — A_p

Mile 735R½ — 4 miles east of Glenrock, Wyo.
Converse County — NE ¼ of SE ¼, Sec. 12, T33N, R75W

This fording place sometimes was used as an alternative to Bisonette's ferry or Reshaw's bridge, over the North Platte River. The location was determined from a manuscript map by Paul

C. Henderson.
USGS map, Glenrock, Wyo., 1:24,000, 1949 ed.

EMIGRANT FORD — B$_p$
Mile 737R½ — 1.7 miles east of Glenrock, Wyo.
Converse County — SE¼ of NE¼, Sec. 3, T33N, R75W

This fording place also was used occasionally to cross the North Platte, as an alternative to the Bisonette ferry or the Reshaw bridge.

Author's note. The location is from a manuscript map by Paul C. Henderson.

USGS map, Glenrock, Wyo., 1:24,000, 1949 ed.

FERDINAND V. HAYDEN MONUMENT
(Site 4 — Deer Creek Vicinity Map)
Mile 738.9 — Converse County, Wyo.
NW¼ of NW¼, Sec. 4, T33N, R75W

This granite monument, in the Glenrock City Park, rests on a concrete base. Below a bronze Oregon Trail medallion are the words: "To All Pioneers / Who Passed This Way / And / In Memory Of / Ferdinand V. Hayden / Chief U.S. Geological Survey Of The Territories / 1867-78 / Born At Westfield Mass. 1829."

The monument was erected in 1931 by William H. Jackson, pioneer photographer of the West, who was a bullwhacker for a freighting outfit on the Oregon Trail and Hayden's official photographer in the years 1870-78.

Author's note, July 25, 1972. The monument appears to have been moved from its mapped location (1949), and the bottom three lines have been obliterated.

USGS map, Glenrock, Wyo., 1:24,000, 1949 ed.

DEER CREEK STATION (Site)
(Site 3, Deer Creek Vicinity Map)
Mile 739.0 — Converse County, Wyo.
NE¼ of NE¼, Sec. 5, T33N, R75W

A trading post, consisting of a store, blacksmith shop and post office, was established here in 1857 by Joseph Bisonette. It served as a stage and Pony Express station and was burned by Sioux Indians in 1866. Earlier there had been an emigrant campground in this vicinity. This was an important point on the stage line to Salt Lake City, although it was never first class.

Sir Richard Burton, 1860. ". . . Deer Creek, a stream about thirty feet wide . . . The station boasts an Indian agent, Major Twiss, a post office, a store, and of course a grog-shop. M. Bissonette, the owner of the two latter and an old Indian trader, was the usual creole, speaking a French not unlike that of the Channel Islands and wide awake to the advantages derivable from travellers. . . . large straggling establishment . . . I wish my enemy no more terrible fate than to drink excessively with M. Bissonette. . . . The good creole, when asked to join us, naively refused . . . a delay of fifteen minutes and we were hurried forwards." [56: 154]

William H. Jackson, August 17-18, 1866. Mentions burning of the station by Indians, with the loss of three lives. [201: 126]

O. Allen, 1859. "Deer Creek—Trading post at this point . . ." [8: 63]

John D. McDermott, 1966. ". . . in 1857, Twiss suddenly moved the agency to the mouth of Deer Creek. . . . Bissonette followed . . . established another trading complex. His store, blacksmith shop, and post office were his visible means of support . . . employed fourteen clerks and teamsters . . . by peddling liquor along with the rest of his merchandise, he cornered the agency trade. . . ." P. 57: ". . . President Lincoln removed Twiss from office in 1861. Bissonette remained at Deer Creek for another four years. . . ." P. 58: Bisonette lost stock to raiding Sioux in the fall of 1865, and, "His resources depleted and his life endangered, the trader fled with his family to Fort Laramie. During the summer of 1865, the Indians burned Deer Creek Station." Note: W. H. Jackson definitely places the burning on August 18, 1866. His freight train reached the station on the 17th, at which time he "Bought sugar at 75 cents a pound," and the next entry noted the station was "burned at daybreak, at least 3 men killed and scalped." [160:IV, 56-58]

Author's note, July 25, 1972. As nearly as could be determined, an oil well is now pumping at the site of the Deer Creek Station. The steel post set by Bishop and Henderson could not be found.

Concerning the emigrant campground, there are these comments:

John C. Fremont, July 26, 1842. ". . . reached the mouth of

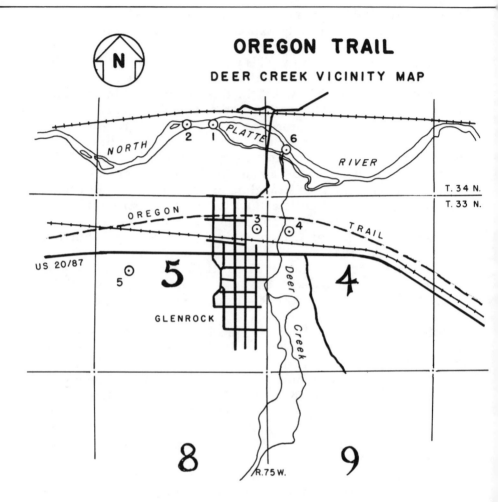

OREGON TRAIL

DEER CREEK VICINITY MAP

NOTES

1. BISONETTE FERRY   4. F. V. HAYDEN MONUMENT
2. RESHAW'S BRIDGE   5. THE GLEN ROCK
3. DEER CREEK STATION   6. INDIAN FORD

MILES

ALH '72

Deer Creek, where we encamped . . . abundance of rich grass . . . [stream] twenty feet broad, and well timbered with cottonwood of an uncommon size. . . ." [202:I, 238]

William Taylor, June 16, 1846. ". . . camped on deer creek. . . ." [275:I, 126]

James A. Pritchard, June 8, 1849. ". . . Deer Creek—a fine camping spot. The Stream is large & handsom & said to contain an abundance of Fish." [317: 87]

J. Goldsborough Bruff, July 16, 1849. ". . . to Deer Creek, which we crossed, passing through hundreds of tents, wagons, camp fires, and people of every age & sex, congregated on its banks, and turned down to the right, camped on the banks of Platte, at the Ferry . . . [July 17] The abandonment and destruction of property here—at Deer Creek, is extraordinary . . . Discarded effects generally rendered useless. . . ." [52: 44-45]

Osborne Cross, 1849. Description of campground. [101: 106-08]

Howard Stansbury, 1852. Description of campground. [361: 60]

Thomas Christy, June 4, 1850. "Deer Creek . . . Lovly place to camp. . ." [71: 34]

William J. Ghent, 1934. ". . . Deer Creek (769 miles), always during the life of the Trail a favored camping place because of its plentiful supply of water, wood and grass." [149: 135]

USGS map, Glenrock, Wyo., 1:24,000, 1949 ed.

NORTH PLATTE (BISONETTE'S) FERRY
(Site 1, Deer Creek Vicinity Map)
Mile 739R½ — Converse County
NW¼ of SE¼, Sec. 32, T34N, R75W

This was a primitive ferry made from six or eight dugout canoes floored over with timbers. It was made to carry wagons, and was propelled across the river by oars (Gould) or pulled with a line (Stansbury). A ferry operated here in 1849 and 1850, and was mainly of service to the gold rush traffic.

J. Goldsborough Bruff, July 16, 1849. "Ferry ⅓ of a mile here, made and tended by 3 or 4 men, is composed of 8 *dug-outs,* above the mouth of the Creek . . . kept by 3 men . . . Ferry-boat or canoes,—of cotton-wood; and grooved timber pinned over, connecting them, forming a rail-way to run the wagons on." P. 601, Note 169, H-3: "This ferry is kept by 3 men from Iowa.

They are emigrants, but think this is a speculation worth their attention . . . an inclined plane is cut in the bank on this side, for a landing, and, the opposite shore is low. The animals are swum over. . . ." This note also contains information from the diary of Charles Gould (1849), typescript, Newberry Library, pp. 37-38, as follows: "The boats are constructed of six 'dug-outs' fastened together, worked by oars. . . ." [52: 44-45]

Howard Stansbury, July 25, 1849. "Just above the mouth of this stream, there was a ferry over the North Fork of the Platte . . . rudest and simplest kind. The ferry-boat was constructed of seven canoes, dug out from cotton-wood logs, fastened side by side with poles, a couple of hewn logs being secured across their tops, upon which the wheels of the wagons rested. . . . rude raft was drawn back and forth by means of a rope stretched across the river, and secured at the ends to either bank. Frail and insecure . . . yet all the wagons were passed . . . [in] two hours, without . . . accident . . . many . . . heavily laden . . . an emigrant had been drowned here, the day before . . . [tried] to swim his horse made the twenty-eighth victim . . . charge for ferriage was two dollars for each wagon. . . . considering that the ferrymen had been for months encamped . . . exposed . . . [to] wandering savages . . . by no means extravagent." [361: 60-61]

Irene D. Paden, 1943. "It was commonly accepted . . . that the well-to-do trains ignored the Deer Creek ferry and, trekking two more days upstream, crossed at the Mormon or Upper Ferry." [298: 194]

Dale L. Morgan, 1959. The Deer Creek ferry is covered in the section on "The Lower Ferries of the Upper North Platte." [274: 148-89]

Author's note, July 25, 1972. The site of the ferry—a stretch of quiet water above an island—is best viewed from the CB&Q railroad embankment west of Glenrock Station.

USGS map, Glenrock, Wyo., 1:24,000, 1949 ed.

RESHAW'S BRIDGE (Site)p
(Site 2, Deer Creek Vicinity Map)
Mile 739R½ — Converse County, Wyo.
NW¼ of SE¼, Sec 32, T34N, R75W

A log bridge was constructed over the North Platte River, about 2,600 feet above the present road bridge. It was evidently poorly built and washed out in the spring of 1852 or 1853. It was the first bridge to be built over the North Platte River and a great convenience to emigrants despite its flimsy nature and the considerable toll charged.

Wallace Stegner, 1964. "John Richard, the same Frenchman who had guided the Mississippi Saints from Fort Laramie to Pueblo in the summer of 1846, had built a bridge across the North Platte at Deer Creek in 1851. This, and the more substantial one that replaced it in 1853, had put the Mormon ferry twenty-seven miles above out of business. . . ." [363: 244]

John D. McDermott, 1966. "In 1851 John Richard and several other squaw men built two toll bridges, one over the Laramie near Fort Laramie and one over the North Platte near the mouth of Deer Creek. Both were engineering failures but financial successes. When the last of the two went the way of a spring flood, Richard looked for another site. . . ." [160:IV, 54]

Author's note, July 25, 1972. No evidence of the bridge remains. The full name of its builder is John Baptiste Richard, the surname pronounced in French to sound like RE-shaw.

USGS map, Parkerton, Wyo., 1:24,000, 1949 ed.

INDIAN FORD — C
(Site 6, Deer Creek Vicinity Map)
Mile 739R — Converse County, Wyo.
NW¼ of SW¼, Sec. 33, T34N, R75W

This fording place was used by Indians in crossing the North Platte River. It may have been used by emigrants also, during periods of low water. The location is from a manuscript map by Paul C. Henderson.

USGS map, Glenrock, Wyo., 1:24,000, 1949 ed.

PARKER AND RINGO GRAVES[P]
Mile 742.5 — 2 miles West of Glenrock, Wyo.
Converse County — SW¼ of NW¼, Sec. 1, T33N, R76W

These two graves are marked by native stones. The northern stone is incised: "J. P. Parker / Died / July 1, 1860 / Age 41. Ys / Iowa." The southern stone is incised simply "M Ringo." They both face west, the graves are covered with stone flagging and the site is protected by a fence of iron pipe.

Author's note, July 25, 1872. No details are available concerning these burials. There is a Pony Express marker nearby, and the fence bears a label, "Restored by / B.S.A. / Troop 81 / Casper, Wyo. / Aug. 1965." The USGS map designates this site as "Cem."—it is 150 feet north of the old U.S. Highway 26/87.

Reference. "The Death of Martin Ringo" in *Overland Journal* 5/1 (Winter 1987), 16-38.

USGS map, Parkerton, Wyo., 1:24,000, 1949 ed.

ADA MAGILL GRAVE

Mile 745.3 — Adjacent to the old highway at Parkerton, Wyo.
Converse County — NW¼ of NE¼, Sec. 9, T33N, R76W

This grave is marked by a red sandstone monument incised "Ada / The Daughter Of / G. W. & N. C. Magill / Died July 3, 1864," and enclosed by a fence of welded iron pipe. An Oregon Trail monument (1913) stands beside the grave. It is another reminder of the terrible toll disease took of the emigrants in the late Oregon Trail period. Little Ada died of dysentery.

William J. Ghent, 1934. "In Converse County . . . at a spot close to the Big Muddy and near the grave of an emigrant's child, Ada Magill, who died July 3, 1864, in Sept. 1913 a stone post on a cement base." This refers to the Oregon Trail monument originally sited directly in front of the grave, but since moved to one side. [149: 251]

Jim Fenex, 1971. Tells of the removal of this burial from the original site which was on the alignment of the first automobile highway, built in 1911-1912. [136: 279-81]

Gregory M. Franzwa, 1972. ". . . little Ada became ill with dysentery at Ft. Laramie and had to lie in the jolting wagon during the long hard journey to Glenrock. During the night of July 2, 1864, her condition worsened . . . she was 6 years old. The grave was piled with stones, then surrounded by a crude wood fence. . . ." [141: 248]

Author's note, July 25, 1972. There is a Pony Express marker near the headstone, and a sign on the fence stating: "Ada Magill / Restoration of gravesite / by Boy Scout Troop 48 / Casper, Wyoming 5-26-63."

USGS map, Parkerton, Wyo., 1:24,000, 1949 ed.

CROSSING OF MUDDY CREEK_p
Mile 748.5 — 4 miles west of Parkerton, Wyo.
Converse County — NW¼ of NW¼, Sec. 1, T33N, R77W

The task of fording Muddy Creek appears to have been difficult at times. There are several streams in the vicinity— Muddy Creek, often called "Crooked Muddy Creek" by the emigrants, which was the main stream; Dry Muddy Creek; and Elkhorn, or "Little Muddy Creek."

Osborne Cross, 1849. Mentioned the use of a raft in crossing Crooked Muddy Creek. [101: 110]

Thomas Christy, 1850. Found the stream "bad to cross." [71: 35]

Sir Richard Burton, 1860. ". . . arrived at a station, called the 'Little Muddy Creek' . . . a wretched place, built of 'dry stones,' viz, slabs without mortar, and the interior was garnished with certain efforts of pictorial art, which were rather *lestes* than otherwise. The furniture was composed of a box and a trunk, and the negative catalogue of its supplies was extensive,—whiskey forming the only positive item." [56: 155]

William J. Ghent, 1934. "A few miles beyond [Deer Creek] they crossed Muddy Creek, which in 1849 marked the westward range of the cholera epidemic. [149: 251]

USGS map, Lockett, Wyo., 1:24,000, 1961 ed.

RESHAW'S BRIDGE_p
Mile 761R1 — 3 miles northeast of Casper, Wyo.
Natrona County — SW¼ of NW¼, Sec. 36, T34N, R79W

Reshaw's wooden bridge spanned the North Platte River at what is now Evansville, Wyo. It was built by John Richard (Reshaw) in 1852, and served as a toll bridge off and on until the spring of 1865, when Richard sold his interests at the site. In its later years, the bridge was not profitable, due to the competition offered by Guinard's bridge, farther upstream.

This was an important river crossing in its day. It ended the need to ford or ferry a very dangerous river. This structure put the "Mormon Ferry" out of business.

Thomas S. Williams, April 1855. ". . . the very morning we got to the bridge on the Platte river, the [Indians] had taken 75 head from Racheau and the traders at that point." [156: 238]

Sir Richard Burton, 1860. ". . . we debouched upon the bank

of the Platte, at a spot where once was the Lower Ferry. . . . A wooden bridge was built at this point some years ago, at an expense of $26,000, by one Regshaw, who, if report does not belie him, has gained and lost more fortunes than a Wall Street professional 'lame duck' . . . the indispensable store . . . drank our whiskey with ice . . . passed a deserted camp, where in times gone by two companies of infantry had been stationed; a few stumps of crumbling wall, broken floorings, and depressions in the ground were the only remnants. . . ." [56: 155-56]

Irene D. Paden, 1943. "In '49 a few travelers noted a precarious bridge three miles below the site of the later bridge near the ferry. It had been built by a fur company and was apparently of no importance or use to the emigrants. Diaries of the sixties . . . mention an Upper and a Lower Platte Bridge, placing them six miles (and two hours travel over a heavy sand hill) apart. Probably the lower bridge was constructed at a better location. . . ." [298: 198]

John D. McDermott, 1965. Provides a biography of John Baptiste Richard, with information on his bridge-building. [160:II, 289-303]

John D. McDermott, 1966. "When the last of the two [the bridges at Deer Creek and Fort Laramie] went the way of a spring flood, Richard looked for another site. This time Bissonette joined the group, becoming one of eight partners. The new bridge, a sturdy wooden structure of twelve arches, spanned the North Platte River near the present town of Evansville, Wyoming.

"The bridge builders found affluence. By charging as much as five dollars a wagon during high water, the owners were forty thousand dollars richer by the end of June, 1853. . . ." P. 55: ". . . Richard bought out the rest of his partners in a few years. Bissonette apparently sold his share in April 1854. . . ." [160:IV, 54-55]

Author's note, July 25, 1972. The river bank where Reshaw built his bridge is now laced with informal roads which weave among large cottonwood trees. The site is evidently a dumping ground and trysting place for the nearby communities. The river is, at that point, a slow-moving, brown flood about 100 yards in width. From the bridge site, Reshaw's Houses were 750 feet distant on Az. 158 degrees true, and Camp Davis was 2,200 feet distant on Az. 209 degrees true (SE¼ of SE¼, Sec. 35, T34N, R79W).

USGS map, Casper, Wyo., 1:24,000, 1961 ed.

CROSSING (FORD) OF NORTH PLATTE RIVER
Mile 765.8 — 4 miles northeast of Fort Caspar Natrona County, Wyo. — SW¼ of SE¼, Sec. 34, T34N, R79W

Emigrants could ford the North Platte River here only in times of low water. When that was not possible, it was necessary to improvise a ferry, use the Mormon Ferry (after 1847), or use the Platte Bridge (after 1858). A sod fort, used in 1858-1859, stood 600 feet south of the ford. This was always an important crossing place, and it was never entirely replaced by ferry or bridge.

John C. Fremont, July 28, 1842. "Two miles from our encampment we reached the place where the regular road crosses the Platte. There was two hundred feet breadth of water . . . the channels were generally three feet deep, and there were large angular rocks on the bottom, which made the ford in some places a little difficult. Even at its low stages this river cannot be crossed at random, and this has always been used as the best ford." [202:I, 239]

James W. Nesmith, July 24, 1843. ". . . To the crossing about noon . . . Drove across in the afternoon without difficulty. [290: 343]

Samuel Penter, 1843. ". . . North Platte, we tied all the wagons together. Someone had a long rope which was tied to the ring of the first wagon and men on the other side helped the train across. [311: 59]

William Taylor, June 18, 1846. "Came to the Crossing of platt not fordable . . . [June] 19. Remained trying to cross our cattle . . . [June] 20. Do [ditto] 16 more waggons came up [June] 21. got all over Rafted the waggons Swam the Cattle. . . ." [275:I, 126]

William J. Ghent, 1934. "The Casper crossing was usually fordable, but at times of high water required a ferry." [149: 135]

USGS map, Casper, Wyo., 1:24,000, 1961 ed.

PLATTE BRIDGE STATION (FORT CASPAR)
Mile 766.2 — 0.4 mile west of the fairgrounds at Casper, Wyo. Natrona County — SW¼ of SW¼, Sec. 7, T33N, R79W

Fort Caspar was a military post established at the crossing of the North Platte River, on the outskirts of present Casper, Wyo. From its establishment in 1858 as a two-company post, it was successively known as Mormon Ferry Post, Platte Bridge Station (after the building of Guinard's bridge), and Fort Caspar, in honor of Lt. Caspar Collins. It was abandoned in October 1867 and immediately burned by the Indians. It was a key point in maintaining emigrant traffic and communications up the Sweetwater Valley.

Irene D. Paden, 1943. ". . . 1858 . . . a prosaic military encampment, known as Mormon Ferry Post . . . The little fortress antedated the bridge by a few months . . . It was located about two hundred sixty-five yards southwest of the bridge and ferry site and was equipped to maintain a hundred soldiers . . . the first name . . . supplanted . . . by Platte Bridge Station; but its final . . . Fort Caspar, was bestowed after the heroic death of Lieutenant Caspar Collins . . . There are no ruins. There is nothing of the fort left to see." [298: 198]

Herbert M. Hart, 1963. Photographs of the reconstructed fort. [167: 83-85]

Robert W. Frazer, 1965. ". . . established in May, 1862 . . . Platte Bridge Station, consisting of adobe buildings, was erected at the same spot—the common crossing place—in 1858. From July 29, 1858, to April 20, 1859, troops were stationed there to protect emigrant trains, to keep open communications with Salt Lake City, and to facilitate movement of supplies for the Utah expeditionary force . . . garrisoned by regular troops . . . 4th U.S. Artillery . . . in May, 1962, . . . troops of the 6th U.S. Volunteers . . . provided to protect the crossing and the telegraph line from the Indians.

"In the spring of 1865 . . . the Indians sought to halt all traffic along the Oregon Trail. On November 21, 1865, Major General John Pope, commanding the department, ordered that henceforth the post be known as Fort Caspar, in honor of First Lieutenant Caspar Collins, 11th Ohio Cavalry, killed in the Platte Bridge Station Battle, on July 26, 1865. . . . first garrisoned by regular troops on June 28, 1866 . . . The name 'Caspar' was often spelled 'Casper' in government reports, and in that form was applied to the town which later grew up. The post was rebuilt and enlarged in 1866. Abandoned on October 19, 1867, when it was replaced by Fort Fetterman. Immediately after Fort Caspar was abandoned, the buildings and the bridge across the North Platte were burned by the Indians. The fort has been reconstructed and the site is now a park." [142: 179-80]

William Judge, 1971. A brief article for Wyoming history

buffs. [210: 281-83]

Author's note, July 25, 1972. Two granite monuments stand in front of the reconstructed portion of the fort (the southwest corner); one commemorating the Mormon Ferry, and the other, Louis Guinard's bridge.

USGS map, Casper, Wyo., 1:24,000, 1961 ed.

MORMON FERRY MONUMENT
Mile 766.3 — ½ mile NW of the fairgrounds, Casper, Wyo.
Natrona County — SW¼ of SW¼, Sec. 7, T33N, R79W

A ferry was established by the Mormons in 1847 and operated through 1851 for the benefit of emigrants wishing to cross the North Platte River during high water. The monument locates the Mormon Ferry as 1 mile south of the Fort Caspar site (NW¼ of Sec. 18), but recent research places this crossing at or near the emigrant ford in the SE¼ of Sec. 34, T34N, R79W. The ferryboat consisted of two dugout canoes 30 feet long, with a three-foot beam, planked to carry wagons. The fee charged was from four to five dollars per wagon.

In terms of time saved, and in safety of lives and property, the Mormon Ferry benefited the emigrants greatly, while the cash obtained from this business helped the Mormons to finance their new settlement at Great Salt Lake.

Lewis Barney, June 1847. ". . . to the upper crossing of the Platt River. Here we had considerable trouble as the river was very high and rapid. Colonel Markham and I made a raft of old dry logs on which we crossed three wagons. There were two or three other rafts made but the current being too strong the rafts were abandoned. It was decided to make two large canoes and leash them together for a ferry boat. This being decided myself and several others were sent up the river seven miles, to a grove of large cottonwoods. We selected two large trees, 3 ft. through. Of these, we made two large canoes, thirty feet long. We then cut two other trees and hewed them down to two inches thick, and straightened the edges making planks of them 14 inches wide, and 30 ft. long. We then loaded them on our wagons and drove back to camp. We then leashed the two canoes together and fastened the two planks on the canoes lengthwise. Then we launched them in the river and ran a wagon on the planks that were far enough apart to be under the wheels of the wagon. We

A ferry of the type used along the upper North Platte River.

then ran it across the river which was quickly and easily done. In this way, the wagons were all soon over; the stock we swam across.

"We were now ready for another start. At this time there was a company of Oregon emigrants who came up and wanted us to ferry them over the river. This we soon did, there being 60 or 70 wagons of them, for which they paid flour, bacon and groceries. By this means our stock of provisions were greatly replenished." [25: 16]

James A. Pritchard, June 10, 1849. "At 9 AM we reached the Ferry. I[t] was kept by some Mormons from Salt Lake who had come clere there to keep ferry for the season. We found about 175 wagons ahead of us & we had to take our turn. We however joined another company or 2 & constructed a raft to cross our wagons on. After several efforts we succeded in crossing 2 wagons, but we found the current so strong and the Raft so heavy and unwiealdy that we abandoned the project and awaited our turn which came in on Wednesday morning." (They had arrived on Sunday.) Pp. 152-53, Note 4D: The ferry was established in 1847, and operated each year through 1852, during the season of high water. "In 1849 the Mormon ferrymen reached the river on May 27 and began ferrying, 3½ miles east of Casper, next day. They continued until late July." [317: 88]

Osborne Cross, July 2, 1849. ". . . raft was hastily put together . . . [but two men were lost by drowning, and it soon became evident the time and risk were not justified, for] . . . Mormon ferry could be hired for four dollars per wagon. . . ." P. 116: ". . . river is not over four hundred yards wide . . . very rapid." [101: 112, 116]

Thomas Christy, June 5, 1850. "Upper Platte Ferry . . . Arrived at the ferry 3 o'c PM, and got our wagons taken right across . . . There is four boats running here. . . ." [71: 35]

John B. Hill, June 21, 1850. ". . . we ferried our wagons across the North Platte, and had to pay five dollars for each." [180: 36]

Irene D. Paden, 1943. "Twenty-eight miles from Deer Creek was the Upper or Mormon Ferry of the North Platte, near modern Casper. . . . crossing in pre-prairie-schooner days was three miles down from the later ferry site . . . In 1847 the well organized Mormon migration faced the river. They built pine-pole rafts capable of carrying an empty wagon . . . two wagon trains from Missouri had arrived . . . A bargain was struck by which the Mormons ferried the Missourians for $1.50 per load and the privilege of buying provisions at Missouri prices." [298: 195-98]

Wallace Stegner, 1964. ". . . Mormons . . . worked all night to ferry the Gentiles for a fee . . . on June 14, Brigham delegated Thomas Grover and eight others to stay behind, improve and operate the ferry. . . ." P. 244: States that the Mormon Ferry was put out of business by the building of John Richard's bridge at Deer Creek in 1851. [363: 143]

Author's note, July 25, 1972. A granite monument at the reconstructed Fort Caspar was erected in 1932 to commemorate "The Mormon Ferry. . . ."

USGS map, Casper, Wyo., 1:24,000, 1961 ed.

OLD PLATTE BRIDGE (GUINARD'S)
Mile 766.3 — ½ mile northwest of the fairgrounds, Casper, Wyo.
Natrona County — NW¼ of SW¼, Sec. 7, T33N, R79W

A log bridge 13 feet wide and 1,000 feet long was built by Louis Guinard in 1858 at the site of the Mormon Ferry on the North Platte River. It was operated as a toll bridge until the abandonment of Fort Caspar in 1867, when the superstructure was promptly burned by the Indians. The bridge provided a safe crossing at a key point on the Oregon Trail, facilitating the movement of emigrants, freight and military traffic during a turbulent period.

O. Allen, 1858. "Platte Bridge—Trading post and blacksmith shop at this point; if the river is fordable keep upon the south side of the river to avoid sand banks on the north side." [8: 63]

Sir Richard Burton, 1860. "Our station lay near the upper crossing or second bridge, a short distance from the town. It was also built of timber at an expense of $40,000, about a year ago, by Louis Guenot, a Quebecquois, who has passed the last twelve years upon the plains. He appeared very downcast about his temporal prospects . . . the usual toll is $0.50, but from trains, especially Mormons, the owner will claim $5; in fact, as much as he can get without driving them to the opposition lower bridge [Reshaw's], or to the ferry boat . . ." P. 161: ". . . [next morning] we hitched up, crossed the rickety bridge at a slow pace, and proceeded . . . to ascend the left bank of the Platte. . . ." [56: 156, 161]

William H. Jackson, August 18, 1866. "We crossed at once over the very finest, if only because it was the first—bridge yet encountered, a sturdy and workmanlike structure of logs . . ." [201: 127]

William J. Ghent, 1934. "Here, at the last crossing of the North Platte, there was a telegraph station, and also a toll bridge, which had been built by a Canadian squaw man, Louis Ganard. . . ." [149: 227]

Irene D. Paden, 1943. ". . . in the winter of 1858-59, a bridge presents itself . . . The bridge was long, narrow, unbeautiful, and supported by piers made of cribbing filled with rocks. It waded slowly across the Platte on these bulky legs and was finished in time for the migration of '59." (The remaining evidences of the bridge—mounds of stone from its piers—are described, 198-99.) [298: 198]

John D. McDermott, 1965. "During the late 1850s Louis Guinard built a new bridge across the North Platte about seven miles above Richard's, and in a few years drew most of the emigrant travel." [160:II, 301]

William Judge, 1971. States that Platte Bridge was 1,000 feet long, 13 feet wide and supported on 28 cribs 30 feet apart. It was burned by Indians in 1867. [210: 281-83]

Author's note, July 25, 1972. The mounds of stone left from the deteriorated bridge piers have been covered with earth to protect them. The first is 100 feet behind the monument which commemorates the "Site of / Old Platte Bridge / built by /

Louis Guinard / 1858-59 / Immediately south and / west are the sites of / Platte Bridge Station / First overland telegraph, stage and Pony / Express stations on / the Old Oregon Trail / Erected by / Natrona County Historical Society / July 26, 1930"

An investigation on June 17, 1982, revealed remnants of a second line of pier-mounds paralleling the bridge alignment on the east. This hints at earlier construction nearly on the same site.

USGS map, Casper, Wyo., 1:24,000, 1961 ed.

BATTLE OF RED BUTTES[P]
Mile 764.6 — About 1 miles west of Fort Caspar
Natrona County, Wyo. — SE¼ of SE¼, Sec. 11, T33N, R80W

A military train of five wagons was destroyed on August 26, 1865, in the Battle of Red Buttes. The train was traveling toward Platte Bridge Station (later, Fort Caspar), under escort of Sgt. Amos Custard and 10 troopers. Twenty men who remained with the wagons were killed. Three men of an advance guard of five got through to the post. The overwhelming of the wagon train by Sioux and Cheyenne Indians followed failure of a relief attempt by Lt. Caspar Collins, who was killed with four of his men in an ambush at the west end of the bridge.

William J. Ghent, 1934. "On the same day [July 26, 1865], a few miles distant, a troop train of three wagons was captured and burned and all but three of its twenty-five soldiers and drivers were killed." [149: 229]

Irene D. Paden, 1943. "On July 26, 1865 . . . Four miles out on the Telegraph Road the train was attacked . . . nineteen mutilated bodies found with the charred remains of the Custard wagon train were buried in one long grave. It was not marked . . . the exact location is not known. Monuments to their memory have been placed at an arbitrarily selected spot . . . often called the Red Buttes fight." [298: 200-01]

LeRoy R. Hafen, 1938. "At 2 A.M. on July 26 word came to Platte Bridge that a wagon train of five wagons escorted by ten soldiers was traveling toward the post from Sweetwater Station. Nothing was done to warn the train or send relief under cover of darkness. . . . Despite warnings, Sergeant Custard with the wagon train continued to move down the river toward Platte bridge. When about three miles from the post he sent out an advance party of five men. Three of these finally reached the post alive. As the Indians began to surround the train, the sergeant corraled his wagons and succeeded in holding off the Indians for about an hour. But he was overpowered and all the men were killed." [156: 335-36]

Tom Nichols, 1971. Retells the story of Sgt. Custard's fight. [293: 294-95]

Author's note, Aug. 25, 1972. The site of the battle has not been positively identified, but monuments have been arbitrarily placed at three locations: on the north side of the river, about a mile west of the Platte Bridge site (SE¼ of SE¼, Sec. 11, T33N, R80W); also on the same side of the river about four miles west of the Platte Bridge site (NW¼ of SE¼, Sec. 16, T33N, R80W), and on the south side of the river, at Red Buttes Village (SE¼ of SW¼, Sec. 22, T33N, R80W). The latter is obviously on the wrong side of the river, but was intended to be convenient to Highway 220.

USGS map, Emigrant Gap, Wyo., 1:24,000, 1960 ed.

RED BUTTES CROSSING
Mile 773.6 — 12 miles southwest of Casper, Wyo.
Natrona County — SW¼ of NE¼, Sec. 3, T32N, R81W

This is the uppermost fording place of the North Platte River, at Bessemer Bend. It is immediately below the Red Buttes. This crossing of fur trade days was also used by early emigrants when the stage of the river allowed; however, it was seldom resorted to after the ferries and bridges became available at downstream sites.

A campsite of the returning Astorians, March 12, 1812, was 5,000 feet due east of the crossing, on the south bank of the river (NW¼ of NE¼, Sec. 2, T32N, R81W).

Rufus B. Sage, Spring, 1842. ". . . a ride of thirty miles [from Deer Creek] brought us to the place where the Oregon Trail crosses the Platte; and, after fording the river, we encamped upon the opposite side.

"The stream, at this point, is about three hundred yards from bank to bank, and, at the time of our crossing it, swimming deep for a small portion of the way.

"In ordinary stages, the water is but little over three feet deep, and the ford perfectly safe and practicable. The partial melting of the mountain snows had increased the size and velocity of its current, and rendered our passage slightly dangerous and difficult. The bed appeared to be rocky, and in some places rough,—requiring much caution in crossing wagons to prevent them from overturning." [338:IV, 319]

Lewis Barney, June 1847. "followed the Oregon road until we came to the upper crossing of the Platt River." The method of crossing is described." [25: 16]

Author's note, July 25, 1972. The place name—Red Buttes-which has survived from the early days of the fur trade, refers to the dull red hills flanking the canyon of the North Platte River between Coal and Bessemer mountains. The Red Buttes are in T32N, R81W, with the eastern portions in Sections 11, 12, 13 and 14; and the western in Sections 9, 10, 15 and 16.

Interesting early descriptions were recorded by Rufus B. Sage (338:IV, 320) and Rev. Samuel Parker (301: 74)

USGS map, Emigrant Gap, Wyo., 1960 ed.

U.S. MAIL STATION NO. 28$_P$
Mile 773.9 — 12¼ miles southwest of Casper, Wyo. Natrona County — NE¼ of NW¼, Sec. 3, T32N, R81W

The Red Buttes Mail Station stood on a prominent bench above the west bank of the North Platte River, probably on the site now occupied by the foundations of the "Old Goose Egg Ranchhouse," made famous by Owen Wister. There is an Oregon Trail monument nearby.

O. Allen, 1848. "Red Buttes, U.S. Mail Station No. 28—The road leaves the river at this point . . ." [8: 64]

Frances S. Webb, 1965. "Goose Egg Ranch Still Lives In Memory" is a brief account of the old ranchhouse and its passing. [Annual Wyoming Edition of the *Casper Star Tribune*: 14]

Author's note, July 25, 1972. The Oregon Trail monument at this point is of granite, 9" by 23" by 49", bearing a bronze Oregon Trail medallion and incised: "Red Buttes / Of Oregon Trail Fame Where / Westward Travelers Left The / North Platte River / A Tribute To Pioneer Emigrants / From / Casper Literary Club / 1930." The monument is set quartering to the Bessemer Road, about 1,100 feet northwest of the bridge over the North Platte River.

USGS map, Emigrant Gap, Wyo., 1:24,000, 1960 ed.

EMIGRANT GAP
Mile 774.0 — 12 miles west of Casper, Wyo.
Natrona County, NE¼ of Sec. 10, T33N, R81W

Emigrant gap is a shallow pass through the ridge now called Emigrant Gap Ridge. It is of little importance on the emigrant route since most traffic followed the route later known as the "Telegraph Road," along the North Platte, after crossing the river near present Casper.

William Clayton, 1848. "Road turns south and rises a long hill . . . Ascent gradual. Many singular looking rocks on the south side. Descent rough and crooked. Towards the foot, road very uneven." [78: 14]

Irene D. Paden, 1943. Quoting Wyoming historian, A.J. Mokler: ". . . you can take the Emigrant Gap Road . . . It wasn't used until 1865, but it saw a lot of traffic. . . . The older trail runs into it about twenty-five miles out . . . the old one starts right down the river. . . ." P. 202: "A later generation of indigenous Casperites have named it Emigrant Gap, one of a long series of Emigrant Gaps." [298: 199, 202]

USGS map, Emigrant Gap, Wyo., 1:24,000, 1960 ed.

POISON SPRING$_P$
Mile 777.5 — 1.9 miles west of Poison Spider School
Natrona County, Wyo. — NW¼ of SW¼, Sec. 20, T33N, R81W

This is a mineral-laden spring one-quarter mile left of the emigrant road. With an adjacent pool, it was considered poisonous to stock. It was a particularly feared landmark.

William Clayton, 1848. "Mineral spring and lake. Considered poisonous. No bad taste to the water, unless the cattle trample it. In that case it becomes black, and is doubtless poisonous. . . ." [78: 14]

Osborne Cross, July 6, 1849. ". . . in sight of the Red hills . . . encampment . . . a mile from the road, below an alkali swamp and mineral spring . . . very cold, and its taste that of stone-coal. . . ." [101: 118]

J. Goldsborough Bruff, July 23, 1849. ". . . to the bed of a creek with springs in it: ('Mineral Springs') . . . As the mineral springs were supposed to be poisonous, I would not allay the mule's thirst at the risk of their lives." [52: 36]

Thomas Christy, June 6, 1850. "Mineral Spring and Lake Not

much poisonous." Repeats Clayton's warning about stirring up the mud." [71: 36]

Irene D. Paden, 1943. ". . . Poison Spider Creek, all the wrong colors for respectable water and very scummy, but wholesome in comparison with the neighboring supply." [298: 202]

Author's note, July 26, 1972. Approximately 3.6 miles farther, at Mile 781.1, the alternate routes from the vicinity of present Casper, Wyo., came together in the SE¼ of Sec. 2, T32N, R82W, on Iron Creek.

The Oregon Trail is a single track from the junction to near Independence Rock, and it was found uniformly marked along that 35-mile segment by six-inch square concrete posts about 40 inches high, bearing a bronze medallion: "Oregon Trail, 1843-1869"—facing on the unimproved road which closely parallels the "trail." The posts were set by the Bureau of Land Management, in conjunction with the Wyoming Historical Society.

USGS map, Emigrant Gap, Wyo., 1:24,000, 1960 ed.

ROCK AVENUE
Mile 784.5 — 8½ miles southwest of Poison Spider School
Natrona County, Wyo. — SE¼ of SE¼, Sec. 14, T32N, R82W

From "Poison Spring Creek Pass," the road descends for 0.3 mile in a left turn which changes its direction 90 degrees, bringing the lower 500 feet of the road parallel to a ragged ridge of rock which was known as "The Devil's Backbone." Thus, the road was in a defile between that feature and the ridge just descended. The ridge is a conspicuous landmark which has been greatly damaged by recent road construction.

William Clayton, 1848. "Rock Avenue and steep descent—The road here passes between high rocks, forming a kind of avenue or gateway, for a quarter mile." [78: 14]

J. Goldsborough Bruff, July 23, 1849. "Passed through a very singular defile, called 'Rock Avenue' about 50 ft. wide, and some 200 long. . . . After emerging from the Defile, the road descended a very steep hill." [52: 50]

Sir Richard Burton, 1860. ". . . we descended a steep hill, and were shown the Devil's Backbone. It is a jagged, broken ridge of huge sandstone boulders, tilted up edgeways, and running in a line over the crest of a long roll of land . . . like the vertebrae of some great sea-serpent." [56: 162]

Irene D. Paden, 1943. ". . . a hideous stretch of deformed rock strata bursting jaggedly from the torn earth . . . Howard R. Egan wrote about it in '47 . . . 'about eight miles from the lake [on Poison Spider Creek] there is a steep descent from a bluff, and at the foot there is a ridge of sharp-pointed rocks, leaving only a narrow space for the wagons to pass, and the road is very rough.' . . . Mr. Mokler [a Wyoming historian] said . . . that the descent had been named Poison Spider Creek Pass. There are lots of names carved around on the rocks . . . the two older roads met at the Poison Spring Creek Pass . . . went through the Rock Avenue together." [298: 203]

Author's note, July 26, 1972. Reconstruction of the road at this point appears to have destroyed all trace of the original Oregon Trail. Very few names remain along the parallel wall of the "Devil's Backbone"—portions of the inscribed cliff have been blasted away to obtain stone for road building, which, at this point, was little better than calculated vandalism.

The prominent ruts Paul Henderson noted as graven into the sandstone near the bottom of the hill appear to have been destroyed in the reconstruction.

USGS map, Clarkson Hill, Wyo., 1:24,000, 1951 ed.

WILLOW SPRINGS_p
Mile 792.0 — 16 miles southwest of Poison Spider School
Natrona County, Wyo. — NW¼ of NW¼, Sec. 9, T31N, R83W

These free-flowing springs are at the head of Willow Creek. There was a campground near the lower spring, at the emigrant road, but other springs about a mile up the draw were used when traffic was heavy. This was the feature most often noted by emigrants on the route between the crossing of the North Platte and Independence Rock.

John Boardman, July 25, 1843. "Nooned at Willow Spring, where Stewart's Company made meat." [37: 104]

Overton Johnston, July 1843. "On the 25th we came to Willow Springs . . . clear cold water, rising in a little green valley." [208: 79]

Miller-Reed, July 10, 1846. ". . . encamped at the Willow Springs good water but little grass . . . the Main Spring 1½ miles above." [275:I, 259]

Heinrich Lienhard, 1846. "At noon we stopped at the so-called Willow Springs to allow our animals some rest, grass, and water; and afterward we continued on our way a few more hours." [229: 83]

William Clayton, 1848. "'Willow Spring' About three rods west of the road, at the foot of willow bushes. Water cold and good—grass plenty, but creek some miry." [78: 14]

James A. Pritchard, June 14, 1849. ". . . Willow Spring. Here we took a cool refreshing drink." [317: 90]

Osborne Cross, July 7, 1849. ". . . arrived at the Willow spring . . . a small stream of fine, pure, cold water . . . from the head of a small ravine . . . [named] from the number of small willows about it." [101: 119]

J. Goldsborough Bruff, July 24, 1849. ". . . to a *Slew,* Willow Spring . . . rill and cool springs. Plenty of young grass." [52: 51]

O. Allen, 1858. "Willow Spring and Branch—This spring is at the head of the branch in a hollow." [8: 64]

William J. Ghent, 1934. "One delightful camping place is almost always mentioned—Willow Creek Spring, with pure, cold water, good, plentiful grass and a willow grove." [149: 136]

Irene D. Paden, 1943. ". . . Willow Springs at a distance of twenty-six miles from the ferry. In years of little travel it was the perfect oasis . . . the water never failed." [298: 205]

Author's note, July 26, 1972. Abandoned ranch buildings stand at Willow Spring, which no longer appears drinkable. As early as 1860, Richard Burton noted a lodgment there, ". . . a little doggery boasting of a shed and a bunk, but no corral." It had just been plundered of edibles. [56: 1630].

USGS map, Benton Basin NE, Wyo., 1:24,000, 1951 ed.

PROSPECT (RYAN) HILL
Mile 793.0 — Extends SW one mile from Willow Springs
Natrona County, Wyo — SE ¼ of Sec. 8, T31N, R83W

This hill required a 400-foot climb up a hog-back between two shallow draws. The grade averages 7.5 percent (rises 7.5 feet per 100 feet of horizontal distance.) The landmark was popularized by the Mormons through William Clayton's *The Latter-day Saints' Emigrants' Guide.*

William Clayton, 1848. "'Prospect Hill' (Summit). Pleasant view of the surrounding country, to the Sweet Water mountains." [78: 14]

J. Goldsborough Bruff, 1849. "In one mile from the last camp [Willow Spring] we ascended a high hill, from the summit of which is a grand prospect of the surrounding country, and hence it is named 'Prospect Hill'." [52: Note, 292]

Irene D. Paden, 1943. "Another mile [from Willow Spring] brought the emigrants to the summit of Prospect Hill . . . first view of the Sweetwater Mountains." [298: 206]

USGS map, Benton Basin NE, Wyo., 1:24,000, 1951 ed.

UNNAMED ALKALI SLOUGH_P
Mile 798.6 — Near the head of Fish Creek
Natrona County, Wyo. — SE¼ of SW¼, Sec. 23, T31N, R84W

Stock frequently mired in this alkali swamp while they were grazing. It is one of many dangerous localities along this part of the Oregon Trail.

William J. Scott, August 14, 1846. "Look out about 12 miles the other side of the willow Springs the Soap factory it looks like it was solled on top and if you step on it you will go under head and years and if not washed off it will take the hair off." [275:II, 639]

William Clayton, 1848. "Bad slough.—Plenty of grass, but little water." [78: 14]

Author's note, July 26, 1972. The swamp has been turned into a reservoir by construction of an earthen dam across the lower end.

USGS map, Benton Basin NE, Wyo., 1:24,000, 1951 ed.

GREASEWOOD (HORSE) CREEK
Mile 803.0 — 12 miles northeast of Independence Rock
Natrona County, Wyo. — NW¼ of NE¼, Sec. 1, T30N, R85W

This small stream was known to the emigrants both as "Sage Creek" and "Greasewood Creek." It became "Horse Creek" when a stage station was established there. The campground here was noted for its sagebrush as well as its good water.

Heinrich Lienhard, 1846. "At Sage Creek, where we arrived in good time, we pitched camp. . . . This creek flowed by rapidly in its narrow bed, and its water was clear and good tasting. The grass unfortunately had been completely grazed off by the cattle of the emigrants who had camped here before us, so that there was little left for ours. The creek doubtless took its name Sage from the great quantities of the large wild plants of this species, which seem to thrive well on the sandy slopes." [229: 83]

William Clayton, 1848. "Grease-wood creek, 6 feet wide 1 ft. deep. Very little grass, and no fuel but wild sage." [78: 14]

J. Goldsborough Bruff, July 25, 1849. "'Grease Wood Creek.' Swift rill of cool mineral water." [52: 52]

Angelina Farley, Aug. 27, 1850. "Camped by the side of a small running brook. The smell of the so called sage is almost intolerable to me." [133: Ms. Diary]

O. Allen, 1858. "Grease Wood Creek and crossing—Grass limited; good water, sage brush for fuel." [8: 64]

Author's note, July 26, 1972. A search of the area around the crossing produced no trace of the Horse Creek Station which once stood there; however, very good Oregon Trail ruts were found to the left (east) of the present road.

USGS map, Fenton Basin SW, Wyo., 1:24,000, 1951 ed.

WAGON TRAIN DEBRIS
Mile 809L2 — In the Pathfinder Reservoir
Natrona County, Wyo. — SW¼ of NW¼, Sec. 3, T29N, R85W

Debris from a number of groups of burned wagons was discovered in a rough oval measuring 300' x 400'. The center of the oval was 300 feet south of an iron stake placed by Paul C. Henderson.

The circumstances which resulted in the destruction of this sizeable wagon train are unknown, but the positioning indicated a "forted-up" party.

Henry R. Herr, July 13, 1862. "Camped 25 miles from Ft. Laramie. Heard the Indians at South Pass were very unfriendly having completely butchered some 40 soldiers and a large number of emigrants." July 15: "We are expecting a Govt train from Ft. Laramie to escort us to the mountains. A number of Govt soldiers and whole train of emigrants were completely butchered at Sweetwater som 200 miles." [175: Ms Diary] (No confirmation of the foregoing rumor has been found, but it is too early to have been of the Platte Bridge fight—that was in 1865.)

Author's note. A marginal notation on Paul C. Henderson's manuscript map states: "Iron pipe marker placed at time of discovery. Groups of burned emigrant wagons discovered 1931." The site is in the Pathfinder Reservoir (on the Sweetwater River) and the evidences of this disaster were noticed when the water level was lowered; it may have been the event which generated the rumor heard by Henry Herr.

The wagon train destroyed here may have deviated from the regular Oregon Trail alignment in order to find grass for the stock.

USGS map, Sanford Ranch, Wyo., 1:24,000, 1959 ed.

SWEETWATER STATION$_p$
Mile 813.9 — 1 mile east of Independence Rock
Natrona County, Wyo. — NE¼ of SE¼, Sec. 10, T29N, R86W

This was a one-company fortified military post at the bridge over the Sweetwater River. It was one of several such posts established during the Civil war to protect emigrants and to maintain the telegraph line.

Robert S. Ellison, 1930. A watercolor by William H. Jackson of "Sweetwater Station near Independence Rock" depicts the post. Independence Rock is in the background. [130: 11]

Edness K. Wilkins, 1971. Indicates the post was established by Co. D., 11th Ohio Volunteer Cavalry, as a post for 40 men. The station had blockhouses at opposite corners and a 15-foot palisade. There was a bridge over the Sweetwater River at this point.

This was the headquarters station of Lt. Caspar Collins, who had detachments at Three Crossings, Rocky Ridge (St. Marys), and South Pass (Burnt Ranch). [397: 287-93]

USGS map, Fort Ridge, Wyo., 1:24,000, 1951 ed.

SALERATUS (PIAYA) LAKE
Mile 814R — One mile northeast of Independence Rock
Natrona County, Wyo. — Common Corner
Sections 2, 3, 10 & 11, T29N, R86W

This is an alkali deposit, or "pan," about a quarter-section in size, from which the Mormons obtained a soda compound for use in baking.

Sir Richard Burton, 1860. ". . . to the west of the road a curious feature, to which the Mormon exodists . . . gave the name of Saleratus Lake. . . . one of a chain of alkaline springs . . . Cattle drinking of the fluid are nearly sure to die . . . appearance. . . . [as if] solidly overfrozen . . . on a near inspection the icy surface turns out to be a dust of carbonate of soda, concealing beneath it masses of the same . . . solidified by evaporation. The Latter-Day Saints . . . laid in stores of the fetid alkaline matter . . . for their bread. . . . Near the lake is a deserted ranch which once enjoyed the title of 'Sweetwater Station.'" [56: 163-64]

Wallace Stegner, 1964. In June 1847, "Lorenzo Young and others gathered pailfuls of the efflorescent white bicarbonate of soda—'saleratus'—for the women to try out in baking, but it made bread of a suspiciously green cast . . . had to be used in moderation." [363: 150]

USGS map, Independence Rock, Wyo., 1:24,000, 1951 ed.

INDEPENDENCE ROCK
Mile 814.8 — 48 miles southwest of Casper, Wyo.
Natrona County — SE¼ of SE¼, Sec. 9, T29N, R86W

This is an oval-shaped outcrop of granite, oriented northwest-southeast. It is 1,900 feet long, 700 feet wide, and has a maximum relief of 128 feet above the valley floor. From a distance it resembles a massive turtle. Standing convenient to the emigrant road, it served as a bulletin board almost from the beginning of white travel in the area.

Independence Rock is the most noted landmark west of Fort Laramie. It was a place to look for word of friends ahead, or leave word for those coming on behind, and beyond those practical uses, it satisfied the human need to be known.

Rev. Samuel Parker, August 7, 1835. "Passed Rock Independence. . . . This is the first massive rock of that stupendous chain of mountains which divides North America and forms together with its barrens on either side a natural division. This rock takes its name from the circumstances of a company of fur traders suspending their journey and here observing in due form the anniversary of our national freedom." [301: 75]

Rufus B. Sage, Spring 1842. "Independence Rock is a solid and isolated mass of naked granite, situated about three hundred yards from the right bank of Sweet Water. It covers an area of four or five acres, and rises to a height of nearly three hundred feet. The general shape is an oval, with the exception of a slight depression in its summit where a scanty soil supports a few shrubs and a solitary dwarf pine.

"It derives its name from a party of Americans on their way to Oregon, under the lead of one Tharp, who celebrated the

Independence Rock, as seen from the trail. The Sweetwater River is in the foreground.

fourth of July at this place,—they being the first company of whites *that ever* made the journey from the States, *via* South Pass." Footnote: "Tharp and his party have not been identified . . . name probably dates from the sojourn of Thomas Fitzpatrick and companions at its base on July 4, 1824."

Sage's remarks continue: "The surface is covered with names of travellers, traders, trappers, and emigrants, engraved upon it in almost every practicable part, for the distance of many feet above its base—but most prominent among them all is the word, 'Independence,' inscribed by the patriotic band who first christened this lonely monument of nature in honor of Liberty's birthday.

"I went to the rock for the purpose of recording my name with the swollen catalogue of others traced upon its sides; but, having glanced over the strange medley, I became disgusted, and, turning away, resolved, *'If there remains no other mode of immortalizing myself,* I will be content to descend to the grave *unhonored and unsung!'*" [338:IV, 323-24]

John C. Fremont, August 1, 1842. ". . . encamped one mile below Rock Independence. This is an isolated granite rock, about six hundred and fifty yards long, and forty in height. Except in a depression of the summit, where a little soil supports a scanty growth of shrubs, with a solitary dwarf pine, it is entirely bare. Everywhere within six or eight feet of the ground, where the surface is sufficiently smooth, and in some places sixty or eighty feet above, the rock is inscribed with the names of travelers. Many a name famous in the history of this country, and some well-known to science, are to be found mixed among those of the traders and of travelers for pleasure and curiosity, and of missionaries among the savages. Some of these have been washed away by the rain, but the greater number are still very legible." Pp. 273-74, August 23: ". . . Rock Independence . . . Here, not unmindful of the custom of early travelers and explorers in our country, I engraved on this rock of the Far West a symbol of the Christian faith. Among the thickly inscribed names, I made on the hard granite the impression of a large cross, which I covered with a black preparation of India rubber, well calculated to resist the influence of wind and rain. It stands amidst the names of many who have long since found their way to the grave, and for whom the huge rock is a giant grave stone." Note 75: ". . . political opponents [later used] . . . this incident as evidence . . . [that he was] a Roman Catholic during the presidential campaign of 1856." [202:I, 247, 273-74]

Overton Johnson, July 26, 1843. ". . . Independence Rock . . . south side, next to the stream, which runs within ten yards of its base, it is almost covered with the names of different persons. . . . It was called Independence Rock, by Mr. Wm. Sublet, an old Indian Trader; who several years ago, celebrated here the 4th of July." [208: 79-80]

William T. Newley, July 28, 1843. "We reached the Independent Rock about 10 o'clock a.m. The rock about 200 feet high and about 1400 yards around it. There is a number of names engraved on it." [292: Diary]

James W. Nesmith, July 28-30, 1843. ". . . at Independence Rock . . . had the pleasure of waiting on five or six young ladies to pay a visit to Independence Rock. I had the satisfaction of putting the names of Miss Mary Zachary and Miss Jane Mills on the southeast point of the rocks, near the road, on a high point. Facing the road, in all the splendor of gunpowder, tar and buffalo greese, may be seen the name of J. W. Nesmith, from Maine, with an anchor. Above it on the rock may be found the names of trappers, emigrants, and gentlemen of amusement, some of which have been written these ten years. The rock is an unshappen pile, about a half mile long, and half that breadth, and 100 feet high, and is accessible at three or four places. . . . Sweetwater River runs at the foot of it about fifty yeards distant." [290: 343-44]

Matthew C. Field, Summer 1843. "Rode with Tilghman to the Rock, where we penetrated deep into its center through the gaping fissures, and drank from a spring that is there hidden.

"From the numerous names inscribed on the rock Tilghman assisted me copying the following. Many others are obliterated, and many are made in such hieroglyphican mystery that they are wholly illegible. The female names are, many of them, sweethearts of the wanderers, except some of the newest, which may have been left by ladies of the Oregon party." (There follows two pages of names, with this interesting comment: "Wm L. Sublette, with Moses Harris, on express, Jan. 1827, again on July 4th, 1841 when the rock was christened.") [137: 174-77] (The year probably should have been 1831, as Parker indicated the christening preceded his 1835 visit.)

Samuel Parker, July 4, 1845. "Wrote my name on Independence Rock this morning." [302: Ms. diary]

Samuel Hancock, 1845. "After two days farther travel we encamped near Independence Rock, which curiosity we visited and found inscribed on its eternal sides the names of many of the company who passed by in the first emigration, besides many others, doubtless of mountaineers and trappers. According to our estimation this rock occupies an area of two or three acres and is about a hundred and fifty feet high having other peculiarities of interest to the traveler." [162: 20]

James Mathers, July 7, 1846. ". . . encamped on the bank of Sweetwater about a mile below Independence Rock. . . . 8th stopped a short time at Independence Rock as we passed." P. 259: Miller Reed diary, July 11-13, 1846. "Sat. 11 made this day 20 Miles to Independence Rock Camped below the Rock. . . . Mo 13. left the Rock after Reading many Names." [275:I, 226]

Margaret M. Hecox, 1846. ". . . on the third day of July, we encamped in the shadow of Independence Rock. . . . The next day being the 4th of July we concluded to lay by and celebrate the day. The children had no fireworks, but we all joined in singing patriotic songs and shared in a picnic lunch. Some spent considerable time carving their names on the great rock. This seemed to be the rule of all emigrants passing that way." [172:

32]

Heinrich Lienhard, 1846. "Soon we arrived at Independence Rock, known to all emigrants, and about which I had read in Dr. Wislizenus' description of travels in the Rocky Mountains in the year 1839. I didn't measure the rock at that time, but it is perhaps one hundred feet long, forty feet wide, and thirty feet high, forming a kind of oval with rounded edges. Its sides were covered all around with names of emigrants and hunters who passed here. They reached up to such a height that it was a mystery to me how they could have put them up there. Most of the names had been painted in large letters in black or red on the brownish granite rock; only a few were carved into it. Independence Rock seemed to stand guard at the entrance to a gigantic, ancient volcanic crater." [229: 85]

William Clayton, 1847. "Independence Rock and ford—on the north side of the river—about six hundred yards long, and a hundred and twenty wide, composed of soft granite." [78: 15]

Robert Canfield, July 4, 1847. On Independence Day this party fired a cannon from the top of the rock, and planted a flag there. [63: 3]

James A. Pritchard, June 15, 1849. "This morning all the curious were clambering to the top of Indipendance Rock I among the rest. I saw name to the number of several thousand—some graven some painted. I did not follow their example. It is an isolated elevation composed of masses of granite rock piled one upon another, about one hundred feet high, and about one mile in circumference, located on the northern bank of the Sweetwater river." [317: 90-91]

Osborne Cross, July 8, 1849. ". . . at Independence rock . . . is of granite, about five hundred yards long, one hundred fifty wide, and forty yards high. . . . This rock bears the name of almost everyone who can take time to carve or write his name on it. There is nothing very remarkable about it . . . looking, as it were, like some huge monster rising from the ground." [101: 122]

J. Goldsborough Bruff, July 26, 1849. ". . . reached 'Independence Rock' . . . at a distance looks like a huge whale. It is being painted & marked every way, all over, with names, dates, initials, &c—so that it was with difficulty I could find a place to inscribe on it:—'The Washington City Company July 26, 1849.'" P. 606, Note 197 . . . H3: "It is covered over every accessible portion, with names, initials, dates, &c, in black and red, scratched and painted. It was only at the expense of marking over half-

The name of an emigrant from 1846 is daubed on Independence Rock with the mixture of pine tar and hog fat used to grease wagon axles. Such inscriptions are durable in sheltered locations.

obliterated names, that for the information of friends in the rear, and to gratify my men, I painted about 4 feet above the base—'WASHINGTON CITY COMPY July 26, 1849.'" [52: 52, 606]

Howard Stansbury, July 31, 1849. ". . . passed the far-famed 'Independence Rock,' a large rounded mass of granite. . . . It was covered with names of the passing emigrants, some of whom seemed determined, judging from the size of their inscriptions, that they would go down to posterity in all their fair proportions." [361: 65]

Thomas Christy, June 8, 1850. "Passed by Independence Rock. This is a remarkable natural curiosity mostly on account of its peculiar shape and magnitude. Ther are many names of visitors painted in various places on the east end. It is about six hundred yds long and hundred and twenty wide, composed of hard granite. It is ovel or round on the top." [71: 38]

Angelina Farley, Aug. 29, 1850. "Passed Independence Rock covered almost all over with names of travelers." [133: Diary]

Cecilia E. Adams, 1852. "Stopped for dinner opposite Independence Rock. It is a great curiosity, but we were so tired that we could not go to the top of it. It is almost entirely covered with names of emigrants." [2: Ms. Diary]

J. J. Connor, 1853. Noted that the 24 names of his party were put on the Rock. [87: Ms. Diary]

Maria A. Parsons, June 30, 1853. "Mr. Belshaw and I climbed the Rock. I felt very dizzy when I reached the top. There I saw hundreds of names, not one I knew." [31: Ms. diary]

E. J. Galtra Farrington, 1853. ". . . there are upwards of several hundred names inscribed on the top and sides of it, all have a curiosity to climb on its top." [135: 9]

J. C. Couper, 1857. "Passed Independence Rock 1800 feet in length and about half in width. Among the many names inscribed on its surface Wm. Sublette a leader of Sir Wm. Stewarts party in 1843." [95: 11]

Sir Richard Burton, 1860. ". . . at Rock Independence . . . It crops out of an open plain, not far from the river bed, in dome shape wholly isolated, about 1000 feet in length, by 400-500 in breadth; it is 60 to 100 in height, and in circumference 1.50 to 2 miles. Except upon the summit where it has been weathered into a feldspathic soil; it is bare and bald: a scanty growth of shrubs protrudes however from its poll. The material of the stern looking dome is granite, in enormous slabs and boulders, cracked, flaked, seared and cloven. . . . The Indians have named it Timpe Nabor, or the Painted Rock. . . . In the present day, though much of the writing has been washed away by rain, 40,000-50,000 souls are calculated to have left their dates and marks from the coping of the wall to the loose stones below this huge sign post. There is, however, some reason in the proceeding: it does not in these lands begin and end with the silly purpose . . . leave in their vermillion outfit, or their white house-paint or their brownish-black tar—a useful article for wagons—a homely but hearty word of love or direction upon any conspicuous object. Even a bull or a buffalo's skull . . ." [56: 164-65]

Robert S. Ellison, 1930. A monograph on Independence Rock, with an extensive list of names appearing on it. [130: passim]

William J. Ghent, 1934. ". . . Independence Rock . . . numerous stories have arisen in regard to its naming." P. 256, Note 4: ". . . Mr. Camp is probably right in his suggestion that as Fitzpatrick

Independence Rock from the west.

cached his furs near the Rock on or about July 4, 1824, the incident prompted the giving of the name." P. 251: "The west face of Independence Rock was marked with an inscription; on the north face, on July 4, 1920, a bronze tablet was set, commemorative of the organization of a lodge of Masons on the Rock on July 4, 1862; and in the same year another bronze tablet, presented by Mr. Henry D. Schoonmaker, was also set in the Rock. The inscription on the last-named tablet carries the quite erroneous statement that the name of the famous landmark was given 'by emigrants who celebrated Independence Day here July 4, 1825.'" [149: 136, 251 & 256]

WPA Writers Project, 1939. "Fremont in 1842 innocently left a mark that was later to embarrass him; remembering that many whose names and initials were there had already died, he thought of the formation as a giant gravestone and left a large cross on it. . . . At some later time a group of migrants who were hostile to Roman Catholicism dynamited the rock at this point to destroy what they considered a symbol of that sect. At the same time when Fremont was a candidate for the Presidency, the fact that he placed the cross here was used to inflame feeling against him." [146: 188]

Irene D. Paden, 1943. "Asahel Munger, a missionary Oregon bound in 1839, was told by Harris . . . mountain man, that the name Independence was bestowed upon it in 1830 by trappers of the American Fur Company who happened to spend the Fourth of July camped in its shadow." P. 120: "The enterprising Mormons sometimes had a man or two at the Rock who would undertake to inscribe a name and date for varying prices up to five dollars, depending on location." [298: 120, 209]

Wallace Stegner, 1964. "While they [John Brown and William Woodruff] were on top, a party of Missourians came to the foot of the rock and dug a hole and buried somebody. They noted the name later: Rachel Morgan, aged twenty-five . . . When they had added their own names to the rock, and prayed—'the first Latter-day Saint[s] that ever went onto that rock or offered up prayers according to the priesthood.'" [363: 151]

Robert L. Munkres, 1968. An article for Wyoming history buffs. [284: 23-40]

Author's note, July 26, 1972. At the northwest corner of Indepdence Rock is an inscription: "OLD OREGON TRAIL," in eight-inch letters on the sloping base of the rock. The best names found, and the only really early ones, were at the southeast corner of the rock, particularly in and around the cave.

In a cove on the west side of the rock is a 15' by 20' plot fenced with ornamental iron and identified only by a letter "S" on the gate. It is probably a burial plot but headstones were not evident in the tangle of brush within the fence.

A rest area has been developed at the northwest corner of the rock and about 500 feet of the base has been protected with fencing. Despite the protection, recent name-writing has obliterated almost all trace of older inscriptions. There are nine bronze tablets set into the Rock at that point, commemorating: Ezra Meeker, missionaries Whitman and Spaulding, the Masons' lodge, the rock itself, Fr. Pierre Jean DeSmet, the Mormon pioneers, Rev. Jason Lee, Dr. Grace Raymond Hebard and Anderson Deckard.

USGS map, Independence Rock, Wyo., 1:24,000, 1951 ed.

CROSSING OF SWEETWATER RIVER
Mile 815.0 — South of Independence Rock
Natrona County, Wyo. — NW¼ of NW¼, Sec. 15, T29N, R86W

At this point the emigrants crossed the Sweetwater River for the first time. A bridge at Sweetwater Station served trail traffic of the late period.

William Clayton, 1848. "Independence Rock and ford . . ." [78: 15]

James A. Pritchard, June 15, 1849. "At this point [Independence Rock] we cross the river." It is described as "from 60 to 80 feet wide deep channel, gravelly bed & swift current." [317: 91]

Sir Richard Burton, 1860. ". . . we forded the Sweet-water . . . The Canadian voyageurs have translated the name Sweetwater from the Indian Ping Pa; but the term is here more applicable in metaphorical than a literal point of view . . . the banks are free from the saline hoar, which deters the thirstiest from touching many streams on this line . . ." [p. 167] about seventy feet wide and deep to the axles." [56: 166-67]

William J. Ghent, 1934. "As to the naming of the Sweetwater also there have been many conjectures. Chittenden suggests a French origin. Perhaps Granville Stuart's statement *(Forty Years on the Frontier)* that it was named for 'its beautiful clear cold waters having a sweetish taste, caused by alkali held in solution . . . not enough, however, to cause any apparent injurious effects,' may be the true one." [149: 136]

Irene D. Paden, 1943. "Until after 1849 the Sweetwater ford was immediately at the rock. . . ." [298: 209]

USGS map, Independence Rock, Wyo., 1:24,000, 1951 ed.

DEVIL'S GATE$_p$
(Site No. 1, Devil's Gate Vicinity Map)
Mile 820R — Natrona County, Wyo.
NE¼ of NE¼, Sec. 35, T29N, R87W

This is a prominent landmark approximately one-half mile north of the Oregon Trail, on land belonging to the Tom Sun Ranch.

The feature is a narrow cleft—370 feet deep, 1,500 feet long and as narrow as 50 feet in some places—by which the Sweetwater River breaks through a ridge called the Sweetwater Rocks. It was a gloomy place, and violent also when the water was high, so that a satanic denomination seemed fitting. The gorge can be viewed from former Wyoming Highway 220 (which may still be reached by way of the entrance road to the Tom Sun Ranch). Permission should be obtained at the ranch for any closer approach. A water diversion dam has been constructed midway within the gorge, but it is not conspicuous.

Rufus B. Sage, Spring 1842. ". . . struck the river a few miles above camp, at a place where the stream cuts its way through a high ridge of hills, forming another cañon of three or four hundred yards in length, and about forty broad, called the Devil's Gate, as I afterward ascertained.

"Its walls arose perpendicularly to a height of between four and five hundred feet, and consisted of trap rock, sandstone, and granite." [338:IV, 324]

John C. Fremont, August 2, 1842. "Five miles above Rock

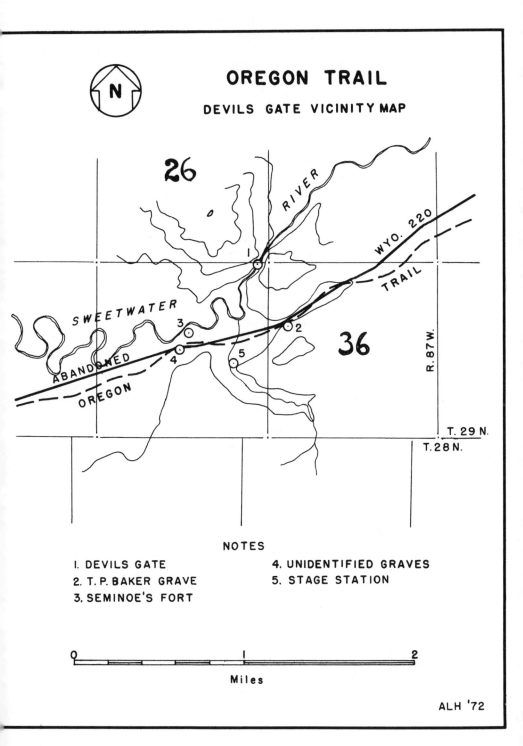

OREGON TRAIL

DEVILS GATE VICINITY MAP

NOTES

1. DEVILS GATE
2. T.P. BAKER GRAVE
3. SEMINOE'S FORT
4. UNIDENTIFIED GRAVES
5. STAGE STATION

Miles

ALH '72

Independence we came to a place called the Devil's Gate, where the Sweetwater cuts through the point of a granite ridge. The length of the passage is about three hundred yards, and the width thirty-five yards. The walls of rock are vertical, and about four hundred feet in height; and the stream in the gate is almost entirely choked up by masses which have fallen from above." P. 249, Note 57: "The name Devil's Gate apparently was quite new. Father DeSmet went to the mountains in 1840 without mentioning it, but on his second journey, in a letter dated 16 Aug. 1841, he said that 'travelers have named this spot the Devil's Entrance.'" [202:I, 247-49]

Matthew C. Field, 1843. "After dinner attempted the passage of Hell Gate, on a bet with Dr. Tilghman, and after an hour's labor was compelled to return on account of the fright of my mule, but the old hunters who came in far enough to look on acknowledged the effort was a gallant one." [137: 174]

James W. Nesmith, July 31, 1843. "Visited the Canyon of the Sweet Water. The cut is in a rock about eight feet wide and 200 feet high. . ." [290: 345]

John Minto, August 17, 1844. "Devil's Gate. It varies in width, I think, from fifty to one hundred feet or more; and the walls, I should estimate, at four hundred or five hundred feet high. I did not attempt to go through . . ." [266: 161]

James Mathers, July 8, 1846. ". . . encamped above the pass of the river between high rocks [three miles beyond Independence Rock]. This is the most interesting sight we have met with on our journey." [275:I, 226]

Heinrich Lienhard, 1846. "This place is known as Devil's Gate, and here on either side was inscribed, as at Independence Rock, a large number of names. Here again I wrote my name, but not in particularly large letters, which very likely have long since disappeared." [229: 85-86]

J. M. Harrison, 1846. ". . . a short distance from Independence Rock was the Devil's Gate where Sweetwater had worn its way through Sweetwater Mtns. We walked down into the passage of the river and looking overhead it looked like we might jump from one wall to the other, it was so narrow at the top . . . climbed mountain [and] saw signs of mountain sheep. Some of the party killed a bighorn sheep." [165: Letter]

William Clayton, 1848. "Devil's Gate—A little west from the road. The river here passes between perpendicular rocks four hundred feet high—this is a curiosity worthy of a traveler's notice." [78: 15]

Devil's Gate, just west of Independence Rock.

James A. Pritchard, June 15, 1849. ". . . in 5 miles come to what is called the deavels gate   It [is] a singular fissure or cannon in the Mountains through which Sweetwater forces its way. The fissure is about 30 feet wide and about one half mile through, with vertical walls from 350 to 400 feet high." [317: 91]

Osborne Cross, July 10, 1849. ". . . Devil's gap. This gap is truly wonderful, being a space not over twenty yards wide and about five hundred feet high, having very much the appearance of being chiselled out by the hand of man rather than the work of nature." [101: 128]

J. Goldsborough Bruff, July 26, 1849. ". . . 'Devil's Gate.'. . . Some of the boys clambered up the rocks on the N. Side of the Gate, and reached some cavernous places, where they fired pistols and threw down rocks, pleased with the reverberation, which was great. I made a careful sketch of this remarkable gorge." [52: 53]

Howard Stansbury, July 31, 1849." 'Devil's Gate.' The space between the cliff, on either side, did not in some places exceed forty feet. The height was from three to four hundred feet." [361: 65]

William J. Ghent, 1934. "A giant boulder near Devil's Gate was inscribed by Capt. Nickerson." [149: 252]

WPA Writer's Project, 1939. "In the early 1860's four women, members of a train camped at this point, climbed to the top of the ridge above the gorge. One of them, 18 years old [Caroline Todd], venturing too close to the edge, fell and was killed. She was buried in the gorge." [146: 189]

Irene D. Paden, 1943. "The emigrants saw this slit in the horizon—fourteen miles away, so they said . . . one of the major landmarks . . . Parties went constantly to the easily accessible brink of the southern overhanging cliff only to find that no one (even when a human chain had been formed to support the outside man) could be found to peer over the overhanging lip of the four-hundred foot drop." P. 214: Describes the river at the Devil's Gate as ". . . a regular gangster of a river, shouting defiance down its own dark alley." [298: 213-14]

Wallace Stegner, 1964. "Where Dan Jones and his companions lived through their rawhide winter in the trader's cabins at Devil's Gate, there is a ranch." [363: 306]

USGS map, Independence Rock, Wyo., 1:24,000, 1951 ed.

T. P. BAKER "GRAVE"
(Site No. 2, Devil's Gate Vicinity Map)
Mile 820.0 — Natrona County, Wyo.
SW¼ of NW¼, Sec. 36, T29N, R87W

Author's note, July 1, 1993. Research during the spring of 1993 by OCTA's master grave sleuth, Randy Brown, has established that this is actually the marker for the grave of Frederic Richard Fulkerson, who died here on July 1, 1849. The grave stone was sketched by J. Goldsborough Bruff. The marking evidently had disappeared over the next fifteen years. Baker inscribed his name at least once more while traveling west of this site.

Tom Sun, age 87 when interviewed in 1972, lived his entire life on the ranch established by his father at Devil's Gate. He was asked about this and other graves in the area, and he said that the Boy Scouts had refurbished the Baker "grave" in 1931. At that time there were three or four graves in a circle of stones on the opposite side of the road and the boys got the stones they piled on the grave from that circle. Thus, the graves once marked by the circle of stones can no longer be distinguished.

The USGS map shows another grave 2,200 feet to the northeast (on the line common to the northwest and northeast quarters of Section 36), but a prolonged search failed to discover it. Sun remembered that grave as a small one—probably that of a child.

Bruff, writing in 1849, described a grave in this pass: ". . . near the outlet a grave attracted my attention . . . Painted on stone at head:—'Frederic Richard, son of James M. and Mary Fulkerson, Aged 18 years . . .'" [52: 52-53]. Farther along the trail, just over the Green River crossing on the Sublette Cutoff, was the grave of the mother, which Bruff also recorded: "Mary, Consort of J.M. Fulkerson, Died July 14, 1847." [52: 74]

USGS map, Independence Rock, Wyo., 1:24,000, 1951 ed.

DEVIL'S GATE STAGE STATION
(Site No. 5, Devil's Gate Vicinity Map)
Mile 820.2 — Natrona County, Wyo.
NE¼ of SE¼, Sec. 35, T29N, R87W

The Devil's Gate Station was also known as "Plant's," for the French-Canadian who ran it. It was mail station No. 29 on the route to Salt Lake City—another in the line of stations established to facilitate the movement of mail and passengers.

Sir Richard Burton, 1860. ". . . muddy station kept by M. Plante, the usual Canadian . . . we supped badly . . ." (There is more on the inadequate accommodations at this overnight stop.) [56: 167]

Author's note, July 26, 1972. There are some foundation stones at the stage station, which is also marked by an iron stake. According to Sun, three graves near the station were washed out by Rush Creek many years ago (the stream passed close to the station on the west side). He also remembered that the grave of a woman was on the slope across the stream from the station, but there no longer is any evidence of it.

USGS map, Independence Rock, Wyo., 1:24,000, 1951 ed.

DEVIL'S GATE (SEMINOE'S) FORT₍ₚ₎
(Site No. 3, Devil's Gate Vicinity Map)
Mile 820.7 — Natrona County, Wyo.
SW¼ of NE¼, Sec. 35, T29N, R87W

This trading establishment consisted of several houses built by Basil Lajeunesse, also known as "Seminoe," prior to 1855 and abandoned before the fall of 1856. The structures were partly demolished for fuel by the Mormons, who sheltered there from early winter storms. In fact, the presence of these buildings undoubtedly saved the lives of many members of Martin's Handcart Company.

Josiah Rogerson Sr., Jan. 4, 1914. In his account of Martin's Handcart Company, 1856: ". . . they finally arrived at Devil's Gate fort about the 1st of November . . . the wagons were banked near the fort . . . All the people who could crowded into the houses of the fort out of the cold and storm. One crowd cut away the walls of the house they were in for fuel, until half of the roof fell in. . . ." [330: news item]

Anonymous, 1929. The fort was built by Basil Lajeunesse, who had been with Fremont and remained in the mountains. He was called "Seminoe" by the Snake Indians among whom he lived for a time (he had married a woman of that tribe). [13: 237-38]

LeRoy R. Hafen, 1938. "Mr. Kerr and others recently from this city [Salt Lake City] were stopping at Seminoe's Fort waiting for the escort." P. 238: Thomas S. Williams, April 20, 1855: "Three or four days before I got to Devil's Gate, a large war party of Indians had driven off all of Semino's horses, and all of Pappan's and the mail mules, making a clean sweep of all animals at that point." [156: 220, 238]

USGS map, Independence Rock, Wyo., 1:24,000, 1951 ed.

UNIDENTIFIED BURIALS
(Site No. 4, Devil's Gate Vicinity Map)
Mile 820.8 — Natrona County, Wyo.
Near center of Sec. 35, T29N, R87W

This reburial site contains the remains from graves exposed by construction work during the building of Wyoming State Highway 220.

Author's note, July 26, 1972. The 8' x 30' fenced plot is on the south side of the old highway, opposite the entrance to the Tom Sun Ranch. It contains three monuments—all facing north. The eastern stone—a granite, 7" x 25" x 60"—is incised, below a bronze Oregon Trail medallion: "To The Pioneers / 1830-1870 / Buried Here On The / Tom Sun Ranch / Ezra Meeker / Often Visited This Spot / Erected By / Oregon Trail Memorial / Association 1930."

The middle stone, also granite (7" x 24" x 41"), is incised:

"The Oregon Trail / 1841 Devil's Gate One-Fourth Mile East / Split Rock 20 Miles Northwest / Erected By The Historical Landmark Commission Of Wyoming / 1943."

The western stone, which also carries a bronze Oregon Trail medallion, is incised: "In Honor Of / The Pioneer Women / Buried Here / In Unmarked Graves / 1836-1870 / Erected 1930 / By Business And / Professional Women's / Club of Casper."

USGS map, Independence Rock, Wyo., 1:24,000, 1951 ed.

MARTIN'S COVE
Mile 823R1 — 2 miles west of Tom Sun Ranch
Natrona County, Wyo. — NE¼ of SW¼, Sec. 27, T29N, R87W

This is a protected pocket on the southern flank of the Sweetwater Rocks, where a portion of Capt. Edward Martin's Mormon Handcart emigrants took shelter from wintery storms early in November 1856, while awaiting assistance from Salt Lake City. Many died there from cold and exhaustion.

The Mormon pioneers paid a terrible price, in terms of human life, in 1856. Between Council Bluffs and Salt Lake City, Martin's Company lost between 135 and 150 persons, and Willie's Handcart Company lost 66.

This monument to the handcart pioneers is in Salt Lake City.

Josiah Rogerson Sr., Nov. 30, 1913. A reminiscent account by a survivor. [329: news item]

Josiah Rogerson Sr., Jan. 4, 1914. A continuation of the previous article, presenting extensive excerpts from the diary of Dan W. Jones, one of the volunteers who went out from Salt Lake City to the relief of the handcart emigrants. He stayed the remainder of the winter at the abandoned trading post at Devil's Gate (Seminoe's), in charge of a detachment which looked after the property abandoned there. A roster of the heads of families and unattached persons of Martin's Company is included, and also information on the building of the handcarts and equipping of these travelers. [330: news item]

LDS Church Historian. Items on the Martin Company in the journal, as follows:

"April 18, 1852, p. 1: "Hand Cart & Wheelbarrow Immigration;" a proposal.

September 26, 1856, p. 1: "Hand Cart Companies;" the first to arrive in Salt Lake City met by a band of music and many brethern and citizens of the settlements.

October 5, 1856, p. 3: "Hand Cart Companies;" mentions those belated on the Plains, with Brigham Young's call for teams and wagons, food, clothes, etc.

October 5, 1856, p. 4: "Hand Cart Companies;" conditions and experiences detailed by Franklin D. Richards, who implored help.

October 15, 1856, p. 2: "Hand Cart Companies;" gives the names of those in the 6th Company—Capt. Edwin Martin's, from England—as published in *Deseret News.*

November 30, 1856, p. 1: "Hand Cart Companies;" President Brigham Young's instructions to the Saints to feed and nurse the poor sufferers of the "Martin Hand Cart Company" that was belated in the snow east of Salt Lake Valley.

November 30, 1856, pp. 9-54: "Hand Cart Companies;" the letters of John Jaques to the *Herald* detailing the awful sufferings of the Martin and Willie Hand Cart companies.

February 1, 1857, p. 4: "Hand Cart Companies;" Brigham Young's statement on the five companies which crossed the plains from the Missouri River to Utah in 1856.

Collateral items referring to this episode, in the journal, as follows:

June 11, 1856, p. 1: Report of Wm. Woodward.

September 26, 1856, p. 2: Report of Elder Dan D. McArthur.

November 2, 1856, p. 3: Repudiation of blame by President Brigham Young.

November 16, 1856, p. 1: Explanation of President Brigham Young.

April 4, 1915, p. 3: Meeting of surviving Handcart Veterans.

November 28, 1926, p. 2: Story of the Handcart Pioneers as told by Andrew Jenson, LDS Church Historian, over Radio KSL. [209: entries]

Irene D. Paden, 1943. ". . . a little recess in the hills where in 1856 an unfortunate company of Mormons were caught by early

Split Rock, a prominent feature west of Devil's Gate.

snows. . . ." The story is given as in Daniel W. Jones' diary. [298: 215-16]

LeRoy R. Hafen, 1960. A definitive work on the Mormon handcart migration prepared from documentary sources. [159: passim]

Bill Bragg Jr., 1972. An account for Wyoming history buffs. [44: 271-73]

Author's note, July 26, 1972. A monument erected by the Utah Pioneer Trails and Landmarks Association, and citizens of Wyoming, June 22, 1933, stands on the north shoulder of abandoned Wyoming Highway 220 at a point 2.0 miles west of the Sun Ranch. It states: "Survivors of Captain Edward Martin's Handcart company of Mormon emigrants from England to Utah were rescued here in perishing condition about Nov. 12, 1856. Delayed in starting and hampered by inferior carts, it was overtaken by an early winter. Among the company of 576, including aged people and children, the fatalities numbered 145. Insufficient food and clothing and severe weather caused many deaths. Toward the end every campground became a graveyard. Some of the survivors found shelter in a stockade and mail station near Devil's Gate, where their property was stored for the winter. Earlier companies reached Utah safely."

The Martins Cove name appears to have been misplaced on the USGS map, appearing on the Independence Rock, Wyo. (1951) sheet, where it is shown too high in the Sweetwater Rocks; it would have been more appropriate to have placed the name on the Savage Peak, Wyo. (1951) sheet.

USGS map, Savage Peak, Wyo., 1:24,000, 1951 ed.

ASTORIAN CAMP
Mile 825R½ — 5 miles west of Devil's Gate
Natrona County, Wyo. — NE¼ of SE¼, Sec. 25, T29N, R88W

This is a campsite used by the returning Astorians on October 12, 1812. The location has been determined from a manuscript map prepared by Paul C. Henderson.

USGS map, Savage Peak, Wyo., 1:24,000, 1951 ed.

SPLIT ROCK STATION
Mile 837.9 — 2 miles east of Split Rock Ranch
Natrona County, Wyo. — SW¼ of NW¼, Sec. 30, T29N, R89W

At this site was a stage station, Pony Express station, telegraph station and a garrisoned point. It is beside the Sweetwater River opposite a noted Oregon Trail landmark, Split Rock.

O. Allen, 1858. "Cut Rock, U.S.M. Station No. 30—Grass in abundance, sagebrush and willows for fuel." [8: 64]

Henry R. Herr, July 30, 1862. "Camped at Split Rock, where there is quartered 50 soldiers for protection of the emigrants. 200 wagons passed today on their way to Salmon River mines [Idaho]. Soldiers composed of 6th Ohio Reg." [175: Ms. Diary]

William J. Ghent, 1934. ". . . a bluff near Split Rock probably Craner Rock, was one of the places inscribed by Capt. Nickerson." [149: 252]

Buelah Walker, 1972. Provides information on the telegraph and Pony Express stations at Split Rock. [386: 274]

Author's note, July 27, 1972. The site of Split Rock Station, between Craner Rock and Sweetwater River, is now a hay meadow, and no evidence of its existence could be found.

A monument erected by the Historical Landmark Commission of Wyoming in 1956 stands beside U.S. Highway 287 at a point 2.2 miles west of Split Rock Ranch. It states: "SPLIT ROCK / A Famous Natural Landmark / Used By Indians, Trappers, And / Emigrants On The Oregon Trail. / Site Of Split Rock Pony Express / 1860-1861, Stage, And Telegraph / Station Is On The South Side / Of The Sweetwater. / Split Rock Can Be Seen As A / Cleft In The Top Of The Rattlesnake Range."

The landmark feature—also known as "Cut Rock"—is located in the SW¼ of the SE¼, Sec. 18, T29N, R90W, in the mountains called the Sweetwater Rocks.

USGS Map, Split Rock, Wyo., 1:24,000, 1951 ed.

"The Old Castle" — a remarkable formation along the trail.

"THE OLD CASTLE" (CASTLE ROCK)
Mile 842L½ — 2 miles west of Split Rock Ranch
Fremont County, Wyo. — SW¼ of SW¼, Sec. 21, T29N,R90W

This is an outcrop of grayish clay which still resembles the crumbling walls of an ancient castle. It has a rectangular appearance as seen from below.

It was used by emigrants as a name-register, although evidently not an important one. No evidence of early use of the name has yet been found.

Sir Richard Burton, 1860. Probably the place pointed out to him as the "Devil's Post-office," and of which he wrote thus: "It has lately been washed with rains so copious, that half the edifice lies at the base of that which is standing." [56: 170] The authors of two prominent guidebooks, [8] and [78], fail to mention this feature.

Henry Jensen, 1972. He states that the name of W. K. Sublette (1849) has been found among the few still readable in the soft material of this landmark. [206: 274-75]

USGS map, Split Rock, Wyo., 1:24,000, 1951 ed.

THREE CROSSINGS STAGE STATION_P
Mile 849.2 — 5 miles east of Jeffrey City, Wyo.
Fremont County — SW¼ of NW¼, Sec. 4, T29N, R91W

The stage station here probably served the early mail route to Salt Lake City.

Sir Richard Burton, 1860. "At 11 A.M. we reached 'three crossings' . . . The little ranch was neatly swept and garnished, papered and ornamented . . . table cloth was clean, so was the cooking, so were the children. . . ." There is much more about the English couple who ran the station. [56: 171-74]

Author's note, July 27, 1972. The location of this stage station is taken from Paul C. Henderson's manuscript map. It was probably abandoned when the military post was established at Mile 850.8. Several sources indicate that stage, Pony Express and telegraph services were all concentrated at the safer place during the period of Indian unrest.

Another feature in this general area is a grave site on the north side of the Sweetwater River in the SE¼ of the SW¼, Sec. 33, T30N, R91W. This site was pointed out by Robert Anderson, a geologist employed by the Bureau of Land Management. Anderson was in the Three Crossings area examining the land for an impending sale. The site may have been a homestead. The grave is rock-covered and the protective railing is down.

USGS map, Black Rock Gap, Wyo., 1:24,000, 1951 ed.

THREE CROSSINGS_P
Mile 850.5 — 4 miles east of Jeffrey City, Wyo.
Fremont County — N½ of Sec. 5, T29N, R91W
and SW¼ of Sec. 31, T30N, R91W

Here the Oregon Trail made three crossings of the Sweetwater River before and while passing through a rocky defile. The crossings, and the canyon, could be avoided by taking either of two alternates, both of which were difficult.

James Mathers, July 10, 1846. "Crossed the creek three times today, and passed thro' a narrow place between two high rocky hills." [275:I, 226]

J. Goldsborough Bruff, July 28, 1849. ". . . we forded the SweetWater river.—Gravelly bottom & swift current. Now a broad road, clouds of sand & impallpable dust:—dimming the

The meadow at Three Crossings bears the trace of the old road as it is about to enter the gorge, out of the picture at right. The stage stations was located on the bench beyond the small tree in left center. The deep sand route carried the travelers through the notch in the center, thus avoiding the three crossings of the Sweetwater River.

atmosphere, and covering and penetrating every thing, over rolling sand hills covered with sage. The river and road now enters a gorge of the mountains. . . . Perpendicular rock walls, from 400 to 600 ft. hight on our right. This is a very narrow and rugged pass,—or cañon, we crossed and recrossed the stream again in 1½ miles. Whirlwind of sand blowing through with a fresh breeze. The rocks here, wherever accessible, are marked all over with inscriptions, as usual. Thick growth of willows on the banks. Plenty remains of broken & burnt wagons here." [52: 56]

Angelina Farley, Sept. 1, 1850. "Crossed the river 3 times and passed between rocky ridges where thousands of emigrants had written their names. Saw three that I knew." [133: diary]

O. Allen, 1858. "Three Crossings of Sweet Water—Good grass may be found east and west of the crossings, at this point you cross the river three times in the distance of a mile and one half." [8: 64]

William J. Ghent, 1934. ". . . at Three Crossings, a granite bluff was marked [by Capt. Nickerson]." [149: 252]

Irene D. Paden, 1943. ". . . within a narrow gorge formed by the range of Granite Mountain and a projecting spur . . . gorge is now dammed . . . A heavy sand road completely circumnavigated the gorge." [298: 218-20]

Author's note, July 27, 1972. This place name—Three Crossings—does not designate a precise location, but a locality consisting of a large meadow and a rocky, gate-like canyon. Two of the crossings were ordinarily made in the meadow and one in the throat of the canyon. However, there were two alternative routes around this difficult place, so that all or part could be avoided, but both involved hard pulling on sandy terrain. Hay ranching has greatly altered the character of the meadow and irrigation works have changed the canyon. The mosquitoes found here were the most voracious encountered anywhere on the Oregon Trail, and they tend to inhibit interest in the locality.

USGS map, Stampede Meadows, Wyo., 1:24,000, 1951 ed.

THREE CROSSINGS STATION (Military)$_P$
Mile 850.8 — 3.8 miles northeast of Jeffrey City, Wyo.
Fremont County — NW¼ of NE¼, Sec. 6, T29N, R91W

A military post at this point was similar to Sweetwater Station, in that it was a fortified, one-company establishment. It also was a telegraph station.

The stage station here was garrisoned during the Civil War to protect emigrants and the telegraph line. The stage line, however, was shifted to the Cheyenne-Rock Springs route when Indian hostilities rendered the Sweetwater Valley too dangerous.

WPA Writer's Project, 1939. ". . . SITE OF THREE CROSSINGS, a telegraph and stage station of the 1860s that was on the north [south] bank of the river, near the mouth of Sage Hen Creek." [146: 190]

Florence Kirk, 1972. In 1928 the bodies of 14 soldiers buried near the old Pony Express station were removed, but one remains; that of "Bennett Tribbett, Co. B—11 Ohio." [219: 275-76]

Author's note, July 27, 1972. The station referred to here was 400 feet northeast of the "Goose Egg Rock," a prominent local

feature.
USGS map "Stampede Meadow, Wyo.," 1:24,000, 1951 ed.

NAMES CLIFF$_P$
Mile 854.4 — 3 miles northwest of Jeffrey City, Wyo.
Fremont County — SW¼ of SE¼, Sec. 32, T30N, R92W

This is another place where emigrants left their names daubed
on the cliff face with wagon tar. The location is from a manuscript
map by Paul C. Henderson.
USGS map, Stampede Meadow, Wyo., 1:24,000, 1951 ed.

NAMES ROCK
Mile 858.0 — 6 miles northwest of Jeffrey City, Wyo.
Fremont County — SW¼ of SE¼, Sec. 36, T30N, R93W

The location of this emigrant name register is from a manuscript map prepared by Paul C. Henderson.
USGS map, Graham Ranch, Wyo., 1:24,000, 1951 ed.

FIFTH CROSSING OF THE SWEETWATER
Mile 858.4 — 6.5 miles northwest of Jeffrey City, Wyo.
Fremont County — SW¼ of SW¼, Sec. 36, T30N, R93W

Here, 0.4 mile west of Names Rock, the Oregon Trail crossed
back over the Sweetwater River to the south side. The location
is from a manuscript map by Paul C. Henderson.
USGS map, Graham Ranch, Wyo., 1:24,000, 1951 ed.

ICE SPRING (ICE SLOUGH)
Mile 862R¼ — 9.5 miles east of Sweetwater Station
Fremont County, Wyo. — NW¼ of SE¼, Sec. 32, T30N, R93W

A marsh occupies a sag in the valley floor, where water collects
and freezes beneath a tundra-like covering of turf. During
Oregon Trail days the ice remained sound and good throughout
the hot summer months because of the insulating effect of its
cover. This feature bordered on the miraculous so far as most
emigrants were concerned. (A few were frankly skeptical.) It was

also a minor comfort to the trail-weary.

William Clayton, 1847. "Ice Spring.—This is on a low, swampy spot of land on the right of the road. Ice may generally be found by digging down about two feet." [78: 15]

James A. Pritchard, June 16, 1849. ". . . we came to an Ice Spring one of the strangest & mos singular in Nature. This Spring as it is called, is rather a bason surrounded by sand plains, about one mile in length & from 150 to 300 yards wide. But does not all contain Ice. The Ice is found about 8 to 10 inches beneath the surface. There is from 4 to 6 inches of water above the Ice, and of turf or sod of grass appearantly floating on the water, upon which you can walk over it. You can stand and shake for 2 or 3 rods Squar. The water above the Ice is pretty strongly impregnated with Alkli. The upper end of the marsh is entirely that kind of water mixture. Tho there is good fresh water in spots. To get to the Ice you take a spade or Ax & cut away the sod & ther strike down & cut it out in Squar blocks. The Ice is clear & pure entirely free from any Alkali and other unpleasant tast. It is from 4 to 10 inches thick, and as good as any I ever cut from the streams in Kentucky. I cut and filled my water bucket & took it with me." [317: 91]

Osborne Cross, July 14, 1849. ". . . alkaline marsh, which may be looked upon as a natural curiosity. It was at this place that by digging into the ground about twelve inches we came to a bed of excellent ice, which was very acceptable to us." [101: 135]

J. Goldsborough Bruff, July 29, 1849. ". . . on right, in the low ground, by digging a couple of feet, ice is obtained. The surface is dug up all about by the travellers—as much from curiosity as to obtain so desireable a luxury in a march so dry and thirsty—this is called the 'ice springs.'" [52: 57]

Angelina Farley, Sept. 2, 1850. "We passed where there is said to be a ice bed." [133: diary]

O. Allen, 1858. "Ice Spring - Good grass, water scarce, wild sage for fuel, ice found by digging in the ground." [8: 64]

Sir Richard Burton, 1860. ". . . the Ice Springs,—of which, somewhat unnecessarily, a marvel is made. The ground, which lies on the right of the road, is a long and swampy trough between two waves of land which permit the humidity to drain down, and the grass is discoloured, suggesting the presence of alkali. After digging about two feet, ice is found . . . accounted for by the fact that hereabouts water will freeze in a tent during July, and by the depth to which the wintry frost extends." [56: 174]

William J. Ghent, 1934. ". . . the marsh stretch known variously as Ice Slough or Ice Springs. . . . Delano, anticipating the skepticism of his readers, explains at some length that the thick growth of high grass, protecting the ice from the sun accounted for the apparent miracle. Randall H. Hewitt . . . in 1862, asserted that the story was a 'cold-blooded romance,' written with the intent to deceive. He was, however, mistaken . . . two residents of the district write the author that they have no doubt the emigrants sometimes found ice there, and one of them suggests the explanation given by Delano. [149: 137]

Irene D. Paden, 1943. "The astonishing part is not that they found ice, but that they were surprised by the discovery. . . . The Mormons noted it in '47, and most of the guidebooks featured it . . . Icy Slough . . . The many people whom we have asked on many occasions are unanimous in stating that there has been no summer ice for years . . . [that] is the information as we received it . . . feel obligated to say that we didn't dig up the slough to find out, and we don't think they did either." [298: 221]

Author's note, July 27, 1972. There is an informational panel at a turnout on U.S. Highway 287, 1.5 miles west of the Ice Spring (called "Ice Slough" on the sign). Paul C. Henderson has recovered ice from the area on a number of occasions, and he has kept a careful record of the dates and conditions, but the slough is now nearly dry and very little ice is formed in winter. It has the appearance of a hay meadow.

USGS map, Graham Ranch, Wyo., 1:24,000, 1951 ed.

SEMINOE CUTOFF (East Junction)
Mile 870.2 — 3 miles southeast of Sweetwater Station
Fremont County, Wyo. — SE¼ of SW¼, Sec. 1, T29N, R95W

This Oregon Trail alternate remained south of the Sweetwater River, thus avoiding four crossings and the "Rocky Ridge." It took its name from Basil Lajeunesse, a squawman who was known as "Seminoe" by the Shoshoni Indians, with whom he lived.

O. Allen, 1852. "Here the roads fork and join near the last crossing of Sweetwater; take the north road, grass and water scarce at these springs [Warm Springs], sage brush for fuel." [8: 64]

USGS map, Sweetwater Station, Wyo., 1:24,000, 1953 ed.

WARM SPRINGS (Seminoe Cutoff)
Mile 872.5 — 3½ miles south of Sweetwater Station
Fremont County, Wyo. — NE¼ of NE¼, Sec. 15, T29N, R95W

This is a group of tepid springs from which a nearby stage station later took its name. The station site is 1,300 feet southwest of the springs, and a "Cold Spring" was 700 feet southeast of the station. The locations are all from a manuscript map by Paul C. Henderson.
USGS map, Happy Spring, Wyo., 1:24,000, 1953 ed.

SIXTH CROSSING OF THE SWEETWATER RIVER_p
Mile 875.5 — 3.4 miles southwest of Sweetwater Station
Fremont County, Wyo. — SE¼ of SE¼, Sec. 6, T29N, R95W

The location of this Oregon Trail crossing is from a manuscript map prepared by Paul C. Henderson.
USGS map, Sweetwater Station, Wyo., 1:24,000, 1953 ed.

SEVENTH CROSSING OF THE SWEETWATER RIVER_p
Mile 879.3 — 6½ miles southwest of Sweetwater Station
Fremont County, Wyo. — NE¼ of NE¼, Sec. 15, T29N, R96W

The site of this Oregon Trail crossing has been determined from a manuscript map prepared by Paul C. Henderson.
USGS map, Barras Springs, Wyo., 1:24,000, 1953 ed.

EIGHTH CROSSING OF SWEETWATER RIVER_p
Mile 880.1 — 7 miles southwest of Sweetwater Station Fremont
County, Wyo. — NE¼ of NW¼, Sec. 15, T29N, R96W

The location of this Oregon Trail crossing is from a manuscript map by Paul C. Henderson.
USGS map, Barras Springs, Wyo., 1:24,000, 1953 ed.

ST. MARY'S STATION_p
Mile 884.1 — On Sweetwater River below the "Rocky Ridge"
Fremont County, Wyo. — NW¼ of SW¼, Sec. 19, T29N, R96W

This stage station, later a garrisoned point, has been remembered longer than most in the Sweetwater Valley, probably because of its unusual name.

Sir Richard Burton, 1860. "'Foot of Ridge Station,' near a willowy creek, called from its principal inhabitants, the Muskrat. The ridge from which it derives its name is a band of stone that will cross the road during tomorrow's ascent. . . . The station rather added to than took from our discomfort: it was a terrible unclean hole; milk was not procurable within thirty-five miles . . . there was no sugar, and the cooking was atrocious . . . not sorry when the night came, but then the floor was knobby, the mosquitoes seemed rather to enjoy the cold, and the bunks swarmed with 'chinches'." [56: 175-76]

William H. Jackson, August 30, 1866. ". . . stopped at recently abandoned St. Mary Station and gathered wood." [201: 131]

William J. Ghent, 1934. ". . . at the site of St. Mary's Station a slate slab was set up [by Capt. Nickerson]." [149: 252]

WPA Writers' Project, 1939 ". . . SITE OF ST. MARY'S TELE-GRAPH STATION, also called Rocky Ridge." [146: 192]

Irene D. Paden, 1943. ". . . a small marker for the site of old St. Mary's stage station, usually referred to as St. Mary's Crossing. . . . no evidences remaining of the old station house." [298: 226] Author's note, July 28, 1972. A seven-inch square stone post, set on the slope of the bluff north of the Sweetwater River, is incised on its south face, "Old / Oregon / Trail / 1913 / St. Mary / Station," and on its east face, "HGN / 1914." This marker is 20 feet above the road, in a situation which appears neither disturbed nor habitable; however, there is occupational debris on the flat below the road about 500 feet east of the marker.

It is stated that St. Mary's was a military post with a small garrison during the Civil War period. [397: 287-93]

USGS map, Barras Springs, Wyo., 1:24,000, 1953 ed.

SARAH A. THOMAS GRAVE (Seminoe Cutoff)$_p$
Mile 885.1 — 13 miles southwest of Sweetwater Station
Fremont County, Wyo. — SW¼ of NW¼, Sec. 14, T28N, R97W

Sarah A. Thomas died June 6 or 29, 1854. Her grave is about ⅛ mile southeast of Emigrant Springs, on the Seminoe Cutoff. The springs are 1,700 feet south of the northwest corner of Sec. 14. These locations are all from a manuscript map by Paul

C. Henderson.
USGS map, Lewiston Lakes, Wyo., 1:24,000, 1953 ed.

ROCKY RIDGE
Mile 889R&L — 14 miles west of Sweetwater Station Fremont County, Wyo. — Sec. 21, 27, 28 & 35, T29N, R97W

This is a particularly stony ridge flanking the Sweetwater on both sides of the river. The axis is on a NW-SE direction and emigrants following the original Oregon Trail (here north of Sweetwater) had to pass over this barrier.

Virgil Pringle, July 13, 1846. ". . . we ascended the high lands to the right of the river, the highest ground we have been on . . . Passed several fine springs on the high lands." [275:I, 176]

James Mathers, July 13, 1846. "Traveled 16 miles over high hills and through intervening valleys crossing two small brooks, three ponds, one small branch of the Sweetwater . . . road . . . generally good, except two or three places where it is rocky." [275:I, 227] William Clayton, 1848. "Rough, rocky ridges— Dangerous to wagons, and ought to be crossed with care." [78: 16]

James A. Pritchard, June 17, 1849. "We traveled up the river several miles & left it cross what is called Stony Ridge—A very high elevation . . . several fine springs breaking out of the top of the mountain." [317: 92]

J. Goldsborough Bruff, July 31, 1849. ". . . ascended the high hill, moved over it, and ascended another, very stony and rough, requiring care of the teamsters:—then over some hard level road, and minor stony ridges." [52: 59]

Author's note, July 28, 1972. The Oregon Trail route over this ridge is absolutely impassable for ordinary passenger vehicles. In case of a breakdown or accident there is no assistance within a reasonable walking distance. *This is a remote and dangerous area.*
USGS map, Lewiston Lakes, Wyo., 1:24,000, 1953 ed.

UPPER MORMON SPRING (Seminoe Cutoff)$_p$
Mile 890.2 — 18 miles southwest of Sweetwater Station Fremont County, Wyo. — NW¼ of NW¼, Sec. 24, T28N, R98W

The location of this campground, on the Seminoe Cutoff, has been determined from a manuscript map by Paul C. Henderson.

USGS map, Lewiston Lakes, Wyo., 1:24,000, 1953 ed.

MORMON CEMETERY
Mile 898R¼ — 23 miles west of Sweetwater Station
Fremont County, Wyo. — SE¼ of SE¼, Sec. 36, T29N, R99W

Many casualties of the Mormon handcart migration are buried in this trailside cemetery.
USGS map, Radium Springs, Wyo., 1:24,000, 1953 ed.

UNIDENTIFIED GRAVES$_P$
Mile 901.0 — 4.5 miles northeast of Burnt Ranch
Fremont County, Wyo. — SW¼ of SE¼, Sec. 5, T28N, R99W

These trailside burials are probably from the period 1845-60. The location is from a manuscript map by Paul C. Henderson.
USGS map, Atlantic City, Wyo., 1:24,000, 1953 ed.

MORMON MAIL STATION (Seminoe Cutoff)$_P$
(Site 1, Burnt Ranch Vicinity Map)
Mile 903.4 — Fremont County, Wyo.
NW¼ of SE¼, Sec. 26, T28N, R100W

This station, on Brigham Young's mail route to Salt Lake City, was important to the story of communication with the Mormon community there.
Author's note, Sept. 9, 1972. The foundation of this station is on the west bank of Meadow Creek, at the crossing of the Seminoe Cutoff below Oregon Slough (0.4 mile south of the Burnt Ranch monument). Foundation stones and occupational debris have been found at the site.
A manuscript map by Paul C. Henderson notes this as "Mormon Mail Station—1854 (South Pass Station)."
USGS map, Continental Peak, Wyo., 1:24,000, 1958 ed.

BURNT RANCH STATION$_P$
(Site 2, Burnt Ranch Vicinity Map)
Mile 905.0 — Fremont County, Wyo.
NW¼ of NE¼, Sec. 26, T28N, R100W

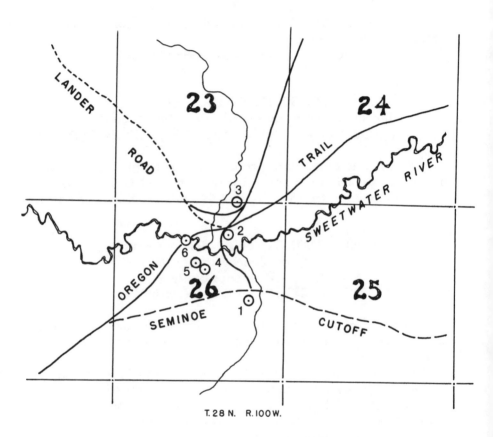

OREGON TRAIL

BURNT RANCH VICINITY MAP

T. 28 N.   R. 100 W.

NOTES

1. MORMON MAIL STATION
2. BURNT RANCH MONUMENT
3. MILLER, ET. AL., GRAVES
4. NINTH CROSSING
5. BARNETTE & BRYAN GRAVES
6. OLD BRIDGE

MILES

ALH '72

Variously known as Gilbert's Station, Upper Sweetwater Station, South Pass Station, possibly as South Pass City, and—after 1868—Burnt Ranch (from the success of Indians in burning it), this station was at the last crossing of the Sweetwater River. It was here that the Seminoe Cutoff rejoined the original Oregon Trail, and here also Lander's Road diverged from it.

Because of its importance in the protection of emigrant and other traffic, this station was a particular objective of Indian harassment.

O. Allen, 1858. "Last crossing of Sweet Water at Gilbert's station and Forks of Lander Pacific Wagon Road, U.S. Mail Station No. 31 . . .'." [8: 65]

Sir Richard Burton, 1860. "Near this spot, since my departure, has been founded 'South Pass City,' one of the many mushroom growths which the presence of gold. . . ." [56: 178]

Henry R. Herr, Aug. 3, 1862. "South Pass City, N.T. Rocky Mtns. At Sweetwater River there is 100 soldiers camped. Sunday evening 50 head of mules were stolen and several men shot dead by Indians. Indians here are bad." [175: diary]

The marker at Burnt Ranch is discolored from the rubbing of range cattle.

William H. Jackson, Aug. 30, 1866. "Laid over a day at South Pass station to fix broken wagon tongue." [201: 132]

William J. Ghent, 1934. ". . . site of the Burnt Ranch station of a later day." Notes that Capt. Nickerson set a stone at the site. [149: 138, 252]

WPA Writers' Project, 1939. ". . . a stage and telegraph station of the early days, was twice burned by Indians." [146: 193]

Bureau of Land Management, 1967. ". . . Burnt Ranch, also known as Gilbert's Station and South Pass Station. This historic site served as a rest stop for the Concord stage, a Pony Express Station, and a telegraph relay station. From 1862 to 1868, a unit of the 11th Ohio Volunteers was garrisoned at this site to protect the emigrant trains and stages using Lander's cut-off and the Old Oregon Trail. Shortly after the troops abandoned the station, it was burned to the ground by Indians. Later rebuilt, it was burned again—hence the name 'Burnt Ranch'." [54: folder]

Author's note, Sept. 9, 1972. The Burnt Ranch monument is a slate post—well greased by the rubbing of range cattle—which states only: "Burnt Ranch / Oregon Cal. / Trail / 1913." It stands about 100 feet west of a large cellar hole which may have been under the station building. According to Paul C. Henderson, there were emigrant campgrounds both east and west of the station site (Virgil Pringle's diary indicates the upper campground extended up to a mile above the Ninth Crossing.)

USGS map, Atlantic City, Wyo., 1:24,000, 1953 ed.

LANDER'S ROAD (EAST JUNCTION)ₚ
(See Burnt Ranch Vicinity Map)
Mile 905.1 — Fremont County, Wyo.
NE¼ of Sec. 26, T28N, R100W

An alternate route for Oregon Trail traffic from Burnt Ranch to Fort Hall was in use after 1859. Built by Frederick West Lander, an engineer of the Department of the Interior, it was the only portion of the Oregon Trail route deliberately built as a road for the use of the emigration.

Henry R. Herr, Aug. 3, 1862. "South Pass City, N.T. . . . We took the Lander Cut-off here [it] being 100 miles shorter . . . there are 150 wagons including the Gov't train & as it is dangerous to travel alone can only make 20 miles a day with them." [175: diary]

Elizabeth A. Stone, 1924. ". . . Frederick West Lander, an engineer in the Department of the Interior . . . estimated cost . . . seventy thousand dollars . . . workmen, under a contractor . . . William F. McGraw . . . out with a military escort the previous fall, but reached South Pass too late to begin . . . winter the party scattered . . . summer of 1858 work was begun . . . Twenty miles of heavy pine forest was cleared, ten miles of willows, and upward of four hundred thousand cubic yards of earth was excavated." [368: 64]

E. Douglas Branch, 1929. Provides biographical information on Lander. [45: 174-75]

Peter T. Harstad, 1968. General information on the Lander Trail. [166: 14-28]

USGS map, Atlantic City, Wyo., 1:24,000, 1953 ed.

CHARLES MILLER (et. al.) GRAVES_P
(Site 3, Burnt Ranch Vicinity Map)
Mile 905R¼ - Fremont County, Wyo.
SE¼ of SW¼, Sec. 23, T28N, R100W

A group of unmarked graves is on the ridge east of Slaughterhouse Gulch. One of these is the grave of Charles Miller, Lander's meteorologist, who was killed by a Mormon in 1858. Only five graves can be clearly discerned, but there may be more.

These are probably only a few of the many burials in this vicinity.

Author's note, Sept. 9, 1972. These graves were located from information provided by Paul C. Henderson. The fact that Miller is among them is all that is known about the burials here.

USGS map, Atlantic City, Wyo., 1:24,000, 1953 ed.

NINTH CROSSING OF SWEETWATER RIVER_P
(Sites 4, Burnt Ranch Vicinity Map)
Mile 905.1 — Fremont County, Wyo.
N½ of Sec. 26, T28N, R100W

One crossing leads directly to the Mormon Mail Station on Oregon Slough (probably a later connection to the Seminoe Cutoff). The other now is marked by a rickety and unsafe wooden bridge, and appears to be the original crossing.

Virgil Pringle, July 14, 1846. ". . . to the last crossing of Sweetwater where we made our noon halt." [275:I, 176]

Sir Richard Burton, 1860. Notes the crossing as ten miles from South Pass. [56: 178]

USGS map, Atlantic City, Wyo., 1:24,000, 1953 ed.

BARNETTE & BRYAN GRAVES_P
(Site 5, Burnt Ranch Vicinity Map)
Mile 905R — Fremont County, Wyo.
SW¼ of NW¼, Sec. 26, T28N, R100W

These are the graves of Joe Barnette, who died Aug. 26, 1844, and a Mrs. Bryan, who died in July 1845, probably the 25th. Lost sight of since the 1930s, the two graves were rediscovered by Lawrence Eno among sagebrush on the bench south of Sweetwater River. Mrs. Bryan's headstone is shown on the opposite page.

USGS map, Atlantic City, Wyo., 1:24,000, 1953 ed.

Lawrence Eno of New York City made this picture of the Bryan grave in the summer of 1982.

This ramshackle bridge marks the site of the ninth crossing of the Sweetwater River.

4

South Pass to Caldron Linn

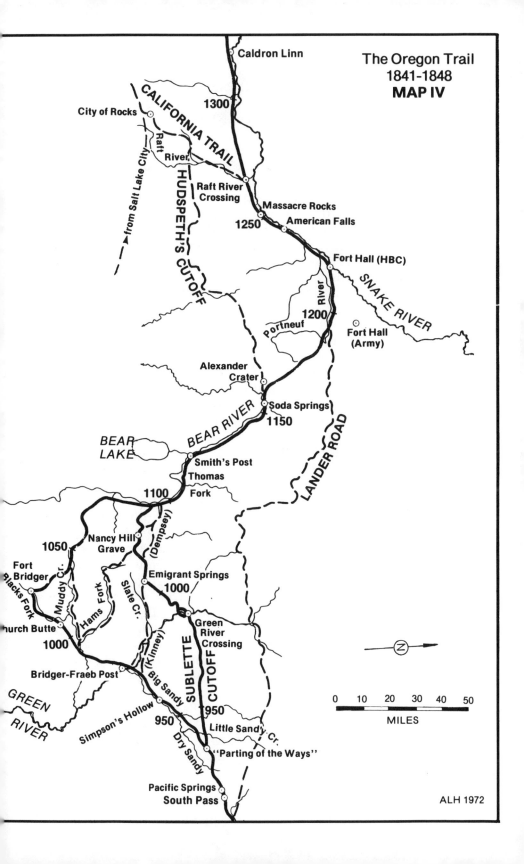

The Oregon Trail
1841-1848
MAP IV

Caldron Linn

1300

City of Rocks

CALIFORNIA TRAIL

Raft River

Raft River Crossing

HUDSPETH'S CUTOFF

from Salt Lake City

Massacre Rocks

1250

American Falls

Fort Hall (HBC)

SNAKE RIVER

Portneuf River

1200

Fort Hall (Army)

Alexander Crater

Soda Springs

1150

BEAR RIVER

LANDER ROAD

BEAR LAKE

Smith's Post

Thomas

1100

Fork

Nancy Hill Grave

1050

(Dempsey)

Fort Bridger

Blacks Fork

Muddy Cr.

Hams Fork

Slate Cr.

Emigrant Springs

1000

Church Butte

1000

(Kinney)

Green River Crossing

SUBLETTE CUTOFF

Bridger-Fraeb Post

Big Sandy

GREEN RIVER

Simpson's Hollow

950

Dry Sandy

950

Little Sandy Cr.

"Parting of the Ways"

Pacific Springs

South Pass

0 10 20 30 40 50

MILES

ALH 1972

SOUTH PASS
Mile 913.9 — Summit of the Continental Divide
Fremont County, Wyo. — SW¼ of NW¼, Sec. 4, T27N, R101W

This is a shallow pass on the continental divide. The crest is approached from the east on an imperceptible grade, but the descent on the west is fairly steep. Two monuments now stand in a fenced enclosure of several acres, and railroad tracks now intrude upon an otherwise wild scene.

Symbolically, this is the most important landmark on the Oregon Trail because it marked the emigrant's arrival at the frontier of the Oregon country. It was also the key to the entire overland route and its half-way point.

Rev. Samuel Parker, Aug. 10, 1835. "The passage through these mountains is in a valley so gradual in the ascent and descent that I should not have known that we were passing them had it not been that as we advanced the atmosphere gradually became cooler. At length we saw the perpetual snows upon our right hand and on our left, elevated many thousand feet above us. . . . There would be no difficulty in the way of constructing a railway from the Atlantic to the Pacific Ocean, and probably the time may not be very far distant when trips may be made across the continent as they have been made to Niagara Falls to see Nature's wonders." [301: 76-77]

Overton Johnson, Aug. 7, 1843. ". . . over the dividing ridge, through the Grand Pass." [208: 85]

Theodore Talbot, Aug. 22, 1843. "Today we set foot in Oregon Territory. . . . 'The land of promise' as yet only promises an increased supply of wormwood and sand." [374: journal]

James A. Pritchard, June 18, 1849. "About 4 p.m. we stood upon the Summit leavel of the Rocky Mountains . . . now upon the dividing Ridge or to use a more forcible figure 'the Backbone of the North American Continent'—And from which the waters flow into the Atlantic & Pacific Ocean. . . . The Platau of the South Pass is from 15 to 20 miles wide—and as you approach the Summit level or the point of culmination it is gradually narrowed down. And the summit level lies immediately between 2 low hills from ¾ to one mile apart, which rise about 150 feet above the plain." [317: 93]

Osborne Cross, July 17, 1849. South Pass, which had nothing to mark it . . ." [101: 140]

J. Goldsborough Bruff, Aug. 1, 1849. ". . . to noon halt,—just about the length of the train beyond the culminating point of

Ezra Meeker, who went west in 1852, placed this monument on the continental divide in 1906.

This small slate marker, placed by Capt. Nickerson in 1916, is the only other marker in South Pass.

the SOUTH PASS of the Rocky Mountains, threw our banner to the breeze, on this elevated and notable back-bone of Uncle Sam's . . . The only marks to designate this particular point, are 3 knolls of decripitating white stone, 2 on the left, and 1 on the right of the trail; left hand ones about 50 yards apart, and the other one 100 yards from them." [52: 60]

William J. Ghent, 1934. ". . . South Pass, which Chittenden puts at 947 miles from the start, and Fremont at 962 . . . at once the approximate halfway post of the journey and also the entrance to what was then known as Oregon." P. 252: Concerning the markers, ". . . a stone slab placed in 1916 by Captain Nickerson," and, . . . one to Mrs. Whitman and Mrs. Spalding, placed by Ezra Meeker." (He has them reversed.) [149: 139, 262]

Author's note, Sept. 9, 1972. About 40 acres at the summit (elevation 7,412 feet) have been fenced to exclude cattle. The summit monument set by Ezra Meeker is a pinkish sandstone a foot thick, two feet wide and round-topped; the Whitman-Spalding monument is an irregular slab of black slate 2 inches thick, a foot wide and two feet high.

USGS map, Pacific Springs, Wyo., 1:24,000, 1958 ed.

PACIFIC SPRINGS$_P$
Mile 916.5 — 2.7 miles west of South Pass
Fremont County, Wyo. — SE¼ of SW¼, Sec. 1, T27N, R102W

The Pacific Springs make their appearance in the valley leading westward from South Pass. They are 300 feet lower than the pass and create an extensive marsh which appears as a green oasis in a bleak, dry landscape. The landmark was often noted by emigrants because it was the first of those western waters toward which they had been striving.

William T. Newley, Aug. 7, 1843. "We left Sweetwater and in 8 miles struck a large spring in Oregon and camped on a small branch." [292: diary]

Overton Johnson, August 7, 1843. ". . . encamped by a marsh, which is one of the sources of Green River." [208: 85]

Samuel Hancock, 1845. ". . . we came to a place where there was good grass and again established our camp; here we soon found an ox mired in apparently solid ground, and in extricating him, observed a peculiarity of the earth which seemed to be floating on the surface of the water, for in walking on it, one would be impressed with the belief, from its waving, rocking motion; this is a somewhat justifiable conclusion as there is an abundance of water in this locality which is known as the Pacific Spring." [162: 20-21]

James Mathers, July 14, 1846. ". . . came to a marshy prairie made by springs from which issues a brook running to the S.W." [275:I, 227]

Miller-Reed diary, July 18, 1846. ". . . 2 miles below on the west Side is the green Spring which You Can See from the Sumit." [275:I, 260]

Charles Stanton, July 19, 1846. ". . . came to a fine spring, with the grass looking green about it. The managers of our company finding it rather boggy, thought the cattle would get mired should they attempt to feed upon the rich herbage, and concluded to go on . . . was the green spring, the first water that flows westward." [275:II, 619]

J. M. Harrison, 1846. "Near summit passed Pacific Spring, the first water flowing into the Pacific." [165: letter]

William Clayton, 1848. "Pacific creek and springs.—Abundance of grass any where for a mile. Good water, and plenty of wild sage for fuel." [78: 16]

James A. Pritchard, June 18, 1849. "Two miles west of the Pass is the Pacific Springs. It rises in a hollow and oozes in from both sides for a mile or more. It is nothing more or less than a perfect Quagmire or marsh, covered with a mat or turf of grass, Sufficiently strong to bear an Ox with ease. So soft is the mud and water that I could shake 25 or 30 feet in diameter." [317: 94]

J. Goldsborough Bruff, August 1, 1849. ". . . we pushed on to the 'Pacific Springs'—fountain source of the Pacific streams . . . camp'd ½ mile above springs in a moist bottom, with rivulet." [52: 62]

Sir Richard Burton, 1860. "The springs are a pond of pure, hard, and very cold water surrounded by a strip of shaking bog, which must be boarded over before it will bear a man." He had more to say about the stage station already in existence at the springs, adding that "the shanty was a trifle more uncomfortable than the average; our only seat a kind of trestled plank." [56: 180]

William H. Jackson, Sept. 1, 1866. "All camped together at Pacific Springs, the first trading post on the western side of the watershed." [201: 132]

Irene D. Paden, 1943. A description of the spring, which appeared thus: "In its mossy border it looked like a huge mirror flush with the turf." P. 236: ". . . log houses . . . date from staging days, when they constituted the important Pony Express and stage station called Pacific Springs . . . are four buildings—two on each side of the old road—widely spaced so that they form the four corners of a rough rectangle. The house faces the old store and barn. The blacksmith shop stares across at the stables. It is now the John Hays horse ranch, and the buildings are in everyday use. In front of the store a sheep wagon idled in the sun." [298: 234, 236]

Author's note, Sept. 9, 1972. The buildings, noted on the USGS map as the "Old Halter and Flick Ranch," are now abandoned. Three of the four buildings described by Mrs. Paden remain, but the fourth—apparently the stage station—is gone, with its location marked by foundations stones shadowed by tall sage.

USGS map, Pacific Springs, Wyo., 1:24,000, 1958 ed.

SOUTH PASS EXHIBIT
Mile 919R¼ — 5 miles west of South Pass
Fremont County, Wyo. — SW¼ of NE¼, Sec. 10, T27N, R102W

This roadside exhibit is 500 feet east of Wyoming State Highway 28. There is a particularly good view of South Pass, Pacific Springs, and Oregon Buttes, five miles to the east, from this point. Several new informational panels and a large parking area were installed by the Bureau of Land Management in 1992.

This site has no historical significance beyound the overview of the South Pass region afforded to highway travelers.

USGS map, Pacific Springs, Wyo., 1:24,000, 1958 ed.

PIONEER GRAVE
Mile 920L½ — 6½ miles west of South Pass
Fremont County, Wyo. — SE¼ of NE¼, Sec. 2 1, T27N, R102W

This grave, shown on Paul Henderson's manuscript map as unidentified, is now known to be the burial place of Charlotte R. Dansie, 33; infant son Joseph, and Caroline Meyers, 25. (Franzwa)

USGS map, Pacific Springs, Wyo., 1:24,000, 1958 ed.

FALSE PARTING OF THE WAYS MONUMENT
Mile 924.5 — 24 miles northeast of Farson, Wyo.
Sublette County — NE¼ of SE¼, Sec. 26, T27N, R103W

A fenced area one-half mile long is adjacent to a parking area along Wyoming Highway 28. It contains fine Oregon Trail ruts and two monuments. The southwestern marker calls attention—incorrectly—to the "Parting of the Ways." In actuality, it marks the deviation of the Green River-South Pass stage road from the route of the Oregon Trail.

The "Parting of the Ways" monument at this place gives unwarranted support to a major historical error which should be corrected; however, the site has genuine historical value as a convenient display of Oregon Trail ruts.

Author's note, July 18, 1972. In addition to the "Parting of the Ways" monument (a 7" x 24" x 6' granite, with incised text), there is another 500 feet northeast. Set by the Historical Landmark Commission of Wyoming in 1950, it is incised: "The Oregon Trail / In Memory Of Those Who / Passed This Way

To / Win And Hold The West."

The rut display, already fenced for preservation, is in a remarkably scenic setting. Paul Henderson called attention to the error being perpetuated at this point, and information available for the true Parting of the Ways bears out his contention (see Mile 932.3).

USGS map, Hay Meadow Reservoir, Wyo., 1:24,000, 1958 ed.

The false Parting of the Ways marker actually locates a minor junction west of South Pass.

PLUME ROCKS
Mile 926R¼ — 23½ miles northeast of Farson, Wyo.
Sublette County — Center of SW¼, Sec. 27, T27N, R103W

This eroded clay formation parallels the Oregon Trail 1.5 miles east of the crossing of the Dry Sandy. It is a minor landmark—less spectacular than its name would indicate.

J. Goldsborough Bruff, Aug. 3, 1849. ". . . on our right, about 300 yds. distant, some low clay bluffs, of a dark dingy red hue, and singularly plume-formed projections on top, from the effects of the elements." [52: 63]

USGS Map "Hay Meadow Reservoir, Wyo.," 1:24,000, 1958 ed.

DRY SANDY CROSSING_P
Mile 927.5 — 22 miles northeast of Farson, Wyo.
Sublette County — NE¼ of NE¼, Sec. 29, T27N, R103W

The Dry Sandy is the first stream reached after leaving Pacific Springs. It is crossed below a broad basin which tends to collect subsurface water. Thus, in dry seasons, water could be had here by digging in the stream bed, but it was tainted with alkali. There was a stage station here in later years.

Above: The Oregon Trail crossing of the Dry Sandy. Below: One of the "tanks" dug by the forty-niners for watering livestock still survives, just west of the crossing of the Dry Sandy.

This was a much-feared locality, where emigrants stopped only when absolutely necessary.

Miller-Reed diary, July 18-19, 1846. ". . . about 6 miles from this spring [Pacific] is dry Sandy which you will avoid as Several Cattle got poisoned by drink the water in the pools." On the following day, the loss of three cattle was attributed to the water at Dry Sandy. Three more died two days later. "[275:I, 260]

William Clayton, 1848. "Dry Sandy.—The water brackish, and not good for cattle. Very little grass, but no wood." [78: 16]

Osborne Cross, July 17, 1849. ". . . compelled to stop on the banks of Dry Sandy . . . water and grass very scarce." [101: 140] Howard Stansbury, August 1849. "Encamped for the night on the banks of Dry Sandy, where we had to dig in the bed of the stream for water; but a very scanty supply was obtained." [361: 70]

O. Allen, 1858. "Dry Sandy—spring east of the crossing in the bed of the creek, the water is brackish and poisonous to stock, fuel scarce, and little or no grass." [8: 65]

Irene D. Paden, 1943. "This disappointing watercourse is ordinarily all that its name implies; but we, like the Forty-niners, were regarding it in the summer of a wet year, and the hot, sandy bottom; between steep banks boasted a string of unappetizing stagnant pools. The emigrant ford is right at the bridge." [298: 236-37]

Author's note, Sept. 9, 1972. There is no longer any bridge at the Dry Sandy crossing and the several watercourses (with three- to four-foot cutbanks) are impassable. The ruin of the Dry Sandy Stage Station is evident south of the Oregon Trail, where a stone foundation 16 feet long, occupational debris and one of L. C. Bishop's iron stakes can be seen.

On the other side of the trail, which here has several close-spaced tracks just west of the stream, are the water-filled pits of several of the "dug-tanks" such as the one described by Joseph G. Bruff, who wrote on August 3, 1849: "Crossed 4 dry sandy ravines, and reached a tank, within 10 paces of the trail, on the right;—It was dug square, containing good cool water, with probably fine clay held in suspension, giving it much the appearance of cream tartar water (solution). A pearl-colored micacious clay (2 ft down to surface of water, water 1 foot deep, well 3 ft. square)." [See 52: 63]

Paul C. Henderson indicates there was an emigrant campground on the flat east of the crossing of Dry Sandy.

USGS map, Hay Meadow Reservoir, Wyo., 1:24,000, 1958 ed.

PARTING OF THE WAYS
Mile 932.3 — 15 miles northeast of Farson, Wyo.
Sweetwater County — SE¼ of NW¼, Sec. 4, T26N, R104W

At this point in an open, sagebrush plain, the Oregon Trail continued to the southwest and the Sublette Cutoff (properly, Greenwood Cutoff) veered right to cross the Little Colorado Desert on a shortcut to the Bear River.

The cutoff was opened in 1844. It saved about 46 miles over the route through Fort Bridger, but it included 50 waterless miles and was not popular until the gold rush period. It was here that emigrants had to decide whether to gain a few miles or favor their livestock.

James Mather, July 16, 1846. After camping at "Little Sandy" (the Dry Sandy, by his distance from Pacific Springs), he wrote: "Our company separated to-day, eight waggons takeing the common rout and the others with Major Cooper took what is called the cutoff." [275:I, 227]

Dr. T. Pope Long in a letter dated July 19, 1846, wrote: "The Oregon route may be considerably shortened by avoiding Fort Bridger, and passing a stretch of forty five miles without water but most companies go that way."—by Bridger. [275:II, 623]

From the *Oregon Spectator*, May 13, 1847: "We would advise the immigrants after recruiting upon Sweetwater to take Greenwood's, "cut off' into Bear River Valley, by doing which they will save a detour of several days journey." [275:II, 729]

James A. Pritchard, June 19, 1849. "We nooned today at the forks of the road. The left hand of which led to Fort Bridger and to Salt Lake, and the right hand road led to the *Sublett* or Greenwood cutoff a distance of 19 ms from the South Pass. Here we took the right hand road." P. 155, Note 48: Shows that only 5 of the first 12 trains in 1849 took the cutoff. "The disadvantage of this route was the long, waterless stretch of more than 50 miles from the Big Sandy to Green River. Pritchard uses both the old and new names for the cutoff. Bruff's map disallows the propriety of calling the Greenwood Cutoff the Sublette Cutoff, applying the latter name to a route approximating what became the Lander Cutoff. Bruff says in his diary on August 2, "It is call'd by the emmigrants, very improperly, 'Sublette's Cut-off,' but it was discovered by another mountaineer,—Greenwood [in 1844]; and should be called 'Greenwood's CutOff.' [William L.] Soublette had discovered and traveled a short cut higher up, from near the base of 'Fremont's Peak,' to Fort Hall, which is

Above: Only a small rock, placed by Bruce McKinstry and L. C. Bishop, marked the true Parting of the Ways. Even that disappeared during the 1970s. Below: Wilma Haines examines a marker for the Sublette Cutoff, in the desolate landscape just west of the Parting of the Ways.

only practicable for mules, and now probably nearly obliterated."
P. 147, Note 20: ". . . Solomon [Sublette], gave to Joseph E.
Ware the information which led Ware in his *Emigrants' Guide to
California* (St. Louis, 1849) to 'take the liberty' of renaming the
old Greenwood Cutoff west of South Pass the 'Sublette Cutoff.'"
(Pritchard mis-identified the Sublette as Andrew W., second
youngest of the five brothers.) [317: 94, 147, 155]

J. Goldsborough Bruff, August 3, 1849. *"(Forks of road 4 or 5
miles before reaching 'Little Sandy')* The road forks,—left branch
to Fort Bridger, Salt Lake &c. and the right is the cut-off route.
At the Forks of the road . . . had a meeting, when all of them
followed me on the 'Cut-off 'except 2 ox wagons . . . A great
many trains have already preceded us on this route—broad &
well beaten trail . . . at the Forks there was a stick driven in the
ground, with a board nailed on it, plastered with notices, of
what companies, men, &c. and when, they had passed, on either
route; & desiring friends in the rear to hurry up, &c. A notice
requested travelers to throw stones up against the base, to
sustain the stick." [52: 66]

Osborne Cross, 1849. Took the cutoff because he thought it
least used in 1849. [101: 141]

Thomas Christy, June 15, 1850. "At 3 o'c we arrived at the
junctions of the Fort Hall & Salt Lake roads, distant 17 miles
from P Springs. Here we judged from the appearance of the
roads that the greatest emmigration had gone by way of Salt
Lake, so we concluded to take cut off (Subletts) on account of
grass, as ther was not so many going that way." [71: 44]

WPA Writers' Project, 1939. "While the majority of the
emigrants for many years went southwest from this point to Fort
Bridger, others made short cuts, turning west over routes followed
by the fur traders, the chief of which was known as Sublette's
Cutoff. It was not popular." [146: 196]

Author's note, Sept. 9, 1972. A small marker of red sandstone,
about 12" x 15" with a rounded top, was placed at this important
trail junction by McKinstry and Bishop in 1956. It is marked with
a left-pointing arrow, followed by "F. Bridger," and a right-
pointing arrow, followed by "S. Cut off." The vegetation at the
site is sparse sagebrush, and the vista is very open.

An entry in Bruff's diary for Aug. 10, 1849, concerning a grave
he saw at the crossing of the Sublette Cutoff over Ham's Fork,
shows that the cutoff was in use in 1847. He copied from the
marker: "Died July 2 1st, 1847, Mr. Beverly Appron."

USGS map, Parting of the Ways, Wyo., 1:62,500, 1958 ed.

LITTLE SANDY CROSSING (Sublette Cutoff)
Mile 937.0 — 18 miles northeast of Farson, Wyo.
Sweetwater County — Center of NE¼, Sec. 2, T26N, R105W

This was the first good water beyond Pacific Springs. The water at Dry Sandy crossing was suspect, and thus avoided if possible.

James A. Pritchard, June 19, 1849. "We crossed the Little Sandy filled our casks with water." [317: 94]

J. Goldsborough Bruff, Aug. 4, 1849. "At 6 A.M. we rolled on over Little Sandy, & Westerly . . ." [52: 67]

Thomas Christy, June 15, 1850. ". . . 4 m. brought us to Little Sandy. Here we filled our water cans and drove about 3 miles and camped." [71: 44]

USGS map, Big Sandy Reservoir SE, Wyo., 1:24,000, 1969 ed.

LITTLE SANDY CROSSING (Fort Bridger Route)ₚ
Mile 940.9 — 7 miles northeast of Farson, Wyo.
Sweetwater County — NE¼ of SW¼, Sec. 28, T26N, R105W

Those travelers who followed the road to Fort Bridger found the Little Sandy crossing to be the first good water since Pacific Springs. A stage station was established on the west bank of the stream about 1,500 feet from the crossing. The ruin of this Little Sandy Station has 13 graves nearby.

Early references to the route at this point are found in the following:

William T. Newly, Aug. 8, 1843. [292: diary]
Theodore Talbot, Aug. 24, 1843 [374: journal]
Pierson B. Reading, Aug. 8, 1843. [319: journal]
Samuel Parker, July 10, 1845. [302: diary]
USGS map, Eden Reservoir East, Wyo., 1:24,000, 1968 ed.

BIG SANDY CROSSING (Sublette Cutoff)
Mile 943.1 — 9.7 miles north of Farson, Wyo.
Sweetwater County — SE¼ of NE¼, Sec. 11, T26N, R106W

The 45 miles of Little Colorado Desert between the Big Sandy River and the Green River were without water, except for pools left by infrequent rains. Thus, the Big Sandy Crossing was a particularly important watering place, where all available containers were filled. The Argonauts, in their haste, were tempted to chance the desert crossing, where the Oregon emigrants usually took the safer, roundabout route by Fort Bridger. The Little Colorado Desert is still an isolated, dangerous locality; travelers should not attempt to travel its unimproved roads without special equipment.

James A. Pritchard, June 20, 1849. ". . . we reached an crossed Big Sandy at 7 AM—The starting point to cross the Greenwood or Sublett's cutoff . . . our intention in the first place to stop here and rest our mules till evening. Then start and make a night travel across this desert of 45 ms. without water as the practice has heretofore been . . . [but decided] as the day was cool to take with us water for our mules & selves and travel till night which would bring us nearly to Green River. And then depend upon the dew to water our animals that night, and make the trip early next morning. At a distance of 7 ms we found a pool of water to the left of the road . . . [from] raines. Here we watered . . . country . . . leavel, Slightly undulated, no timber, but plenty of wild Sage. . . . road is firm . . . untill you get within 15 miles of Green River. . . . there on to the river . . . cut up very much by deep ravines." [317: 94-95]

J. Goldsborough Bruff, Aug. 4, 1849. "This stream is a larger edition of Little Sandy: wider bottoms, bounded by cliffs, above the road: and having long low banks of sand. The grass in the bottoms grazed off . . . The 'Wolverine Rangers,' Capt. Potts, had been camp'd on the opposite side of us, in the bottom, just above the road, and had broken up a wagon, leaving the sides &c for the benefit of our cooks. We also found on their campground several hundred weight of fat bacon, beans, lead, iron, tools, a cast-iron stove, &c. . . . Having filled up our water kegs and canteens, at 4 P.M., we left, for the *long drive,* variously estimated, from 35 to 55 ms. without water." [52: 67-68]

Thomas Christy, June 16, 1850. "Two miles further brought us to Big Sandy. Crossed over and traveled down the river two miles. Found good grass. Camp . . . concluded to stay here until tomorrow morning, when we will start on the desert, a distance of 35 miles some say, others 43 . . . [p. 46, June 17] Filled up all our water vessels for the desert. We will start in an hour or less and try it and see if it is as large an Elephant as is represented." [71: 45-46]

Sir Richard Burton, 1860. He notes that beyond Big Sandy lies "a *mauvaise terre,* sometimes called the First Desert, and upon the old road water is not found in the dry season, within forty-nine miles—a terrible *journada* for laden wagons with tired cattle." [56: 185]

USGS map, Eden Reservoir West, Wyo., 1:24,000, 1968 ed.

WILLIAM ASHLEY'S CAMP
Mile 946R1½ — 3½ miles north of Farson, Wyo.
Sweetwater County — NE¼ of NW¼, Sec. 10, T25N, R106W

This is the site of Gen. Ashley's camp of March 16, 1825, on the Big Sandy River. The location is from a manuscript map by Paul C. Henderson.

USGS map, Eden Reservoir West, Wyo., 1:24,000, 1968 ed.

BIG SANDY CROSSING (Fort Bridger Route)p
Mile 949.3 — Farson, Wyo.
Sweetwater County — SE¼ of SE¼, Sec. 28, T25N, R106W

Emigrants on the trail through Fort Bridger crossed the Big Sandy River here. This also was the site of a stage station.

Sir Richard Burton, 1860. ". . . stream Wagahongopa, or the Glistening Gravel Water. We halted for an hour to rest and dine; the people of the station, man and wife, the latter very young, were both English, and of course Mormons; they had but lately become tenants of the ranch." [56: 185]

Irene D. Paden, 1943. ". . . Big Sandy was, of itself, clear and wholesome, but during rush years was fouled by the rotting flesh of animals that died trying to fill their baggy hides with green willow from the banks." [298: 238]

Wallace Stegner, 1964. ". . . at Farson, on the Little Sandy. Here is a spot for a Mormon to pause at . . . here [June 28, 1847] that the pioneers camped to confer with Jim Bridger." [363: 305]

Author's note, July 28, 1972. The two monuments on the west side of U.S. Highway 187, in Farson, are: a granite slab with a Pony Express medallion, incised, "The Site Of / Big Sandy Station / Gift Of Andrew Arnott / To The State Of Wyoming," and a blunt obelisk of concrete carrying a bronze tablet which refers erroneously to "Little Sandy Crossing." The station site is about 400 feet east of the stream crossing and faces on the main street of Farson.

USGS map, Farson, Wyo., 1:24,000, 1963 ed.

CHARLES HATCH GRAVE_P
Mile 951L1 - 2 miles southwest of Farson, Wyo.
Sweetwater County — NW¼ of Sec. 6, T24N, R106W

This grave is on the west bank of the Big Sandy River, atop the 50-foot bluff which borders the stream. The location is on range land back of irrigated hay fields. It is a pioneer grave of the gold rush era.

Author's note, Sept. 9, 1972. The headstone is marked, "In Memory / Of Charles / Hatch HO / Died June 12, 1850." Scratched in lightly to the right of the top two lines is, "Killed by Indians." There is a footstone

The grave of Charles Hatch, near Farson, Wyo.

and remnants of a woven-wire fence. The headstone is 3" x 10" x 14" above ground, and cracked across the middle. There may be another gravesite about 100 feet south of the Hatch grave.

Delmer Brooks, from Farson, has stated that a land-leveling operation on his ranch just outside of town uncovered a segment of the Oregon Trail. Beneath the sod, the soil within the track was powdery. In it he found a brass Army button.

USGS map, Farson, Wyo. 1:24,000, 1968 ed.

SIMPSON'S HOLLOW (SIMPSON'S GULCH)
Mile 959L½ — 9½ miles southwest of Farson, Wyo.
Sweetwater County — SW¼ of NW¼, Sec. 31, T24N, R107W

On October 5, 1857, Mormon riders under Lot Smith captured a train of 23 wagons loaded with subsistence supplies for Gen. Albert Sidney Johnston's army, then advancing upon Utah. The wagons and freight were burned at this place, which was probably named for train-master Lew Simpson of the Russell, Majors & Waddell Company.

This was a colorful episode of the Mormon War. Destruction of this and two other trains, with a loss of 368,000 pounds of rations, was a serious blow to the invading force, preventing them from reaching Salt Lake City that fall.

Charles A. Scott, Oct. 5, 1857. ". . . Our rear followed by a party of mounted Mormons—News received of the burning of a supply train, by Mormons on the Big Sandy."

(A note from the same source states: "Altogether two trains, consisting of 75 wagons, were burned by Lot Smith, a major in the Nauvoo Legion. William A. Hickman, *Brigham's Destroying Angel* (New York, 1872), 120; T.B.H. Stenhouse, *The Rocky Mountain Saints* (Salt Lake City, 1904), 368; Ray B. West, Jr., *Kingdom of the Saints* (New York, 1957), 258." [370: 164]

Sir Richard Burton, 1860. "After twelve miles driving we passed through the depression called Simpson's Hollow, and somewhat celebrated in local story. Two semicircles of black still charred the ground; on a cursory view they might have been mistaken for burnt-out lignite. Here, in 1857, the Mormons fell upon a corralled train of twenty-three wagons, laden with provisions and other necessaries for the Federal troops, then halted at Camp Scott awaiting orders to advance. The wagoners, suddenly attacked, and, as usual, unarmed,—their weapons being fastened inside their awnings,—could offer no resistance, and the whole convoy was set on fire except two conveyances, which were left to carry back supplies for the drivers till they could reach their homes. On this occasion the *dux facti* was Lot Smith, a man of reputation for hard riding and general gallantry. The old saint is always spoken of as a good man who lives by 'Mormon rule of Wisdom' . . . no blood was spilt . . . They still boast loudly of the achievement, and on the marked spot where it was performed, the juvenile emigrants of the creed erect dwarf graves and nameless 'wooden' tomb-'stones' in derision of their enemies." Speaking of the other train burned somewhere between Green River Station and Hams Fork Station, Burton writes, P. 192: ". . . the black stains had bitten into the ground like the blood marks in the Palace of Holyrood—a neat foundation for a structure of superstition. Not far from it was a deep hole, in which plunderers had 'cached' the iron-work which they were unable to carry away." [56: 186, 192]

USGS map, Simpson Gulch SE, Wyo., 1:24,000, 1968 ed.

UNIDENTIFIED GRAVES
Mile 959L¾ — 9½ miles southwest of Farson, Wyo.
Sweetwater County — NW¼ of SE¼, Sec. 31, T24N, R107W

This is a group of emigrant graves on the bluff above the Big

Sandy River, northeast of the mouth of Simpson Gulch. There was a fording-place at the mouth of the gulch.

Irene D. Paden, 1943. ". . . the graves in the stretch of river bank where the coulee of Simpsons Hollow opens out to the Big Sandy . . . herder . . . Yes, there were graves there—quite a lot, he told us, getting more and more indistinct as years passed until now he remembered where to find only one or two. As a boy he had considered it almost a trail cemetery." [298: 239]

Author's note, Sept. 9, 1972. According to Karen Buck Rennells, members of a local historical group found graves in this vicinity during the summer of 1972, calling them casualties of the burning of the government supply train (but it is a matter of record that no lives were lost in that incident).

Delmer Brooks, a rancher contacted at Farson, remembers seeing graves in the vicinity when he was a boy. He stated that a branch of the Oregon Trail came down the east bank of the Big Sandy River to a ford near the mouth of Simpsons Hollow, hence the traffic up the gulch.

USGS map, Simpson Gulch SE, Wyo., 1:24,000,1968 ed.

BIG TIMBER STATION
Mile 966.2 — 17 miles southwest of Farson, Wyo.
Sweetwater County — NE¼ of SW¼, Sec. 19, T23N, R108W

Big Timber station stood at a three-way junction in the Oregon Trail. The Slate Creek-Kenney route bore off to the right (west) of the primary route, and a little used route to a lower crossing of the Green River forded the Big Sandy River about 400 feet south of the station (departing left from the primary route). The station stood on the lip of a sandy bench, about 25 feet above the marshy river bottom.

Irene D. Paden, 1943. "Just where the Fort Bridger road swung over to touch the Big Sandy for the second time, the emigrants of the fifties found a fork in the trail. By turning right they might travel Kinney's Cutoff, favored above the Sublette Cutoff because of its commendable manner of arriving at water every fifteen or twenty miles. At the fork was a trading post of logs elegantly roofed with poles and brush." [298: 238]

USGS map, Gasson Bridge, Wyo., 1:24,000, 1963 ed.

LOMBARD FERRY_p
Mile 974.2 — 23.7 miles southwest of Farson, Wyo.
Sweetwater County — SE¼ of Sec. 18, T22N, R109W

A commercial ferry was developed at the site of this early Oregon Trail crossing of the Green River. Evidences of the ferry are said to remain, but the area is relatively inaccessible. It is 2.2 miles above the mouth of the Big Sandy River, and probably was the most important of many crossing places in the vicinity.

Irene D. Paden, 1943: "Later companies crossed almost at the mouth of the Big Sandy at what was called the Lombard Ferry." P. 241: "There were one or two fords, but they could be used only before the spring floods, or late in the summer. The professional guides could force the wagons through the current by tripling teams and using a dozen or so mounted outriders. So narrow was the 'safe' strip of gravel bar where they felt their precarious way that a deviation of ten feet meant loss of a wagon . . . in the summer of '47, came the ubiquitous Mormon and his ferryboats. By '49 several were needed at the main crossings. It was a money-making venture . . . three to four dollars a wagon." P. 242: "The crossing used in later years by the wagons bound for Fort Bridger became known as the Lombard Ferry . . . its western landing . . . marked by the ruins of several stone buildings and a snubbing post to which the ferry ropes were attached." [298: 240-42]

Author's note, Sept. 8, 1972. The site was not reached. Unfortunately, it was approached from the Little Colorado Desert, on the north side of the Green River, where the existing jeep trails are unsuited to passenger car travel. The approach should be from Granger, Wyoming. The name of the ferry is derived from the Lombard Buttes, west of the Green River.

Paul Henderson believed the early Oregon Trail crossing (ford) to be 1.3 miles above the mouth of the Big Sandy River; that is, in the NW¼ of Sec. 29, T22N, R109W, or nearly a mile below the ferry site. References to the early crossing are:

Pierson B. Reading, Aug. 11, 1843. [319: journal]
William T. Newley, Aug. 10- 11, 1843. [292: diary]
Theodore Talbot, Aug. 25-26, 1843. [374: journal]
Samuel Penter, 1843. [311: recollection]
Edward Parrish, Aug. 27-28, 1844. [305: diary]
Samuel Parker, July 13-14, 1845. [302: diary]
Dale L. Morgan, 1960. [274: April, 51-69]
Mrs. Paden makes this comment concerning the early crossing

of the Green River: ". . . traders' caravans and the early wagon trains skirted the desert proper to the southeast, remaining near the Big Sandy until well within the angle of its confluence with the Green and then striking up the east bank of the great river about twenty miles to a crossing near the mouth of Slate Creek." [298: 240]

William Ghent considered the Green River crossing to vary greatly. He says: "The main Trail kept down the general course of the Big Sandy until it approached the Green, when it broke into a number of branches. To judge from the diarists, the Green crossing was anywhere from the mouth of Big Sandy to fifteen miles above it." [149: 140]

USGS map, Thoman School, Wyo., 1:24,000, 1963 ed.

GREEN RIVER STATION$_p$
Mile 976.0 — 20 miles northeast of Granger, Wyo.
Sweetwater County — SW¼ of NW¼, Sec. 29, T22N, R109W

This stage station was one mile northwest of the mouth of the Big Sandy River, according to a manuscript map prepared by Paul C. Henderson.

USGS map, Lombard Buttes, Wyo., 1:24,000, 1963 ed.

BRIDGER-FRAEB TRADING POST (Probable Site)
979L2 — 17½ miles northeast of Granger, Wyo.
Sweetwater County — NW¼ of Sec. 8, T21N, R109W

This trading post was established by Jim Bridger and Henry Fraeb, shortly before the death of the latter. Bridger and his new partner did not see fit to continue at that location, so the useful life of the post was probably less than a year (1841-1842). It was west of the Green River, below Dry Creek. It was gone before the emigration reached a substantial volume, although a few mention the site.

Miller-Reed diary, July 25, 1846. ". . . down green River about 4 miles to Bridgers New fort where we turned to the right to Black's fork. . . . the fort is now vacant, Bridger having removed to his old Fort on Black's fork." Pp. 430-31, have an extended discussion of Bridger's two forts. Presumably this one was built on Green River in August 1841 and, after Fraeb's death, Bridger and his new partner, Louis Vasquez, relocated on Black's Fork

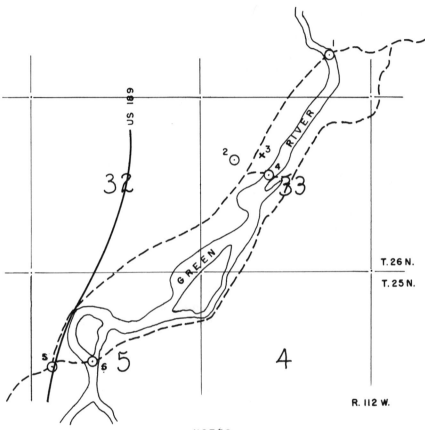

OREGON TRAIL

NAMES HILL VICINITY MAP

NOTES

1. GREEN RIVER FORD
2. UNIDENTIFIED GRAVES
3. BURNED WAGONS
4. THE MORMON FERRY
5. NAMES HILL
6. MOUNTAIN MEN'S FERRY

ALH '72

in 1842—first on a bluff, but, in the summer of 1843, in the valley bottom at the present Fort Bridger site. [275:I, 261, 430-431]

USGS map, Lombard Buttes, Wyo., 1:24,000, 1963 ed.

GREEN RIVER CROSSING_P
Mile 981L4 — 16½ miles northeast of Granger, Wyo.
Sweetwater County — SE¼ of SE¼, Sec. 17, T21N, R109W

This crossing of the Green River is four miles below the mouth of the Big Sandy River. It was used by those who preferred to cross the Big Sandy at the site of Big Timber Station, and thus descend the cast bank of the Green to this crossing. The location is from a manuscript map prepared by Paul C. Henderson.

Dale L. Morgan, 1960. This crossing is described in his discussion of the Green River ferries of the forty-niners. [274: April, 51-69] Refer to the Lombard Ferry for additional information on the Green River crossings.

USGS map, Lombard Buttes, Wyo., 1:24,000, 1963 ed.

GREEN RIVER FORD (Approximate Location)
(Site 1, Names Hill Vicinity Map)
Mile 985.0 — Lincoln County, Wyo.
SE¼ of Sec — 28, T26N, R112W

This crossing of the Green River was available to emigrants after the spring freshet had subsided. The actual point of crossing varied somewhat from year to year, as the gravel bars changed, but it was essentially at the mouth of Steed Canyon, south of LaBarge, Wyo.

It was a very important crossing to early emigrants before the gold rush; less so after commercial ferries were established here in 1849.

James A. Pritchard, June 21, 1849. "We found our way into the river bottom by a precipitous and difficult decent from the top of a very high bluff." P. 156, Note 50: "The Green was high and swift in in 1849, and no one seems to have forded before Samuel McCoy on July 29." [317: 96]

J. Goldsborough Bruff, Aug. 5, 1849. ". . . sort of bold rugged promontory, the base of which rests in the bottom of Green

River valley. . . . look down on the perilous descent the wagons had to make. . . . It was however deep sand, lumps of clay, and loose stones & fragments of slate. From the crest down to base, right and left, were fragments of disasters, in the shape of upset wagons, wheels, axles, running gear, sides, bottoms, &c. &c.— Nothing daunted, we double-locked, and each teamster held firmly to the bridle of his lead mules, and led down, in succession, till the whole train reached the valley below, about ½ of a mile. . . . We followed the base of these tall heights, for some distance . . . over deep dusty irregular small hills, on left side of the river, and then turned W to the river; drove in, on its pebbly bottom,—hub deep, and rapid, turned down stream about 150 yds. to a gravel bank, above water, crossed that in about the same distance, and then across the stream again, obliquely 50 yds. to the opposite shore. We drove down the valley ¼ mile, and camped." [52: 70-71]

Irene D. Paden, 1943. ". . . cutoff branched into several terminals at the Green, five of which we know, the ferries were not of necessity near any one of them . . . came over the cliff where it was easiest to get down . . . ferries crossed where river banks and current would permit. In early days it was usually two to four miles from the spot where the teams rushed into the river to the nearest ferry." [298: 256]

Author's note, Sept. 7, 1972. The location given here for the ford is Paul Henderson's; it would be the highest point of crossing. It is likely that crossings were made at various points for a mile downstream—according to conditions in the different years and seasons. In this regard, the early users of the Sublette Cutoff tended to arrive at the Green River after the waters had fallen, and hence forded without difficulty, but the forty-niners, particularly those who pushed hard, had to contend with high water—which required them to ferry.

USGS map, Names Hill, Wyo., 1:24,000, 1968 ed.

UNIDENTIFIED GRAVES
(Site 2, Names Hill Vicinity Map)
Mile 985.8 — Lincoln County, Wyo.
SW¼ of NW¼, Sec. 33, T26N, R112W

This is a group of emigrant graves on a low ridge on the Buck Ranch. Through now unmarked, the location is known. There are indications that a number of wagons were burned nearby.

These are probably burials of the gold rush period. Additional research is required, particularly in connection with the wagon debris.

J. Goldsborough Bruff, Aug. 7, 1849. "A grave, in the bottom, 300 yds. below camp:—'S.R. Webb, Died Aug. 1, 1849, from Selma, Ala.'" The camp was opposite the middle crossing, or Mormon ferry. [52: 73]

Ela Holden, 1927. "Mr. and Mrs. Roney Pomeroy, Mrs. Pomeroy's brother, Robert McIlvain, and wife, who had recently arrived from Kansas, made up an exploration party and leaving home early one Sunday morning they followed the old emigrant road north to where the road crossed Green River about eight or nine miles from Fontenelle. Near this ford they found a meadow which had served as a camping ground in the days when gold seekers crossed the plains. The party found a pile of scrap wagon irons indicating the burning of a wagon train and on higher ground above the meadow was a group of graves marked by boards and endgates of wagons. Mute evidence of a massacre.

"Many years later a Mrs. Ira Dodge wrote an article for publication in *Recreation Magazine* in which she described the group of graves, also sending snapshots of same and a copy of the then legible names on the headboards. Mrs. Dodge received a letter from an old lady living in the East in which the lady wrote that the name copied from one of the graves was that of her father, who had left his home in the East to go West with a party of forty-niners when she was a child and that no information had the family received from the husband and father after he left South Pass. The mother had died without knowing the fate of her husband and the writer, a child when her father left, was now an old lady." [183: 53]

Author's note, Sept. 7, 1972. These graves, on the present Buck Ranch, were obliterated by a former owner who stacked hay on the low ridge where they were.

MORMON FERRY — GREEN RIVER
(Site 4, Names Hill Vicinity Map)
Mile 985.8 — Lincoln County, Wyo.
SE¼ of NW¼, Sec. 33, T26N, R112W

This "drifter," or current-operated ferry, was placed in operation near the end of June 1847, at the middle crossing of the Green River (opposite the Buck Ranch). It was operated the following summer also.

This commercial ferry was a great improvement over the previous practice of fording or improvising a ferry from logs or wagon boxes.

James A. Pritchard, 1849. Crossed at the Mountain Men's ferry June 21, 1849. Note 50: "Mormons who this year manned ferries both on the Salt Lake Road and on the Sublette Cutoff had not yet arrived; they set out from Salt Lake City June 12, but seem unrecorded at this upper crossing before June 30." [317: 156]

Osborne Cross, July 19, 1849. ". . . Green River . . . trail passes down a very steep hill into a deep, sandy gorge which runs to the Mormon ferry." July 20: "The Mormon ferry is about five miles above where we crossed the river, at the foot of a range of high clay bluffs." The distance between ferries is either mis-stated, or the temporary ferry of the mountain men had been moved downstream. [101: 143]

Thomas Christy, June 18, 1850. "There is a ferry here, one boat. It being throng[ed] we concluded to travel down two miles . . ." [71: 47]

John B. Hill, July 1850. ". . . Green River . . . The ferry-man allowed too many passengers to get into the boat, and the water came within two inches of the gunwale. He ordered every man to stand steady, and we stood, as the boat was liable to swamp. . . . A rope with pulleys on it was stretched across the river, and the current carried the boat across. When we were nearly across, the upper edge of the boat dipped a sheet of water an inch deep, from end to end, and I thought the boat would be swamped instantly, turn over upstream, cover all of us under water and drown the last one of us. . . . a few of us jumped to the lower side of the boat, and it was righted at once. . . . At that time Green River was booming." [180: 39]

Irene D. Paden, 1943. "Where the bottoms suddenly widen again we found a group of ranch buildings [present Buck ranch] between us and the river. Our maps showed an old ford at this point, and we drove in. . . . annexing a couple of men . . . as guides to the river bank, and one of the men said that he had heard of a ford . . . back of the sheep corral. . . . Near the fence stood the stone slab that marked the ford. It was dirt encrusted and forgotten." This is one of the slate markers placed by Captain Nickerson." [298: 260-61]

Dale L. Morgan, 1960. An account of the ferries on the Sublette Cutoff. [274: Oct., 167-203]

Author's note, Sept. 7, 1972. Chester Buck, who owned the property where the "Mormon Ferry" is located, pointed out the site. Local tradition has it that Pinckney Sublette was drowned at this ferry, but the error in this is apparent in 160:I, 373-75. The story of the exhumation of the supposed remains of Pinckney and their removal to St. Louis for use in a suit over the Sublette estate, is told by Holden, 183: 62-66. The remains were later returned to Wyoming and reburied near the mouth of Fontenelle Creek.

Author's note, May 1993. Recent information indicates there may have been as many as a dozen ferry crossings across Green River in a space of five miles from the Buck Ranch downstream. USGS map, Names Hill, Wyo., 1:24,000, 1968 ed.

NAMES HILL
(Site 5, Names Hill Vicinity Map)
Mile 987.4 — Lincoln County, Wyo.
NW¼ of SW¼, Sec. 5, T25N, R112W

This is a sandstone cliff several hundred feet long, on the west bank of the Green River. Here emigrants cut names and dates. Names Hill is famous for its "Jim Bridger" signature.

J. Goldsborough Bruff, Aug. 7, 1849. ". . . we moved on: and winding down the bottom, in about 2½ ms. reached an ascent, rather steep, but not high, and just at the foot, on right of trail-20 paces from it, vertical cliffs of a mouse-colored sandstone, on the face of which was engraved with a fine-pointed instrument, an Indian diagram, representing 43 rifles, nearly vertical, and a chief and horse, apparently separated from 4 other Indians and a horse laying down, by a stream with a small fork to it . . . drew it." [A finished sketch published in the *Annual Report* of the Smithsonian Institution (1872), 409-12]. P. 74: "On the Plateau, above, on left of trail, a grave, with sand-stone slab, engraved thus:—'Mary, Consort of J. M. Fulkerson, Died July 14, 1847.' The grave was covered with sand-stone slabs." [52: 74]

Elizabeth A. Stone, 1924. "Only second in importance is Names Rock, a light-colored boulder [cliff] about twenty feet high and one hundred feet wide, that stands seven miles north of the mouth of Fontenelle Creek and about six miles west of Green River. The meadows below were the camping place of many travelers, who climbed the hill to cut in the soft Rock

Above: Site of the Mountain Men's Ferry, on the Green River. Below: The "signature" of Jim Bridger at Names Hill is protected by chain link fencing.

names and dates, many of which are still legible. The name of the scout Jim Bridger is here inscribed, either by a companion, as he could not write, or by some subsequent traveler." [368: 63-64]

Ela Holden, 1927. "Names Hill, located near the old campground, has served as a bulletin board for trapper, scout and gold seeker as the smooth surface is covered with names and dates of those that passed that way." [183: 53]

William J. Ghent, 1934. ". . . on the face of the bluff known as Names Hill, near one of the Green crossings, an inscription was made, and slate slabs were set up at two of the crossings." This refers to Capt. Nickerson's marking of the Oregon Trail in Wyoming. [149: 252]

Irene D. Paden, 1943. "Names Hill—a precipitous, almost over hanging cliff made of great, jutting, flat-surfaced and sharp-edged rocks. At the base sage grew raggedly. We easily found the inscription 'James Bridger—Trapper—1844,' while many other names crowd the available space." P. 260: "At Names Hill the bottoms are wide, but just below the cliff presses close to the river for a short stretch and the modern road has been blasted through at the water's edge." [298: 259-60]

Author's note, Sept. 7, 1972. The portion of the rock face which has Bridger's name on it is enclosed with chain-link fencing. About 150 feet north, at the mouth of a little draw, is a granite monument, incised: "Names Hill / The Old / Green River Crossing / And Rendezvous On The / Old Oregon Trail / Gift Of / First National Bank / Kemmerer, Wyo. / To The State Of Wyoming." The short, steep grade by which the trail climbed up, from where the monument is, to the bench above has been damaged by pipeline or cable laying. No trace remains of the Indian art sketched by Bruff.

Jim Bridger was illiterate, and his "signature" was either carved for him or is spurious.

USGS map, Names Hill, Wyo., 1:24,000, 1968 ed.

"MOUNTAIN MEN'S FERRY" — GREEN RIVER
(Site 6, Names Hill Vicinity Map)
Mile 987.3 — Lincoln County, Wyo.
NE¼ of SW¼, Sec. 5, T25N, R 112W

This ferry was maintained by mountain men from Fort Bridger during the season of high water in the Green River. It accommodated the gold rush traffic over the Sublette Cutoff. Four canoes joined into a raft made up the ferry boat, which operated near Names Hill. (The location may have changed from time to time.) It was an important crossing, although probably less reliable than the Mormon Ferry upstream.

James A. Pritchard, June 21, 1849. "We reached the river at 11 A.M., four miles above the ferry . . . we found there 24 wagons before us, 14 of which were crossed by night. I succeded in effecting a hire of the boat for the night, which was not objected to by those who were ahead of me. We were to furnish the hands to man the boat and pay him $1.50 pr wagon or he would furnish the hands & charge $3.00 pr wagon—prefered the former as we had men . . . who could beat his best hands with ease , . . by 12 we had the whole train over. . . . The ferry Boat was constructed of 4 small Canoes which were roughly rafted togeather. The ferry is kept by some Frenchmen who live in lodges made of skins and proped up with poles. They have Indian Squaws for wifves. . . . Green River is a bold rapid stream about 350 to 400 feet wide with a good deal of water for a stream of its size." P. 156, Note 50: "So far as is known, there had been no commercial ferry on the Green River in 1848, but mountain men supplied from Fort Bridger and associating with the Snake Indians saw the possibilities . . . David Cosad . . . June 15, 1849 . . . wrote: 'There are about 40 French men . . . they keep a ferry which we had to pay $3.00 for Each Wagon' None of the 'French' ferrymen is named in 1849, but next year John Steel found Jim Baker and one McDonald owners of a ferry." [317: 96, 156]

Osborne Cross, July 20, 1849. "The wagons were ferried across. . . . two ferries here, which are only temporary. The Mormon ferry is about five miles above where we crossed the river, at the foot of a range of high clay bluffs." (Either this is a mis-statement of distance or this lower ferry had been shifted downstream during the month following Pritchard's crossing.) [101: 143]

Thomas Christy, June 18, 1850. ". . . down two miles. There is two boats. We will get our turn between now and sundown. . . . 5 oclock all across safe." [71: 47]

Author's note, Sept. 7, 1972. The identification of this crossing is based on Henderson's map position; nothing was found at the site.

USGS map, Names Hill, Wyo., 1:24,000, 1968 ed..

SOUTH BEND STAGE STATION
Mile 996L1¼ — Granger, Wyo.
Sweetwater County — NW¼ of NE¼, Sec. 32, T19N, R111W

Identified here are two buildings, one complete and one ruin. Neither of them are in agreement with an available description of the original South Bend Stage Station with regard to construction or situation. Nor does either structure appear to be as old as is claimed on the monument west of the buildings. If they are Overland Stage related, it is unlikely they antedate 1862, and there remains a possibility that neither is even that old.

Sir Richard Burton, 1860. ". . . reached Hams Fork . . . and there we found a station. The pleasant little stream called by the Indians Turugempa, the 'Blackfoot Water.' The station was kept by an Irishman and a Scotchman—'Dawvid Lewis': It was a disgrace; the squalor and filth were worse almost than the two—Cold Springs and Rock Creek—which had called our horrors, and which had always seemed to be the *ne plus ultra* of western discomfort. The shanty was made of dry-stone piled up against a dwarf cliff to save backwall, and ignored doors and windows. The flies—unequivical sign of unclean living!—darkened the table and covered everything put upon it." These outraged impressions continue. [56: 192]

WPA Writers' Project, 1939. Granger, Wyo. "The Overland Stage Station established here is still standing." [146: 101]

Author's note, Sept. 7, 1972. The purported South Bend Stage Station stands in a fenced plot, facing old Highway 30 about mid-way between the bridge over Black's Fork and the main street which parallels the railroad tracks. The 200-foot square plot deeded to the State of Wyoming contains two structures and a monument. The former are both of stone: one, 20' x 30', is in good condition, with a gabled, shingle roof and exterior plaster; while the other, 20' x 30', is a ruin attached to the main building at the west rear, and without a roof. The granite monument states: "The Old / South Bend / Stage Station / Built In 1850 / Gift Of / E.J. Brandly / And Family / To The State Of Wyoming / In Memory Of / Mrs. E.J. Brandly / On The Oregon Trail / And Pony Express."

A number of facts indicate that the structures given to the state are not as old as claimed: (a) Neither the site nor the structures agree with Sir Richard Burton's description of 1860,

The incongruous ruin of what is known as the South Bend Stage Station, in Granger, Wyoming.

(b) The structures are aligned with the town streets, which are laid out as a grid, oriented according to the direction of the railroad tracks. (The railroad was built through during the summer of 1868.) (c) An examination of door and window casings of the intact structure, and the framing and beams of the ruin, showed only wire nails (manufacture of such nails began in 1892—hand-made square nails would be expected in an 1850 structure, and machine-forged square nails after 1865), (d) The main building is architecturally unusual; that is, its cut-stone walls, brick chimneys, and gabled roof represent a type of contruction common where railroad transportation was available, but unlikely in an isolated 1850 stage building.

It would seem that there is reason to question the statement that these structures are 1850 vintage stage buildings. Further research is in order.

Paul C. Henderson's manuscript map indicates the original Oregon Trail passed more than a mile west of the present town of Granger.

USGS map, Granger, Wyo., 1:24,000, 1961 ed.

HAMS FORK CROSSING_p

Mile 996.0 — 1½ mile west of Granger, Wyo.
Sweetwater County — SE¼ of NW¼, Sec. 30, T19N, R111W

This crossing of the original Oregon Trail is at a point 1.2 miles above the mouth of Hams Fork, and probably near the location of the fur trapper's rendezvous of 1834. The Mormon route in 1847 stayed east of the Oregon Trail from Green River to Hams Fork, passing through the limits of the present town of Granger. The U.S. bridge built on that route in 1857 or 1858 was about 500 feet above the mouth of Hams Fork.

References to the route in this vicinity are found in the following:

William T. Newley, Aug. 11, 1843. [292: diary]
Pierson B. Reading, Aug. 12, 1843. [319: journal]
Theodore Talbot, Aug. 28, 1843. [374: journal]
Edward Parrish, Aug. 28, 1844. [305: diary]
Samuel Parker, July 13-14, 1845 [302: diary]

The naming of Hams Fork is covered by John E. Baur [160:IX, 193]

USGS map, Granger, Wyo., 1:24,000, 1961 ed.

EMIGRANT SPRING

Mile 1006.0 — 18 miles west of Fontenelle, Wyo.
Lincoln County — NW¼ of NW¼, Sec. 13, T23N, R115W

This spring issued from the base of a cliff near the head of Emigrant Creek, a headwater of Slate Creek. The country here is rolling, sage-covered and treeless. It was, nevertheless, an important camping place, near the point of merger of the Slate Creek route with the Sublette Cutoff.

Elizabeth A. Stone, 1924. "At Emigrant Springs, near the postoffice called Supply, is a slate slab marked 'Oregon Trail, 1843-1915.' In the sagebrush near this stone are the graves of several emigrants with unmarked slabs above them." [368: 65]

William J. Ghent, 1934. "At Emigrant Springs, in Lincoln

County, to which the Trail came up from its southward dip to Fort Bridger, a slate slab was placed. . . ." [149, 3253]

Irene D. Paden, 1943. ". . . Sublette Road. It descends to the headwaters of Slate Creek and there coincides for a few miles with the Kinney Trail. It passes Emigrant Springs—yes, another. . . ." [298: 262]

Mrs. Chester Buck, 1972. The earliest readable name on the cliffs above Emigrant Springs is "Joseph Hildt, July 4, 1852," as recorded by the Lincoln County Historical Society. [53: list]

Author's note, Sept. 8, 1972. The spring has been turned into a stock-watering pond and probably bears no resemblance to the watering place the emigrants knew. A search of the area failed to locate either the slate marker or the graves, but they could have been missed in the giant sagebrush—up to eight feet tall—which surrounds the spot.

USGS map, Round Mountain, Wyo., 1:24,000, 1969 ed.

JOHNSTON SCOUT ROCK (Sublette Cutoff)
Mile 1006L¾ — 18 miles west of Fontenelle, Wyo.
Lincoln County — NE¼ of NE¼, Sec. 23, T23N, R115W

This large block of sandstone is one of several which have tumbled from the cliff above. It bears emigrant names and dates, among them "T.C. Johnston L.A. Cary 1860 Scouts," from which the rock has come to be known locally as the Johnston Scout Rock. It is adjacent to the Kinney Cutoff (Mile 1032) about a mile south of the junction with the Sublette Cutoff at Emigrant Spring. This is typical emigrant rock art; in this case, not yet spoiled by modern doodling.

Mrs. Chester Buck, 1972. Members of the Lincoln County Historical Society copied the readable names found on the Johnston Scout Rocks during a summer field trip in 1972. The earliest was that of W.A. Williams, dated July 1850; and the latest was "John Rawson, May 5, 1888"—a span of 38 years. [53: list]

Author's note, Sept. 8, 1972. The rock is about 12 feet high, 10 feet wide and 20 feet long, and its neighbor is of about the same size but standing on end. Most of the readable names are on sheltered surfaces.

USGS map, Round Mountain, Wyo., 1:24,000, 1969 ed.

CHURCH BUTTE ("Solomon's Temple")
Mile 1007.0 — 10 miles southwest of Granger, Wyo.
Uinta County — SW¼ of Sec. 25, T18N, R1113W

Church Butte is a soft sandstone formation about 1,000 feet in diameter which rises 75 to 100 feet above the level of Black's Fork Valley. Weather has sculptured this mound into shapes which the emigrants likened to familiar and imagined things. There was a stage station west of the butte.

John Boardman, Aug. 12, 1843. ". . . crossed Black's Fork and passed Soloman's Temple a surcular mound of clay and stone of the shape of a large temple and decorated with all kinds of images: gods and godesses, everything that has been the subject of the sculptor: all kinds of animals and creeping things, etc. A magnificent sight . . ." [37: 106]

The stone upon which the Church Butte plaque is mounted is so eroded that the tablet seems to be floating on air.

Sir Richard Burton, 1860. ". . . we passed Church Butte, one of the many curious formations lying to the left hand or south of the road. This isolated mass of stiff clay has been cut and ground by wind and rain into folds and hollow channels which from a distance perfectly simulate the pillars, groins and massive buttresses of a ruinous Gothic cathedral. The foundation is level, except where masses have been swept down by the rain, and not a blade of grass grows upon any part. An architect of genius might profitably study this work of nature." [56: 194]

WPA Writers' Project, 1939 ". . . compressed of blue and black sandstone, rise 75 feet above the level of the surrounding hills and resemble a cathedral." [146: 98]

Author's note, Sept. 7, 1972. The weathering of the gray sandstone of this feature has been so great that no readable names could be found. The cast iron plaque which has been fixed in the base, at the point nearest the road, is nearly eroded out, appearing to stand in high relief. The text states: "Church

Butte / Erected July 2, 1930 / In Honor Of The / Mormon Pioneers / Who Passed This Point / Early In July 1847 / And In Subsequent Years.

USGS map, Church Butte, Wyo., 1:24,000.

BURNED WAGON TRAIN (Possible Site)ₚ
Mile 1007.0 - 12 miles southwest of Granger, Wyo.
Uinta County — SW¼ of SW¼, Sec. 35, T18N, R113W

Areas of char and remnants of wagon hardware found at this site are the basis for the tentative presumption that a wagon train was burned here. Further investigation of this site is warranted.

Author's note, Sept. 7, 1972. B. L. Singer, a retired employee of the Mountain Fuel Supply Co. (a pumping station operator), who now lives near Name Rock, supplied directions for locating the site of what he believed to be a burned wagon train. In past years he had recovered many small items of wagon hardware as the wind blew away the light soil. He had also observed areas of char.

No char could be found at the site in 1972, but a number of square nails were recovered, along with a handmade screw and bolt and some unidentifiable iron fragments. The location is exactly upon the trace of the Oregon Trail. This may be the place where another military wagon train was burned by Mormons in 1857. (See Sir Richard Burton's comment on p. 257).

USGS map, Millersville, Wyo., 1:24,000, 1965 ed.

NAME ROCKₚ
Mile 1017.5 — 20 miles southwest of Granger, Wyo.
Uinta County — SW¼ of NE¼, Sec. 33, T17N, R113W

This is a long, low rock face used by emigrants as a name register, but few readable names remain. There is said to be a grave nearby.

Author's note, Sept. 7, 1972. This feature, which is noted on the USGS quadrangle sheet, is about 400 feet long with an exposed face not over 20 feet high. The remaining names are done in wagon tar (none were seen which dated earlier than the 1860s, but the examination was not thorough).

According to B. L. Singer there was a gravesite on the high

Above: Dome-like projections overhang the face of Name Rock, affording protection for pioneer signatures. Below: the Johnston Scout Rocks, "near Emigrant Spring on the Slate Creek Cutoff.

ground which projects into the valley north of Name Rock, about 950 feet distant on Az. 326 degrees true. Surface evidences have been obliterated by jeepers who have developed a road over the ridge at that place. The grave location is in the NW¼ of the NE¼, Sec. 33.

USGS map, Millersville, Wyo., 1:24,000, 1965 ed.

PLACE OF BLACK'S DEATH
Mile 1024.4 — 2½ miles northeast of Fort Bridger, Wyo.
Uinta County — NW¼ of Sec. 26, T16N, Rl 15W

Indians killed a trapper named Black in 1832. It is from him that the Blacks Fork River takes its name.

Heinrich Lienhard, 1846. "In the evening, while I was writing in my diary, a red-headed mountain-man [who has been identified as Joseph Reddeford Walker] asked me whether I was writing a journal. When I admitted that I was, he said that it might interest me to know that 14 years ago, at this spot, over there in the willow thickett, a man named Black had been killed by a band of 50 Blackfoot Indians. For some time, he had courageously defended himself and killed or wounded several of them before they succeeded in doing away with him." Lienhard's party was camped two miles below Fort Bridger and south of the stream (Blacks Fork). [229: 94]

USGS map, Mountain View, Wyo., 1:24,000, 1964 ed.

HAMS FORK CROSSINGS (Sublette Cutoff)
Mile 1025.0 — 8½ miles (lower) and 12¼ miles (upper)
northwest of Kemmerer, Wyo.
Lincoln County — SW¼ of SW¼, Sec. 1, T22N, RI 17W (lower)
Sec. 23, T23N, R117W (upper)

The Sublette Cutoff has two branches here, and these are the points where they passed over Hams Fork.

James A. Pritchard, June 24, 1849. "The descent on the west side [of Commissary Ridge] was so abrupt we were compelled to let our wagons down in part by attaching ropes and letting the men hold on behind. At the foot of the hill we came to what is called Hams fork of the Bear [Green] River, it is about 50 feet wide at this place with a strong current . . . We had to raise our wagon beds 8 or 10 inches to keep the water out." [317: 98]

Thomas Christy, June 20, 1850. ". . . arrived at Hams Fork of Bear [Green] River . . . Crossed it and ascended a long steep hill." [71: 49]

Irene D. Paden, 1943. "Emil Kopac, who has devoted years to a study of the Sublette country, says that both Sublette's Trail and the later Kinney's Trail fork into two divisions before entering the east side of the valley of Hams Fork. The two sectors of Kinney's Trail join again at the river so that there are but three crossings . . . The northern of the two branches of Sublette's Trail crossed Hams Fork at the confluence of Robinson's Creek and followed along its course a short distance. The southern ascended a ridge but soon joined its fellows . . ." [298: 262-63]

Author's note. The Sublette Trail was not field-checked in this vicinity because of poor access. It is likely that reservoir construction has obliterated one or both of these crossings.

FORT BRIDGER (First Trading Post Site)ₚ
Mile 1026.3 — 0.9 mile north of Town of Fort Bridger, Wyo.
Uinta County — NW¼ of NW¼, Sec. 33, T16N, R115W

Trading houses of a temporary nature were established prior to July 1842 on the prominent bench fronting on Blacks Fork just south of the present Wall Reservoir. This post appears to have been abandoned in 1843; however, there was a return to Blacks Fork before 1844, but probably to a different site.

This first trading post appears to have been of little consequence insofar as the emigrants were concerned. There is no evidence that they received material assistance there.

Overton Johnson, August 13, 1843. ". . . we arrived at the Trading House of Messrs Vasques and Bridger . . ." [208: 86]

James W. Nesmith, 1843. ". . . most of our company and men arrived at Fort Bridger, on Black's Fork, Monday, August 14." [290: 347]

Pierson B. Reading, August 14, 1843. "Came 12 miles up stream and camped near Ft. Bridger a small temporary fort buit by a Mr. Bridger, an old trapper." [319: journal]

William T. Newley, Aug. 14, 1843. "We reached Fort Bridger at noon in 8 miles. Lay by rest of day. Mr. Carey's daughter Katherine died. 15. We burry the little girl and travel 8 miles." [292: diary] Theodore Talbot, Aug. 30, 1843. "Came nearly west along Black's Fork passing under the bluff on which Vasquez's and Bridger's houses are built. We found them deserted. . . . they are built of logs plastered with mud . . ." [374: journal]

John Boardman, Aug. 1843. "13. Arrived at Bridger & Vasquez's Fort, expecting to stay 10 or 15 days to make meat, but what our disappointment to learn the Sioux and Cheyenne had been here, run off all the buffalo, killed 3 Snake Indians and stolen 60 horses." [37: journal]

Edward Parrish, Aug. 30, 1844. ". . . camped near the Green River Fort, known as Bridger's Fort. The water and grass are fine. . . . Capt. Walker conducted us to the place of encampment and then returned to his own wigwam among his own Indians of the Snake tribe." [305: reminiscence]

John Minto, Aug. 1844. "On the twenty-ninth we made a good drive to the vicinity of Fort Bridger . . . here a considerable number of mountain men, and some professional gamblers, who went from place to place . . . to prey upon the trappers and hunters. These latter generally have native women, and their camps are ornamented with green boughs and flowers. In some we find men playing cards; near others shooting matches are in progress." P. 166: "James Bridger was doing his own trading . . ." How "quick and sharp at a bargain" Jim was, is evident from Minto's experience. P. 209: "August 31 we drove away late from Fort Bridger . . ." [266: 164, 166, 209]

Robert S. Ellison, 1931. "While Bancroft and others state that Fort Bridger was established in 1842, Bridger is said to have spent considerable time in that vicinity for many years prior to 1842. For instance, Basil Clement (Claymore) refers to 'Fort Bridger on the Black Fork' in 1841 in a statement made to Charles Edmund Deland in 1899." [131: 9-10]

Irene D. Paden, 1943. "There is evidence that he had completed something in the way of building by the summer of 1842, because an eccentric minister, Williams by name, returning from Oregon, passed on July 3rd of that year and made mention of reaching Bridger's fort. By December 10, 1843, Bridger who could neither read nor write, had a letter sent to Pierre Chouteau, Jr., the head of a large fur-trading company in St. Louis, announcing: 'I have established a small fort, with a blacksmith shop and supply of iron, in the road of the emigrants on Black Fork of Green River, which promises fairly. In coming out here they are in need of all kinds of supplies, horses, provisions, smithwork, etc. They bring ready cash from the states, and should I receive the goods ordered, will have considerable business in that way with them, and establish trade with the

Indians in the neighborhood who have a good number of beaver among them.'" [298: 246-47]

Author's note, Sept. 12, 1972. Information from Paul Henderson indicated that he had found evidences of Bridger's first trading post on the bluff 0.9 mile from the town of Fort Bridger on Az. 342 degrees true (on the edge of the present town dump). Much of the indicated area had recently been turned into a borrow-pit from which road maintenance materials had been taken. The site may have been destroyed entirely.

USGS map, Fort Bridger, Wyo., 1:24,000, 1964 ed.

The entrance to the Army's Fort Bridger.

FORT BRIDGER (SECOND TRADING POST SITE)
Mile 1026L1 - At Fort Bridger State Park, Wyo.
Uinta County — SW¼ of SW¼, Sec. 33, T16N, R115W

This Fort Bridger was built perhaps as early as 1844, on the bottomland where the army's Fort Bridger was later established (1858). Materials from the earlier post may have been utilized in the construction of the four log houses and enclosures. This post was sold to the Mormons in 1853, enlarged by them and burned in 1857 on the approach of a U.S. military force.

As the second of a series of essential way stations along the Oregon-California-Utah trails, this was a place where some supplies could be obtained, essential blacksmith work could sometimes be done, and where worn-out oxen, mules and horses could be exchanged for serviceable animals.

The state of Wyoming has built a replica of the old fort to the rear of the museum in tha park. Continued archaeological study has pinpointed its exact location to the rear of the museum building.

J. M. Harrison, 1846. "We found Fort Bridger a small stockade used as a rendezvous for trappers & Indian trade. We saw a small band of domesticated mountain goats & sheep." [165: letter]

Miller-Reed diary, July 27, 1846. ". . . encamped in a beautiful Grass bottom about ½ mile below Bridgers Old Fort now occupied by Bridger and Vascus." [275:I, 26 1]

James Reed, July 31, 1846. Calls Bridger and Vasquez "two very excellent and accommodating gentlemen, who are the proprietors of this trading post." P. 280: "They now have about 200 head of oxen, cows and young cattle, with a great many horses and mules; and they can be relied on for doing business honorably and fairly." [275:I, 279, 280]

Heinrich Lienhard, 1846. "Fort Bridger consisted of two block-houses surrounded by palisades 10 feet high. It could hardly be defended for long against a determined attack. Bridger probably used it more for a trading post . . ." P. 96: "There were two roads from Fort Bridger: the old one via the so-called Soda Springs and Fort Hall, and the new one called Captain Hasting's Cutoff, which was said to be much shorter and which led past the Great Salt Lake. Many parties ahead of us had chosen this route. . . . we, too, preferred it." [229: 95-96]

William Clayton, 1848. "'Fort Bridger': . . . Altitude, 6,665 feet. You cross four rushing creeks, within half a mile, before you reach the Fort, and by traveling half a mile beyond the Fort, you will cross three others, and then find a good place to camp. The Fort is composed of four log houses and a small enclosure for horses. Land exceedingly rich—water cold and good, and considerable timber." [78: 17]

Howard Stansbury, Aug. 11, 1849. ". . . to Fort Bridger—an Indian trading-post, situated on the latter stream, forming several extensive islands, upon one of which the fort is placed. It is built in the usual form of pickets, with the lodging apartments and offices opening into a hollow square, protected from attack from without by a strong gate of timber. On the north, and continuous with the walls, is a strong high picket-fence, enclosing a large yard, into which the animals belonging to the establishment are driven for protection from both wild beasts and Indians. . . . received with great kindness . . . by . . .

Major James Bridger. . . . courteously placing his blacksmith-shop at my service."

P. 228: "Thursday, September 5 . . . Fort Bridger on Black's Fork of Green River. This is a trading post. . . . and is owned and conducted by Messrs. Vasquez and Bridger. . . . Black's Fork, upon which the fort is situated, is a considerable stream of excellent, clear, sweet water, which rises in the Bear River Mountains, and discharges its waters into Green River. . . . A mile and a-half above the fort, it divides into four streams, which unite two miles below, forming several islands, upon the westernmost of which the fort is beautifully located, in the midsts of a level, fertile plain, covered with a luxuriant growth of excellent grass. Numerous groves of willows and cottonwoods with thickets of hawthorn, fringe the margins of the stream, and afford fuel and timber for the necessities of man, and shelter for cattle. . . . The emigrant road forks here." [361: 74, 228-29]

Andrew Jensen, 1913. "In the year 1853, President Brigham Young purchased from James Bridger, what was claimed by that early mountaineer and trapper to be a Mexican grant of land, together with some cabins known as Fort Bridger. . . . The Utah pioneers of 1847 found it an important way station. Mr. Bridger claimed to hold a tract of country thirty miles square, under the Mexican government, to which the land belonged when he built his fort and made his improvements. But by the Mexican laws he was only allowed nine miles square, and to this he was undoubtedly legally and justly entitled. This claim, or ranch, of nine miles square, with the fort, known as Fort Bridger, and whatever improvements that were made thereon, Mr. Bridger sold to President Brigham Young, and gave a deed for the same, receiving therefor eight thousand dollars in gold. Brigham Young subsequently erected a stone fort and corrals for the protection of animals, and made other improvements on the ranch at an expense of about twelve thousand dollars. From 1853 to 1857, Fort Bridger was quite an important 'Mormon' outpost." [207: 32]

Robert S. Ellison, 1931. Quotes Edwin Bryant, who wrote on July 17, 1846, as follows concerning the location of Fort Bridger: "Its position is in a handsome and fertile bottom of the small stream on which we are encamped, about two miles south of the point where the old wagon trail, via Fort Hall, makes an angle and takes a northwesterly course." (This junction appears to have been north of the site of Bridger's first post, and probably came into being because there was then no reason to go farther south). Pp. 9-32 provide a brief history of Bridger's post from the beginning to its abandonment by the Mormons. [131: 9-32]

William J. Ghent, 1934. "The Mormon Pioneers of 1847, who had met Bridger going east, at the Big Sandy, reached the 'fort' only to find the blacksmith shop destroyed by fire and apparently nothing being done to restore it." P. 142: "Until February 1848 Fort Bridger was in Mexican territory . . ." [149: 141-42]

Author's note, July 9, 1972. The so-called "Mormon Wall" is evidently a reconstruction for which portions of two Army buildings (the commissary-storehouse and the old guardhouse) were removed. Cobbles from the original wall may have been used in the reconstruction.

Reference. Robert L. Munkres, "Fort Bridger," in *Overland Journal*, 8/2 (1990), 25-34.

USGS map, Fort Bridger, Wyo., 1:24,000, 1964 ed.

ALFRED CORUM GRAVE
Mile 1029.0 — 14 miles northwest of Kemmerer, Wyo.
Lincoln County — NE¼ of NE¼, Sec. 3 1, T23N, R117W

This marked grave from gold rush days is on the Sublette Cutoff.

J. Goldsborough Bruff, Aug. 10, 1849. "And at the heights about 5 mi. beyond [Hams Fork] another on the left and close to the trail—on a board—'Sacred to the memory of Alfred Corum who died July 4th, 1849 Aged 22 years.' And 300 yards further, also on the left,—'Margaret Campbell, departed, July 28, 1848, aged 36 yrs. 4 mos. 28 days.'" [52: 83]

Irene D. Paden, 1943. "The only other two [burials] identified are those of A. and J. Corum." [298: 266]

USGS map, Kemmerer, Wyo., 1:62,500, 1954 ed.

NANCY HILL GRAVE
Mile 1029.8 — 14 miles northwest of Kemmerer, Wyo.
Lincoln County — SE¼ of SE¼, Sec. 30, T23N, R117W

This is the marked grave of Nancy Hill, who died on the Sublette Cutoff in 1852.

Irene D. Paden, 1943. ". . . are several graves still recognizable among these mountains. . . . Nancy Hill's . . . some one shot the date right off the old stone. . . . [but] we know the date anyway.

It was 1847. . . . He [a rancher named Connely] and Mr. Jones told us a good bit, and I filled in the rest of the tragic story from two old newspaper clippings which were given me to read that same evening. In the year 1900 Ed Sutton, whose ranch we had passed about two hours earlier, was visited by a stranger—a Mr. Wright. He had been at the last resting place of Nancy Hill and had come down to this neighbor to enlist friendly interest for the lonely grave on the mountain. He was to have married her. . . . had traveled in her wagon train. In the fifty-three years . . . since he had helped bury her he had returned three times . . . once in the seventies, once in the nineties, and now again. . . . Nancy Hill was a goddess of a girl, close to six feet tall and magnificently healthy. She was well in the morning. She was dead at noon. She was barely cold when they buried her. The wagon with her grieving relatives went on . . . Her lover remained. He was mounted and could catch the wagons. He stayed a day or two at the grave . . . Close to this grave Mr. Wright knew of seven more . . . We soon came to the grave, at the head of Robinson's Hollow. It was about fifty yards from the road. Small gray sage and greasewood but a foot high crowded close." [298: 265-66]

Author's note, Aug. 3, 1982: Recent research by Reg P. Duffin has established beyond reasonable doubt that Nancy J. Hill died July 5, 1852, and not in 1847 as frequently stated. It also appears that the present markers, which are not originals, may have been incorrectly placed during efforts to restore the Hill and Corum graves. Duffin's thorough and convincing findings are available in *Overland Journal,* July 1983, "Here lies Nancy Hill"; and Fall 1986, "The Nancy Hill Story; Final Chapter."

USGS map, Kemmerer, Wyo., 1:62,500, 1954 ed.

SMITHS FORK CROSSING_p
Mile 1097.5 — 0.9 mile northwest of Cokeville
Lincoln County, Wyo.
Unsurveyed (Lat. 42° 05' 40"N, Long. 110° , 56', 45"W)

This stream was crossed with considerable difficulty early in the season, but often unmentioned by those arriving later.

John C. Fremont, Aug. 22, 1843. ". . . in about three miles from our encampment, we reached Smith's Fork, a stream of clear water, about 50 feet in breadth. It is timbered with cottonwood, willow, and aspen, and makes a beautiful debouchment through a pass about 600 yards wide, between remarkable mountain hills, rising abruptly on either side, and forming gigantic columns to the gate by which it enters Bear river valley." Note 46: ". . . editor Dale L. Morgan believes that Jedediah—who penetrated the area in 1824-1825—is the likelier choice" over Thomas L. Smith, as the one for whom the stream was named. [202:I, 473]

James A. Pritchard, June 25, 1849. ". . . struck Bear river valley at 3 P.M. In 6 or 8 ms came to Thomas's [Smith's] fork of Bear River. We found it to deep to be forded with safty without raiseing our wagon beds some 15 or 18 inches. So the remainder of the afternoon was spent in cutting down cotton wood trees and cribing up our wagon beds. We lashed the timbers & beds fast to the Axels of the wagons." There are more details of this difficult crossing. [317: 99-100]

Thomas Christy, June 21, 1850. ". . . to Smith's Fork. Here we had to cross four branches all about the same size, not 4 rods apart." [71: 50]

Irene D. Paden, 1943. ". . . it divided its current among several channels, thus making it barely possible to ford . . . My notes taken in 1935 record four . . . in 1938 we modestly contented ourselves with three. They are seasonal." [298: 270]

USGS map, Cokeville, Wyo., 1:24,000, 1967 ed.

THOMAS FORK CROSSING$_P$
Mile 1108.6 — 1.2 miles west of Border, Wyo.
Bear Lake County, Idaho — SE¼ of NE¼, Sec. 9, T14S, R46E

The crossing of Thomas Creek, which resembled a sluggish canal, was particularly difficult for early emigrants because of the steep, muddy inclines into and out of the stream. The problem was solved by the building of toll bridges there in the 1850s.

The crossing is a mile west of the Wyoming-Idaho state line and there is an Idaho State information panel (No. 229) at a parking area nearby. There is a very good view of Oregon Trail ruts ascending the hill west of the stream—often called "Talma's Fork" in fur-trade literature.

James A. Pritchard, June 27, 1849. ". . . one of the tributaries of Bear river [Thomas Fork]. Here we had to block up our wagons. After crossing the creek the road turns up a high long hill . . . 6 miles . . . to where the road strikes the river again."

The Bear River flows through level ground at the mouth of Thomas Fork.

[317: 101]

J. Goldsborough Bruff, Aug. 15, 1849. ". . . cross the stream (Thomas' fork) Found the banks deep and soft, and narrow inclined planes in different places, where the wagons had forded, and worn them in deep bad ruts . . ." [52: 89]

Thomas Christy, June 22, 1850. ". . . to Thomases Fork. There we had to raise the loads in our wagons to keep the provisions from getting wet." [71: 51]

Irene D. Paden, 1943. "The stream is deeply cut and carries a full current. The wagons were worried across with ropes and plenty of man power, occasionally turning turtle on the up pull . . . travelers of the fifties who found toll bridges erected over Smith's and Thomas' forks . . ." [298: 270]

Gregory M. Franzwa, 1972. "By the early 1850s there were two bridges across the Thomas Fork, the owners of which each levied a dollar for passage." [141: 291]

USGS map, Border, Wyo.-Ida., 1:24,000.

INDIAN GRAVE_P
Mile 1111.6 — 4 miles west of Border, Wyo.
Bear Lake County, Idaho — SE¼ of Sec. 1, T14S, R45E

This is the burial place of an Indian woman killed in a fall from a horse on June 27, 1849.

James A. Pritchard, June 27, 1849. "The wife of the Old Chief of whom I have been speaking was thrown from her horse today and killed. And a boy who was rideing behind her was also thrown and his arm broken. She was buried according to their custome. She was put into the ground & all her things were put with her, and an equal share of all their provisions. They then shot the horse and put him into the grave for the woman to ride. They then fired a few guns into the grave & put up a most piteous howling, weeping, and waleing—and in that state of agony departed from the place." [317: 101]

J. Goldsborough Bruff, Aug. 15, 1849. "Saw a grave on the 3d hill side on left [after crossing Thomas Fork], about 3 ms. from creek. On the head was a rude wooden cross, on which was pencilled:—'An Indian Squaw; June 27th, 1849, Kill'd by a fall from a horse, near this place: Calm be her sleep, and sweet her rest. Be kind to the Indian.'" [52: 89]

USGS map, Pegram, Ida., 1:24,000.

SMITH'S TRADING POST_P
Mile 1120L? — About 5 miles south of Montpelier, Idaho
Bear Lake County — Near NW Cor., Sec. 36, T13S, R44E

This post was established by Peg Leg Smith in 1848 on the east bank of the Bear River, below the outlet of Bear Lake. It consisted of four log cabins which were abandoned prior to 1850. This may have replaced an earlier trading house at or near the same location.

This way station was of some assistance to forty-niners and others traveling the Oregon-California trail.

John Minto, Sept. 1844 (at Fort Hall). "Pegleg Smith, a man widely known as one of the most reckless of his class . . . now neatly dressed in Navy blue, and would have been judged a steamboat captain in Saint Louis . . . a Catholic priest came out, and Mr. Smith passed before him, lifting his hat and receiving a few low spoken words which I supposed was such a blessing as would be given on a feast day." [266: 216]

Nicholas Carriger diary, July 26, 1846. ". . . Passing a Trading house on the river . . ." The continuing mileage to the Soda Springs would place this post about where Peg Leg Smith was reported to have established it in 1848. [275:I, 155]

James A. Pritchard, June 27, 1849. ". . . Smith's trading post. . . .

This Old Smith who lives here has a cork leg—a rough looking man he is too. The place is better known as Smith's trading post. A Salt Lake Mormon & wife were here for the purpose of trading with the Emmegrants, & several Frenchmen." Pp. 157-158, Note 57: Provides a lengthy synopsis of information on Smith and his post, including this: "His trading post on the Bear dates from 1848. In April of that year Joseph L. Meek, eastbound with dispatches from Oregon, was given a letter in which Pegleg announced his intention of establishing at the Big Timbers on Bear River just such a trading post as Pritchard and others came upon in 1849; this appeared in the St. Joseph *Adventure* of May 19, 1948." Note continues with a summary of pertinent 1849 diary entries. [317: 101, 157-58]

Osborne Cross, 1849. "July 25. . . . Smith's trading house, which is about thirteen miles distant. I crossed Thomas's fork and left the river . . . over high hills . . . arrived at the trading house about two." P. 152, "July 27 . . . Mr. Smith, the trader, visited us and was extremely kind . . . having a fine beef killed." P. 155, there is mention of "Brown's trading house on Bear River," as if it was near Smith's. [101: 150-51, 152, 155]

J. Goldsborough Bruff, Aug. 15, 1849. "The old mountaineer,— 'Peg Leg Smith,' came into camp: he has a cabin on the bank, some distance below, and trades with cattle, whiskey, &c. His leg was injured and he out knife & amputated it himself, and afterward dressed [it], and fortunately recovered." P. 618, "He has fitted a wooden leg—(hence the appelation, by his comrades,) and a socket to the stirrup, permits him to ride as smartly as ever." The story of his injury is repeated as in *Hutchings' Illustrated California Magazine*, V (1860-61), 147-50, 420-21. [52: 90, 618]

Irene D. Paden, 1943. "The emigrants found Peg-leg friendly, hospitable, and apparently innocuous." Repeats Isaac Wistar's improbable story of a murderous brawl at Independence. [298: 272-73]

Alfred G. Humphreys, 1966. Implies that Peg Leg Smith settled in Bear River Valley soon after 1841. However, this biographical sketch of Thomas L. (Peg Leg) Smith provides no documentation for a residence in the Bear River Valley prior to 1848.

Gregory M. Franzwa, 1972. "The fort consisted of four log cabins and some Indian lodges. It was established with the idea of farming the fertile land of the Bear Valley, but there was obviously more fertility in the emigration of 1849." [141: 249]

Author's note, July 8, 1972. An Idaho State information panel has been placed beside highway US30N overlooking the site of Smith's trading post (which is thought to have been where the Union Pacific railroad tracks now run).

USGS map, Montpelier, Idaho, 1:24,000, 1967 ed.

MONTPELIER CREEK CROSSING
Mile 1123.8 — Montpelier, Idaho
Bear Lake County — NE¼ of SW¼, Sec. 3, T13S, R44E

This stream was variously known as "Tullick's Fork" (for Samuel Tullick, a fur trapper), and "Fuller's Fork," but now Montpelier Creek. At or near this stream a route used by the Mormons veered to the west, short-cutting the northward loop of Bear River by passing through Emigration and Strawberry canyons in present-day Caribou National Forest on their way to Utah.

Charles Preuss, 1846. On the map compiled from the notes gathered on John C. Fremont's 1843 expedition, this stream is shown as "Tullick's Fork"—a name which had survived from the fur trade. [315: map, Section V]

Thomas Christy, June 22, 1850. "Camped close to Fuller's Fork, but we rued this before morning . . . musquetoes." [71: 51] Irene D. Paden, 1943. "At Montpelier was a trading post, now commemorated by a marker. There is a local tradition (substantiated by deep wheel gouges) that some of the wagons came down the hills directly at the marker . . . not a main stem of traffic." [298: 273]

USGS map, Montpelier, Ida., 1:24,000, 1967 ed.

HOOPER SPRING
(Site 6, Soda Springs Vicinity Map)
Mile 1153R2 — Caribou County, Idaho
SE¼ of SE¼, Sec. 36, T8S, R41E

This is a large hot spring on Soda Creek, northeast of Chester Hill. It is an oval-shaped pool, covered by a pavilion roof. Local residents drink the water. These springs were probably seen by very few emigrants because of their positioning away from the route of travel.

John C. Fremont, Aug. 25, 1843. ". . . along the base of the

William H. Jackson's 1871 photo shows there was a pavilion over the Hooper Spring a century ago—there still is.

ridge which skirts the plain, I found at the foot of a mountain spur, and issuing from a compact rock of a dark-blue color, a great many springs . . . the water of which was collected into a very remarkable basin, whose singularity, perhaps, made it appear to me very beautiful. It is larger—perhaps fifty yards in circumference; and in it the water is contained at an elevation of several feet above the surrounding ground by a wall of calcareous *tufa*, composed principally of the remains of mosses, three or four, and sometimes ten feet high. The water within is very clear and pure, and three or four feet deep, where it could be conveniently measured near the wall; and, at a considerably lower level, is another pond or basin of which the gas was escaping in bubbling columns at many places. This water was collected into a small stream." [202:I, 481-82]

WPA Writers' Project, 1939. "Many springs . . . most of them cold . . . Hooper, a mile north of town . . . close by is the Champagne Spring, and to the north is the Mammoth Soda Spring . . . Stampede Park . . . a natural amphitheatre . . . flowing into the park is Eighty Percent Spring. There was formerly a bottling plant at Ninety Percent Spring, near Stampede Park . . ." [298: 104-05]

Author's note, July 8, 1972. The Hooper Spring is reached by going north from US30N, 2.2 miles on East Third Street. The Ninety Percent Spring was jokingly called the "Anti-poligamy Spring" by Gentiles, according to Beadle's *The Undeveloped West*.

USGS map, Soda Springs, Ida., 1:62,500, 1948 ed.

WAGONBOX GRAVE
(Site 4, Soda Springs Vicinity Map)
Mile 1153R⅓ — Caribou County, Idaho
SE¼ of NE¼, Sec. 12, T9S, R41E

This is a reburial, around which the town cemetery has developed. The original burial site is about a half-mile southeast.

A family, (father, mother and five children) was killed by Indians in 1861. They were buried in their wagon box at the crossing of Little Spring Creek, by an emigrant party led by George W. Goodheart.

WPA Writers' Project, 1939. "Just south of town, where Little Spring Creek crosses the road, is the spot where a family of seven was killed by Indians; the cemetery in which these persons were buried, with their wagon box serving as a coffin, is west of town." [146: 104]

Author's note, July 8, 1972. The bodies were uncovered in the course of improvement work within the town of Soda Springs.

USGS map, Soda Springs, Ida., 1:62,500, 1948 ed.

STEAMBOAT SPRING
(Site 3, Soda Springs Vicinity Map)
Mile 1154.5 — Caribou County, Idaho
NE¼ of SW¼, Sec. 11, T9S, R41E

Steamboat Spring was the principal feature of a group of mineral springs now covered by the water of Soda Point Reservoir. Its location can be detected by the agitation of the surface of the reservoir when calm (about 2,500 feet distant from the Monsanto Pavilion, Soda Springs Country Club golf course, on Az. 108 degrees true). It is not a true geyser, but it was an important landmark of fur trade and emigration days.

The Steamboat Spring was photographed by Malcolm S. Smith on October 25, 1990, while the Soda Point Reservoir was drained for routine maintenance. The activity remains, but the cone is gone—dynamited before the reservoir filled in 1924, according to local information, to see if the activity could be increased. It didn't work.

Rufus B. Sage, November 1842. "A few hundred yards below these [the Soda Springs], is another remarkable curiosity, called Steamboat Spring. This discharges a column of mineral water from a rock-formed orifice, accompanied with subterranean

sounds like those produced by a high-pressure steamboat."
[338:V, 138]

John C. Fremont, Aug. 25, 1843. "In a rather picturesque spot, about 1,300 yards below our encampment, and immediately on the river bank, is the most remarkable spring of the place. In an opening on the rock, a white column of scattered water is thrown up, in form like a *jet-d'eau*, to a variable height of about three feet, and, though it is maintained in a constant supply, its greatest height is attained only at regular intervals, according to the action of the force below. It is accompanied by a subterranean noise, which, together with the motion of the water, makes very much the impression of a steamboat in motion; and, without knowing that it had been already previously so called, we gave to it the name of *Steamboat Spring*. The rock through which it is forced is slightly raised in a convex manner, and gathered at the opening into an urn-mouthed form, and is evidently formed by continued deposition from the water, and colored bright red by oxide of iron. . . . It is a hot spring, and the water has a pungent and disagreeable metallic taste, leaving a burning effect on the tongue . . . the temperature . . . of the Steamboat spring 87 degrees." [202:I, 477-78]

Overton Johnson, Sept. 7, 1843. ". . . about a half mile below [the Soda Springs] . . . a Spring where the water (which is quite warm), at intervals of fifteen seconds, is thrown several feet in the air." [208: 88]

James A. Pritchard, June 29, 1849. "The Steam Boat Springs are about ½ mile below, the water of it are a little warmer than the others and escapes out of the ground through a crevis or apiture in the stone about the size of a man's head. The effervescing gasses, being somewhat confined beneath the ledges of stone, presents this puring appearance." [317: 102]

Osborne Cross, Aug. 1, 1849. ". . . at the side of the river . . . the celebrated spring, generally known as 'Steamboat Spring' . . . water seems to rise out of the river through a tube . . . of carbonate of lime which is about three feet high . . . a rattling noise not unlike the escaping steam from a steam pipe. It is not loud, but such is the similarity of the sound that it has received the name of 'Steamboat Spring' forced up by the pressure of the gas below." [101: 158]

J. Goldsborough Bruff, Aug. 17, 1849. "Passed the 'Steamboat Spring,' named from the resemblance of the sound it gives, to that of a steamboat's paddles, under water. It is a circular tumuli of about [5] ft. diam. and about [3] ft. high; bubbling & jetting

USGS Photo Archives

Steamboat Spring as photographed by R. W. Richards, c. 1911. This area is now under the waters of the Soda Point Reservoir.

clear sparkling water, as the hissing gases escape. The mound is of dark flesh color. *(S.B. Spring is near the bank of stream)* An old cedar stands near the spr'g, the trunk & branches of which are carved and penciled all over, as high up as can be reached, with names, &c. These springs are really worth a travel so far to see." [52: 91]

Thomas Christy, June 24, 1850. ". . . springs & one fourth of a mile [beyond] is the noted Steam Boat Springs." [71: 53]

Isaac VanD. Mossman, 1853. "One of the curiosities of our journey was the celebrated 'Steamboat Springs," near Bear River, one hot enough to boil an egg in the alloted four minutes, and the other not a hundred feet away, with water of ice-cold temperature, each of them puffing and blowing like a steamboat." [280: 3]

WPA Writers' Project, 1939. "Steamboat Spring two miles west of town, now emerges at the bottom of an artificial lake . . . still boils up through 40 feet of water and explodes at the surface." [146: 104]

Irene D. Paden, 1943. "Of them all, the only hot spring

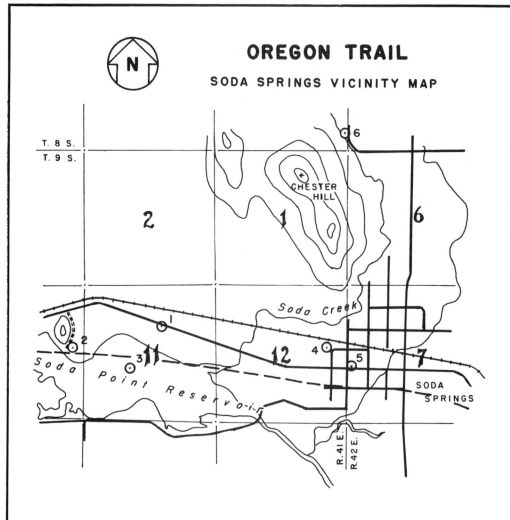

OREGON TRAIL

SODA SPRINGS VICINITY MAP

NOTES
1. INFORMATIONAL PANELS   4. WAGONBOX GRAVE
2. HOT SPRING CONES   5. OREGON TRAIL MONUMENT
3. OLD STEAMBOAT   6. HOOPER SPRING

MILES

ALH '72

recorded was the famous Steamboat Spring . . . Reams of paper used in describing this eccentric landmark . . . now submerged." [298: 275]

USGS map, Soda Springs, Ida., 1:62,500, 1948 ed.

CAMP CONNOR & SODA SPRINGS
(Site 1, Soda Springs Vicinity Map)
Caribou County, Idaho — Sec. 11, T9S, R41E

This is the original townsite of Soda Springs. It was developed adjacent to Camp Connor, established in 1863 by Gen. Patrick E. Connor to protect emigrants and Idaho miners from Indian attack. In 1870 Brigham Young relocated the town to its present site, about 1¾ miles to the east. Both the camp and the original town were probably very close to the "soda" and "beer" springs, in an area now covered by the waters of Soda Point Reservoir. The informational panels—Numbers 158 and 218, 1.5 miles west of Soda Springs on U.S. Highway 30N—are approximately opposite the camp, town and springs.

Rufus B. Sage, Nov. 1842. "The valley of Bear river affords a number of springs strongly impregnated with various mineral properties, which cannot fail to excite the curiosity and interest of the traveler. They are found upon the left [northeast] bank of the stream, a short distance below a small affluent from the north.

"Two of them are situated in a small grove of cedars, within a short distance of each other.

"In passing their vicinity the attention of the traveler is at once arrested by the hissing noise they emit; and on approaching to ascertain the cause, he finds two circular-shaped openings in the surface, several feet in diameter, and filled with transparent fluid in a state of incessant effervescence, caused by the action of subteranean gases.

"The water of the one he finds on tasting to be excellent natural *soda,* and that of the other, slightly acid and beer-like;— the draught will prove delicious and somewhat stimulating, but, if repeated too freely, it is said to produce a kind of giddiness like intoxication. These singular natural curiosities are known among the trappers as the Beer and Soda springs, names not altogether inappropriate.

"Besides the above-described, there are a number of others in this vicinity of equal mineral character, as well as several hot springs, varying in temperature from blood to that of extreme boiling heat." [338:V, 138]

John C. Fremont, Aug. 25, 1843. ". . . the famous *Beer Springs* . . . a basin of mineral waters enclosed by the mountains . . . A pretty little stream of clear water enters the upper part of the basin from an open valley in the mountains, and, passing through the bottom, discharges into Bear river. Crossing this stream, we descended a mile below, and made our encampment in a grove of cedar immediately at the Beer springs, which, on account of the effervescing gas and acid taste, have received their name from the voyageurs and trappers of the country, who, in the midst of their rude and hard lives, are fond of finding some fancied resemblance to the luxuries they rarely have the fortune to enjoy. . . . There is a confusion of interesting objects gathered together in a small space. [202:I, 476-82]

Overton Johnson, 1843. Description. [208: 87-88]

James W. Nesmith, 1843. Description. [290: 349]

John Boardman, 1843. Description. [37: 110]

Samuel Hancock, 1845. "These soda springs are well worthy a notice, possessing all the properties of pure soda water; one of them particularly attracted our attention and admiration, the water gushing out in foam about six times a minute, through a rock which has been formed by the action of the water; this rock is quite uniform in shape and the aperture through which the soda water flows is round and perhaps three inches in diameter, giving the jet an imposing appearance as it gushes at intervals, falling gracefully back into its natural fountain in sparkling streams then wasting itself in every direction around. We used this water in making our bread and found it answered all the purposes of yeast, so we carried a quantity away as a substitute for it." 162: 23-24]

J. M. Harrison, 1846. ". . . road comparitively level to Soda Springs. . . . Some had the form of a cone or crater on a small scale. Some cones entirely dry . . . ground sounded hollow. Many of the company professed to relish it but I could not drink it." [165: letter]

Virgil Pringle, Aug. 2, 1846. ". . . to Soda Springs and camp to enjoy the novelties of the place which are many and interesting." [275:I, 178]

William J. Scott, Aug. 14, 1846. ". . .the Sody Spring is aquite acuriosity thare is agreat many of them just boiling rite up out of the ground take alitle sugar and desolve it in alitle water and then dip up acup full and drink it before it looses it gass it is furstrate I drank ahol of galon of it   you will see several Spring Spouting up out ove the river." [275:II, 639]

James A. Pritchard, June 29, 1849. ". . . reached . . . the Soda or Beer Springs. These are so called on account of the acid tast and effervessing gasses contained in the waters. It is a place of very great interest. The water is clear and sparkling, and in many places t[h]rown several feet in the air. The water is constantly boiling up with a kind [of] hissing nois. There are a great number of springs bursting out of the ground but the principal one is near the river and comes out at the edge of the water near the lower part of the grove. The Springs are situated in a fine seeder Grove with a stony foundation. The Steam Boat Springs are about ½ mile below." [317: 102]

J. Goldsborough Bruff , Aug. 17, 1849. ". . . noon'd near the celebrated 'Soda and Beer Springs' . . . several of these springs were within my corral.—One near my mess-fire.—the water was fine, only needed lemon syrup, to render it perfect soda water. These mineral springs are very numerous, many wells & springs boiling up & shooting jets." [52: 91]

Angelina Farley, Sept. 16, 1850. ". . . passed a Soda spring. The water tastes like soda after the life is gone out of it. . . . around where the water ran over it looked a dark coperas color." [133: diary]

John B. Hill, 1850. Mentioned a Frenchman living at the Soda Springs. [180: 40]

Thomas Christy, June 24, 1850. ". . . an Indian (Snake) village in Soda Bend of Bear River. One half mile farther is the Soda, Beer and Cold Springs." [71: 53]

Idaho Historical Society, n.d. Reference Series Leaflet 63 covers the establishment of Camp Connor, and 182 provides 17 pages of quotations concerning the Soda Springs (1833 to 1953). [195: items 63 & 182]

Author's note, July 8, 1972. There is a monument on the lawn of the courthouse square, fronting on U.S. Highway 30N, which states: "1863 / General Patrick Edward Connor / U.S.A Cavalry Infantry / 53 Families And Others / Founded Soda Springs / Built Fort To Protect Emigrants / County Seat Oneida County 18641867." This is in the SW¼ of SW¼, Sec. 7, T9S, R42E. (Site 1, Soda Springs Vicinity Map).

USGS map, Soda Springs, Ida., 1:62,500, 1948 ed.

HOT SPRING CONES_P
(Site 2, Soda Springs Vicinity Map)
Mile 1155.5 — Caribou County, Idaho
SE¼ of NE¼, Sec. 10, T9S, R41E

Two low, rust-colored cones, one dry and the other still discharging some water, are at the west end of the Soda Springs Country Club golf course. They are east of the minor road leading to the Monsanto Pavilion. These are the remaining visible evidences of the "Soda Springs." (The Hooper Spring north of town is of a different type.)

Irene D. Paden, 1943. "In the hills the springs are of the pothole variety, but we were told that towards the river we should find them more impressive . . . waters of the Bear are now backed over many acres of flat land . . . came to a struggling golf course . . . with great cones of porous rock, ten feet high and more formed by mineral deposit and containing the famous springs." [298: 274]

Author's note, July 8, 1972. Evidently the larger cones seen by Mrs. Paden 28 years ago were destroyed during extension and improvement of the golf course.

USGS map, Soda Springs, Ida., 1:62,500, 1948 ed.

WILLIAM HENRY HARRISON MONUMENT
Mile 1157.9 — 5.2 miles west of Soda Springs, Idaho
Caribou County — SW¼ of SW¼, Sec. 8, T9S, R41E

This stone slab is in the shape of the map of Idaho. It is incised, "In Honor of William Henry Harrison of Massachusetts Who Lost His Life on the Oregon Trail About 1850 Erected by His Niece Mrs. Alura F. H. Beardsley 1931." It is in a field adjacent to an abandoned section of U.S. Highway 30N. The reverse side mentions the nearby "massacre" site. This monument does not appear to be related to a specific event at or near the site, except for the reference to the "massacre"; instead, it reflects a general familial concern.

Author's note, July 8, 1972. The monument has been vandalized by removal of the Oregon Trail medallion. It stands in a wheat field, 20 feet beyond the highway right-of-way, and is protected by a fencing made of salvaged bridge steel.

USGS map, Soda Springs, Ida., 1:62,500, 1948 ed.

POSSIBLE "MASSACRE" SITE$_p$
Mile 1158L1½ — 1.5 miles due south of Alexander Station
Caribou County, Idaho — SW¼ of NE¼, Sec. 19, T9S, R41E

This sagebrush-covered flat on the west bank of the Bear River, is where local information places the destruction of a wagon train, (date unknown).

Overton Johnson, 1843. Noted evidences of Indian conflict in this vicinity, but lack of details makes it impossible to ascertain if emigrants were involved. [208: 88]

Author's note, July 8, 1972. Ray Jorgeson, a rancher who has lived all life in the immediate vicinity, states that wagon parts and human remains had been found there, but he could not recall by whom. The back side of the William Henry Harrison monument refers to this event.

USGS map, Soda Springs, Ida., 1:62,500, 1948 ed.

SODA POINT$_p$
Mile 1158L1⅓ — 4¾ miles southwest of Soda Springs, Idaho
Caribou County — Summit in N½, Sec. 20, T9S, R41E

This is the northernmost extremity of the ridge around which the Bear River was forced in its course from Bear Lake to the Great Salt Lake. It was a landmark of the Oregon Trail from its earliest days.

John C. Fremont, Aug. 26, 1843. "The mountain, which is rugged and steep, and, by our measurement, 1,400 feet above the river directly opposite the place of our halt, is called the *Sheep Rock* probably because a flock of the common mountain sheep *(ovis montana)* had been seen on the craggy point." [202:I, 483]

J. Goldsborough Bruff, Aug. 18, 1849. "This remarkable cliff is surmounted by a high round hill, studded with pines & verdure Height 1000 feet . . . Deep below, within these basaltic walls, the clear cold waters of the river rush and roar, hastening to mingle with the Salts of the Great Salt Lake, some 90 odd miles. . . . A broken place in the bank, filled with detritus, permitted us, by a troublesome path, to reach the stream and dip up water." [52: 92, 619]

USGS map, Soda Springs, Ida., 1:62,500, 1948 ed.

EAST JUNCTION, HUDSPETH'S CUTOFF
Mile 1159.0 — 6.2 miles west of Soda Springs, Idaho
Caribou County — SE¼ of SE¼, Sec. 12, T9S, R40E

This is the point of departure of the Hudspeth-Meyers route from the original Oregon Trail. This cutoff was popular with the Argonauts. It was also the place where the first California party left the Oregon Trail to make their way down the Bear River.

James A. Pritchard, 1849. Note 59 states: "Here, at the great bend of the Bear, was the point of departure for the Hudspeth Cutoff, opened just 20 days later [July 20, 1849] by a company of Missourians captained by Benoni M. Hudspeth and guided by John J. Meyers . . . first direct forecast of what became the Hudspeth Cutoff was by Levy Scott, who in 1846 had helped pioneer the Applegate Cutoff to Oregon; in a letter of October 25, 1847, printed in the Oregon City *Oregon Spectator,* November 11, 1847, he expressed belief that a cutoff could be made from the end of the Greenwood Cutoff to the head of Raft River. Jesse Applegate . . . In a waybill printed in the *Spectator,* April 6, 1848, similarly said, 'From where Greenwood's Cutoff enters the Bear river valley on a direct course (nearly E. & W.) to the head of Cajeux creek is less than 100 miles, by the road it is 225. There is nothing to prevent wagons from making this cutoff, but some 6 or 7 miles of rough road in descending into Cache valley; this might be examined and its practicability determined in a day or two.' . . . Henry R. Mann, writing on July 24, 1849, of the emergence upon Raft River of 'Messrs. Hedspeth and Meyers of the Jackson Co. Mo. Co.,' said, 'They intended to come out at the head of Mary's River, but not understanding their true latitude have struck the old road before it crosses the dividing ridge to the Basin. They would have made some 200 miles on the old road had they succeeded, but as it is they have made almost nothing. They were almost thunderstruck, when upon emerging they found they were only 70 miles from Fort Hall.'" [317: 159-60]

William J. Ghent, 1934. "Here the earliest California emigrant route—the one taken by Bidwell's company—parted . . . ran southwest and south, following the general course of the Bear. [149: 143]

Irene D. Paden, 1943. Gives the Hudspeth Cutoff a full chapter treatment. [298: 308-22]

Mrs. Paul Campbell, 1968. Biographical information on "Benoni Morgan Hudspeth." [59: 9-13]

The Alexander Crater, as seen through a telephoto lens.

USGS map, Soda Springs, Ida., 1:62,500, 1948 ed.

ALEXANDER CRATER$_p$
Mile 1159Ll — 7.3 miles west of Soda Springs, Idaho
Caribou County — N½, Sec. 14, T9S, R40E

This flat cone stands about 100 feet above the level and barren plain west of the Bear River. Hudspeth's Cutoff—the most-traveled route after 1849—passed over the southern shoulder of this volcanic feature. It was a prominent landmark noted by many emigrants.

John C. Fremont, Aug. 26, 1843. ". . . I was attracted by the singular appearance of an isolated hill with a concave summit, in the plain, about two miles from the river . . . at the summit of the hill, I found that it terminated in a very perfect crater, of an oval, or nearly circular form, 360 paces in circumference and 60 feet at the greatest depth. The walls, which were perfectly vertical, and disposed like masonry in a very regular manner, were composed of a browncolored scoriaceous lava, evidently the production of a modern volcano." [202:I, 483-84]

Overton Johnson, Sept. 7, 1843. ". . . we passed on the left, a large, hollow mound, the crater of an extinguished volcano." [208: 89]

Osborne Cross, Aug. 2, 1849. Noted that the hills "bore evident signs of having once been volcanoes." [101: 161]

Thomas Christy, June 25, 1850. ". . . leaving the Fort Hall road

on our right . . . running west. Passed Old Crater. . . ." [71: 54]
USGS map, Soda Springs, Ida., 1:62,500, 1948 ed.

FORT HALL (ARMY POST)_p
Mile 1200R9 — 8 miles east of Blackfoot, Idaho
Bingham County — Center of NE¼, Sec. 24, T3S, R36E

The Army's Fort Hall was established in May 1870 to control
the Indians of the Snake River Valley. It was on Lincoln Creek.
William J. Ghent, 1934. ". . . in May 1870, the Government
established a Fort Hall, often known as 'New Fort Hall,' about
twenty five miles northeast of the old trading post, and on
October 12 of that year set aside the Fort Hall Indian Reservation . . . on territory including the new fort." [149: 145]
Item (e) in the Idaho Historical Society Reference Leaflet on
this site notes the establishment of a military post on Lincoln
Creek in 1870. [195: No. 63]
USGS map, Yandell Springs, Idaho, 1:62,000, 1955 ed.

CANTONMENT LORING_p
Mile 1215R¼ — 12 miles southwest of Blackfoot, Idaho
Bingham County — NW¼ of SW¼, Sec. 26, T4S, R33E

This temporary military post was established in 1849, four
miles northeast of Fort Hall (HBC), by the Regiment of Mounted
Rifles. It was commissioned to protect traffic on the Oregon
Trail
J. Goldsborough Bruff, Aug. 19, 1849. ". . . genteel-looking
Panak . . . offered to guide us to the Cantonment . . . nearly
surrounded by slews & marshes . . . difficult to reach after dark.
Rode several miles over very deep sand, interspersed with sage
bushes; then across a long grassy bottom, and finally reached
the water & marsh, and rode around—as it appeared to me, in
the dark, several times, and at length reach'd some wagons and
a tent, among willow bushes . . . guide informed me that they
(the Indians) were not allowed to go in at night. So I went on
a few paces, met a soldier and enquir'd who commanded the
post, and he informed me that it was Col. Andw. Porter, of the
Mounted Rifles. I was quickly at his Markee . . . 'Cantonment
Loring'—as this post is called, is situated 6 ms. above Fort
Hall,—on Snake river. A quadrangular PicketFort is laid off

here.—(330 by 136 feet). The cotton-wood logs are laid down, for the commencement of the bastions—intending to built them up of logs, and the curtain—or walls, of picket, or perpendicular logs, close together. At present, the command is sheltered in tents & a few rough sheds. Admirable neatness & discipline observed. . . . Col. Porter has been most indefatigable—came here but a few days ago, with a small command, and has done so much . . . Guard mounting & all the regular duties of a garrison, applicable to such a position are strictly observed." [52: 100-02]

Osborne Cross, 1849. Selection of the site. [101: 170-71]

Howard Stansbury, August 1849. Describes the relationship to Fort Hall. [361: 92-93]

John B. Hill, 1850. Describes relationship to Fort Hall. (180: 41]

John Mullan, Dec. 19, 1853. Describes the relationship to Fort Hall. [282: 333-34]

Jennie Broughton Brown, 1932. Presents correspondence from Edgar M. Ledyard, concerning his attempt to locate the post. "Major Cross in 1849 . . . three miles above Fort Hall . . . occupied in 1849-50 by two companies of the Rifle Regiment." [48: 310, 373-75]

Irene D. Paden, 1943. In 1935 she accompanied Dr. Minnie Howard in search for the site: "A short period of excitement punctuated our search as we found and explored the excavations at Loring Cantonment, the old military post which we knew to be about three miles from the fort." [298: 283]

Item (h) in Idaho Historical Society Reference Leaflet 63 notes the establishment of Cantonment Loring in 1849. See also items (f) and (g) for other temporary posts in the area. [195: No. 63]

USGS map, Pingree, Idaho, 1:24,000, 1955 ed.

FORT HALL (WYETH-HBC)ₚ
Mile 1217.4 — 15 miles northwest of Pocatello, Idaho
Bannock County — NE¼ of NE¼, Sec. 6, T5S, R33E

Fort Hall was a stockaded trading post 80 feet square erected by Nathaniel J. Wyeth in 1834 on the east bank of the Snake River, between the mouths of the Portneuf and Bannock rivers. It was sold to the Hudson's Bay Company in 1837; rebuilt in 1838 by encasing the log work with adobe bricks, and abandoned

Above: This monument to Fort Hall—the most massive marker on the Oregon Trail—is on U.S. Highway 91. Below: Ruts of the Oregon Trail lead across the Fort Hall Bottoms toward the site of the old fort. A gravel access road has since been built on top of this segment of the trail.

in 1856 because of the increasing hostility of the Indians in that area. After 1849, the post served the emigrant trade almost entirely. It was one of the important way-stations on the Oregon Trail, ranking with forts Laramie, Bridger, and the Whitman Mission.

Jason Lee, July 14, 1834. ". . . came 4 or 5 m. and camped where the Capt. is going to build a Fort." P. 242: "Wednes. July 30, 1834. Capt. Wyeth's Fort is not yet finished. . . . This Fort is in Lat. 43° 14' N. but Lon. is not yet ascertained. It is on Lewis' Fork in an unpleasant situation being surrounded with sand which is sometimes driven before the wind in as great quantity as snow in the east." P. 243: "Left the Fort at 11 o'clock A.M. . . . after a few hours march camped on Portneuf . . ." [225: 145, 242-43]

Osborne Russell, July 16, 1834. "Here Mr. Wyeth concluded to stop build a Fort & deposit the remainder of his merchandise: leaving a few men to protect them and trade with the Snake and Bonnack Indians. On the 18th we commenced the Fort which was a stockade 80 ft. square built of Cotton wood trees set on end sunk 2½ feet in the ground and standing about 15 feet above with two bastions 8 ft. square at the opposite angles. On the 4th of August the Fort was completed. And on the 5th the 'Stars and Stripes' were unfurled to the breeze at Sunrise in the center of a savage and uncivilized country over an American Trading Post." Russell's date of arrival is in error—Lee, Townsend and Wyeth agree on the 14th. [337: 5]

John K. Townsend, July 1834]. "On the 14th we traveled but six miles when a halt was called, and we pitched our tents upon the banks of the noble Shoshone or Snake River. . . . The next morning we moved early, and soon arrived at our destined camp. This is a fine large plain on the South Side of the Portneuf [this is an error; note Lee's comment upon leaving Fort Hall that "after a few hours march" westward, they camped on the Portneuf], with an abundance of excellent grass and rich soil. The opposite side of the river is thickly covered with large timber of the cottonwood and willow, with a dense undergrowth of the same, intermixed with serviceberry and currant bushes. "Most of the men were immediately put to work felling trees." [379: 210]

Nathaniel J. Wyeth, July 14, 1834. "Went down the river about 3 miles and found a location for a fort and succeeded and killed a Buffaloe near the spot. 15. Commenced building the fort . . . 6th. Having done as much as was requisite for safety to the Fort

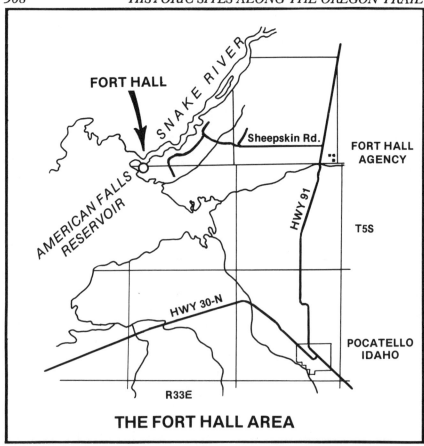

THE FORT HALL AREA

and drank a bale of liquor and named it Fort Hall in honor of the oldest partner of our concern. We left it and with it Mr. Evans in charge of 11 men and 14 horses and mules and three cows." [406: 227]

Rev. Samuel Parker, September 4, 1835. "Today I received a letter from Fort Hall containing an invitation from Mr. A. Baker to spend the winter." This was received on Big Lost River, Idaho. [301: 101] F.A. Wislizenus, 1839. "The fort lies hard by the river, and is built in a square of about eighty by eighty feet, suggestive of a barracks . . . except that the outer walls, ten to twelve feet high, are constructed in this case out of partly baked brick instead of wood. A small cannon is in the courtyard. The clerks of the fort were Mr. Armedinger [Ermatinger] and Mr. Walker.

"Fort Hall lies on the left bank of the Snake River, between the mouths of the Blackfoot and Portneuf Creeks." [405: 106-07, 520-521]

Rufus B. Sage, November 9, 1842. "Fort Hall is located upon the left bank of Snake river, or Lewis' Fork of the Columbia, in a rich bottom near the delta formed by the confluence of the Portneuf with that stream, in lat 43° 10′ 30″ north, long. 112° 20′ 54″ west.

"In general structure it corresponds with most of the other trading establishments in the country. It was built by Capt. Wythe of Boston, in 1832 [1834], for the purpose of furnishing trappers with their needful supplies in exchange for beaver and other peltries, and to command the trade with the Snakes." [338:V, 141-42]

John Boardman, August 11, 1843. ". . . Fort Hall is situated in a large plain on Snake River & built of Squaw cakes of mud baked in the sun; it is inferior to Fort Laramie . . . there was neither meat, flour nor rice to be had. Nothing but sugar and coffee at 50 cents per pint." [37: 111]

James W. Nesmith, August 28, 1843. ". . . arrived at Fort Hall . . . Grant, manager . . . He sells at exhorbitant price; flour, 25 cents per pint; sugar, 50: coffee, 50; rice 33⅓. Part of the company went on with pack animals, leaving their wagons." [290: 349-50]

Overton Johnson, September 13, 1843. ". . . we arrived at Fort Hall. . . . Fort Hall is built of the same material . . . as the Forts on the Platte are." [208: 89]

Samuel Penter, 1843. ". . . Fort Hall. There we found the wagons of the emigrants of 1842." [311: 60]

John C. Fremont, September 18, 1843. ". . . we were agreeably surprised, on reaching Portneuf river, to see a beautiful green valley with scattered timber spread out beneath us, on which, about four miles distant, were glistening the white walls of the fort. [143: 161]

John C. Fremont, September 22, 1843. "Except that there is a greater quantity of wood used in its construction, Fort Hall very much resembles the other trading posts which have been already described to you, and would be another excellent post of relief for the emigration. It is in the low, rich bottom of a valley, apparently 20 miles long, formed by the confluence of Portneuf river with Lewis's fork of the Columbia, which it enters about nine miles below the fort, and narrowing gradually to the mouth of the Pannack river, where it has a breadth of only two or three miles." Fremont discusses the value of a military post to protect and succor the emigrants and states his position, "112° 29′54″ 43° 01′30″ . . . 4,500 feet." [202:I, 520-21]

John Minto, September 1844. Records his not-very-auspicious arrival at Fort Hall. P. 216: ". . . there was one small common room used by trade transients. . . . Grant was, I think, a coarser man than Bridger, but carried more outside polish of manner. He gave me fair treatment in trade, however, furnishing a strong saddle horse for my gun, and finding I could get the bullet moulds for it, he gave me an Indian saddle for that." Describes Pegleg Smith, whom he saw there (see Mile 1120, Smith's Trading Post). [266: 215]

Samuel Parker, July 30, 1845. "To Fort Hall on Snake River. 31—Laid by at Fort Hall." [302: diary]

Virgil Pringle, August 7, 1846. "Pass the fort and camp four miles below on Port Neuf. Find the fort located on a rich, fertile plain, well watered with springs and creeks and some scattering timber." [275:I, 178-79]

J. M. Harrison, 1846. ". . . arrive Fort Hall. Hudson Bay Co. Fort carried on a considerable trade with surrounding Indians." [165: letter]

James A. Pritchard, July 2, 1849. "Fort Hall is occupied by English traders. They pack their goods from Astoria and other trading points on the Pacific coast of Oregon. The buildings are composed of Sun dried brick. They have vast herds of Cattle & horses & Mules. They milk a great number of Cows and make a great deal of butter & cheese. Their stock runs at large. . . . There are several families liveing here—some French, some English, and some Americans." [317: 105]

Osborne Cross, August 8, 1849. ". . . Fort Hall, a trading establishment . . . This place is about three miles below where two companies of the rifle regiment have chosen for the site of their new post. It is built of clay and much in the form of Fort Laramie, having a large sallyport which fronts the Portneuf, with its walls extending back towards the banks of Snake river. There is a blockhouse at one of the angles. The buildings inside are built against the side of the wall and of the same materials. The main building is occupied by the proprietor, while the others are intended for storerooms and places for the hands . . . rooms are all small and by no means comfortable . . . but a small door and window. . . . Captain Grant . . . been here fourteen years . . . I presume the troops . . . will not be required to occupy this post very long." P. 172: "The two drawings of the outer and inner side of Fort Hall . . . will give you a correct idea of their rude construction." [101: 170, 172]

Howard Stansbury, August 1849. "Five miles to the north, Fort

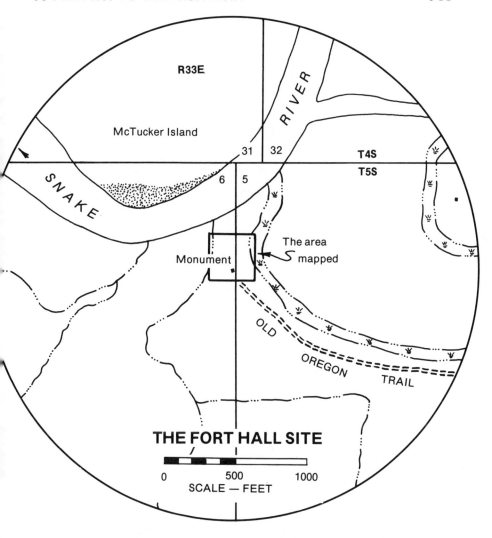

THE FORT HALL SITE

SCALE — FEET
0   500   1000

Hall, with its whitewashed walls, is plainly in view. The 'Three
Buttes' rise in the distance, while the PortNeuf, with its bright
sparkling waters, flows at our feet. The scene was one of
surpassing beauty. . . . we left Fort Hall on our left, and five
miles beyond it terminated our journey, at Cantonment Loring."
[361: 92-93]

J. Goldsborough Bruff. August 24, 1849. ". . . at 2 p.m. bade
them adieu [at Cantonment Loring] and started for Ft. Hall,
which we reached at 5 p.m. Road level, but crooked & marshy,
with several gravelly bed[s] of streams to cross . . . I walked back

Osborne Cross sketched Fort Hall as he saw it in 1849. The exterior view is above, interior below.

to the Fort, entered the Great Portal, walked across the open square, and up a pair of stairs, to a balcony, and at the door of an upper apartment met Capt. Grant, the former Hudson Bay commander." There is some mis-information about Capt. Thing, an employee of N. P. Wyeth. ". . . Grant . . . rebuilt the fort, as it now stands, of adobes, &c." There is a sketch of the exterior on p. 103. P. 104: "Grant is permitted, by Col. Porter to retain his old home, and gives him charge of some stores in the lower apartments of the Fort. The old Captain is very English, and anti-Yankee. . . . observed that he knew nothing about the treaty, had not seen it." P. 106: ". . . I descended the steps into the courtyard, and when we had reached the well,—in the centre, (a square wooden structure about 3 ft. above ground—with a hinged scuttle to it). . . ." P. 626, Note 293: "This adobe quadrangular structure is very similar to Fort Laramie—though much smaller, and appears to have more wood in its construction. The walls are in a very dilapidated state—and on the N.W. side are shored up with timbers. The main entrance, in the South Eastern wall, is a large double gate, with a small gate within one of the others." [52: 102-03, 106, 626]

A. J. Allen, 1850. "Fort Hall in charge of Mr. Grant and his associate, McDonald." [6: 164]

John B. Hill, 1850. "Before we got to Fort Hall we had to go through seven miles of deep sand. . . . we could see Fort Lowren five miles north of the road and five miles above Fort Hall." [180: 41]

Henry J. Coke, September 5, 1850. "When I reached the Fort (this is a real *nom de guerre* for a very ordinary mud edifice, walled in with adobes), Mr. Grant. . . ." [83, 218]

John Mullan, December 19, 1853. ". . . Cantonment Loring, so called in honor of Colonel Loring of the rifle regiment, and occupied in 1849 and 1850 by two companies . . . about five miles above Fort Hall." [282: 333]

Thompson C. Elliott, 1908. "Doc" Newell's taking of wagons from Fort Hall to the Whitman Mission in 1840 is explained. [125: 106-07]

Jennie Broughton Brown, 1932. "After his first visit in 1906, Mr. Meeker carried on a considerable correspondence trying to locate the true site of the historic fort . . . in 1916, on his third visit he was successful. . . . As early as 1912 the people of Blackfoot had celebrated at the old site in honor of their Jason Lee Memorial Church, and three years later, Miles Cannon, Idaho historian, was conducted there by an Indian, a former government scout . . . remained for Ezra Meeker to identify and verify the place, which he did in 1916 . . . on July 27, 1920, was held there a special dedicatory service attended by representative citizens of Pocatello and Blackfoot . . . dedicated with an inscribed marker a cairn of stones erected by the Boy Scouts in

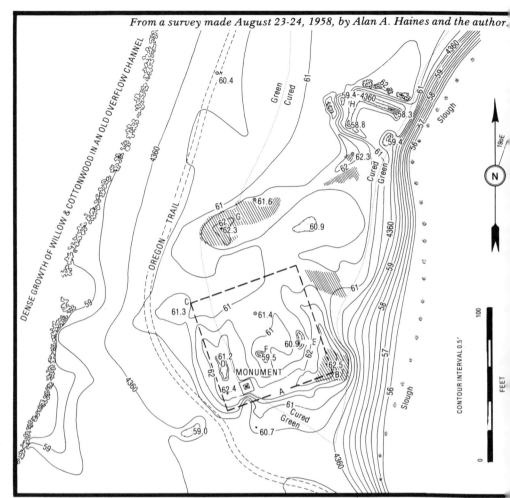

TOPOGRAPHIC MAP OF THE SITE OF FORT HALL

The Fort Hall monument is located within the site of the original enclosure, outlined by heavy dashes. The marker is 720 feet south and 30 feet west of the position shown for the northeast corner of Section 6, T5S, R33E. The riverbank is about eight feet above the Snake River during normal summer river conditions. Excavation revealed evidence of the gate at A, bastions at B and C, buildings at D and E, the well at F, and a later Hudson's Bay Co. building at G. (That was possibly within the fort when it was later extended from 80' square to about 80' x 120'.) The cross-hatched areas are bare adobe soil. A light dotted line shows the sharp demarcation between the green and the cured vegetation.

commemoration of the first Protestant sermon preached in the intermountain region. The lava monument, although without any inscribed marker, was on that occasion in evidence on the true site of Fort Hall."

Pp. 367-68: "The opinion prevails among many people that the Oregon Trail Memorial Association has a deed and title to the site of old Fort Hall . . . such is not the case. . . . W. P. Havenor, at present 1932] county surveyor of Bannock County, Idaho, was at one time engaged to make a survey to determine the true site of the old fort. He reported that it was on the section line between Sections 5 and 6, Township 5 south, Range 33 cast, Boise Meridian. As the Fort Hall monument is twenty-seven feet west of the section line, the Association petitioned Congress for a title to Lot 1, Section 6, Township 5 south, Range 33 east, Boise Meridian, Bannock County, Idaho, containing in all about eighty acres . . . the land in question is a part of the Fort Hall Reservation, and is Indian property . . . the Tribal Council of the Fort Hall Indians is favorable [to cession of a small tract for Park purposes] . . . pertinent to note . . . Lot 1 in Section 6, previously referred to, contains 36.6 acres granted to the United States government for the American Falls Reservoir purposes under Act of Congress approved May 9, 1924. . . . under supervision of the United States Reclamation Service. The grant, however, carried a reservation of an easement to the Fort Hall Indians, 'To use the said lands for grazing, hunting, and fishing, and gathering of wood, and so forth, the same way as prior to this enactment, insofar as such uses shall not interfere with the use of said land for reservoir purposes.'" Details of a plan to build a beacon-tower on the site as a memorial—this presumed flooding of the site, but American Falls Reservoir was not built so high. The Chief Engineer of the project said later it never would be flooded.

P. 380: The Oregon Trail Association, Idaho Unit, reorganized December 29, 1931. P. 381: ". . . plans for the centennial celebration of the founding of Old Fort Hall in 1934; lastly to secure by 1934 some fitting memorial structure in honor of the old fort." [48: 363, 367-68, 380-81]

William J. Ghent, 1934. ". . . to Fort Hall (1288 miles) . . . a general refitting and re-forming place . . . where men changed their minds as to their destination. . . . Here also the Oregon-bound emigrants of 1841 and 1842 left their wagons because they were told that no vehicle could be taken farther. . . . Miles Cannon says that in 1838 it [Fort Hall] was rebuilt, possibly on

Young Alan Haines stands before the monument erected by Ezra Meeker, located within the foundation traces of old Fort Hall. Right: That monument has since been replaced with this one, from which the bronze tablet has been removed.

a different location.

"Mr. Cannon says that the spot was six miles above the mouth of the Portneuf, Chittenden says nine miles, and Major Osborne Cross, who visited it in 1849, about fifteen miles." P. 146: "At Washington, on September 9, 1869 . . . award of the two Commissioners, which gave $450,000 to the [Hudson's Bay] Company and $200,000 to its auxiliary [for all claims in Oregon]." [149: 143, 146]

Irene D. Paden, 1943. "In 1855 the company abandoned it, and the material of its walls was soon torn down and utilized again in the construction of a stage station known as 'The Adobes' some three miles distant at the Spring Creek bridge. The great flood of '62 finished the razing of the fort, and its location gradually faded from the public memory. . . . in 1906, Ezra Meeker raised money for a monument . . . mistakenly at the Adobes. Ten years later Mr. Meeker relocated the exact site. . . . in 1920, the monument was correctly placed . . . public forgot again . . . In 1934, the centennial of its founding was celebrated in Pocatello with all the furor imaginable but with no mention . . . of its actual location." P. 281: young Shoshone girl then showed us the old ford over Clear Creek and pointed to wagon ruts running straight down the bottoms." P. 282: ". . . Dr. Minnie Howard . . . accompanied Ezra Meeker when he succeeded in locating . . . she was positive that they [the foundations] were not under water." P. 283: ". . . the site was hidden under a four-foot growth of wheat grass . . . partial clearing where stood Ezra Meeker's monument . . . on a very slight elevation." P. 284: (Dr. Howard, speaking of her visit in 1916: "We wanted to get all the proof we could . . . so, after we checked the size and shape of the outline of the walls and the position of the well . . . picked the inner angle of the walls . . . dug there . . . buffalo bones with knife hacks in them, great bolts from the wagon door into the fort, lime, fragments of stove grate and some bottle glass . . . some broken pieces of blue English china . . . we stood within the confines of Fort Hall itself." [298: 280-84]

Albert J. Partoll, 1951. "In spring of 1840 he [Angus McDonald] was assigned to Fort Hall (there until autumn of 1847). Then transferred to the Flathead . . ."

"An event in the affairs of Fort Connah during 1856 was the arrival of trade goods from Fort Hall . . . which was abandoned owing to Indian troubles." Fort Hall was closed in 1856 by order of Chief Factor Dugald McTavish—see testimony of Angus McDonald, September 25, 1865, in *British and American Joint Commission*, III, 162; and of Dugald McTavish, April 10, 1865, *Ibid.*, 206. [309: 138, 407]

Frank C. Robertson, 1963. A general treatment of the history of Fort Hall. [327: passim.]

Idaho Historical Society, Reference Leaflet. This four-page folder covers the establishment of Fort Hall and its history from the viewpoint of fur trade economics. [195: No. 121]

Idaho Historical Society, Reference Leaflet. This two-page folder contains a paragraph summary of Fort Hall history. [195: No. 62]

Anonymous, 1968. A general article which confuses the Fort Hall trading post with the later Fort Hall stage station. [15: 28-31] Author's note, July 7, 1972. The Fort Hall site was found covered with a denser stand of rye grass than on either of two previous visits—in 1951 and 1958. A portion of the old Ezra Meeker monument, which was standing at the site 21 years ago, is now lying alongside the more pretentious column of mortared stone which replaced it, but the bronze tablet is missing.

There are very good Oregon Trail ruts across the Fort Hall Bottom east of the fort site.

On U.S. Highway 91, at a point one-half mile south of the Fort Hall Indian Agency, are two markers: a mortared stone monument on the east and an Idaho State information panel on the west. USGS map, Springfield, Idaho, 1:24,000, 1955 ed.

FORT HALL STAGE STATION ("The Adobes")
Mile 1223L1 — 12 miles northwest of Pocatello, Idaho
Bannock County — In Sec. 18, T5S, R33E

A stage station was built 2½ miles southwest of Fort Hall with materials taken from the fort after its abandonment. The stage station site, which was on Spring Creek, is now under the waters of the American Falls Reservoir. The transference of building materials created a strong local belief that the original Fort Hall was on Spring Creek—an idea which has no basis in fact.

Jennie Broughton Brown, 1932. "J. N. Ireland had created a stage station near a crossing of one of the streams by the fort, but due to the difficulty in fording in seasons of high water the stage route was impractical. Ireland then decided to build a stage station on higher ground two and a half miles southwest on Spring Creek. As he needed lumber, he took most of the timbers from the old fort and constructed the buildings later known as Ben Holliday's 'Adobes,' at the Spring Creek Bridge. The only thing left on the old site was the adobe walls, which were outside of the timbered stockade, and were easily razed by waters of the great flood which covered the bottoms [in 1862 and 1864]."

At Pocatello, Meeker "made the statement that, in his opinion, the most pretentious monument on the Oregon Trail should be erected at the site of old Fort Hall . . . [He] solicited a fund which he placed in the treasury of the Women's Study League . . . used to fashion two monuments of native lava rock, one of which still stands on the high school grounds, marked 'Oregon Trail' [although the trail did not pass through Pocatello] . . . The other lava monument, designed to mark the site of old Fort Hall, was placed on the site of 'The Adobes,' at Spring Creek bridge, where it remained until 1920 when it was removed to the true site of old Fort Hall, where it still may be seen." [48: 335, 262-63]

USGS map, Michaud, Idaho, 1:62,500, 1934 ed.

AMERICAN FALLS
Mile 1241.0 — West of "old town" of American Falls, Idaho
Power County — SW¼ of SE¼, Sec. 30, T7S, R31E

The Snake River forms American Falls when it drops about fifty feet in six- to-ten-foot steps. The cataract flows over and between basalt fragments of a ridge of rock which compress the stream to a width of 250 yards. The site of the falls is now immediately below the 87-foot (dam which impounds the waters of American Falls Reservoir, Idaho.

John C. Fremont, September 24, 1843. ". . . *American Falls* of Snake River . . . The river here enters between low mural banks . . . By measurement, the river above is 870 feet wide, immediately contracted at the fall in the form of a lock, by jutting piles of scoriaceous basalt, over which the foaming river must present a grand appearance at the time of high water. The evening was clear and pleasant, with dew . . ." (Illustration on p. 524.) [202: 522-24]

James A. Pritchard, July 5, 1849. ". . . we passed the great American falls. The fall must be 40 or 50 feet in about 70 or 80 yards. There is no more than from 6 to 10 feet perpendicular fall at any place. The roaring of the waters can be heard for many miles. They rush with great velocity over and through the vast lumps that lay in massive piles in the channel. There is a solid mass of Black volcanick rock forming a complete butment on either side of the river. This Stone is a composition of Volcanic Stone, sinder, & smelted Oar of some sort . . . river [is] 250 yards [wide]. [317: 109]

Osborne Cross, August 10, 1849. ". . . to the American falls . . . in a short distance [the river] is precipitated over huge blocks to resume its course. . . . In the center of the falls there is a ledge of rocks dividing the river into two parts." [101: 76]

J. Goldsborough Bruff, August 26, 1849. "The 'American Falls' . . . are very pretty cascades, but with more rapids and froth than fall of water, at this season . . . I sketched the Falls & scenery." [52: 111]

Jennie Broughton Brown, 1932. "When American Falls dam was built, the reservoir covered the townsite . . . what action should be taken regarding the graves of several pioneers . . . American Falls Women's Club had surrounded with a fence the plot containing the group of five or six graves and had erected a monument . . . Reclamation Service removed the monument to the courthouse grounds, but advised against

removal of the bones . . . some opposition . . . Oregon Trail
Memorial Association . . . local D.A.R. . . . agreed with the
Women's Club that the graves were better respected to leave
them undisturbed . . . now lie beneath the waters of the lake."
[48: 376]

WPA Writers' Project, 1939. ". . . a favorite camping spot on
the trail in this area . . . The dam is a mile wide and has a
maximum height of 87 feet. The reservoir it creates is 12 miles
wide, 26 miles long, and covers an area of 56,000 acres. The cost
of the dam was $3,060,000." [146: 108]

Irene D. Paden, 1943. "In very early trapping days a boatload
of American trappers were caught in the pull of a fifty-foot fall
on the Snake River and plunged over to their death . . .
name . . . commemorates the tragedy." [298: 287]

Author's note, Aug. 23, 1972. A monument of basaltic stone
on the east bank of the Snake River, between the dam and the
powerhouse, has a plaque which states: "Oregon Trail / 1842-
1883 / Erected by / American Falls / Women's Club / 1915.

USGS map, American Falls, Ida., 1:24,000.

INDIAN SPRINGS$_p$
Mile 1245L1¾ — 4 miles south of American Falls, Idaho
Power County — NE¼ of SE¼, Sec. 18, T8S, R31E

This spring was the focus of an emigrant campground. A hotel
was later established at this point.

WPA Writers' Project, 1939. ". . . where pools and baths are
available . . . mineral hot springs." [146: 108]

Irene D. Paden, 1943. "Below the town [of American Falls],
some two miles, the trail crosses the highway at an angle, going
into the knolls which lie away from the river. It passes a spring
surrounded by a maze of old camp roads, goes near the Indian
Springs Hotel. . ." [298: 287]

USGS map, Indian Springs, Idaho, 1:24,000.

MASSACRE ROCKS
Mile 1250.7 — 10 miles southwest of American Falls, Idaho
Power County — NW¼ of NE¼, Sec. 6, T9S, R30E

Here are two rock masses, with just enough gap between them
to allow the passage of emigrant wagons. This was a likely

A — *Where the Newman train was nooning on August 9, 1862, when word arrived of an Indian attack on the train ahead; assistance was sent.* B — *The Adams train was found looted.* C — *The Smart train, attacked at the same time, made a running fight to a strong position near Massacre Rocks.* D — *The killed were buried at the southern end of Massacre Rocks—three burials on the 10th and two on the 11th.* E — *The campground of the trains which combined for safety.* F — *Here a scouting force of emigrants found Indians with stolen stock on August 10, and had to retreat toward the Snake River.* G — *The low ridge where the survivors took refuge among juniper trees until rescued by an Iowa train. All the trains moved on to the Raft River on the 11th.*

looking place for an Indian ambush. However, the somber name is not the legacy of such an event, but stems from several related clashes which occurred some distance away on August 8 and 9, 1862. The dead were buried near the rocks.

The site was not even an important landmark for the

Above: The Snake River above Eagle Rock. The Adams train was attacked while traversing the bench on the right. Below: Register Rock has been protected with this shelter, to assure continued legibility of the old emigrant inscriptions.

emigration, and the sinister name did not appear until well after the turn of the century. It is an inappropriate but firmly established usage.

Hamilton Scott, Aug. 9-11, 1862. 8/9—While his train was nooning below American Falls, word arrived that Indians were robbing emigrants four miles ahead. Scott's party went to their assistance but found the Adams train looted. They found one emigrant dead, two wounded and several missing, and the wagons without teams. Taking the wagons in tow, the rescuers moved ahead four miles to a campsite near Massacre Rocks. At that place they found the Smart train, which had been attacked at about the same time a mile in advance of the Adams train, but they had fought their way on to the vicinity of Massacre Rocks, with the loss of two men killed. 8/10—Thirty-five men followed the Indians to recover the lost stock, found their camp on Cold Creek, nine miles away (actually six miles) and were attacked, having to retreat three miles under fire with the loss of two killed and two missing, in addition to several wounded. 8/11— The five dead recovered from the three incidents were buried at the south end of Massacre Rocks, after which the combined wagon trains—five had gathered for safety—moved on to Raft River. 8/12—Miss Adams died of her wound and was buried at Raft River. [347: diary]

Jane A. Gould, Aug. 10-11, 1862. 8/10—The train she was with reached American Falls about noon of the day the party of men went out to recover stock. Leaving the falls about 2 p.m., this ox train met refugees from the Cold Creek fight along the emigrant road about 4 p.m. They were asked to help recover the two dead men and brought them on to the camp near Massacre Rocks, "5 miles ahead" (actually, 4.5 miles). 8/11—The two bodies they had brought in "were buried this morning with the three others" before the combined trains moved on to Raft River. 8/12— Captain Adams' daughter died and was buried in a wagon box. [151:diary]

John C. Hilman, August 11, 1862. In this letter, written by a member of the third ox train to come up to the scene of the original attack, it is noted that darkness obliged them "to camp on the very ground . . . red with the bloodof innocent men and women." Moving on at daybreak they reached the place, five miles distant, where two other ox trains—Captains Newman and Kennedy—were gathered with survivors of the Adams and Smart trains. 8/10—Thirty men went in pursuit of the Indians and found them seven miles distant. At the first fire from the Indians two-thirds of the men turned and ran—three killed (only two bodies recovered) and five wounded. 8/11—The combined trains, totaling 200 wagons and 700 people, moved on to Raft River, "after burying the dead." [181:letter]

John R. Adkinson, 1967. In this reminiscent account of a member of Captain Newman's company, it is noted that there were two small horse or mule trains ahead of his ox train on 8/9. Receiving word of the attack on the one nearest, three miles ahead, they went to their relief and found the survivors in "the bluffs and rocks just below the falls" (on the Snake River, immediately above Eagle Rock). The other train, which was attacked a mile beyond, made a running fight to the vicinity of Massacre Rocks where they corraled for a successful defense. The relieving ox train camped nearby. 8/10—Three dead were buried and a party went out to recover lost stock, were attacked and driven to the shelter of a low ridge near the river. 8/11—A small party organized to bring in the bodies from the Cold Creek fight got only two, and they were buried in the road with the others, before the combined trains moved on to the Raft River. [4: 9-11]

H. C. Ellis [undated]. 8/9—They were nooning when a rider came, telling of an Indian attack four miles ahead. Forty men rode to relieve the beleaguered train. The survivors were helped on to a campsite (near Massacre Rocks) where they found a mule train that had escaped the Indians. 8/10—Thirty-six men followed the Indian trail into a valley south of the emigrant road, had a fight and retreated two miles to the shelter of some juniper trees. [129: letter]

Alvin Zaring [undated]. 8/9—Nooned four miles below American Falls, where a rider informed them of the attack on a train four miles ahead. Went to the relief of that party and hauled their wagons on to a camp four miles beyond (near Massacre Rocks). There they found a small horse train that had been attacked. 8/10—The Indians were pursued and found nine miles from camp. In the fight that followed, the emigrants were driven three miles. 8/11—Buried five dead men and drove to Raft River. [410: account]

Henry R. Herr, August 29, 1862. ". . . Passed 5 graves of emigrants murdered Aug. 9, 1862." September 3: "Snake River, passed graves of five Indians killed by emigrants." [175: diary]

Jennie Broughton Brown, 1932. "Another spot always associated with the section of the road near Fort Hall is Massacre Rocks, a few miles farther west than American Falls on the

Oregon Trail. In that narrow defile between the rocky cliffs many pioneers were ambushed and killed by the Indians. On October 16, 1927, was dedicated there a granite monument with a bronze marker bearing the following inscription: 'In this defile on August 10, 1862, a band of Shoshone Indians ambushed an emigrant train bound for Oregon, killing nine white men and wounding six. Erected by the Sons of Idaho, 1927." Other information on p. 378 is also inaccurate. The monument referred to was removed in the course of highway improvement work and there is no intention of replacing it. [48: 377-78]

WPA Writers' Project, 1939. A very romantic and inaccurate account which also presumes an ambush at Massacre Rocks. [146: 109-10]

Irene D. Paden, 1943. ". . . we drove squarely between the Masacre Rocks . . . formed an ideal spot for ambush . . . particular incident which gave the rock its name happened in the summer of '62." There follows the story of the attack on the Adams train as given by diarists. [298: 287-88]

Idaho Historical Society, Reference Leaflet. General information on Indian attacks in the vicinity during 1862 is given, including two more first-hand accounts of the incidents near Massacre Rocks. (These agree closely with the accounts briefed previously.) [195: No.234]

Author's note, August 23, 1972. According to Tom Dilly of American Falls, a lifetime resident of the area, newspaper reporter and member of the Bannock County Historical Society, the "Massacre Rocks" name was coined by American Falls business men in 1927 to promote tourist interest. This agrees with the fact that the name does not appear on early maps, nor in early accounts.

The opening between the Massacre Rocks was enlarged considerably by blasting in 1958, in preparation for the building of an interstate highway (not yet completed at that point).

The locations for the various events of the Massacre Rocks incident are as follows:

Attack on the Adams train, NE¼ of SW¼, Sec. 22, T8S, R30E.

Attack on the Smart train, NE¼ of NE¼, Sec. 28, T8S, R30E.

Start of the Cold Creek fight, SW¼ of SW¼, Sec. 20, T8S, R31E.

Dilly remembers seeing evidences of the graves south of the Massacre Rocks (about 50 feet, he believes), but was unable to relocate them during a visit to the area in 1972. His recollection goes back more than 60 years, at which time he was a small boy.

USGS map, Neely, Idaho, 1:24,000.

REGISTER ROCK
Mile 1252.8 — 12 miles southwest of American Falls, Idaho
Power County — NE¼ of SW¼, Sec. 12, T9S, R29E

This half-buried boulder, 25 feet in diameter, holds many names and dates of emigrants. It is enclosed with chain link fencing and protected from weathering by an octagonally roofed pavilion. Many of the early notations remain legible, particularly those which were incised. Unprotected rocks in the vicinity have been vandalized. This is a particularly well-protected and accessible example of the rock-art of the emigration.

WPA Writers' Project, 1939. "Emigrant Rock . . . a stone 20 feet high on which early travelers left their autographs. Some of the names are carved into the rock and even some of those painted with axle grease as early as 1849 are still visible." [146: 110]

Irene D. Paden, 1943. "Two miles from Massacre Rocks, down a hollow, is the old Rock Creek Camp. The wagons crossed the streamlet at the foot of the descent, traversed the little flat, and pulled out again up several deeply cut gorges. Jutting up in the hollow are rocks which fairly exude names and dates. Among others we found the one word, Mann [Henry R. Mann]." [298: 288]

Author's note, August 23, 1972. The sign under the shelter states: "Register Rock / While cooking fires smoked, and livestock / watered and grazed, the early pioneer / took time to etch his passing on this and / other rocks in the area. / Register Rock was a scheduled resting / spot along the Oregon Trail, and has / been preserved by the Idaho Department of Parks to enable the visitor a chance / to enjoy an experience of the past."

This campground on the Oregon Trail is now a part of Idaho's Massacre Rocks State Park. The small stream which provided water here was known to the emigrants both as "Fall Creek" and "Rock Creek."

USGS map, Yale, Idaho, 1:62,500, 1959 ed.

COLD WATER CAMPGROUND_p
Mile 1258.0 — 6.4 miles east of Yale, Idaho
Power County — SW¼ of Sec. 19, T9S, R29E

This Oregon Trail campground was located at a good spring.

Author's note, August 22, 1972. This site was identified by Max Bruce of the Bureau of Land Management Office in Burley, Idaho. The spring is now part of a ranch crowded in between the new Interstate Highway I-86, and old U.S. Highway 30N. Probably much of the campground is covered by the roads.

Near this point is the Frymier Field ("Bonanza Bar," a gold placer of 1878), of which tailing piles remain across the Snake River. The location is 1.3 miles to the northeast, in the NW¼ of Sec. 20 and SW¼ of Sec. 17, T9S, R29E. These diggings are visible from I-86.

USGS map, Yale, Idaho, 1:62,500, 1959 ed.

CROSSING OF RAFT RIVER$_p$
Mile 1265.0 — 1.8 miles south of Yale, Idaho
Cassia County — NE¼ of NW¼, Sec. 7, T1OS, R28E

Beyond this relatively easy river crossing the track divided, the left branch being the "California Trail," which also served traffic bound for Oregon by the southern route, laid out by the Applegates, and the right branch continuing down the Snake River as the "old" Oregon Trail.

It was at this point that the emigrant had to make his most important decision—whether to go to California or Oregon, and if the latter, by which portal.

Osborne Russell, September 22, 1838. "We arrived at a stream called Cozzu (or Raft River)." P. 170, Note 149: "Raft River was called the 'Cassia' by Ferris, and 'Casu' by Wyeth. Jason Lee says it '. . . received its name from the circumstances that some of the traders were obliged to make a raft to cross it in high water.' Certainly the name must have been given early for Peter Skene Ogden notes in his journal (p. 356): 'Monday, March 20th [1825]. I sent two men with traps to examine Raft River.'" [337: 93, 170]

Rev. Samuel Parker, August 7, 1843. ". . . to Ferry's Creek. [301:diary]

John C. Fremont, September 26, 1843. ". . . on a stream called Raft river, *(Riviere aux Cajeux,)* . . . on the left, the ridge in which Raft river heads is about 20 miles distant, rocky and tolerably high." Note 64: ". . . JCF is one of the few early travelers to correctly render the name *cajeux,* applied at an early date by the French peasantry to small rafts." [202:I, 526]

William Taylor, July 25-26, 1846. ". . . to Casua Bad Road 26 Left the Oregon Road." [275:I, 127]

Virgil Pringle, August 10, 1846. ". . . to the Casue or Raft River . . . at this place the Oregon and California road fork." [275:I, 179]

J. M. Harrison, 1846. "Shortly after leaving Fort Hall we came to where the California road turned off. A number of our company took this road the most of them we believe intending to turn off on the Applegate route to the Willamette Valley." [165: account]

James A. Pritchard, July 6, 1849. ". . . descended into the bottom of Raft River. It is a small stream with a smooth strong current and gravelly bed . . . it is at the crossing of this stream that the Oregon & California roads separate." [317: 110]

Osborne Cross, August 11, 1849. ". . . we crossed Ogden's river at twelve o'clock. The road turns off to the south for California . . ." [101: 179]

J. Goldsborough Bruff, August 27, 1849. ". . . reach'd Raft river, forded it, and just over on our right, a grave just where the Oregon trail turns off right, over basaltic cliffs - 'To the Memory of Lydia Edmonson who died Aug. 16, 1847, Aged 25 years.'" [52: 111]

Hamilton Scott, August 12, 1862. "Miss Adams, the lady who was wounded in the fight with the Indians, died last night and was buried this morning. Some of the trains take the California Road this morning. We keep the old Oregon road." [347: diary]

Walter E. Meacham, 1947. Traffic bound for Oregon by way of the Applegate (southern) route turned off on the California Trail at the Raft River. [257: 9]

Idaho Historical Society, Reference Leaflet. Describes the northern end of the California Trail. [195: No. 63]

Idaho Historical Society, Reference Leaflet. Mentions establishment of Smith's Camp at the mouth of the Raft River in 1864. [195: No. 52]

Author's note, September 30, 1972. An information panel concerning this crossing has been placed at the I-84 rest stop, 10.1 miles west of the Raft River. The junction of the Oregon and California trails was on the west bank of the Raft River at a point one mile south of I-84. It came into existence in 1846 when Jesse Applegate branched off from the original Oregon Trail in order to open a new route to the Willamette Valley by way of the southern reaches of the territory. However, the new route immediately became more important to California-bound traffic (which followed Applegate's track half-way), and it soon came to be known as the "California Trail."

A small cove near the junction served as a campground and three emigrant graves there have been vandalized.

USGS map, Yale, Idaho, 1:62,500, 1952 ed.

MARSH CREEK CAMPGROUND$_p$
Mile 1281.1 — 5 miles due east of Declo, Idaho
Cassia County — NW¼ of NW¼, Sec. 27, T10S, R25E

This Oregon Trail campground was used by emigrants from John C. Fremont's exploration on, but it is now obliterated by agricultural use.

John C. Fremont, September 27, 1843. ". . . we encamped at a considerable spring, called Swamp Creek, rising in low grounds near the point of a spur from the mountain."

USGS map, Rupert SE, Idaho, 1:24,000, 1964 ed.

5

Caldron Linn to Ladd Canyon

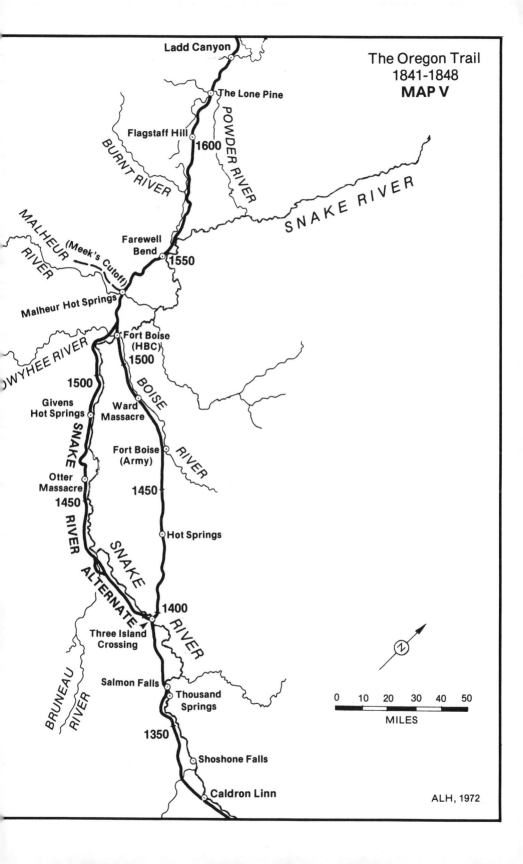

The Oregon Trail
1841-1848
MAP V

Ladd Canyon

The Lone Pine

Flagstaff Hill

1600

POWDER RIVER

BURNT RIVER

SNAKE RIVER

MALHEUR RIVER

(Meek's Cutoff)

Farewell Bend

1550

Malheur Hot Springs

OWYHEE RIVER

Fort Boise (HBC)

1500

1500

BOISE RIVER

Givens Hot Springs

Ward Massacre

SNAKE

Fort Boise (Army)

Otter Massacre

1450

1450

RIVER

Hot Springs

SNAKE

ALTERNATE

RIVER

1400

Three Island Crossing

BRUNEAU RIVER

Salmon Falls

Thousand Springs

1350

Shoshone Falls

Caldron Linn

0   10   20   30   40   50
MILES

ALH, 1972

CALDRON LINN$_p$
Mile 1318R¼ — 1.6 miles east of Murtaugh, Idaho
Twin Falls County — NE¼ of SE¼, Sec. 5, T11S, R20E

This is a narrow chute by which the Snake River descended 40 feet into a pool with such violence as to suggest the old Gaelic word, "linn," which can mean either a waterfall or a steep ravine; and that, preceded by "caldron," provided an apt description of the effect upon the stream at that point.

This particular obstacle symbolized the disappointing nature of the Snake River as the Astorians knew it. Travelers by land were less impressed, and, now that the Snake River has been harnessed and is nearly dry much of the year, there is no spectacular torrent to give meaning to the name.

Washington Irving, 1882. Wilson Price Hunt's party arrived here on October 18, 1811. ". . . they had arrived at a terrific strait, that forbade all further progress in the canoes, and dismayed the most experienced voyageur: The whole body of the river was compressed into a space of less than thirty feet in width, between two ledges of rocks, upward of two hundred feet high, and formed a whirling and tumultuous vortex, so frightfully agitated as to receive the name of 'The Caldron Linn.' Beyond this fearful abyss the river kept raging and roaring on, until lost to sight among impending precipices. [199:II, 372]

Idaho Historical Society, Reference Leaflet. From Milner Dam on the Snake River—"Almost eight miles down the channel (and about 6, measured directly) from Milner, the river drops through a falls known to the original explorers there as Caldron Linn. A linn is a pool below a falls, the term coming from Scotland . . .

"Almost a year later, on September 29, 1812, Robert Stuart and a party of Astorians returning east to the United States, came back to the Caldron Linn . . . [of which he wrote] '. . . at the Caldron Linn the whole body of the River is confined between 2 ledges of Rock somewhat less than 40 feet apart & Here indeed its terrific appearance beggars all description— Hecate's caldron was never half so agitated when vomiting even the most diabolical spells, as is this Linn in a low stage of water & its bearing in idea such proximity of resemblance to that or something more infernal, I think well authorizes it to retain the new name it has, more particularly as the *tout ensemble* of these 30 miles has been baptised the Devils Scuttle Hole.'

"Caldron Linn includes nearly half of another fall of 80 feet before Dry creek enters a mile below." [195: No. 289]

The Snake River at Caldron Linn.

Author's note, August 22, 1972. Due east of Murtaugh is an information panel (Idaho No. 284) which describes the Hunt party's experience at Caldron Linn, adding: "Today no road reaches the spot and the name is forgotten." The Oregon Trail passed close to Caldron Linn, but it does not seem to have been known to the emigrants.

The rapid where Ramsey Crooks' canoe was lost, with the drowning of his steersman, Antoine Clappine, is five miles up the river in the center of the NW¼ of Sec. 30, T10S, R21E. The locality was identified in 1938 through the finding of traps and guns which appear to have fallen into the river from the wrecked canoe.

USGS map, Murtaugh, Idaho, 1:24,000, 1965 ed.,

STRICKER STORE
Mile 1327.6 — 10 miles southwest of Twin Falls, Idaho
Twin Falls County — NW¼ of NW¼, Sec. 23, T11S, R18E

This is a one-room log cabin, 18' x 20', standing on the north bank of Rock Creek where the emigrant route reaches that

The Stricker Store on Rock Creek, near Twin Falls, Idaho. This pioneer building was established as a stage station on the Oregon Trail.

stream. It is sod-roofed, and a sheet metal covering now protects the sod. It has a veranda-type porch facing the creek. There is a two-room cellar behind the building, and a stone monument stands nearby. It is the only original stage station remaining from the line which connected Utah and Idaho in prerailroad days. It was not a Pony Express station, as sometimes stated, and its principal use seems to have been as a store.

WPA Writers' Project, 1939. "Trading Station . . . for years the first west of Fort Hall. It was a camping site, a Pony Express station, and then in 1863 a settlement. The old store still stands. [146: 112]

Author's note, August 22, 1972. The historical marker on Highway 30, at Hanson, Idaho, states: "Historical Spot / Strickers Store And Rock Creek /Stage Station. Five Miles South. One / Mile West. First trading post to be / established west of Fort Hall on / the Old Oregon Trail in 1863 / Erected 1937 by Sons and Daughters of Idaho Pioneers / Dedicated to the State of Idaho."

The Stricker Store is located at what was, of necessity, a campground for emigrants. Rock Creek was the first water after leaving the Snake River near present Murtaugh, Idaho—nineteen miles by air.

Reference. Ralph W. Macy, "Stricker's Store," in *Overland Journal*, 4/2 (Spring 1986), 25-35.

USGS map, Stricker Butte, Idaho, 1:24,000, 1965 ed.

SHOSHONE ("CANADIAN") FALLS
Mile 1337R5 — 4 miles northeast of Twin Falls, Idaho
Twin Falls County, in SW¼ of Sec. 31, T9S, R18E

This is a waterfall of 212 feet which could occasionally be heard by emigrants on the Oregon Trail, five miles away. The Twin Falls, two miles east (up the Snake River) appears to have been unknown to them. However, few emigrants were even aware of this mighty cascade. There was little incentive to stray from the trail in a region where game was scarce and the Indians were considered treacherous.

Osborne Cross, August 15, 1849 (at Rock Creek). ". . . could easily hear the sound of a waterfall . . . much surprised to learn the next day that within ten miles of this place there is a cascade which is not surpassed by the Niagara falls. . . . Lieutenant Lindsay to the place, who pronounced it one of nature's great wonders." P. 185: . . . name [Canadian Falls] said to have been given them by a priest many years since, they decided on that of the Great Shoshonie falls, instead of Canadian, as being the most appropriate. The road does not pass there . . . nearest point is not less than eight or ten miles . . . [five miles from the emigrant route]." [101: 184]

Idaho Historical Society, Reference Leaflet. "In contrast to Thousand Springs and Salmon Falls, almost no one noticed Shoshone and Twin Falls, located off the regular route of travel. Two men and the guide from an expedition of mounted riflemen, who examined more of the country along the river, heard Shoshone Falls and went to great effort to get all the way down the canyon there, August 15, 1849. They made a relatively accurate estimate of the height of the falls—until then called Canadian Falls—and decided to rename the place Shoshone Falls. An Indian had shown Canadian, or Shoshone, Falls to the expedition's guide years before. [195: No. 184, 2]

Gregory M. Franzwa, 1972. "Proceed to an overlook area and observe the falls. Note the results of a cruel harnessment, but at least at Shoshone what is left of the water is allowed to pass over the brink. The Snake drops 212 feet over a horseshoe-shaped rim about 1,000 feet wide. Visitors may walk on the rocks of the brink, where only a few isolated streams plunge to the deep pool below. At one time the water roared over the entire escarpment

virtually unbroken. Thomas J. Farnham, in 1843, said that the roar could be heard three miles away." [141: 319-20]
    USGS map, Twin Falls, Idaho, 1:24,000, 1964 ed.

CROSSING OF ROCK CREEK (Probable)_P
CROSSING OF ROCK CREEK (Probable)$_P$
Mile 1338.2 — 2.5 miles southeast of Twin Falls, Idaho
Twin Falls County — SW¼ of NW¼, Sec. 26, TIOS, R17E

This natural crossing of Rock Creek, a stream which slashes across the Snake River Valley from the mountains to the river, in a narrow rent in the volcanic rocks which are everywhere else too precipitous and deep for wagons. The crossing appears to have been on an Indian trail, and was the only practicable ford of a serious barrier to wagon travel.
    John C. Fremont, September 29-30, 1843. ". . . we encamped about 5 o'clock on Rock creek—a stream having considerable water, a swift current, and wooded with willow. . . . in its progress toward the river, this creek soon enters a chasm of the volcanic rock, which in places along the wall presents a columnar appearance; and the road becomes extremely rocky whenever it passes near its banks. It is only about twenty feet wide where the road crosses it, with a deep bed, and steep banks covered with rocky fragments, with willows and a little grass on its narrow bottom. . . . The fragments of rock which had been removed by the emigrants in making a road where we ascended from the bed of this creek were whitened with lime." [202:I, 527-28]
    Samuel Parker, August 9, 1845. Calls this stream "Stony Creek." [302: diary]
    Osborne Cross, August 14, 1849. ". . . arrived at Rock creek and continued down its banks to a bend where the road diverges. . . . The bottom of this creek, as well as its banks, was of volcanic formation . . . stream itself not more than fifteen feet wide . . . canyon . . . many places fifty to one hundred feet high and varying in width from one hundred to two hundred yards." [101: 182-83]
    WPA Writers' Project, 1939. "A natural cave in the wall of Rock Creek Canyon (R) was the first jail in Twin Falls County . . . until a Federal statute made it illegal to keep persons below the surface of the earth." [146: 113]
    Irene D. Paden, 1943. "The pioneers, cutting across a bend of the Snake, came to it [Rock Creek] far upstream, turned down its east bank, and skirted the steep brink for eight miles before

Some of the "Thousand Springs" tumble into the Snake River.

a suitable place was found for the descent. The creek itself was but twenty feet wide." [298: 331]

Author's note, November 18, 1972. The problem of the crossing of Rock Creek was discussed with Dr. Merle D. Wells, who had just made a careful reconnaissance along the stream to determine where the emigrants might have crossed it. He found only one natural crossing, which is at a bend, as Major Cross noted. The canyon was particularly impassable below the present townsite of Twin Falls, and neither of two other sites suggested [141: 320] seemed practical for wagons. These places are 0.8 and 1.2 miles upstream from the probable crossing.

USGS map, Twin Falls, Idaho, 1:24,000, 1964 ed.

THOUSAND SPRINGS
Mile 1363R½ — 5.9 miles south of Hagerman, Idaho
Twin Falls County, Sec. 8, T8S, R14E

In this area a series of streams burst out from beneath the rimrock on the north side of the Snake River and cascade into it. They were once numerous enough to merit the name, "Thousand Springs," but much of the water is now diverted to a hydroelectric plant. This was a landmark of considerable interest to the emigrants, who are credited with naming the feature.

John C. Fremont, September 30, 1843. "Immediately opposite to us, a subterranean river bursts out directly from the face of the escarpment, and falls in white foam to the river below . . . views annexed [p. 529] . . . in measuring the river, which is 1,786 feet in breadth, with banks 200 feet high . . . a beautiful basin of clear water, formed by the falling river, around which the rocks were whitened by some saline incrustation. Here the Indians had constructed wicker dams . . . the main stream, which, issuing from between strata of the trap rock in two principal branches, produced almost a torrent, 22 feet wide, and white with foam . . . temperature of the spring was 58 degrees . . . river was 51 degrees. The perpendicular height of the place at which this stream issues is 45 feet above the river, and 152 feet below the summit [rimrock]." [202:I, 528-30]

Osborne Cross, August 16, 1849. ". . . we came to where the water burst forth from the rocks in many places . . ." [101: 187]

Idaho Historical Society, Reference Leaflet. "Many of them [missionaries and settlers] recorded their impressions of nearby Thousand Springs . . . The designation . . . in fact, goes back to this time. . . . Beginning in 1852, a route on the north side of the river from a crossing just above Thousand Springs came into use. Some emigrants forded the river, but most who crossed there used a ferry. In 1852 and 1853 the ferry did not amount to much, although those who used it had to pay $6.00 to take advantage of a better route. . . . By 1879, improved service was offered there by Payne's Ferry." P. 3: "Before irrigation, around 15 percent of the water discharged from Thousand Springs (and from many other large springs of the region) came from the Lost River country, where the Big Lost River, Little Lost River, and Birch Creek sink into the broad lava-filled plain. Still more water came from rain and snow that fall in the valley above the springs, where the lava beds act as an enormous reservoir for water storage. Most of the water for Thousand Springs came from Snake River at the forks near Rexburg: much of the stream flow goes underground there . . . reappears a great many years later in and around Thousand Springs. More recently, irrigation on the north side of Snake River has increased the water supply for these springs around 40 percent." [195: No. 184, 2]

Author's note, August 21, 1972. Most of these springs are now harnessed for power and only a few continue to cascade down to the river as they used to. The Snake River Trout Co. uses water from these springs in its trout ranching operation, which is said to be the largest of its kind. An information panel has been placed on U.S. Highway 30 opposite the springs.

USGS map, Thousand Springs, Idaho, 1:24,000.

UPPER SALMON FALLS
Mile 1366.0 — 3.4 miles south of Hagerman, Idaho
Twin Falls County — NW¼ of NE¼, Sec. 2, T8S, R13E

The Salmon Falls consisted of two rapids, about five miles apart, where the Indians gathered to spear the salmon which were so obstructed in their ascent of the Snake River that they could be taken with ease.

Salmon could be bartered from these Indians, which was a great help to the emigrants, many of whom had used up most of the food they had brought with them.

Idaho Historical Society, Reference Leaflet. Provides 10 excerpts from other diaries of travelers who visited the Salmon Falls prior to 1853. These accounts are by Wilson P. Hunt (1811), Robert Stuart (1812), Narcissa P. Whitman (1836), Sarah W. Smith (1838), Asahel Munger (1839), Overton Johnson and William H. Winter (1843), Charles Preuss (1843), Theodore Talbot (1843), Osborne Cross (1849), P. V. Crawford (1851), John S. Zeiber (1851), and Clarence B. Bagley (1852). The comment is also made: "Long before white trappers explored the region, upper and lower Salmon Falls had been a major Indian campground; although Boise River provided the main Shoshoni salmon fisheries, Salmon Falls served great numbers of Indians farther up the valley of the Snake, because that was as far upstream as salmon could ascend." [195: No. 184]

Author's note, August 21, 1972. The lower Salmon Falls is 1.8 miles north of Hagerman, Idaho. It, like the upper falls, has been dammed for hydro-electric power production. The location of the Lower Salmon Falls is in the SW¼ of SW¼, Sec. 2, T7S, R13E.

USGS map, Hagerman, Idaho, 1:24,000, 1950 ed.

THREE-ISLAND CROSSING
Mile 1397.4 — 2 miles southwest of Glenns Ferry, Idaho
Elmore County — NW¼ of NE¼, Sec. 1, T6S, R9E

William H. Jackson painted the Three Island Crossing as it appeared when approached by emigrants heading west.

Today's Three Island Crossing, as seen from the state park on the north bank of the Snake River.

This is a crossing of the Snake River near present Glenns Ferry, Idaho, by which the emigrants reached the north side of the river and a better road to Fort Boise. The crossing touched only two of the three islands which are set in a widening of the river at that point.

Always a dangerous crossing, its use avoided a rough, dry trail on the south side of the Snake River; thus, most emigrants tried to cross here.

James W. Nesmith, September 10, 1843. "Encamped on an island in the river . . ." September 11: ". . . Crossed the river this morning without difficulty . . ." [290: 35]

John C. Fremont, October 3, 1843. "About 2 o'clock we arrived at the ford where the road crosses to the right bank of the Snake River. An Indian was hired to conduct us through the ford, which proved impracticable for us, the water sweeping away the howitzer and nearly drowning the mules, which we were obliged to extricate by cutting them out of the harness. The river here is expanded into a little bay, in which there are two islands, across which is the road of the ford; and the emigrants had passed by placing two of their heavy wagons abreast of each other, so as to oppose a considerable mass against the body of water. The Indians informed [us] . . . one . . . in attempting to turn some cattle. . . . [was] carried off and drowned . . . we had a resource in a boat. . . breadth [of the river] of 1,049 feet . . . from six to eight feet deep . . ." [201:1, 532-33]

William D. Stillwell, 1844. "We left our wagon at the upper crossing of Snake River, where the Emigrant road crossed the Snake River at Three Islands." [367: letter]

Samuel Parker, August 14, 1845. "To Snake River—crossed very deep to hind wheels—7 yoke to a wagon." [302: diary]

Samuel Hancock, 1845. "The next day we arrived at the crossing of Snake River, when two men of the company forded it for the purpose of hunting on the other side, and did not return that night; in the morning four men went in search of them, and found blood and the traces of something being dragged on the ground; they followed this and found the body of one of these men divested of its scalp, clothing, gun, etc. After looking around and making the most diligent search for the other and seeing no trace of him, they concluded that he had shared a similar fate, and burying the comrade already found as best they could, returned to camp. We now made preparation for crossing the river, which was very rapid and deep, and perhaps 200 yards wide; the crossing was effected by proping up the wagon beds above the reach of the water and having three men on horseback by the team of the first wagon, to which the others were all chained each to the preceding one, and with a man on horseback to keep the teams straight, we reached the opposite bank safely, though some of the smaller cattle were forced to swim." [162: 26]

Osborne Cross, August 19, 1849. ". . . undertake to cross the river here . . . opposite two small willow islands and thought it practicable, as the water in depth would not come up to the wagon beds. . . . current was discovered to be strong . . . [one man drowned]. . . . cutting down the banks one of the wagons was then tried . . . [abandoned the attempt] . . . remained on the left bank." [101: 193-94]

WPA Writers' Project, 1939. "The Bannock chief, Buffalo Horn, terrorized this area in 1878, burning the stage station which stood at the foot of King Hill and murdering three miners on Dead Man's Flat." [146: 116]

Irene D. Paden, 1943. "Not all travelers, either in early days or later, crossed the river near Glenn's Ferry . . . long, deadly dry trek around the bend. . . ." [298: 336]

Idaho Historical Society, Reference Leaflet. Three pages of quotations from early travelers concerning the Three Island Crossing. [195: No. 185]

Author's note, August 21, 1972. At 1.7 miles northwest of the crossing, on the north side of U.S. Highway 20/30, is a monument inscribed: "To all pioneers who passed / over Three Island Crossing / and helped to win the West / erected 1931 / by Troop One Boy Scouts of / America / Roslyn, New York / Scoutmaster E.K. Pietsch." This monument, in the NW¼ of SE¼, Sec. 26, T5S, R9E, has been vandalized by gunfire.

The freight road from Salt Lake City to Boise, opened in 1863, was greatly improved in 1871 by the establishment of a ferry three miles upstream from the ford of emigrant days. This new crossing, 1.1 miles east of Glenns Ferry, Idaho, is the source of the town's name. Evidences of the old ferry installation can be seen about 600 feet downstream from the bridge which now spans the Snake River at that point. The ferry site is in the NW¼ of SW¼, Sec. 28, T5S, R10E.

An Idaho State Park, located on the north bank of the Snake River below the Three Island Crossing, has museum exhibits complementing the pioneer history of the area.

USGS map, Glenns Ferry, Idaho, 1:24,000, 1947 ed.

UNNAMED HOT SPRINGS
Mile 1417.0 — 9 miles east of Mountain Home, Idaho
Elmore County — SW¼ of SW¼, Sec. 16, T3S, R8E

This was a camping place for emigrants, attracted by several hot springs which occupy a basin 1,000 feet across at the head of Hot Spring Creek.

James W. Nesmith, September 13, 1843. "Passed the Hot

Spring about noon. Water almost boiling." [290: 351]

Peter H. Burnett. "On the 14th of September [1843] we passed the Boiling Spring. Its water is hot enough to cook an egg. It runs out at three different places, forming a large branch, which runs off smoking and foaming . . ." [55: 81]

John C. Fremont, October 5, 1843. ". . . to a group of smoking hot springs, with a temperature of 164 degrees. . . . The rocks were covered with a white and red incrustation; and the water has on the tongue the same unpleasant effect as that of the Basin spring on Bear River. They form several branches, and bubble up with force enough to raise the small pebbles several inches. . . . These springs are near the foot of the ridge, (a dark and rugged looking mountain) . . ." [202:I, 534]

William D. Stillwell, 1844. "The first night [after leaving Three Island Crossing] we camped at the hot & cold springs about half way to Boise River . . ." [367: letter]

Irene D. Paden, 1943. ". . . passed the hot springs and came to Canyon Creek. Here was the site of the original settlement of Mountain Home . . . according to local tradition, in the early eighties a Commodore Jackson [located there] and Mountain Home was just what its name implies—his home in the mountains . . . became a stage and freighting stop, and he ran it as he pleased . . . he picked up his town, post office and all, and moved it over to the new railroad, leaving the stage line flat but keeping the name." [298: 336-37]

Author's note, August 21, 1972. The original site of Mountain Home station was 8¼ miles northeast of the present town, at the place where Rattlesnake Creek breaks out of the mountains. It was in the NW¼ of NW¼, Sec. 6, T3S, R8E. The spring was under the floor of the building.

USGS map, Mountain Home, Idaho, 1:62,500, 1956 ed.

CROSSINGS OF BRUNEAU RIVER (South Alternate)
Mile 1428.0 — 4½ miles northwest of Bruneau, Idaho
Owyhee County — (Upper) NW¼ of SW¼, Scc. 9, T6S, R5E
(Lower) NW¼ of SW¼, Sec. 35, T5S, R4E

There are few references to the crossing of the Bruneau River by those emigrants who elected to remain on the south side of the Snake River. This probably indicates that those crossings were not especially difficult.

Osborne Cross, 1849. Mentions the crossing. [101: 199] Idaho

Historical Society, Reference Leaflet. Item (c) notes the existence of a military post at the mouth of the Bruneau River in 1866. [195: No. 63]

Author's note, August 20, 1972. The lower crossing is now flooded by a power dam.

USGS maps, Bruneau, Idaho, 1:24,000, 1947 ed.

Mouth of Bruneau, Idaho, 1:24,000, 1946 ed.

OTTER MASACRE SITE (South Alternate)
Mile 1450.2 — 15 miles southeast of Murphy, Idaho
Owyhee County — SE¼ of NE¼, Sec. 1. T4S, R1W

The site where the Elijah Otter party was destroyed by hostile Indians on September 9, 1860, has formerly been placed west of Sinker Creek (NE¼ Sec. 12, T3S, R1W) on the basis of testimony offered by Miles Cannon in 1921. That location is marked on many maps, including the current USGS topographical sheet, Sinker Butte, Idaho, 1:24,000, 1948 ed.

However, Dr. Merle W. Wells and Larry Jones have discovered, from emigrant diaries not available earlier, that the Otter "massacre" took place near Castle Butte and adjacent to the Snake River. The description of the site appears to fit the Morgan place on Castle Creek.

The attack by local Indians on the Otter wagon train of 44 persons on September 9, 1960, resulted in the death of 11 persons during the siege of two days, and in the dispersal of 33 others—of whom 17 subsequently died or were killed by Indians. This encounter stands as the blodiest of record involving Indians and emigrants in the Snake River Valley during that troubled decade which preceded the Snake River War.

Henry M. Judson, 1862. This Oregon-bound emigrant made the following entries in his diary: "4 Sep. 62. About 12 o'clk we reach Castle Creek so called from some singular looking rocks having the appearance of old dilapidated castles and other ruins—soon Capt K's train arrives and corrals near us—after remaining an hour & a half we are ordered to hitch up & drive on a mile or so for better grass—we comply & find grass higher than our heads & just abreast of the castle rock—on the other side of the corral runs the creek a small crooked stream. . . . 5 Sep 62 I should have mentioned yesterday that it is said the Indians beseiged a party of 30 or 35 men on the very spot on which we were corralled & killed all but 3 after a 3 day fight—

some report seeing nearly a whole skeleton on the ground—I myself saw a skull & probably could have found more by searching. . . ." [210A: diary]

Miles Cannon, 1953. This account is based on information obtained in interviews with two survivors of the massacre—Mrs. Joseph Meyes and her daughter, Mrs. Martin, both of Salem, Oregon—as well as the official reports of Army officers sent to rescue the survivors. Statements are also given by pioneer residents and an Indian involved in the massacre. [59: 133-44]

J. M. Harrison, undated. Has information on the death of Trimble (an event preceding the Otter affair), and more on this is available in Morgan, 1963:II, 602. [165: letter]

Owyhee Historical Society, 1969. Provides excerpts from contemporary newspaper coverage of the event. [297: leaflet]

Lawson Stockman, 1859. This is an obviously hearsay account which is in error in a number of important aspects. However, it likely is representative of the stories which circulated in Oregon following the massacre (the cannibalism aspect alone was enough to excite considerable interest). [236: 164]

Jennie Broughton Brown, 1932. A less-complete version of this event than that of Miles Cannon. It is also incongruous in a number of respects and entirely undocumented. [48: 329]

Wm. H. McNeil, undated. "Boise Massacre," quoted from *Dufur* (Ore.) *Dispatch*, 1896. "Dan Butler joined another group of volunteers who rode up to Boise to punish Indians for the massacre Sept. 13, 1860 of eight wagons of emigrants and 54 people, who surrounded the train in an all-day battle all one night and all the next day. Some of the emigrants scattered over the prairie and became lost and starved to death. The mangled, mutilated bodies of the emigrants was one of the most revolting sights Dan Butler had ever witnessed!" [256: 240]

Author's note, August 20, 1972. While examining the marked "Otter Massacre Site" near Sinker Creek, a cairn of gray sandstones was discovered about 700 ft. southwest of the USGS marker. Two of the stones have the word "Otter" incised on them (one also has five recognizable letters of the word massacre). The stones of the cairn appear to have been plucked from a low ridge nearby—one was placed with the lettering inverted—and other stones from the same place were used to form a cross on the ground near the cairn. The present owners of the Naha Ranch had no knowledge of the cairn, or even that there might be a historically-important site on the bench above them.

The grave of Jacob Reuben, the original settler and one of

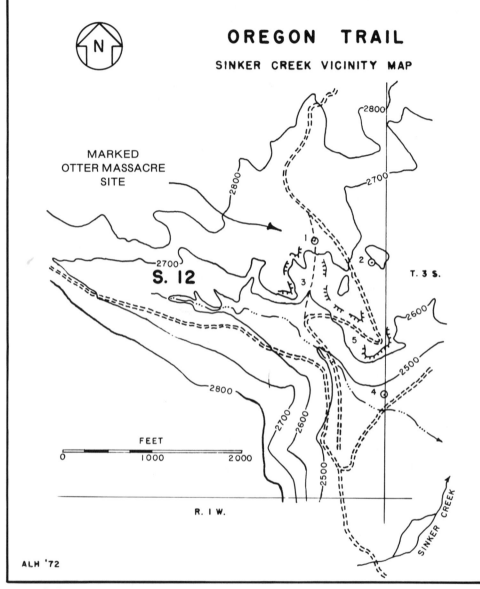

1. Location of the Otter Massacre as shown on the USGS map, Sinker Butte, Idaho.
2. Position of cairn with marked stones.
3. Ruts of the Oregon Trail ascending a steep gulley.
4. Gravesite of Jacob Reuben, an early settler.
5. Stagecoach road supported on a dry-masonry wall.

Miles Cannon's informants, is near Sinker Creek, south of the site. At the town of Murphy, Idaho, in front of the courthouse, is a monument which reads: "Erected to the memory / of the Otter Massacre / 1860 / Forty four persons ambushed by Shoshoni Indians, either killed or / scattered, most awful human experience / Site ten miles east on Sinker Creek / erected by / Sons and Daughters of Idaho Pioneers / 1935."
USGS map, Sinker Butte, Idaho, 1:24,000, 1948 ed.

BONNEVILLE POINT
Mile 1452.0 — 12½ miles southeast of Boise, Idaho
Ada County — SE1/¼ of Sec. 24, T2N, R3E

This is the elevation from which Capt. B.L.E. Bonneville in 1833 saw the Boise, or "wooded" River, named earlier by French-Canadian voyageurs. The Indian trail he was following soon became the Oregon Trail.

John C. Fremont, October 7, 1843. we came suddenly in sight of the broad green line of the valley of the Rivière Boisée (wooded river), black near the gorge where it debouches into the plains, with high precipices of basalt, between the walls of which it passes, on emerging from the mountains. . . . the river, which is a beautiful rapid stream, with clear mountain water, and, as the name indicates, well wooded . . . delighted this afternoon to make a pleasant camp under fine old trees again . . . in the fur trade, a small party of men under [John Reed, built] . . . a little fort on

This monument stands on Boenneville Point.

this river, were surprised and massacred . . . the stream owes its occasional name of *Reid's river* [to that event of January 1814]." [201:I, 536-37]

Irene D. Paden, 1943. "Here, so historians more or less agree, is where Captain Bonneville's party exclaimed in French over the lovely wooded river (*rivière boisée*) that lay ahead. A massive monument to the memory of that first moment of discovery crowns the flattish point . . . few . . . ever see it." [298: 338, 339]

Gregory M. Franzwa, 1972. Gives the text on the monument as follows: "From this old Indian trail, later known as the Old Oregon Trail, Capt. B. L. E. Bonneville's party, on first sighting the river in May 1833, exclaimed, 'Les bois, les bois, voyes les bois!' meaning, the woods, the woods, see the woods! Capt. Bonneville, therefore named the stream Rivière Boise, also indirectly the mountains and the city." [141: 332-33]

USGS map, Indian Creek Reservoir, Idaho, 1:24,000, 1957 ed.

FORT BOISE (ARMY)
Mile 1465R2 — Boise, Idaho
Ada County — SW1/¼ of SW1/¼, Sec. 2, T3N, R2E

Fort Boise was established by Oregon and Washington volunteers in 1863 to protect traffic on the Oregon Trail and the miners flocking to the gold mines of Idaho. This Army post was an important base of operations during Gen. George Crook's successful campaign against the Snake River Indians (1866-1868), and Gen. O. O. Howard's suppression of the dissident Bannocks in 1878. It was deactivated in 1913 and turned over to the U.S. Public Health Service in 1919.

Some historic buildings are used by the Veterans Administration, while others provide a depot for the Idaho National Guard. The grounds also serve as a city park.

Idaho Historical Society, Reference Leaflet. Item (a) provides information on this post. [195: No. 63]

USGS map, Boise South, Idaho, 1:24,000, 1954 ed.

GIVENS HOT SPRINGS (South Alternate)ₚ
Mile 1483.6 — 9 miles southeast of Marsing, Idaho
Owyhee County — NE¼ of NW¼, Sec. 21, TIN, R3W

Several hot springs rise in the flat along the south bank of the Snake River. They were claimed in 1860 and now provide hot water for a plunge said to be the oldest in Idaho.

Overton Johnson, September 1843. The south side of the Snake River ". . . is nothing else than a wild, rocky, barren wilderness, of wrecked and ruined Nature, a field of volcanic desolation . . . Thirty-two miles below the Hot Branches, we crossed Owyhe River . . . opposite Fort Boise . . ." By trail, 34.6 miles. [208: 93]

Osborne Cross, August 27, 1849. ". . . I visited two hot springs a short distance between the river and the hills. The water was extremely hot—too much so to immerse the fingers. The taste was a little metallic . . . no unpleasant smell . . . presume they come from the same fountain head . . . ground around the springs was extremely dry . . . my horse would sink half-leg deep . . ." [101: 204]

Idaho Historical Society, Reference Leaflet. "Those who could not get across Snake River had to travel the more difficult route opened in 1842 down the south side, but they also found hot springs to marvel at when they passed Givens Springs." [195: No. 50]

Author's note, August 20, 1972. According to the present owners of Givens Hot Springs (now a plunge operated in a pleasant grove), the springs were taken up in 1860 by a man of that name who had seen the springs while traveling to Oregon earlier. Not finding what he wanted in the Willamette Valley, he later backtracked into Idaho. A large resort hotel was subsequently erected, but it burned in 1914. The springs, which are now covered, furnish water at 138 degrees.

Due north 2, 000 feet is the site of Hot Springs Ferry, in the NW¼ of the SW¼ of Sec. 16, T1N, R3W. The ferry is no longer in use. Approximately 2,000 feet distant on Az 25 degrees true is Map Rock, a large boulder on the opposite side of the river which has fine Indian petroglyphs on it. It is in the NE¼ of the SW¼ of Sec. 16, T1N, R3W.

USGS map, Givens Hot Springs, 1:24,000, 1958 ed.

WARD MASSACRE SITE
Mile 1486.8 — 2.1 miles south of Middleton, Idaho
Canyon County — NW¼ of NW¼, Sec. 20, T4N, R2W

On August 20, 1854, at a point 24 miles east of Fort Boise (HBC), Indians attacked and killed all but two of the 20 emigrants traveling toward Oregon in the Alexander Ward train. The survivors were young boys—one of whom was rescued by another party of emigrants, while the other made his way to Old Fort Boise transfixed by an arrow. Military retaliation was prompt and severe, and had grave consequences.

The indiscriminate punishment meted out to the Indians enraged them, causing the abandonment of Forts Hall and Boise and making the Oregon Trail in Idaho unsafe for small parties of emigrants for nearly a decade.

Clinton A. Snowden, 1909. Tells the story as he obtained it from Alexander Yantis, one of the men who came upon the scene of the massacre so soon afterward that they were able to trade shots with the Indians; this describes the rescue of the two Ward brothers (the only survivors) and efforts to punish the Indians. [358:III, 5-8]

Wm. H. McNeil, (undated). Reprints Daniel W. Butler's story of the attempt to punish the guilty Indians. He notes the part of H. P. Isaacs and Orlando Humason, ferry operators near old Fort Boise, in the rescue of the Ward boys and in sending word of the disaster to Fort Dalles. A description of the massacre site, as found by the troops and volunteers, is prefaced by the comment: "It is over 40 years since I visited that spot and yet the horror of the sight is often before my eyes." [256: 414]

J. M. Harrison, undated. This account, which may have been written as early as the 1870s, states: "Twenty miles below Boise City, about opposite Middletown on the south side of the river is the seat of the *Ward Massacre* in the summer of 1854, where all but two lads (who were left for dead but afterwards came to and made their escape), some forty persons in all, men & women & children, were massacred by the hand of the ruthless savages. It appears they had been annoyed by Indians for some time, when while they were moving, the Indians being considerably reinforced made a final charge, the men being few in number were soon killed or mortally wounded (there is a detailed description of the treatment of the victims; and of the rescue of the two boys "by a soldier from Fort Boise." Actually, the rescue was due to the combined efforts of the Yantis party of emigrants and the Fort Boise ferrymen] . . . soldiers made gallows and hung offenders in the vicinity as a warning to all others. . . . gallows stood there until a year ago when they fell down. Bodies gathered up and put in a mass grave . . ." [165: letter]

C. F. Coans, 1922. "Nathaniel Olney, the Indian agent for the Snake River district, accompanied a military expedition which was sent to punish the murderers of the Ward party and protect emigrants who were entering the country in the fall of 1855. The detachment under Major Haller was in the upper Snake Valley during August and September . . ." [82: 23]

Author's note, August 7, 1972. At Ward Memorial State Park, a granite shaft bears the names of 18 persons who were killed there on August 20, 1854. Interesting background to the massacre is provided by a statement which appears in the *Oregon Historical Quarterly*, 23 (March 1922), 3: "The Shoshoni Indians along the Snake River were said to have threatened to kill all those who might fall into their hands, and the fate of the Ward Party, and several men of another party, in the fall of 1854, seemed to be the carrying out of this threat." (Statement of R.R. Thompson to Joel Palmer, September 3, 1854.) Perhaps this was an inevitable climax toward which events had been building for some time. USGS map, Middletown, Idaho, 1:24,000, 1958 ed.

FORT BOISE (HBC SITE)
Mile 1510.7 — 4.7 miles northwest of Parma, Idaho
Canyon County — SW¼ of SE¼, Sec. 26, T6N, R6W

This Fort Boise was a trading post of the Hudson's Bay Company, established on the east bank of the Snake River, below the mouth of the Boise River, in 1834. It was severely damaged by flood waters in 1853 and may not have been reoccupied. As at Fort Hall, the original wooden construction was encased in adobe.

Emigrants were able to purchase some subsistance items at Fort Boise and get assistance in ferrying; also, the Hudson's Bay Company presence served to control the local Indians.

James W. Nesmith, September 19, 1843. "Encamped . . . below the fort. Visited . . . Payette . . . a very agreeable old French gentleman . . . in this country . . . since 1810." [290: 352]

John Boardman, September 30, 1843. "Crossed a small river going down . . . Oregon company had bought all that could be spared . . . Fort Boise is built of mud . . . near the mouth of 2 rivers." [37: 113]

John C. Fremont, October 9, 1843. ". . . arrived at Fort *Boise.* This is a simple dwelling-house on the right bank of Snake River, about a mile below the mouth of Rivière Boisée; and on our arrival we were received with an agreeable hospitality by Mr. Payette . . . in charge . . . all of whose garrison consisted of a Canadian *engage* . . . had made but slight attempts at cultivation . . . a few vegetables . . . post being principally supported by salmon . . . the dairy, which was abundantly supplied, stock appearing to thrive . . . observations, the longitude of the fort is

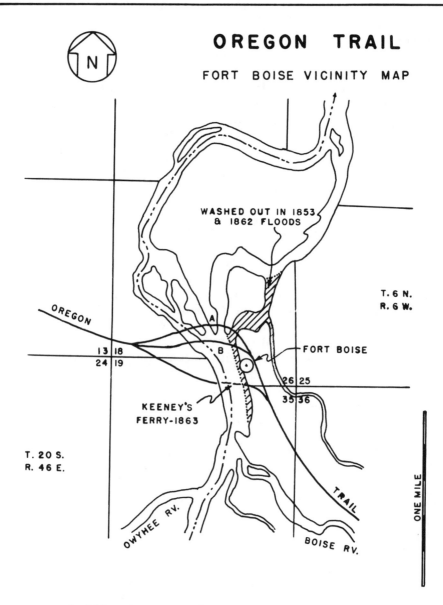

OREGON TRAIL

FORT BOISE VICINITY MAP

WASHED OUT IN 1853 & 1862 FLOODS

T. 6 N.
R. 6 W.

OREGON

FORT BOISE

13 | 18
24 | 19

26 | 25
35 | 36

KEENEY'S
FERRY-1863

T. 20 S.
R. 46 E.

ONE MILE

TRAIL

OWYHEE RV.

BOISE RV.

A. PACK-HORSE FORD (WHITMAN, 1836)

B. WAGON FORD (NESMITH, 1843; MINTO, 1844; PALMER, 1847)

ALH '72

116° 47' 00"; latitude is 43° 49' 22" . . . 2,100 feet." [202:I, 537]

John Minto, 1844. ". . . Fort Boise . . . mustered among us enough money to purchase twenty pounds of Oregon flour. The trader in charge refused to sell a little dried elk meat. It was 'for the master,' he said. We forded Snake River at the emigrant crossing below the little adobe trading post. [266: 222]

Osborne Cross, August 29, 1849. ". . . arrived at Fort Boise about five p.m. and encamped on . . . Owyhee about three-quarters of a mile from the trading-post . . . on the opposite side of Snake river and immediately on its banks . . . blockhouses are placed at the corners . . . sallyport or main entrance opens on Snake river. [101: 206]

Irene D. Paden, 1943. "Here a trader named Reid built a fort and, with nine other men, was massacred by Indians in 1813 or 1814 . . . [known as] Reid's River until 1834 . . . McKay . . . built a trading post for himself in what had been the horse corral of the Reid fort . . . year or two later Hudson's Bay Company built Fort Boise slightly below the smaller mouth at the north side of the island. The emigrant ford was immediately below this fort . . . flourishing until the winter of 1853, when a heavy flood crumbled the adobe building into the Snake . . . a new Fort Boise was built at the narrows just above Goose Egg Island, and, in 1868, the Keenan ferry was established there . . ." [298: 340-41]

Kenneth L. Holmes, 1968. The biographical sketch of François Payette contains a good summary of the development of Fort Boise on the pages indicated. [160:VI, 339-42]

Idaho Historical Society, Reference Leaflets. The first is an invaluable aid to the finding of the site of old Fort Boise, and the second notes the existence of a temporary military establishment there in 1855. [195: No's. 29, 63]

Author's note, August 7, 1972. A concrete monument of unique design stands at the approximate site of Fort Boise. It is topped by a lion's head (in color), and the pedestal is ornamented with various devices symbolic of the British influence and the Indian-white confrontations in the area. The monument is marked as "Built by Paul Yaden and Art Yensen Oct. 18, 1971. "

USGS map, Owyhee, Oreg.-Idaho, 1:24,000, 1967 ed.

Osborne Cross sketched the exterior (above) and interior (below) views of Fort Boise when he visited there in 1849.

This unusual monument was erected at the approximate site of the Hudson's Bay Company's Fort Boise.

CROSSING OF SNAKE RIVER (lower)
(See Fort Boise Vicinity Map)
Mile 1510.8 — Canyon County, Idaho — S½, Sec. 26, T6N, R6W

This crossing of the Snake River was at the head of two islands, 1,200 feet below the site of Fort Boise. The river could be forded when the water was low; otherwise, ferrying was necessary. A commercial ferry was operating above the fort as early as 1854.

James W. Nesmith, September 19, 1843. ". . . to Fort Boise . . . wind blowing very hard from the Northwest, we found it impossible to ford the river, as the swells rolled very high. Encamped . . . below the fort." September 20: "Crossed . . . without difficulty, the water being about four feet six inches deep . . ." [290: 352]

John C. Fremont, October 9, 1843. "Here the road re-crosses the river, which is broad and deep . . . with our good boat, aided by two canoes . . ." [202:I, 537]

John Minto, September 1844. "Fort Boise . . . We forded Snake River at the emigrant crossing below the little adobe trading post." [266: 222]

J. M. Harrison, undated. "Down Boise River to junction with Snake River where we crossed over to south side of latter stream near Fort Boise." [165: letter]

Irene D. Paden, 1943. ". . . the emigrants of 1843 and Fremont . . . [had] to borrow or hire the enormous dugout canoes for transporting wagons across the river . . . was still desirable for emigrants to cross Snake River, and so a new Fort Boise was built at the narrows just above Goose Egg Island, and in 1868 the Keenan ferry was established there. Even now, where the old county road to Nyssa crosses the Snake, may be seen the trees that shaded the buildings of the ferry settlement and a portion of the old cable . . . The ford of the Snake was just below the fort, but 'ford' must not be taken to mean that teams pulled the wagons across. It was simply that for years there was no ferry." [298: 341]

Wm. H. McNeil (undated). "Isaac & Humason operated the ferry on the Snake River near Boise . . ." in 1854. An employee at the ferry, Enos Fruit, rode horseback to The Dalles, Oregon, with word of the Ward massacre (see Mile 1486.8). [256: 414]

Idaho Historical Society, Reference Leaflet. ". . . Jonathan Keeney, who operated a ferry near there after 1863, took special interest in the fort and the Oregon Trail crossing there." The map on p. 2, based on the 1867 Oregon boundary survey and the

This is the site of the lower crossing of the Snake River, near old Fort Boise.

1868 Public Land survey, shows the location of the ferry, in the latter year, to be 500 feet south (above) the Fort Boise site. [195: No. 29]

Gregory M. Franzwa, 1972. "The ford was said to be 400 yards below the fort. It struck the head of an island and headed to the left, toward the southern bank of the river. The water was described by Joel Palmer as being deep, but not rapid, with a smooth bottom." Quoting Narcissa Whitman (1836): "Her diary entry for Aug. 22 is as follows: 'Left the Fort yesterday. Came a short distance to the crossing of the Snake river, crossed and encamped for the night. The river has three branches divided by islands, as it was when we crossed before [a reference to the Three Island Crossing]. The first and second places were very deep, but we had no difficulty in crossing on horseback. The third was deeper still, we dared not venture on horseback. This being a fishing post of the Indians, we could easily find a canoe.'" [141: 335-36]

Author's note, August 7, 1972. No evidence remains at the Fort Boise site of either the emigrant ford or the later ferry; however, certain features of the stream correspond so well with early descriptions that there seems to be little doubt as to where

the emigrants crossed.
USGS map, Owyhee, Oreg.-Ida., 1:24,000, 1967 ed.

LYTLE PASS (Oregon Trail Ruts)
Mile 1521.3 — 6 miles southeast of Vale, Oregon
Malheur County — SE¼ of SW¼, Sec. 14, T19S, R45E

A half-mile of deeply worn Oregon Trail ruts courses over the pass through which the emigration was channeled. They are on public land and access is good. An agreement has been reached with the county which should make development of interpretive facilities feasible.

John C. Fremont, October 11, 1843. ". . . we reached the foot of a ridge, where the road entered a dry sandy hollow [Cow Hollow], up which it continued to the head; and, crossing a dividing ridge, entered a similar one." [202:I, 539]

Osborne Cross, August 30, 1849. ". . . road led up through the hills by a narrow gorge for about four or five miles . . . looked as if it had been intended for a public highway." [101: 210]

Irene D. Paden, 1943. "Eventually Cow Hollow gave up the ghost, and the long valley petered out in a draw where the wagons concentrated and the sage-grown ruts were beautiful to behold. It is a good place to see what is left of the Oregon Trail." [298: 343]

Author's note, Aug. 7, 1972. The USGS benchmark 2909 (1903) is west of the present highway, Lytel Boulevard, and 40 feet north of the Oregon Trail, which crossed diagonally over the present highway alignment—west to east—in the pass. On the south side (Cow Hollow), the Oregon Trail appears as two tracks; one deepens rapidly to become an erosion trench four to five feet deep, but the other is less prominent in the sparsely vegetated, sandy soil. The track is less eroded north of the pass.

The Bureau of Land Management has an agreement with the county whereby the county will re-route the highway at the pass, leaving the present road as an interpretive turn-out where the ruts will be fenced against damaging use and made available to those interested in Oregon Trail history.

USGS map, Vale East, Oreg., 1:24,000, 1967 ed.

The grave of John D. Henderson, who died of thirst in 1850, unaware that he was within sight of the Malheur River.

JOHN D. HENDERSON GRAVE
Mile 1526.8 — 0.7 mile south of Vale, Oregon
Malheur County — NE¼ of SW¼, Sec. 29, T18S, R45E

Henderson was buried beside the segment of gravel road which parallels Lytle Boulevard south of Vale. A concrete monument stands upon an angular stone projecting from the foot of a small butte. The burial, if made in front of the stone, is now under the shoulder of the road.

Author's note, August 19, 1972. A bronze plaque on the concrete monument states: "Pioneer Grave / of / John D. Henderson / Died of Thirst / August 9, 1852 / Unaware of Nearness of the Malheur River / Leaving Independence, Missouri, in May 1852, Mr. Henderson / and Companion Name Unknown, Had Completed Only Part of the / Journey When Their Team Died. They Were Compelled to / Continue on Foot Carrying Their Few Possessions. The Twenty Miles / of Desert Separating the Snake and Malheur Rivers / Proved too Great a Struggle for the Weary Travelers." Most of name and date remain readable on the face of the rock below the monument.

USGS map, Vale East, Oreg., 1:24,000, 1967 ed.

CROSSING OF MALHEUR RIVER
Mile 1527.0 — Southeast boundary of Vale, Oregon
Malheur County — NE¼ of NW¼, Sec. 29, T18S, R45E

This crossing was also the place from which those emigrants who elected to follow "Meek's Cutoff" across eastern Oregon left the established Oregon Trail, in 1845. Suffering severely from lack of water on the new route, this party finally crossed the Deschutes River above the site where Sherar's Bridge was later built, continuing to the dalles of the Columbia on much the same route as the Barlow Road north of Tygh Valley.

John C. Fremont, October 11, 1843. ". . . about sunset we reached the *Rivière aux Malheurs,* (the unfortunate or unlucky river), a considerable stream, with an average breadth of 50 feet, and, at this time, 18 inches depth of water. . . . With the exception of a bad place a few hundred yards long, which occurred in rounding had been very good." Note 70, p. 539: ". . . named . . . by Peter Skene Ogden . . . in 1825-26 . . . because property hidden there by employees . . . was stolen." [202:I, 539-40]

Overton Johnson, 1843. Mentions a California-bound party that turned up Malheur River. [208: 94]

John Boardman, 1843. Also mentions the departure of the California-bound party. [37: 114]

Samuel Parker, August 23, 1845. "To Malhure Creek. 24—Took Meeks cut-off." [302: diary]

Betsey Bailey, 1845. Describes hardships on Meek's Cutoff in 1845. [18: letter]

St. Louis *Missouri Republican,* July 17, 1846. Provides information on the party that took Meek's Cutoff in 1845—lists the dead. [103:II, 601]

Osborne Cross, 1849. Mentions the crossing. [101: 210, 214]

Claire W. Churchill, 1928. Tells of a "lost train" which took Meek's Cutoff in 1853. [72: 77-98]

Lawrence A. McNary, 1934. Quotes from the Jesse Harritt diary, tells the Blue Bucket Mine story, and notes the crossing of the Deschutes River as being at the mouth of Buck Hollow Creek. [255: 1-9]

Wm. H. McNeil, undated. Gives the Hall account of the Meek's Cutoff party, and repeats the Blue Bucket Mine story. [256: 147]

USGS map, Vale East, Ore., 1:24,000, 1967 ed.

MALHEUR HOT SPRINGS_p
Mile 1527.3 — ¼ mile east of Vale, Oregon
Malheur County — SW¼ of SE¼, Sec. 20, T18S, R45E

A cluster of hot springs rose on the bank of the Malheur River at the foot of Rhinehart Butte. These springs, which were quite hot, have been used for commercial purposes for many years and are so altered that their original character is no longer apparent. The feature was frequently noted by emigrants and occasionally was useful to them.

James W. Nesmith, September 21, 1843. ". . . on a creek called Malheur. Warm spring on the bank . . ." [290: 352]

John C. Fremont, October 12, 1843. "My attention was attracted by a smoke on the right side of the river, a little below the ford, where I found on the low bank, near the water, a considerable number of hot springs, in which the temperature of the water was 193 degrees. The ground, which was too hot for the naked foot, was covered above and below the springs with an incrustation of common salt, very white and good, and fine grained." [202:I, 540]

Overton Johnson, 1843. ". . . twelve miles, and crossed the Malheur, where there are many Hot springs, rising out of the bank of the stream." He adds that part of the company left them there ". . . to follow the Malheur, a small stream, that empties into Snake . . . [and] pass over the California Mountains." The departure of this California party was also noted by another 1843 emigrant—John Boardman (37: 114). [208: 94]

Osborne Cross, September 2, 1849. ". . . visited the hot springs at Malheur River this morning . . . was 196 degrees. This spring is on the right bank . . . two hundred yards from where the road crosses, and at the end of a range of hills . . . ground around this spring was extremely warm . . . heat could be plainly felt through the boot . . ." [101: 214]

Irene D. Paden, 1943. "In 1845, because of hostile Indians, a family including an expectant mother was left here . . . large and telltale fires were not to be thought of, and they were greatly helped and comforted by the plentiful hot water from a large boiling spring. The spring was nowhere in sight, but we spied a laundry building and trudged up the side hill to look behind it. There, half hidden by lumber and pipes, snorting and bubbling like a witch's caldron, were the hot springs of the Malheur. Never ornamental, they are still utilitarian." [298: 343-44]

Author's note, August 7, 1972. The "Vale Hot Springs" plunge is a boarded-up building standing at the foot of Rhinehart Butte, east of town and adjacent to U.S. Highway 20/26. Five hundred feet east of the plunge, within the angle formed by division of the highway into one-way lanes, stands an informational panel describing the "Historic Oregon Trail / Malheur Crossing."

USGS map, Vale East, Oreg., 1:24,000, 1967 ed.

BIRCH CREEK
Mile 1549.2 — 3 miles south of Farewell Bend
Malheur County, Oregon — SW¼ of SW¼, Sec. 16, T15S, R45E

Here was the first usable water after leaving the Malheur River—a 22-mile haul along which the only water found was at Alkali Springs and Tub Springs—neither of which provided anything drinkable.

John C. Fremont, October 12, 1843. ". . . willows begin to appear in the dry bed of the head of the *Rivière aux Bouleaux* (Birch River) . . . found at its junction with another branch, a little water, not very good or abundant. . ." [202:1, 540]

Osborne Cross, 1849. Mentions Birch Creek. [101: 214]

USGS map, Olds Ferry, Ida.-Oreg., 1:24,000, 1952 ed.

OLDS FERRY
Mile 1551.3 — Snake River, south of Farewell Bend
Malheur County, Oregon — SW¼ of NW¼, Sec. 4, T15S, R45E of Willamette Meridian

This current-operated ferry was established at the time of the Idaho gold rush, to link the Oregon and Idaho sides of the Snake River above Hells Canyon. It was an essential installation in the days before the Snake River had been adequately bridged.

House Committee on Roads, 1925. "In 1862, when gold was discovered in eastern Oregon and southern Idaho, Olds Ferry was established on the Snake River a few miles above the present town of Huntington and the course of traffic passed through the present towns of Weiser and Payette, and for years that route was heavily traveled and the ferry did a big business. Today bridges span the Snake at both towns and the old ferry has about passed into history. [384: 23]

WPA Writers' Project, 1939. ". . . a ferry established in 1862 is no longer operated." [146: 124]

Author's note, August 8, 1972. Hells Canyon Dam, which began production of electrical power in 1968, impounds water which has flooded the site of Olds Ferry. Two Oregon Trail monuments which formerly stood between the Old Oregon Trail Highway and the Snake River, in the vicinity of the two Olds Ferry sites (there was a later location a mile upstream from the original) have been submerged in the reservoir.

There is a photograph showing a covered wagon and team on a barge rigged for operation by the current, in Walter Meacham's *Story of the Old Oregon Trail* (1922), 21. He states that J. P. Olds established the ferry in 1858.

USGS map, Olds Ferry, Idaho-Oreg., 1:24,000, 1952 ed.

FAREWELL BEND
Mile 1551.6 — Southeast corner of Baker County, Oregon
SW¼ of SW¼, Sec. 33, T14S, R45E

This is the place where the Oregon Trail left the Snake River, which had been followed more or less closely from Fort Hall for 330 miles. It was an important landmark for the emigrants.

James W. Nesmith, September 12, 1843. ". . . struck Snake River; said to be the last sight we get of it . . . four miles and struck Burnt River . . ." [290: 352]

John C. Fremont, October 12, 1843. ". . . we descended to the Snake River—here a fine-looking stream, with a large body of water and a smooth current; although we hear the roar, and see below us the commencement of rapids where it enters among the hills. It forms here a deep bay, with a low sand island in the midst; and its course among the mountains is agreeably exchanged for the black volcanic rock." [202:I, 540]

Author's note, August 8, 1972. The rapids noted by Fremont are now beneath the waters of Hells Canyon Dam which rises 330 feet above the bed rock of the Snake River. This installation cost $230 million and produces 1,120,000 kilowatts of electricity. Since 1958 the Idaho Power Company has donated several parcels of land, aggregating 50 acres, to the State of Oregon for development as a state park. The facilities now available at Farewell Bend provide for camping, picnicing and water use.

When the interstate highway, which has replaced the old Oregon Trail Highway, was under construction 15 years ago, earthmoving equipment uncovered a pioneer burial at a point one-quarter mile south of the present Farewell Bend interchange and almost exactly in the center of the southbound lane. A man, woman and two children had been buried in a wagon box. Removal of the remains to a new grave, within the angle created by two forks of the frontage road on the west side of the highway, was supervised by the county sheriff. The new gravesite is marked by a plain concrete post, just across the line in Malheur County (SE¼ of SE¼, Sec. 32).

USGS map, Olds Ferry, Idaho-Oreg., 1:24,000, 1952 ed.

BATTLE SITE (Possible)ₚ
Mile 1553.8 — 2¼ miles north of Farewell Bend
Baker County, Oregon — NW¼ of SW¼, Sec. 20, T14S, R45E

A cross near the old highway over "Huntington Hill" is said to mark the site of a "massacre."

WPA Writers' Project, 1939. "Vantage Point . . . is a hill on which the Indians sometimes lay in ambush for emigrants who camped in the vicinity before starting inland; near this place several small emigrant trains were completely annihilated." [146: 124]

Author's note, August 8, 1972. A Mr. Martin, a retired railroad employee residing at Huntington, Oregon, mentioned the cross on "Huntington Hill" as marking the site of a "massacre." He said that artifacts had been recovered there.

USGS map, Olds Ferry, Ida.-Oreg., 1:24,000, 1952 ed.

WAGON TRAIN DESTRUCTION SITE (Probable)ₚ
Mile 1569.0 — 20 miles east of Powder River, Oregon
Baker County — Sec. 33, TIOS, R42E

A wagon train is said to have been destroyed here in 1860, where the emigrant trail left the headwaters of Burnt River, at the mouth of Kitchen Creek.

Henry R. Herr, September 30, 1862. "Burnt River, Ore. We are now 20 miles from Powder River & 35 miles from the mines. Where we are now camped a large emigrant train was completely butchered by Indians in 1860. Human bones are strewn around the camp and some earthworks were thrown up, done for defense. But one man and one woman reached Powder River out of the whole train, they walking the entire distance. [175: diary]

Author's note. The Burnt River, also called "Burntwood Creek" by some, received its name from Peter Skene Ogden on February 4, 1826. His French-Canadians called it *Rivière Brulé* because of the burnt timber found along it. The Oregon Trail ascended the stream about 15 miles from the point where it was first reached at present Huntington, Oregon. John C. Fremont commented on October 13, 1843, that the valley of the Burnt River "looks like a hole among the hills," adding, "I have never seen a wagon road equally bad in the same space." (202:I, 542-43)

USGS map, Oxman, Oreg., 1:24,000, 1967 ed.

FLAGSTAFF HILL MONUMENT
Mile 1600.0 — 5 miles northeast of Baker, Oregon
SW¼ of NW¼, Sec. 6, T9S, R41E

An 18-foot-high monument of cemented cobbles stands at the crossing of the Oregon Trail over Highway 86, about a half-mile southwest of the summit of Flagstaff Hill, where the trail left Virtue Flat. Particularly good Oregon Trail ruts may be seen descending the hill for 2,300 feet on Az. 300 degrees true from the monument, which is marked simply "1843-1943," below an Oregon Trail medallion. The view of the Baker Valley and the Blue Mountains is excellent.

Author's note, August 8, 1972. There are four other monuments of interest at the town of Baker. One, placed by Ezra Meeker in a triangle adjacent to Main and Auburn streets, is marked "Old Oregon Trail 1843," although it is five miles southwest of the trail. Ezra Meeker regularly placed monuments in the principal towns along the "Oregon Trail Highway" he popularized after the turn of the century. There are two monuments in the Baker city park (south of Campbell Street and a block east of Main): one, erected April 19, 1906, is dedicated to the Oregon Trail, the pioneers and the Provisional Government of Oregon, and the other to the American cowboy and the cattle drives—over the Oregon Trail—which moved eastern Oregon cattle to Wyoming and Nebraska from 1886 to 1890. Another Oregon Trail monument stands beside U.S. Highway 30, 1.2 miles north of Baker, but not on the Oregon Trail. It is "Dedicated to the memory of the early pioneers who passed this way 1843-1853." This monument is 600 feet north of the southwest corner of Sec. 5, T9S, R40E.

The Oregon BLM in 1992 erected an interpretive center atop Flagstaff Hill—certainly the most elaborate one the Oregon Trail. The town and county of Baker take their names from Col. E. D. Baker, a friend of Abraham Lincoln and briefly a U.S. senator from Oregon. He was killed in the Civil War.

USGS maps, Virtue Flat, Oreg., 1:24,000, 1967 ed.
            Baker, Oreg., 1:24,000, 1967 ed.

"THE LONE PINE" (Probable Site)_p
Mile 1603.3 — 1.7 miles northeast of Baker Municipal Airport
Baker County, Oregon — NW¼ of SW¼, Sec. 23, T8S, R40E

A tall pine tree stood at a campground on a "branch of the Powder River"—probably at the first crossing of the Baldock Slough. It was cut down by some member of the emigration of 1843, to the sorrow of later travelers. It was a particularly prominent landmark which had received its name from the Canadian voyageurs of the fur trapping days.

James W. Nesmith, September 27, 1843. crossed the divide and encamped at the lone pine tree." [290: 353]

Peter Burnett, September 1843. ". . . encamped on the branch of the Powder River at the Lone Pine. This noble tree stood in the center of a most lovely valley about 10 miles from any other timber. It could be seen at a distance of many miles. . . the tree was gone . . . had fallen at last by the vandal hands. . . . Some of our inconsiderate people had cut it down for fuel." [55: 81-82]

John C. Fremont, October 15, 1843. "From the heights we had looked in vain for a well-known landmark on the Powder River. . . . It may be that the company who cut it felt justified; but, for many years, those who came after mourned its absence and execrated the 'wretch and vandal' who had destroyed it." [202:1, 543-44]

John Minto, 1844. ". . . supper and breakfast at Lone Pine camp on the bank of Powder River; but some wretch had cut the noble landmark, the pine tree, down." [266: 223]

Maria P. Belshaw, August 28, 1853. "Leave Burnt River . . . came to Lone Tree Spring to left of road." [132: 322]

Gregory M. Franzwa, 1972. After citing further observation regarding the Lone Pine, he states: "Thus it would seem that the great tree was somewhere on the river due north of Baker, unless Fremont was referring to the Baldock Slough, which runs between the airport and the hill. To this day no one knows (or is able to substantiate) the exact location of the old tree. Chances are it stood on the west side of Highway 203, north of Baker, near the airport property. Nobody can come any closer than that." [141: 345-46]

Author's note, August 8, 1972. Upon looking out over the Baker Valley from Flagstaff Hill (where travelers first sighted the Lone Pine), the Baldock Slough appears approximately in the center of the valley. Also, the distance from Burnt River—the last camping place—is 18 miles, which is a long day's travel for oxen. Thus, it seems unlikely the camping place at the tree was any farther (the second crossing of Baldock Slough was three miles more and not in the center of the valley, while the crossing of the Powder River proper was yet another nine miles—entirely beyond Baker Valley). Franzwa's guess that the Lone Tree stood on Powder River west of the Baker Airport is not satisfactory, because the Oregon Trail did not approach the river anywhere in the Baker Valley; instead, it stayed to the eastward, paralleling the river but never coming to it until the North Powder Valley was reached. On the other hand, the Baldock Sough—an old meander of the Powder River—probably appeared very much like a river before so much of it was turned into farm land.

The site of "Slough House," a later stage station, was north of Baldock Slough, on Missouri Flat (Mile 1606.6—SW¼ of SE¼, T8S, R40E).

USGS map, Baker, Ore., 1:24,000, 1964 ed.

POWDER RIVER ("Gentry") CROSSING
Mile 1617.5 — ¼ mile south of North Powder, Oregon
Baker-Union Counties — SW¼ of SE¼, Sec. 22, T6S, R39E

The emigration crossed the North Powder River on what is now the edge of the town of North Powder. This became known as "Gentry Crossing" in stagecoach days. Evidences of the dugway by which the stream was entered still are here.

USGS map, North Powder, Ore., 1:24,000, 1965 ed.

SITE OF 16-MILE HOUSE_p
Mile 1625L⅓ — 7½ miles north of North Powder, Oregon
Union County — 2,300′ east of NW corner, Sec. 20, T5S, R39E

Foundation remains of this stage station are still visible near the head of Clover Creek.

Opposite the stage station, beginning at Mile 1626.9, Oregon Trail ruts are visible for 3,500 feet along the east side of I-84.

USGS maps, North Powder, Oreg., 1:24,000, 1965 ed.
    Craig Mountain, Oreg., 1:24,000, 1966 ed.

EMIGRANT INSCRIPTION_p
Mile 1629R¼ — 11 miles north of North Powder, Oregon
Union County — NW¼ of SE¼, Sec. 30, T4S, R39E

The inscription "D. Dodge 1855" appears on a yellow rock high on the east wall of Ladd Canyon. Local tradition, according to former Oregon State Highway Engineer Bob Rennells, places four or five emigrant graves at the head of Ladd Canyon (Mile 1628.7—NW¼ of NE¼, Sec. 31, T4S, R39E).

USGS map, Craig Mountain, Ore., 1:24,000, 1966 ed.

6

Ladd Canyon to Oregon City

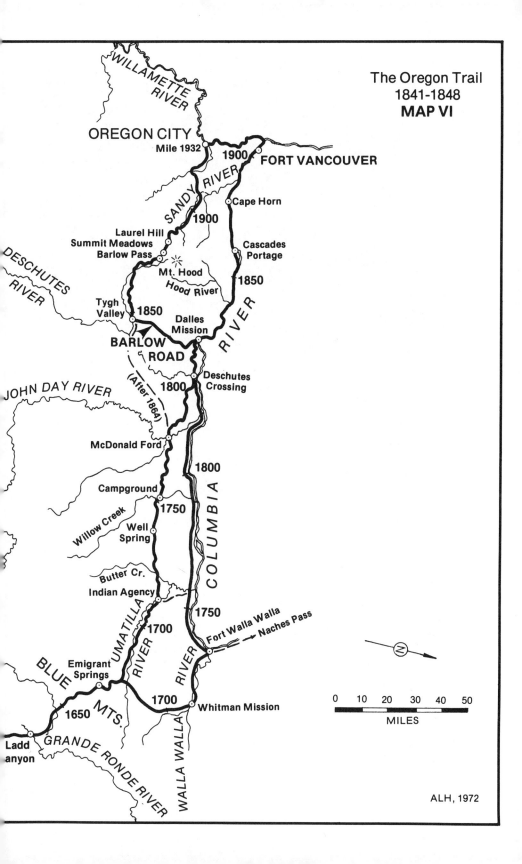

The Oregon Trail
1841-1848
MAP VI

WILLAMETTE RIVER

OREGON CITY
Mile 1932
1900
FORT VANCOUVER

SANDY RIVER

1900
Cape Horn

Laurel Hill
Summit Meadows
Barlow Pass
Cascades
Portage

DESCHUTES RIVER

Mt. Hood
Hood River
1850

Tygh Valley
1850
Dalles Mission

RIVER

BARLOW ROAD

(After 1864)

JOHN DAY RIVER

Deschutes Crossing

1800

McDonald Ford

1800

Campground
COLUMBIA

Willow Creek
1750

Well Spring

Butter Cr.
Indian Agency

1750
Fort Walla Walla → Naches Pass

UMATILLA RIVER

1700

RIVER

BLUE
Emigrant Springs

MTS.
1700
Whitman Mission

1650

GRANDE RONDE RIVER

Ladd Canyon

WALLA WALLA RIVER

N

0 10 20 30 40 50
MILES

ALH, 1972

The water wheel remains from the old Ladd Canyon Stage Station.

LADD CANYON HILL$_p$
Mile 1633.0 — 7½ miles southeast of La Grande, Oregon
Union County — W½ of Sec. 12, T4S, R38E

This was a precipitous descent by which the Oregon Trail bypassed the mouth of Ladd Canyon; dropping into the Grande Ronde Valley by way of the ridge immediately east of the canyon. There was an emigrant campground at the foot of the hill, and, later, a stage station.

John C. Fremont, October 17, 1843. ". . . the wagons had directly descended into the *Rond* by the face of the hill so very rocky and continuously steep as to be apparently impracticable; and, following down their trail, we encamped on one of the branches of the Grande Rond River, immediately at the foot of the hill." [202:I, 545-46] James W. Nesmith, 1843. Noted "the big hill" which obstructed their entry into the valley. [290: 353]

John Minto, 1844. Noted the steep descent into the valley. [266: 223]

Osborne Cross, 1849. Described the descent into the valley. [101: 222]

Maria Belshaw, 1853. Mentioned the descent and the view. [132: 323]

Irene D. Paden, 1943. ". . . Ladd Canyon . . . Here Mr. William Benton put us straight. . . he has lived his eighty years where the wagons dropped down off the mountain into the valley." [298: 345]

Author's note, August 9, 1972. Oregon Trail ruts are still visible on the hillside for 1,000 feet and there is a snubbing tree with rope burns. Part of the Ladd Canyon Stage Station, which was immediately at the bottom of the hill, remains in a ranch building. The emigrant campground, 1,200 feet north of the station, was on an Indian camas meadow. An emigrant grave, marked by a pile of rocks, is in the SW¼ of NW¼, Sec. 12, and another grave, 350 feet from it on Az. 160 degrees true, was destroyed by road construction, according to Oregon State Highway Engineer Bob Rennells. Several graves east of the interstate highway may be connected with post-emigration settlement at this point. An interesting relic of the settlement period is an old waterwheel, built in 1911 by Guy Fuller and William Banton to generate the first electricity in the Grande Ronde Valley.

USGS map, Glass Hill, Oreg., 1:24,000, 1965 ed.

TRADING POST SITE$_p$
Mile 1634L¼ — 6½ miles southeast of La Grande, Oregon
Union County — E½ of SE¼, Sec. 2, T4S, R38E

Information is sparse about this trading post, which antedated settlement of the valley in 1861. An early burial, known locally as the "Copper Kettle Grave," at a point 2½ miles southeast of La Grande (Mile 1638 — SW¼ of SE¼, Sec. 16, T3S, R38E) is also shrouded in mystery.

USGS maps: Glass Hill, Oreg., 1:24,000, 1965 ed.
La Grande SE, Oreg., 1:24,000, 1963 ed.

"OLD TOWN" (La Grande, Oregon)
Mile 1641.0 — Vicinity of First and B Streets
Union County

The Grande Ronde Valley was first settled on this spot in 1861. It was here that the Oregon Trail turned westward to climb out of the valley.

Henry R. Herr, September 30, 1862. Described the new town as "75 log cabins & emigrants with us taking up claims and building houses, 3 stores, beautiful valley 30 miles long." [175: diary]

WPA Writers' Project, 1939. "In 1861 a small group of men retraced the trail from the Umatilla River to stake claims in the valley. Ben Brown . . . built a house on a low bench above the river. Later he converted his house into a tavern, around which a small settlement sprang up, known variously as Brownsville and Brown Town, until the establishment of a post office, when the present name was adopted. . . . In 1884 the . . . railroad was laid straight across the valley, missing the town by a mile, but part of the inhabitants moved . . . creating New Town; the Old Town, as it is still known locally . . . [soon became] part of the city. . . . In 1864 . . . first Union County Courthouse was erected on the site of the Brown cabin and hotel . . . [it has] been occupied as a store, church, and residence since 1876." [146: 128-29]

Author's note, August 9, 1972. La Grande takes its name from the valley, which should properly be spelled *Grand Rond*—the Great Circle. John C. Fremont described the valley thus (October 17, 1843): "About two in the afternoon we reached a high point of the dividing ridge, from which we obtained a good view of the *Grand Rond*—a beautiful level basin, or mountain valley, covered with good grass, on a rich soil, abundantly watered . . . its name descriptive of its form—the great circle. It is one place. . . where a farmer would delight to establish . . . about 20 miles in diameter . . ." (see 202:I, 545). Josiah Beal, who entered the valley in 1847, described it as "like Paradise, ⅓ of it was a swamp at that time. Grass from waist to shoulder high." (see 28: letter of July 1).

There is an Oregon Trail monument at Gangloff Park, north of the town and adjacent to U.S. Highway 30. It is not on the trail.

The stage station at La Grande was in the NE¼ of SE¼, Sec. 7, T3S, R38E.

This is also the place where John C. Fremont's trail diverged from that of the emigrants of 1843. He says: ". . . about noon [on October 18] reached a place on one of the principal streams, where I had determined to leave the emigrant trail, in the expectation of finding a more direct and better road across the Blue Mountains. At this place the emigrants appeared to have

held some consultation as to their further route, and finally
turned directly off to the left; reaching the foot of the mountain
in about three miles, which they ascended by a hill as steep and
difficult as that by which he had yesterday descended to the
Road . . . this . . . after a very rough crossing, issues from the
mountains by the heads of the *Umatilah* . . . we continued our
northern course across the valley, following an Indian trail
which had been indicated to me by Mr. Payette [at Fort Boise] . . .
We passed out of the Grand Rond by a fine road (See 202:1, 545-
47)

USGS map, La Grande SE, Oreg., 1:24,000, 1963 ed.

EMILY DOANE GRAVE_p
Mile 1643.8 — 4 miles west of La Grande, Oregon
Union County — SE¼ of SW¼, Sec. 3, T3S, R37E

This trailside grave may be related to homesteading in the
area rather than the emigration. It is marked "Emily Doane, d.
1868, Age 8." Further research is needed.

USGS map, Hilgard, Oreg., 1:24,000, 1963 ed.

OREGON TRAIL MONUMENT_p
Mile 1646L 1¼ — 6½ miles west of La Grande, Oregon
Union County — NW¼ of SW¼, Sec. 8, T3S, R37E

This monument, more than a mile south of the Oregon Trail,
is a half-embedded field stone with one face flattened to hold
the roughly incised lettering: "Oregon Trail." The track of the
Foster Toll Road passes a few feet south of the monument and
can still be traced by lines of stones thrown out of the wheel
ruts. The monument is now in a field, 500 feet south of Whiskey
Creek Road.

USGS map, Hilgard, Oreg., 1:24,000, 1963

EMIGRANT CAMPGROUND (Hilgard State Park)
Mile 1647L¾ — 6½ miles west of La Grande, Oregon
Union County - S½ of SW¼, Sec. 31, T2S, R37E

Information panels placed in Hilgard State Park by the Union
County Museum Society call the area an emigrant campground.

However, documentation for this assumption has yet to be found. Logging going on in August 1972 at the east edge of the park had uncovered the site where the trail descended to the Grande Ronde River (SE¼ of SE¼, Sec. 31). There were prominent Oregon Trail ruts—rather badly defaced by logging equipment—at that place, and Bob Rennells, the Oregon State Highway Department engineer said there had been a number of rope-burned trees above; but they had been removed prior to that time.

The Pioneer Springs, 1½ miles northwest of Hilgard (at the mouth of Pelican Creek—NW¼ of SW¼, Sec. 30) would have provided a more advantageous camping place.

It was from this vicinity that the ascent of the Blue Mountains began. The name was first used by David Thompson on August 8, 1811, when he wrote: "Beginning to see the Blue Mountains (See 250: 345-46).

USGS map, Hilgard, Oreg., 1:24,000, 1963 ed.

UNKNOWN DEAD MONUMENT
Mile 1663.1 — South edge of Meacham, Oregon
Umatilla County — NW¼ of SE¼, Sec. 3, TIS, R35E

A roadside monument here marks a pioneer burial which probably was made by emigrants using the Oregon Trail. The presence of military buttons with the skeletal remains suggests the burial might be post-Civil War in origin.

This monument at the site of the reburial was intended to commemorate all the unknown dead of the Oregon Trail—its importance is mainly symbolic.

House Committee on Roads, 1925. Concerning the finding of a pioneer burial in the course of road construction at Meacham, Oregon, Walter Meacham entered the following testimony: "When the modern highway was being built over the Blue Mountains, three skeletons were uncovered at the town of Meacham, one of them being a military man, as evidenced by some Army adornments found with the remains. Some cast-iron nails, rusted almost entirely away, were also found, showing that the remains were very old and were no doubt those of some of the members of the early migrations. The remains were carefully and tenderly laid to rest again with military honors by the side of the trail on July 4, 1923, and a fitting monument erected to the memory of the 'Unknown Dead of the Old Oregon Trail,' was installed. That is but one grave, however, of the many thousands, unknown and unmarked . . ." [384: 28]

Irene D. Paden, 1943. "See that leaning post? . . . there they excavated the bodies of a man, woman and little child who had been buried in their wagon. There was nothing to identify them but some buttons and the fact that the wagon still showed that it had been painted blue and yellow." [298: 350]

Author's note, August 8, 1972. A granite monument between the old highway and the railroad track, and presumably upon the reburial site, is marked with a bronze plaque which states: "In Memoriam / Erected 1925 By The / Women's Commercial Club / Of Meacham, Oregon / In Honor Of Those Who Died / Blazing The Old Oregon Trail. "

Also alongside the old highway in Meacham, at a point 200 feet north of the railroad water tank, is an informational panel which carries the debatable statement: "Meacham / First Known As Lee's Encampment, / From Establishment Of A Troop / Camp By Major H. A. Lee In 1844 . . ." The remaining facts, concerning the operation of "Mountain House"—a famous stopover place—and the visit of President Warren G. Harding in 1923, are sound. Franzwa has amplified the error garnered from that panel by adding that the town was, in 1844, "a cantonment of soldiery dispatched by the United States Army to protect the emigrants." (141: 352). The Convention of 1818 with Great Britain, which allowed joint occupancy of the Oregon country, prohibited introduction of the armed forces of either nation, and the first United States troops to enter Oregon Territory did not do so until after the sovereignty was passed to America in 1848. They were men of the Regiment of Mounted Riflemen, who had marched along the Oregon Trail in 1849—Osborne Cross being their most capable journalist. The officer referred to on the panel was Maj. Henry A. G. Lee of the Oregon Rifles, a military force fielded by the Provisional Government of Oregon, not the United States, in January 1848. They were attempting to avenge the Whitman "massacre" and quiet the Indian tribes east of the Cascade Mountains. Following a brief campaign into the country of the Cayuse Indians with Col. Gilliam, Maj. Lee occupied the abandoned Methodist Mission at The Dalles, and that outpost was briefly known as "Fort Lee" in his honor. The Provisional Government of Oregon, which had only come into being July 5, 1843, had no military force at all in 1844, nor any need for one; and the regiment raised in 1848 to chastise the Cayuse was its first and only levy.

The town of Meacham, Oregon, was named for Col. A. B. Meacham, a member of the Modoc Peace Commission who was not killed by those Indians. The town very early capitalized on the colorful events of its freighting and stagecoach past and has done its bit for the legendry of the West (See 298: 350, and 146: 130).

Evidence remains of a cemetery southwest of town and adjacent to the Oregon Trail route (which did not pass through Meacham, although the townsite may have served as a camping place). Only one grave, dated June 16, 1895, can now be definitely identified, and none of the local residents contacted could supply information concerning burials there. If the cemetery contained Oregon Trail burials, the knowledge seems to have been lost.

This should be an appropriate place to mention that Ezra Meeker estimated the deaths along the Oregon Trail amounted to 20,000 out of a total emigration of 300,000. That is nearly 6.8 percent, or put another way, about 10 deaths to the mile. Truly, the trail is America's longest graveyard.

USGS map, Meacham, Oreg., 1:24,000, 1964 ed.

EMIGRANT SPRINGS
Mile 1668.0 — 3 miles northwest of Meacham, Oregon
Umatilla County — NW¼ of NE¼, Sec. 29, TIN, R35E

These springs are at the head of Squaw Creek and are believed to have been discovered by the Oregon-bound missionary, Jason Lee. They were a source of water for emigrants. Highway and pipeline construction have destroyed most of the original spring area, but one small source does remain in the state park.

This is one of a number of sources of good water which dictated where the overnight stops would be on the route over the Blue Mountains.

House Committee on Roads, 1925. "At Emigrant Springs, three miles from Meacham, at a historic spot long known as Lee's Encampment, because of the fact that Jason Lee, the first missionary to come to the Oregon country, had made camp there in 1834, and where thousands of home seekers camped in later years, President Harding formally dedicated the Old Oregon Trail with a great granite monument erected to the memory of the intrepid pioneers who came with the first train of ox teams and covered wagons in 1843." [384: 28]

WPA Writers' Project, 1939. "Emigrant Springs State Park Near the entrance a stone shaft marks a spring said to have been discovered in 1834 by Jason Lee." [146: 130]

Irene D. Paden, 1943. "We passed a sign, 'Emigrant Spring' a night camp or a nooning place? . . . Both—that is, for individual wagons . . . the freighters . . . camped at Two Mile Creek near Meacham." [298: 351]

Author's note, August 10, 1972. The Emigrant Springs used by the pioneers have been lost to highway construction. They occupied the head of that branch of Squaw Creek which flows northward from Emigrant State Park, and were buried under the massive fill by which U.S. Highway I-84 bridges the draw. A vestige of this once important source of water may be seen in a damp swale under the trees 100 feet south of the entrance into the park from old U.S. Highway 30. An 18-inch-square sandstone post incised, "Old / Oregon / Trail / 1843-57," marks the place.

On the east side of the old highway, nearly opposite the residence of the superintendent, is a large boulder bearing a plaque which states: "Dedicated to the Memory Of / The Intrepid Pioneers / Who Came With The First Wagon Train / In 1843 Over The / Old Oregon Trail / And Saved The Oregon Country / To The United States. / Erected By The Oregon Trail Ass'n / July 4, 1923. / Dedicated By / Warren G. Harding / President Of The United States / July 3, 1923." The circumstances of the dedication and its attendant events appear in the 1925 report of the House Committee on Roads (384).

The basis for designating these springs "Lee's Encampment" (see 384, 28) is not apparent in the diary of Jason Lee. The crossing of the Blue Mountains is described (225: 256-57), but without mention of any such camping place upon the summit. The misapplication of the term "Lee's Encampment" to the Meacham Meadows has been discussed in connection with the Unknown Dead monument (Mile 1663.1).

USGS map, Meacham, Oreg., 1:24,000,1964 ed.

DEADMAN PASS
Mile 1671.2 — Southeast of Pendleton, Oregon
Umatilla County — NE¼ of NW¼, Sec. 1, T1N, R34E

This narrow pass, between Buckaroo and Deadman Pass creeks, serves to connect Telephone Ridge and Emigrant Hill. Three separate instances of violent death, involving a total of seven men, occurred here. The specific incident leading to the naming is now unknown.

Deadman Pass was an essential link on the route over the Blue Mountains. It had no name in Oregon Trail days—the colorful appellation developed out of common usage following the Bannock War of 1878.

Larry Smitton, August 11, 1972. From a manuscript he was preparing for the Oregon State Parks Division, Smitton provided information on the factual basis for the name "Deadmans Pass," i.e.:

"During the Bannock War, a small raiding party of Indians gave themselves up and were placed in custody of the Umatilla Indian Agency, which is located just east of Pendleton. A small detachment of cavalry was stationed here at the time. The Bannocks became restive and decided to return to their homes in Idaho. They mounted horses and whooping it up started pell mell for home. Two men with an empty freight wagon and a four-horse team were approaching the pass from the east when they heard the Indians coming in their direction. One of the teamsters quickly cut a horse out of harness, rode bareback down into the timber and hid. The other teamster tried to unharness the remaining three horses to save them, but the Indians arrived and killed him, then resumed their headlong journey eastward.

"When the escaping Indians took leave from the agency, the captain in charge of the cavalry troop hastily issued orders for the men to pursue the fleeing Indians, bring them back but not to kill them. The cavalry left . . . but the captain was not with them. He was big and fat and did not relish the thought of a lot of saddle sores. He quickly prevailed upon a local resident to hitch up his buckboard and accompanied also by a 14-year-old boy, started after the cavalry. When they arrived at Deadmans Pass, there was the empty wagon minus the team, the dead teamster lying in the road. They dragged the dead man off to the side and dug a shallow hole, for a temporary grave, then resumed their journey eastward. The Indians were captured and returned to the agency. Three days later the dead teamster was exhumed and reinterred in the newly laid out cemetery in Pendleton.

"The above story was related to the writer by the younger brother of the 14-year-old (sons of a local resident). The name of this younger brother was Frank Bowman, a well-known resident of Pendleton, now deceased. Bowman obligingly accompanied the writer to Deadmans Pass to show him the location of the shallow grave, but alas, it had been obliterated! In rebuilding the highway [U.S. 30], the shallow grave site was destroyed by heavy earthmoving equipment. The freighter's name was Olney McCoy." [357: ms.]

Author's note, August 10, 1972. The Oregon State Highway Department is currently building a rest area at Deadman Pass in connection with its interstate highway project there. The rest area will have an interpretive panel explaining the historical associations of the site, and a foot trail will allow interested persons to visit an area of fenced Oregon Trail ruts nearby.

USGS map, Cabbage Hill, Oreg., 1:24,000, 1966 ed.

CAYUSE POST OFFICE$_P$
Mile 1678.2 — 11 miles cast of Pendleton, Oregon
Umatilla County — Center of NE¼, Sec. 16, T2N, R34E

This trading post was at a fork of the Oregon Trail, where the right branch went north to the Whitman Mission on the Walla Walla River, and the other westward down the Umatilla River past present Pendleton, Oregon.

Maria Belshaw, 1853. Mentions the descent of Umatilla Hill and the trading post at the bottom. [132: 324]

William J. Ghent, 1934. Quoting from Stephen Penrose concerning the Oregon Trail at this point: ". . . down Cabbage Hill, at first going north to Athena, Weston, and Walla Walla, but later continuing down the Umatilla past Pendleton. . . . It is possible, I think, to determine that the wagon train of '43 came down Cabbage Hill . . ." [149: 147]

Irene D. Paden, 1943. ". . . to Deadman's Gulch, where the 1843 emigrants went to the right (splitting from what was the later trail) and came down Poker Jim Hill. The later trail went along the shoulder of Cabbage Hill near Pendleton, and is plainly visible to the right of the highway. Beginning with the hard-won path of '43, there have been many roads . . ." [298: 346, 348]

Author's note, August 11, 1972. Concerning the trading post at the junction, Larry Smitton, a long-time resident of the area and a history buff, told me that the foundation logs of the post were discovered more than 20 years ago.

USGS map, Cayuse, Oreg., 1:24,000, 1966 ed.

OREGON TRAIL MONUMENT
Mile 1691.0 — Pendleton, Oregon
Umatilla County — N½ of Sec. 9, T2N, R32E

This monument, which stands in front of the Eastern Oregon Hospital and Training Center, between the highway and the railroad, is the one Ezra Meeker placed at Stover's Livery, near the west end of Emigrant Avenue, in 1906. It is of red sandstone, 24" by 24" by 36", incised, "Old / Oregon / Trail / 1843-57." Just when and why it was moved to its present location is not known, but it is now on the Oregon Trail.

Wm. H. McNeil, undated. In speaking of Ezra Meeker's work in placing monuments along the Oregon Trail, he comments, ". . . in 1906 the attention was toward granite monuments in towns. [256: 151]

Author's note, August 11, 1972. The original site, as nearly as can now be ascertained, was in the SW¼ of Sec. 9, and not on the trail.

USGS map, Pendleton, Oreg., 1:24,000, 1966 ed.

WHITMAN MISSION (WAIILATPU)
Mile 1709.6 — 8 miles west of Walla Walla, Washington
Walla Walla County — Center of Sec. 32, T7N, R35E

The emigrants of 1843 and 1844 went by way of Whitman's Mission; in later years only those in need of help (food, blacksmithing or medical attention) went that way. The site of the "Emigrant House," which became a temporary refuge for the weary, the sick and the destitute of the Oregon Trail, is a reminder of the service rendered at this station.

In those years when the Whitman Mission was on the main route to Oregon, the slender resources of that station were inadequate; but later, when only the desperate made the detour from the more direct route of travel, the succor available 200 miles short of the Willamette Valley was invaluable.

James W. Nesmith, October 5, 1843. ". . . started about noon on the trail for Dr. Whitman's . . ." (his party did not stop there but camped four miles beyond). [290: 354]

Peter Burnett, October 10, 1843. Notes only that ". . . we arrived within three miles of Doctor Whitman's mission. . . ." [55: 82] John Boardman, Oct. 13, 1843. ". . . Arrived at Doct. Whitman's after crossing 4 creeks . . . Many of the emigrants here . . . Little provisions at Whitman's. Some corn at $1.00, potatoes 40¢, beef 6¢ . . ." [37: 115]

Overton Johnson, 1843. "Thirty miles from the Umatila, we came to Whitman's Mission . . . [built of] unburnt brick . . . a Mill . . ." [208: 96]

John C. Fremont, October 24, 1843. ". . . passing on the several unfinished houses, and some cleared patches, where corn and potatoes were cultivated, we reached, in about eight miles farther, the missionary establishment of Dr. Whitman, which consisted, at this time, of one *adobe* house—i.e., built of unburnt bricks, as in Mexico . . . We were disappointed in our expectation of obtaining corn meal or flour at this station, the mill belonging to the mission having been lately burnt down." [202:I, 551-52]

William D. Stillwell, 1844. Having come from Spalding's Mission on the Clearwater River by ". . . following the trail to Whitman Station, where Walla Walla now is—we followed the foothills to near Weston, there crossed the ridge & Wild Horse Creek, going west to the Umatilla R. above where Pendleton now is. We crossed the Umatilla at this place, going down on the west side to Butter Creek. Whitman sent an Indian to pilot us thru this place to Wells Springs, then to Willow Creek." [367: letter]

Miles Cannon, 1915. A book-length study of Whitman Mission. [58: passim]

Marvin H. Richardson, 1940. Book-length study of Whitman Mission. [323: passim]

Irene D. Paden, 1943. "From the Cayuse village the emigrants of 1843 and one or two later migrations detoured to the Whitman Mission as a matter of course. After '45 it was not customary." Included are several pages on events at the mission. [298: 354-58]

National Park Service, 1947. "Ever seeking shorter routes, immigrants after 1844 were attracted by new trails farther to the south that bypassed Whitman's station . . . some found Waiilatpu a supply station worthy of a detour to replenish exhausted supplies. The sick could also get medical attention, and the needy could find work that would carry them through the winter. By 1842 Gray had built a house about 400 feet due east of the main mission house. His departure from the mission that year had left the building open for the use of immigrants. Soon it came to be called the 'Emigrant House.' Between it and the mission house a blacksmith shop had been built as early as 1842.

Above: The site of the Emigrant House, Whitman Mission, has been outlined with concrete blocks. The spire of the Whitman Monument is atop the hill in the background. Halfway up that hill is the great grave (below), containing the remains of Dr. Marcus Whitman, his wife, and other victims of the massacre of 1847.

Here wagons could be repaired and oxen and horses shod. In November of that year [1847] the mission community numbered 74 persons . . . of those at Waiilatpu, 50 were emigrants, most of whom had arrived in the 1847 immigration. [After the massacre] . . . the remaining survivors, mostly women and children, were herded into the 'Emigrant House,' where they were held nearly a month." [286: 11-13]

Erwin N. Thompson, 1964. National Park Service study. [376: passim]

USGS map, Walla Walla, Wash.-Oreg., 1:250,000, 1953 ed.

CROSSING OF UMATILLA RIVER
Mile 1712.0 — Echo, Oregon
Umatilla County — NW¼ of SW¼, Sec. 16, T3N, R29E

The emigration crossed the Umatilla River 400 feet above the present bridge. The old Umatilla Indian Agency was established on the east bank in 1851 within the southwest edge of the present town of Echo (NE¼ of SW¼, Sec. 16), and it was burned in 1855 by the Cayuse Indians at the beginning of the Yakima War. Fort Henrietta, a post established by a detachment of the 1st Oregon Mounted Rifles on November 18, 1855, was located on the west bank about 300 feet southwest of the emigrant crossing (NE¼ of SW¼, Sec. 16). It consisted of a stockade with two bastions, and was named for the wife of Maj. Granville O. Haller, 4th U.S. Infantry. The post was abandoned in 1856. There are no visible remnants of either the agency or the fort.

The significance of this crossing was that it put emigrants on the Fremont-Whitman-Harney cutoff, which stayed south of the Columbia River on the dry benchland which gave them a firmer road—but an arid one. The track westward along the Columbia was a sandy one. Some followed the Umatilla all the way down to the "River of the West" in 1844. The cutoff was an Indian route of long standing, but it has been variously identified with John C. Fremont (who used it), Marcus Whitman (who encouraged the emigrants to use it), and Gen. William S. Harney (who had it drawn on the military maps of the area).

John Minto, 1844. This traveler followed the Umatilla River to the Columbia. [266: September, 227]

Wm. D. Stillwell, 1844. He profited from Whitman's advice by ". . . going west to the Umatilla R. above where Pendleton now is. We crossed the Umatilla at this place, going down on the west side of Butter Creek. Whitman sent an Indian to pilot us thru this place to Wells Spring then to Willow Creek, where we again struck the Emigrant Road from Willow Creek to Rock Creek, where we crossed the John Day River. . . ." [367: letter]

James Jory, 1847. Notes that Whitman was directing emigrants by the cutoff. [233: 283]

Maria Belshaw, 1853. Described the buildings at the Umatilla Agency. [132: 324]

Irene D. Paden, 1943. "The general plan of these few later years [after 1845] was to proceed down the Umatilla River and cross forty miles of benchland, shadeless and arid, through which the river found its way to the Columbia. From the mouth of the Umatilla the wagons remained south of the 'Great River of the West' as far as the Dalles. As soon as the incoming settlers became better informed as to the terrain they learned that there was no point in blindly following the Umatilla north . . . [there is] evidence that Dr. Whitman . . . in the habit of meeting the later emigrants at the foot of the Blue Mountains, recommended this new road along the foothills." [298: 354-55]

Robert W. Frazer, 1965. In his discussion of Fort Henrietta, he mentions that, "The agency buildings had been burned previously by the Indians." [142: 128-29]

Wm. H. McNeil, undated. Mentions Fort Henrietta. [256: 240]   USGS map, Echo, Oreg., 1:24,000, 1968 ed.

ST. ROSE MISSION MONUMENT
Mile 1717.0 — 3.7 miles East of Lowden, Washington
Walla Walla County — Sec. 34, T7N, R33E

This granite monument, 10" x 24" by 48", is on the south side of U.S. Highway 12, and is incised as follows: "Here Stood / St. Rose Mission / Also Known As / Frenchtown / 1850-1900 / Land Donation Claim / Of Narcisse Raymond / Cemetery On Hill North / Oregon Volunteers Fought / Indians Dec. 7, 8, 9, 1855 / Chief Peu-Peu-Mox-Mox / Of Walla Wallas Slain / Erected By Home Economic / Clubs Of Walla Walla Co. "

The cemetery mentioned is about 3,000 feet north of the monument (a cross and marble spire may be seen on the crest of a ridge).

It is unlikely that the mission settlement would have been attractive to American emigrants, who had a strong anti-Catholic bias, but the Hudson's Bay Company farm four miles to the south (in Sections 16 and 21, T6N, R34 E) may have been of indirect assistance to them through the produce available at Fort Walla Walla.

The Battle of Touchet River was crucial to the successful conclusion of the Yakima War, during which control of what is now eastern Oregon and Washington was uncertain.

USGS Map, Walla Walla, Ore.-Wash., 1:250,000, 1953 ed.

BUTTER CREEK CAMPGROUND$_P$
Mile 1720.0 — 9 miles west of Echo, Oregon
Umatilla County — SE¼ of NE¼, Sec. 25, T3N, R28E

This emigrant campground was at the crossing of Butter Creek.

Maria Belshaw, 1853. Mentioned this campground. [132: 325]

USGS map, Service Buttes NW, Oreg., 1:24,000, 1968 ed.

FORT WALLA WALLA (HBC)
Mile 1730.3 — At the mouth of the Walla Walla River, Washington
Walla Walla County — Sec. 27, T7N, R31E

This was a stockaded trading post of the Hudson's Bay Company on the east bank of the Columbia River, immediately above the mouth of the Walla Walla River. The site is now under the waters of Lake Wallula, created behind McNary Dam.

The early emigrants received some assistance here (food, transportation down the Columbia River in company boats, and the opportunity to turn in footsore stock for others to be picked up in the Willamette Valley). The ransom of the survivors of the Whitman massacre was effected here through the efforts of British traders.

John Ball, 1832. ". . . arrived at Fort Walla Walla on October 18 . . . the fort was built of upright timbers set in the ground. The timbers were some fifteen or eighteen feet high. A small stockade, with the stations or bastions at the corners for lookouts . . ." [314: 97]

Nathaniel J. Wyeth, October 14, 1832. ". . . near the fort the river Walla Walla was crossed which is about 75 feet wide and about 2 feet deep current moderate . . . the fort is of no strength merely sufficient to frighten Indians   mounting 2 small cannon having two bastions at the opposite corners of a square enclosure having two bastions at the opposite corners of a square enclosure there were 6 whites here." [406: 173]

James W. Nesmith, October 8, 1843. ". . . Fort Walla Walla . . . prospect is dreary . . . near to the fort are sand banks not possessing fertility enough to sprout a pea . . . At the fort we could procure no eatables . . . country looks poverty stricken . . . [290: 355]

Overton Johnson, 1843. ". . . to Fort Walawala . . . procured canoes . . . our minds were constantly filled with anxiety and dread. . ." (One canoe of the flotilla was wrecked at Grand Rapids.) [208: 97]

John C. Fremont, October 26, 1843. ". . . arrived at the Nez Perce fort, one of the trading establishments of the Hudson Bay Company, a few hundred yards above the junction of the Walahwalah with the Columbia River . . . the post is on the bank of the Columbia, on a plain of bare sands, from which the air was literally filled with clouds of dust . . . prevailing high winds . . . emigrants under the direction of Mr. Applegate . . . had nearly completed the building of a number of Mackinaw boats . . . to continue . . . down the Columbia . . . the other portion of the emigration had preferred to complete their journey by land along the banks of the Columbia, taking their stock and wagons . . ." [202:I, 553]

Irene D. Paden, 1943. "It [Fort Walla Walla] was about two hundred feet square, and was built tightly of timbers set on end. At opposite corners, square bastions, supported on sturdy legs, projected out beyond the enclosure . . . found cordial P. C. Pambrun in charge. Two miles before reaching the fort . . . [was the] vegetable garden . . ." [298: 359-61]

Wm. H. McNeil, undated. "At Walla Walla the train split [1843] and those desiring to float down the Columbia in dugouts, canoes, rafts, batteaus, went to Wallula under the guidance of Jesse Applegate and embarked on the various river craft to Celilo Falls where they portaged their possessions to the Dalles . . ." [256: 152]

Leroy R. Hafen, 1965. Notes that Fort Nez Perce (Walla Walla) was established by Donald McKenzie in the fall of 1817. [160:I, 55]

Leroy R. Hafen, 1965-1972. A biographical sketch, "Pierre Chrysologue Pambrun," by Kenneth L. Holmes, provides much information on the fort. Thomas Jefferson Farnham's compliment is noted, as well as "the Frenchman's friendliness to American travelers and his sheer open heartedness in giving them help

Author's note, August 12, 1972. An informational sign in the highway rest area at Wallula junction refers to Fort Walla Walla as "erected in 1818," and pillaged in 1855 at the beginning of the great Indian war in the inter-mountain country.

USGS map, Walla Walla, Wash.-Oreg., 1:250,000, 1953 ed.

CHIMNEY ROCK
Mile 1731L¼ — 16 miles southeast of Pasco, Washington
Walla Walla County — Sec. 34, T7N, R31E

This prominent landmark overlooks the Columbia River. Charles Preuss, Fremont's topographer, made a sketch of this feature. It is on the east bank of the river, just below Fort Walla Walla.

John C. Fremont, October 28, 1843. ". . . down the left bank of the Columbia . . . The sketch of a rock which we passed as we toiled slowly along through deep loose sands, and over fragments of black volcanic rock . . . rapid progress of Mr. Applegate's fleet of boats . . . gliding swiftly down the broad river. . . ." [202:I, 555-56] James W. Nesmith, 1843. Described the feature and recounted an Indian legend concerning it. [290: 356]

USGS map, Walla Walla, Wash.-Oreg., 1:250,000, 1953 ed.

Chimney Rock, a noted Columbia River landmark, is below the mouth of the Walla Walla River.

CAYUSE WAR BATTLEFIELD_P
Mile 1733L½ — 5 miles east of Upper Well Spring
Morrow County, Oregon — SW¼ of Sec. 16, T2N, R26E

On this battlefield the Oregon Volunteers defeated the Cayuse Indians early in 1848, reopening the emigrant route and the Walla Walla Valley. However, the Cayuse War was not concluded until 1850.

John Mullan, 1858. His map locates the battlefield with reference to topographic features. [283: map]

USGS map, Strawberry Canyon NE, Oreg., 1:24,000, 19 70 ed.

UPPER WELL SPRING_P
Mile 1738.4 — South of the Boardman Bombing Range
Morrow County, Oregon — SE¼ of NE¼, Sec. 20, T2N, R25E

The principal Well Spring (there were two) is in the head of Well Spring Canyon, which is a shallow basin of powdery soil serving as an underground reservoir. The spring has been developed for stockwatering purposes. The lower spring (now Tub Spring), also used by emigrants, is 3½ miles northeast, in Juniper Canyon.

These springs provided the water which made the route across the dry benches between Butter and Willow creeks usable by emigrants.

William D. Stillwell, November 18, 1844. In this letter concerning his overland journey in 1844, he writes: "Whitman sent an Indian to pilot us thru this place [from Butter Creek] to Wells Springs then to Willow Creek, where we again struck the Emigrant Road." [367: letter]

P. V. Crawford, August 29, 1851. "Here we find well springs." [100: 164]

Maria P. Belshaw, September 8, 1853. "Came to the Springs . . . [water] proceeds from a mound dug out in the middle plenty of water but not very good . . ." [132: 325]

John Mullan, 1958. This map shows an "Upper Well Spring" and a "Lower Well Spring, "the latter being the feature designated as Tub Spring on modern maps. [283: map]

Osborne Russell, 1848. Concerning the death of Col. Gilliam, whose memorial stone is nearby, Russell adds, ". . . I have received intelligence from the regiment, which started on the campaign in January [1848] . . . The colonel has been killed in camp by an accidental shot from a rifle." [337: 183]

Author's note, August 12, 1972. The Well Spring, which is 200 feet south of the county road paralleling the south boundary of the Boardman Bombing Range, was dry when visited. It has been cased with a perforated barrel which serves to hold back the powdery soil when water is pumped to a nearby stock-watering reservoir.

Across the road and a half-mile to the west is an Oregon Trail cemetery. It is a fenced plot 80' x 206', containing a granite monument and an undetermined number of emigrant graves. A plaque on the south side of the monument states: "In Memory Of / Col. Cornelius Gilliam / Killed At This Spot In Indian War / March 24, 1848 / and the Pioneers Buried Here / Presented By Sarah Childress Polk Chapter No. 6 / D.A.R. Of Polk County Ore.," and another on the north side is marked, "In Memory Of Robert Evan Williams / Buried Sept. 1852 / and Other Emigrants Who Lie Here / Placed By The / Wasco County Pioneers." There are a number of depressions toward the rear of the plot but no grave stones. (According to Larry Smitton, the burials have been vandalized.)

There are evident Oregon Trail ruts north of the cemetery, and remains of a stage station (foundations and well), are in the southeast and northwest quarters of Section 20.

USGS map, Well Spring, Oreg., 1:24,000, 19 68 ed.

WILLOW CREEK CAMPGROUND
Mile 1751.5 — Near the station of Cecil, Oregon
Morrow County — SE¼ of SE¼, Sec. 29, T2N, R23E

This emigrant campground was located at the crossing of Willow Creek.

Wm. D. Stillwell, 1844. ". . . to Willow Creek, where we again struck the Emigrant Road from Willow Creek to Rock Creek. [367: letter]

Maria Belshaw, 1853. Mentioned the campground and also a trading post at that point. [132: 325]

USGS map, Cecil, Oreg., 1:24,000, 1968 ed.

The Upper Well Spring, left, once provided water for emigrants. It now supplies stock water when not entirely dry, as was the case when this photo was made. At right is the ruggedly-constructed Weatherford Marker, now minus the ox yoke which was stolen from atop the cross piece.

WEATHERFORD MONUMENT
Mile 1762.2 — 7.9 miles south of Arlington, Oregon
Gilliam County — SE¼ of SE¼, Sec. 27, T2N, R21E

This marker has been privately placed at the point where the Oregon Trail crosses Highway 13. A 4' x 6' bronze panel hung from a frame of eight-inch welded pipe carries this text: "This Marks The Crossing / Of The / Old Oregon Trail / Used By Pioneers And Settlers / Of The Oregon Territory / This Marker In Honor Of / W. W. Weatherford / 1844-1926 / Who Followed This Route Across / The Plains At The Age of 17 / Driving Oxen And Walking Barefoot / He Later Settled On Shutler Flat / Five Miles South Of This Marker / And Was The First To Engage In / Wheat Farming In Gilliam County / Erected By M. E. Weatherford."

An original ox yoke placed on top of the monument by Weatherford was recently (1972) stolen by vandals who cut the bolts by which it was attached. The bronze panel has been damaged by rifle fire.

An Oregon Trail marker (an enamel sign) is 200 feet east of the monument. Ruts are visible southeast of the highway, but have been plowed out on the northwest side.

USGS Map, Shutter Flat, Oreg., 1:24,000, 1964 ed.

CEDAR SPRING_P
Mile 1768.1 — 2¼ miles north of Rock Creek, Oregon
Gilliam County — SW¼ of SW¼, Sec. 35, T2N, R20E

This trailside spring took its name from the junipers surrounding it.

Author's note, August 13, 1972. There are a few junipers in the flat where the spring is located. A post serving as an Oregon Trail marker indicates that the trail crossed the flat, passed through the present ranch yard and climbed the ridge behind the buildings before splitting around Turner Butte.

USGS map, Turner Butte, Oreg., 1:24,000, 1964 ed.

CROSSING OF JOHN DAY RIVER (McDonaldFord)_P
Mile 1775.0 — 7½ miles south of Blalock, Oregon
Gilliam County — NE¼ of NW¼, Sec. 11, T1N, R19E

Emigrants who took the cutoff over the dry benchland crossed the John Day River here. Those who followed down the Columbia River crossed this stream at its mouth.

John C. Fremont, November 3, 1843. "At noon we crossed John Day's river, a clear and beautiful stream, with a swift current and a bed of rolled stones. It is sunk in a deep valley, which is characteristic of all streams in this region." [202:I, 558]

Osborne Cross, 1849. Mentioned the crossing. [101: 233]

WPA Writers' Project, 1939. ". . . originally called LePage's River by Lewis and Clark for a member of their party, was named in honor of John Day of the Astorians." [146: 136]

Author's note, August 13, 1972. We forded the river afoot in six inches of water for 300 feet. A four-wheel-drive vehicle could have crossed easily at that time. There is an Oregon Trail monument commemorating this crossing 1,400 feet due west (in Sherman County, on the Big Sky Ranch) and 50 feet north of the dirt road by which the ranch is reached from the west. The monument is a rhyolite boulder 30" x 30" by 48" high on a concrete base, and bearing a bronze tablet which states: " 1843—Old Oregon Trail Ford-1863 / Of John Day River / Emigrants On The Old Oregon Trail / Forded The John Day River Near This / Spot From 1843 to 1863 / Thomas Scott Established A Ferry / Near / Here in 1866 / Thousands Of Settlers Passed This Way Until The Completion Of The / Railroad in 1884 / Land Donated by Agnes Merritt." In pebbles

The ford of the John Day River was only six inches deep when this photo was taken.

in the base: "1950 / Sheman [Sherman] County Historical Society."

North of the monument 300 feet is a possible gravesite—a depression with a rock rim, seven feet long and oriented east-west.

There is an Oregon Trail marker at the base of the hill, ¼-mile distant on Az. 330 degrees true. It probably marks the place where the trail ascended to the benchland on the west of the river (the present ranch road goes up a draw which would not have been a practical route for emigrant wagons).

USGS map, McDonald, Oreg., 1:24,000, 1964 ed.

BARLOW ROAD JUNCTION (1864)$_P$
Mile 1778.0 — 19.5 miles east of Biggs, Oregon
Sherman County — NE¼ of SE¼, Sec. 8, TIN, R19E

This is where the latter-day extension of the Barlow Road left the Oregon Trail. The 1864 freighters' route began 3.1 miles west of the McDonald Ford crossing of the John Day River. This cutoff was made possible by the construction of Sherar's Bridge over the Deschutes River, near the mouth of Buck Hollow.

Wm. H. McNeil (undated). ". . . to Webfoot Spring where [in 1864] the road forked 5 miles west of the John Day, one fork followed Grass Valley Canyon to Buck Hollow, Sherar's Bridge (1862) across the Deschutes River, Tygh, Wamic and the Barlow Road. . . ."

There is information on Sherar's Bridge. [256: 157, 235-38]

Author's note. Sherar's Bridge was built as a footbridge in 1860, and was improved to handle wagons four years later. It was constructed at or near the place where the survivors of the Meeks' Cutoff disaster crossed the Deschutes River in 1845. See 302: Oct. 3.

USGS map, McDonald, Oreg., 1:24,000, 1964 ed.

SPANISH HOLLOW$_p$
Mile 1793.0 — 2½ miles northwest of Wasco, Oregon
Sherman County — NW¼ of NE¼, Sec. 31, T2N, R17E

At this point emigrants saw Spanish cattle, probably introduced by Daniel Lee after he established the Dalles Mission in 1838. Oregon Trail ruts and a trail marker are here now.

Wm. H. McNeil (undated). "Spanish Hollow was so named because early day emigrants discoverd two Spanish cows in the hollow leading down from Wasco to Biggs, which the Old Oregon Trail followed." [256: 418]

USGS map, Wasco, Ore.-Wash., 1:62,500, 1957 ed.

OREGON TRAIL MONUMENT
Mile 1800.2 — Near Biggs Junction, Oregon
Sherman County — SE¼ of SW¼, Sec. 8, T2N, R16E

This monument is ¾-mile southwest of Biggs Junction, adjacent to old U.S. Highway 30. It was intended to mark the place where the Oregon Trail came down to the Columbia River after traversing the cutoff from Umatilla River. The marker is a lava boulder 3' x 3' x 3', with a tablet which states: "Near This Point From / 1843 To 1863 / West Bound Emigrants / Caught Their First Sight Of / The Columbia River / Erected By The / Wasco County Pioneer Association 1940. "

The Oregon Trail did not come down Spanish Hollow, as

McNeil indicates (256: 418), but stayed on the ridge west of the hollow; and it was from the point of the ridge that emigrants had their first, grand view of the River of the West.

USGS map, Wishram, Ore.-Wash., 1:62,500, 1957 ed.

DESCHUTES RIVER CROSSING
Mile 1804.0 — 13½ miles east of The Dallcs, Oregon
Sherman County — NW¼ of NW¼, Sec. 26, T2N, R15E

This was a difficult ford at the mouth of the Deschutes River. The site is now submerged by the waters of Lake Celilo, impounded behind the Dalles Dam, and its original character is no longer apparent.

John C. Fremont, November 3, 1843. descended again into the river bottom, along which we resumed our sterile road, and in about four miles reached the ford of the Fall River *(Rivière aux Chutes)*, a considerable tributary. . . . The river was high, divided into several arms, with a Rocky island at its outlet into the Columbia . . . name, which is received from one of its many falls some forty miles up the river. It entered the Columbia with a roar of falls and rapids. . . . The ford was very difficult at this time . . . during the crossing, the howitzer was occasionally several feet under water." [202:1, 558]

James W. Nesmith, 1843. Mentioned the crossing. [290: 358]

John Minto, 1844. Described the crossing and an attempted robbery there. [266: 228]

Osborne Cross, 1849. Mentioned the crossing. [101: 233]

Maria Belshaw, 1853. Noted a ferry in operation there. [132: 326]

Author's note, August 13, 1972. There is an Oregon State Park on the east bank of the Deschutes, south of old U.S. Highway 30, and an information panel on the fill which leads to the east side of the old bridge. It states: "Historic / Oregon Trail / Deschutes River / Crossing / The Oregon Trail Crossed / The Hazardous Deschutes / River At This Point By Float- / ing The Prairie Schooners / And Swimming The Livestock   An Island / At The River Mouth / Was Often Utilized When The Water Was High And The / Ford Dangerous. Pioneer / Women And Children Were / Frequently Ferried Across / The Stream By Native Canoe Men Who Made The Pas- / sage In Exchange For Bright / Colored Shirts And Other / Trade Goods."

Oregon Trail ruts are visible ascending the hill on the west side of the river.

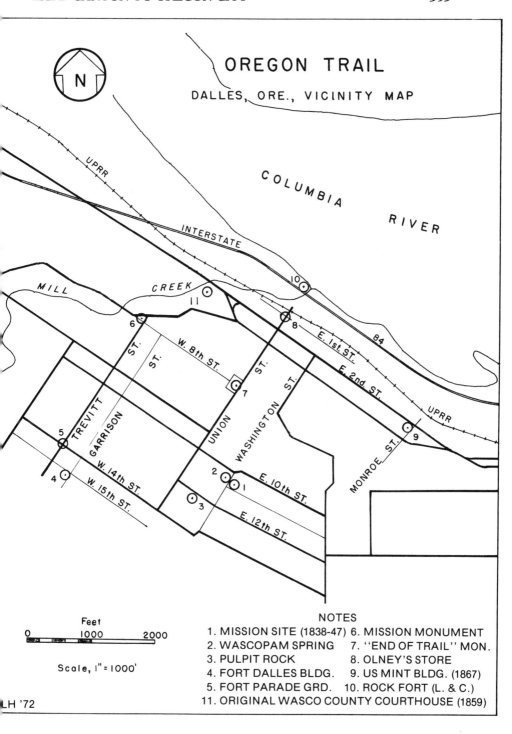

OREGON TRAIL

DALLES, ORE., VICINITY MAP

Feet

0   1000   2000

Scale, 1" = 1000'

LH '72

NOTES

1. MISSION SITE (1838-47)   6. MISSION MONUMENT
2. WASCOPAM SPRING   7. "END OF TRAIL" MON.
3. PULPIT ROCK   8. OLNEY'S STORE
4. FORT DALLES BLDG.   9. US MINT BLDG. (1867)
5. FORT PARADE GRD.   10. ROCK FORT (L. & C.)
11. ORIGINAL WASCO COUNTY COURTHOUSE (1859)

USGS map, Wishram, Ore.-Wash., 1:62,500, 1957 ed.

DALLES MISSION SITE
(Site 1, Dalles, Ore., Vicinity Map)
Mile 1819.0 — Wasco County, Oregon — Sec. 3, T1N, R13E

A mission, one of several maintained by the Methodists in the Oregon Country, was established here by Daniel Lee in 1838. It served as a stopping place for emigrants until its abandonment in 1847, when the property was sold to Dr. Marcus Whitman. In 1843 there were two dwellings, a schoolhouse, stable, barn, garden and cleared fields to greet the way-worn emigrants. This mission appears to have rendered a greater service than Whitman's. Assistance given survivors of the trek over Meek's Cutoff in 1845 probably saved many lives.

John Boardman, October 25, 1843. ". . . arrived at Mr. Perkins Mission . . . found the wagons here." (He had floated down the Columbia from Fort Walla Walla with Applegate's division.) [37: 117]

James W. Nesmith, October 16, 1843. ". . . passed the Dalles. . . . Arrived at the Methodist Mission." (He had come by horseback down the Columbia from Fort Walla Walla.) [290: 358]

Overton Johnson, November 1843. "Wascopin Methodist Mission . . . not yet, we believe, been productive of much, if any, good . . ." [208: 98]

John C. Fremont, November 4, 1843. ". . . encamped near the mission . . . among oaks and other forest trees of the east . . . hospitable and kind reception . . . [by] our country people at the mission . . . Two good-looking wooden dwelling houses, and a large school house, with stables, barn and garden, and large cleared fields between the houses and the river bank, on which were scattered the wooden huts of an Indian village . . ." [202:1, 561]

Samuel Parker, October 7, 1845. "This morning nothing to eat. Got to the mission at dark. Got in a house with my family got something to eat. This was the first day we had done without something to eat but some of the company had been without bread for 15 days and had to live on pore beef without anything else. I will just say pen & tongue will both fall short when they go to tell the suffering the company went through [on Meek's Cutoff]. There my wife and child died . . ." [302: diary]

Osborne Cross, September 14, 1849. ". . . continued our

journey to the Old Mission . . . The Old Mission has gone
greatly to ruin . . . a dwelling house, which we now occupied,
and three more buildings, one of which, opposite the one
fronting on the river, had been used as a school house . . . The
outbuildings have all been destroyed and the whole is going to
decay since the war with the Cayuse . . . There is a fine spring
but a short distance from the house." (Wascopam Spring; see
Dalles, Ore., Vicinity Map, Site No. 2). [101: 234, 236]

Read Bain, 1920. "In March 1838, Daniel Lee and H. K. W.
Perkins selected a site and established a mission at the Dalles.
Daniel Lee took fourteen head of cattle from the Willamette
station over the Cascades reaching the Dalles in October. He
spent most of that winter there, alone. The station prospered
very badly, but the next summer a combined church and home
were added. . . . Bancroft (p. 169) analyzes Lee's motives at
some length in regard to establishing these mission posts; makes
him out a colonizer rather than a missionary . . . stakes of
empire in the name of God." [20: 70]

Irene D. Paden, 1943. ". . . at the modern city of that name,
Daniel Lee, nephew of Jason, had built a mission settlement . . .
[which] 'gave to the valley the cheerful and busy air of
civilization' . . . stood on the Twelfth Street hill just back of the
high school. . . the Lee mission was built thereabouts. A jagged
rocky fragment. . . . Pulpit Rock stands in an intersection of two
streets [see Dalles, Ore., Vicinity Map, Site No. 3] . . . old
mission spring still flows in the school yard." P. 365: Notes that
the museum operated by the Wasco County Historical Society in
the surviving Fort Dalles building (Surgeon's Quarters) has the
mission bell. [298: 364-65]

Herbert M. Hart, 1963. "A detachment under Captain H. A.
G. Lee came here in 1847 during troubles with the Cayuse
Indians. They built a stockade and occupied the Methodist
mission buildings, unofficially calling the whole business Fort
Lee, after their commander." [167: 102]

Robert W. Frazer, 1965. "The Whitman massacre of November
1847, and the Cayuse War which followed it, led to the establishment of a stockade by volunteer troops at The Dalles in January
1848. This post was called Fort Lee for Major Henry A. G. Lee
of the Oregon Rifles [Provisional Government of Oregon—not
United States]; also Fort Wascopam, from the Indian name for
a nearby spring." [142: 127]

Wm. H. McNeil (undated). In 1843, "The Methodist
Missionaries here gave [the emigrants] a warm greeting and

The Methodist Mission at The Dalles, as it appeared in 1845.

provided some fresh meats and other foods and helped them over the Lee cattle trail." [256: 152]

Author's note, August 14, 1972. At the intersection of Trevitt Street and W. 3rd Place, The Dalles, Oregon, there is a triangular plot of grass with a granite monument stating: "The Dalles Indian Mission / Of The / Methodist Episcopal Church / Established In 1833 By / Daniel Lee / Marked By / Willamette University." Note: Despite the implication of the wording on the monument, it does not mark the mission site. The mission buildings were at Washington Street and East 11th, a little more than a half mile to the southeast. They were burned in 1850, after Fort Dalles was built.

The origin of the name by which the Mission settlement, and later, the fort and town, became known is explained by John C. Fremont: ". . . *the Dalles of the Columbia.* The whole volume of the river at this place passes between the walls of a chasm, which has the appearance of having been rent through the basaltic strata which form the valley rock of the region. At the narrowest . . . by measurement, 58 yards, and the average height of the walls above the water 25 feet; forming a trough between the rocks—whence the name, probably applied by a Canadian voyageur. The mass of water . . . passed swiftly between, deep and black, and curled into many small whirlpools and counter currents, but unbroken by foam, and so still that scarcely the sound of a ripple was heard." (see 202:1, 560).

USGS map, The Dalles, Oreg.-Wash., 1:62,500, 1957 ed.

FORT DALLES ("Camp Drum")
(Sites 4 & 5, Dalles, Ore., Vicinity Map)
Mile 1819.0 — Wasco County, Oregon — Sec. 4, T1N, R13E

Fort Dalles, a military post, was established May 21, 1850, on Mill Creek at The Dalles of the Columbia River, as Camp Drum. It was re-designated Fort Dalles in July 1853. When occupied by two companies of the Regiment of Mounted Riflemen, its purpose was to protect emigrant traffic on the Oregon Trail. The post was abandoned in 1867 and disposed of in 1877.

Fort Dalles was the center of Army operations in Eastern Oregon during the 1850s—a turbulent period on the Oregon Trail. After 1861 its role was essentially that of a quartermaster depot.

Irene D. Paden, 1943. ". . . the historical museum . . . was built in 1856 as the surgeon's quarters at old Fort Dalles . . . of an almost indescribable quaintness . . ." [298: 364-65]

Herbert M. Hart, 1963. "On May 13, 1850, two rifle companies came from Fort Vancouver, Washington, to establish a supply depot . . . A 10-mile square reservation . . . soon cut to one mile. By 1851 the new post, Camp Drum, had a 124 by 20 foot log building as an officers' quarters and a 140 by 20 foot frame house for barracks . . . A store house, stable, and sawmill completed the post. In 1853 the post became Fort Dalles, and in 1856 the log buildings were replaced by a semi-circular layout to house a large garrison. Eight companies under Colonel George Wright were sent to Fort Dalles on March 28, 1856 . . ." [167: 102]

Robert W. Frazer, 1965. "The regular military post was first called Camp Drum, probably for Captain Simon H. Drum, 4th U.S. Artillery, killed in the assault on Mexico City, September 13, 1847. It was established by two companies of Mounted Riflemen, under the command of Captain Stephen S. Tucker, by order of Lieutenant Colonel William W. Loring . . . By 1852 a town had grown up around the post, and in 1857 it was granted a charter under the name Fort Dalles — which was soon changed to Dalles City — but listed by the Post Office Department as The Dalles. . . . The last time the post was garrisoned was from March 27 to May 22, 1867. On March 28, 1877, the military reservation was transferred to the Interior Department." [142: 127-28]

Wm. H. McNeil (undated). "In May 1850 Major Tucker . . . proceeded with the erection of the log fort buildings at 14th

The former Surgeon's quarters, a relic of Fort Dalles, now serves as a museum.

and Trevitt streets. L. S. Fritz claimed there were 15 buildings erected." Pp. 1, 2 & 5: A description of the buildings and establishments of the post. [256: 433]

Author's note, August 17, 1972. Spent bullets and Army cartridge cases found on the hillside behind the residence at 2114 Bridge Street indicate the firing range was probably located there. Rock Fort, shown on the Dalles, Ore., Vicinity Map as Site No. 10, was not connected with Fort Dalles; rather, it was a Lewis and Clark campsite on a defensible upthrust of basaltic rock near the bank of the Columbia River.

USGS map, The Dalles, Oreg.-Wash., 1:62,500, 1957 ed.

"END OF THE OLD OREGON TRAIL" MONUMENT
(Site 7, Dalles, Ore., Vicinity Map)
Mile 1819.0 — Wasco County, Oregon — Sec. 3, T1N, R13E

This basalt boulder, 24" by 36" by 48", has a back-sloping top incised, "End / Of The Old / Oregon / Trail / 1843-1906." It is placed inside the Union Street entrance to a small city park. A board over the gate also says, "End of the Oregon Trail."

The boulder is a relic of Ezra Meeker's marking of the Oregon Trail in 1906. It is inaccurate. Even under the broadest interpretation, the overland wagon route ended not here, but at Chenoweth Creek, prior to the opening of the Barlow Road in 1846.

Wm. H. McNeil (undated). Discussing the monument now in the city park at 8th and Union, ". . . End of the Old Oregon Trail . . . 4th and Laughlin School . . . In 1906 the attention was toward granite monuments in towns . . ." [256: 151]

Author's note, August 18, 1972. This monument, which was originally placed by Ezra Meeker in 1906, may have been moved.

The Barlow Road probably originated between the Methodist Mission and Olney's store, in the vicinity of East 3rd and Washington streets, when it was opened by Samuel K. Barlow in 1845-46. However, later travelers left the Oregon Trail at Ten Mile Creek—that distance being east of The Dalles—to cross over to the Barlow, saving some mileage that way. Operated as a toll road after 1846, the Barlow Road was the only wagon road from The Dalles, over the Cascades, to Portland until 1920, with the exception of the years 1876 to 1879 when the Palmer cattle trail along the Columbia was made into a passable summer road.

For general references concerning the Barlow Road, consult the following — 19: 292; 23: 71-81; 24: 260-69; 33: letter; 256: 153; 258: passim.; 275:II, 658, 662-63; and 298: 367-68.

USGS map, The Dalles, Oreg.-Wash., 1:62,500, 1957 ed.

NATHAN OLNEY'S STORE
(Site 8, Dalles, Ore., Vicinity Map)
Mile 1819.0 — Wasco County, Oregon — Sec. 3, T1N, R13E

This log store was established in 1847, on the bank of Mill Creek near where it emptied into the Columbia River. In 1850 Olney was forced to move off the military reservation. He re-established his business at Chenoweth Creek, but evidently soon moved east of The Dalles, to "Olney Creek" (present Fifteen Mile Creek) where emigrants of 1851-53 mention his store.

Except for the trading posts of the Hudson's Bay Company—which were not well adapted to the commerce of the emigration—Olney's store was the first to do business east of the Cascade Range in the Oregon Country.

Wm. H. McNeil (undated) "Capt. Nathan Olney . . . in 1847 he returned to the Dalles to become the first permanent resident and operated the first store . . . in a log hut, on the bank of Mill Creek at First and Union. . . . In the spring of 1850 Maj. S. S. Tucker . . . made Nathan Olney move his log store 'out of town'; so Olney built another log store on Olney (Chenoweth) Creek, about where Highway 30 crosses and continued to trade." [256: 56]

Author's note, December 1986. Olney's residence at Chenoweth (creek resulted in a transitory use of his name on that stream also (see the Maria Belshaw reference of Sept. 15, 1853).

USGS map, The Dalles, Oreg.-Wash., 1:62,500, 1957 ed.

CHENOWETH CREEK ("Crates Point")
**Mile 1822.0 — Northeast of Crates, a suburb of The Dalles, Oregon
Wasco County — NW¼ of NW¼ Sec. 28, T2N, R13E**

Here was a protected harbor at the mouth of the creek where rafts could be built and boats loaded for the voyage down the Columbia River. Here the wagon route ended. A settlement developed on the point of land between Chenoweth Creek and the river after 1850.

Until the Barlow Road was opened in 1846, the mouth of Chenoweth Creek was the end of the overland Oregon Trail, and it remained an important place to the mid-1850s. The settlement there was the precursor of The Dalles.

John C. Fremont, November 6, 1843. "The last of the emigrants had just left the Dalles at the time of our arrival, traveling some by water and the others by land, making ark-like rafts, on which they had embarked their families and households, with their large wagons and other furniture, while their stock were driven along the shore." [202:1, 562]

Josiah Beal, Fall 1847. "We then went about 3 miles farther down the River [below the Dalles Mission] and here we built 2 flat Botes to come down the River. Mr. Bolen was a ship carpenter & had his tools along with him. . . . We soon had our Botes ready to launch. To make them tight us boys were sent out to the timber to gather pitch . . . were filled with contents of our wagons and a few wagons we taken to pieces & stowed in the Bote. Stock driven down Indian Trail . . ." [28: letter]

Maria P. Belshaw, September 15, 1853. "Olney's Creek . . .

Four miles.. ... [below] the Dalles ... many canvas buildings, business lively.. ... six or eight boats on the Columbia ... above the falls." [132: 327]

C.F. Loans, 1922. "Nathaniel Olney, the Indian agent for the Snake River district ... 1855 ..." [82: 23]

Wm. H. McNeil (undated). "In the spring of 1850 Maj. S. S. Tucker ... made Nathan Olney move his log store 'out of town' ... built another log store on Olney (Chenoweth) Creek, about where Highway 30 crosses and continued to trade ..." P. 201: "Crates Point, opposite the Dalles Country Club and at the mouth of Chenoweth Creek, was first known by emigrants as the embarcation point for their journey down the Columbia on rafts, between their first arrival at The Dalles in 1843 and the establishment of the first steamboat service between here and the Cascades in 1848; and to a limited extent even later than 1850. The mouth of Chenoweth Creek was a protected harbor for rafts, batteaux, dugouts, canoes and small barges. Quite a camp of Indians always made their home in that vicinity for that reason. ... There were lots of pine trees in that vicinity which were cut for rafts and hauled by the emigrants to Chenoweth harbor and lashed together in sizes big enough for 6 wagons! The slopes of the banks of the creek made it easy to roll the wagons on to the rafts, remove the wheels and tie them down. The small sail barges, which hauled 4 to 6 wagons, also used the harbor.

"The Hudson's Bay Co. batteau ... which could haul up to 6 tons and carry a dozen passengers or oarsmen, used the protected harbor to haul freight for those desiring to abandon wagons here and go on down the river with what possessions the batteau could handle or carry. Women and children were rowed down the river in canoes or the larger log dugout canoes which would accommodate a dozen people and handled by the Indians who were their master craftsmen." [256: 56, 201]

Author's note, August 4, 1982. The area immediately around the mouth of Chenoweth Creek is occupied by facilities of the Martin Marietta Aluminum Company. Even before that development of the site, its character had been irrevocably altered by the rise of water backed up by the Bonneville Dam.

In addition to the river route through the Columbia Gorge, there was the Jason Lee cattle trail—probably an Indian route—by which the missionaries had taken cattle across the Cascade Range. Of this mountainous trail by way of Lost Lake, Bull Run River and Sandy River, Fremont writes, ". . . the usual road across the mountain required strong and fresh animals, there being an interval of three days in which they could obtain no food." (See 202: 1, 561).

In 1846 Joel Palmer established a rude pack trail down the south bank of the Columbia to the Sandy River, and it was used to move emigrant cattle from the Dalles to the Willamette Valley. (See 256: 153).

USGS map, The Dalles, Oreg.-Wash., 1:62,500, 1957 ed.

TYGH VALLEY GRADE
Mile 1846.4 — ½ mile northwest of Tygh Valley, Oregon
Wasco County — NW¼ of SE¼, Sec. 29-32, T3S, R13E

About 1,000 feet of ruts are visible in this steep ascent, over which the Barlow Road climbed out of the Tygh Valley. Some are partially filled-in by debris from the construction of the Tygh Valley-Wamic Road.

The original Barlow party probably camped on the north bank of Tygh Creek (SW¼ of SE¼, Sec. 4) while the Barlow Road was being built westward toward the White River. The campground is now part of a sawmill development.

USGS map, Tygh Valley, Oreg., 1:24,000, 1962 ed.

WAMIC INFORMATIONAL PANEL
Mile 1851R1¼ — At Wamic, Oregon
Wasco County — NE¼ of NW¼, Sec. 14, T4S, R12E

An informational panel was placed here by the U.S. Forest Service about 1957. It is in the town of Wamic, adjacent to the uncompleted White River Road access to the Mount Hood Loop Highway. It states: "Barlow Road / _____ / This sign is erected at the site / of the old toll gate on the first wagon road / built over the Cascade Range (1845-1846) by / Samuel K. Barlow (1792-1867) an Oregon Pioneer from Kentucky / Mt. Hood Loop Highway."

Wamic is not on the Barlow Road route, and it was not the site of a toll gate. The Barlow, at the closest point, was 1½ miles to the south, and the toll gate was on Gate Creek, 6½ miles distant.

USGS map, Wamic, Oreg., 1:24,000, 1962 ed.

Above: The Columbia river below The Dalles, as seen by Osborne Cross in 1849. The water route contrasted greatly with the Barlow Cutoff. Below is the Tygh Valley as seen from the old road. Barlow's camp was in or near where the log pond is now.

BARLOW TOLL GATE (Eastern)
Mile 1857R½ — On Gate Creek, north of Smock Prairie, Oregon
Wasco County — SE¼ of NE¼, Sec. 35, T4S, R11E

A toll gate was in operation at the Strickland Place from 1846 to 1852. Evidences remain at that point of the road grade, a building foundation, cellar and gate post, although the structural remains may be a residue of settler occupation of the site. While this is the original toll gate on the Barlow Road, additional research is needed; to eliminate the unlikely claim of another locality.

The Oregon Spectator, October 29, 1846. "The Emigration. Those of the emigrants who came by way of the Mount Hood road, have all safely reached the valley of the Willamette . . . the number of wagons and stock that passed the toll-gate on the Mount Hood road. There were one hundred and forty-five wagons, fifteen hundred and fifty-nine head of horses, mules and horned cattle all together, and one lot of sheep . . . I think thirteen . . ."
[275:II, 662-63]

Walter Bailey, 1912. "For two years . . . Captain Barlow personally collected the toll . . . 1848 to 1862 . . . road was leased . . ." [19: 292]

Walter E. Meacham, 1947. "The toll-gate was established east of the mountains at Gate Creek, a tributary of the White River." P. 15: "According to Lige Coalman, long connected with the Barlow Road, the locations [of gates] were as follows: Strickland Place on Gate Creek, 1846-52; Francis Revenue place, 1853-65; Summit House, 1866-70; Two-Mile Camp (3 miles east of Rhododendron) 1871-78; Toll Gate (one mile east of Rhododendron) 1879-1915." [258: 13, 15]

Author's note, August 15, 1972. It would appear as if the Wamic Sign mentioned in the prior site description was placed at the end of the paved road as a matter of convenience rather than historical accuracy, and that local supposition has developed in support of the idea that an early toll gate existed near the town, at about Mile 1851. Further research and correction of the Wamic sign appear to be in order.

USGS map, Rock Creek Reservoir, Oreg., 1:24,000, 1962 ed.

CASCADES OF THE COLUMBIA
Mile 1860.5 — At Cascade Locks, Oregon
Hood River County — Sec. 14, T2N, R7E

This obstruction to navigation of the Columbia River required a three-mile portage. The cascades were occasionally run by loaded craft—even by steamboats—but the practice was dangerous and fraught with accidents. Local Indians assisted in portaging before the portage roads were built in the 1850s.

This was the last dangerous obstacle on the Oregon Trail for those who elected to complete their journey by the Columbia River route.

James W. Nesmith, October 21, 1843. ". . . at the Cascades about ten . . . balance of the day in making the portage . . . high mountains covered with timber, killed by a fire." [290: 358]

John C. Fremont, November 1843. ". . . the river forms a great *cascade,* with a series of rapids, in breaking through the range of mountains . . . gives the idea of Cascades to the whole range; and hence the name . . . in making a short turn to the south, the river forms the cascades in breaking over a point of agglomerated masses of rocks leaving a handsome bay to the right, with several rocky, pine-covered islands . . . halted on the left bank, about five minutes' walk above the cascades, where there were several Indian huts, and where our guides signified it was customary to hire Indians to assist in making the portage . . . the canoe, instruments, and baggage, were carried through (a distance of about half a mile) to the bank of the main cascade, where we again embarked, the water being white with foam among ugly rocks, and boiling into a thousand whirlpools. The boat passed with great rapidity . . . through 2 miles of broken water, we ran some wild looking rapids, which are called the Lower Rapids, being the last on the river, which below is tranquil and smooth—a broad, magnificent stream. On a low point on the right bank . . . were pitched many tents of emigrants, who were waiting here for their friends from above, or for boats and provisions . . . from Vancouver . . . I had noticed their camps along the shore, or transporting their goods across the portage . . . two miles in length; and above, to the Dalles, is 45 miles of smooth and good navigation." [202:I 563-64]

Samuel Parker, Mid-October 1845. "I did not expect to get to the city with my fore sick children and my oldest girl that was sick. I was looking all the time for her to die. I tuck my seat in the canoe by her and held her up and the same at nite when I

The author, second from right, and three colleagues examine a fallen post, all the known remains of the Gate Creek tollgate on the Barlow Road.

came to the cascade falls. I had to make portage of 3 miles. I put my sick girl in a blanket and pack her & only rested once that day. We maid the portage with the help of my fore Indians . . ." [302: diary]

Josiah Beal, 1847. "As soon as the botes were finished, were filled with contents of our wagons and a few wagons were taken to pieces & stowed in the Bote. Stock driven down the Indian Trail. When we got to the cascades we had to unlode our botes and set up our wagons & fill them and make a drive of 5 miles to the lower cascades. The botes were run over the falls and caught below by some Indians that were hired to look after them. At this place Father fell in with John Waymire. He had come up here with supplys to sell the Emegrants in a small bote. He had at this time sold out and father got him to take the family to Portland." [28: letter]

John R. Tice, September 16, 1851. Tice took a steamboat, the *James P. Flint,* 60 feet long, 12-foot beam and five-foot hold, which began service between The Dalles and Cascades on September 4, 1851. From the Cascades, where he found a portage road, there were other boats below continuing the service to Portland. [340: 25]

Maria P. Belshaw, September 15, 1853. ". . . six or eight boats on the Columbia . . . above the falls." September 18, ". . . harbor at Cascades . . . one store, boarding house and gambling house all in one . . . nothing but bitter oaths." P. 329, September 24, ". . . steamer . . . took passage . . ." [The boats then running were the *Multnomah* and *Fashion,* the latter being the rebuilt *J. P. Flint*]. [132: 327, 329]

Wm. H. McNeil (undated). States that steamboat service between The Dalles and Cascades began in 1848, but an item in the Portland *Oregon Daily Times,* September 4, 1851, indicates such service was not available until the fall of 1851. During the early period, "Women and children were rowed down the river in batteaux or the larger log dugout canoes which would accommodate a dozen people and handled by the Indians who were their master craftsmen. The passengers got out at the Cascades, walked the six miles down past the lower rapids where they entered the canoes again to go on down to Milwaukie or Oregon City. The Indians 'lowered' or floated their canoes down on ropes and pulled them back up the rapids the same way . . . Even after the Barlow Road was opened early winter snows often closed it before October emigrants could get over the Cascades and they, too, had to resort to the scows and rafts or abandon their wagons for batteaux and canoes. The cattle and horses were driven over the Lee (Lost Lake) Cattle Trail by the men and boys. [256: 201]

Oscar O. Winther, 1948. "Bradford and Company began work in 1851 on a wooden portage tramway along the north bank of the Columbia River Cascades. Four years later, Colonel Joseph S. Ruckel started a portage wagon road on the south bank of the Cascades. On this roadbed the Oregon Portage Railroad later operated. These portage lines were controlled by the Oregon Steam Navigation Company." [404: 257]

Gregory M. Franzwa, 1972. "The portage at the Cascades was quite necessary in any kind of water. The river at that point was full of great rocks, the ruins of a giant natural bridge across the stream, which collapsed in prehistoric times. The river was so treacherous there as to be impassible to navigation until a series of locks were built a century ago. Now the great rocks are far below the surface, as the Bonneville Dam has raised the water level so that the great Columbia navigation system can function effectively." [141: 372]

Author's note, August 18, 1972. The Port of Cascade Locks now maintains a small park at the abandoned Cascade Locks, and a museum there exhibits Indian artifacts and relics of historical interest, including the tiny "Oregon Pony," a locomotive which once hauled cars back and forth on the six-mile-long portage railway.

The small settlement at the Cascades was attacked by Indians in January 1856, but the siege was quickly lifted by troops from Fort Vancouver. Construction of Bonneville Dam and the consequent raising of the water level has greatly changed the shoreline of the Columbia River here, submerging most of the old portage site.

USGS map, The Dalles, Oreg.-Wash., 1:250,000, 1953 ed.

KLINGER'S CAMP
Mile 1872.4 — 4 miles east of Barlow Pass
Wasco County, Oregon — SE¼ of SE¼, Sec. 2, T4S, R9E

Here was a "hay burner station"—a stopping place for freighters—maintained by a trapper named Klinger. A pile of chimney stones and a Forest Service informational sign mark the site, which is on the White River where the road turned up Barlow Creek toward Barlow Pass.

The importance of this site to history does not stem from its use as a freighter's stopover, but rather from the probability that this is the site of "Fort Deposit." Here, or very near here, William Berry waited out the winter of 1845-46 while guarding the wagons and possessions of the Barlow party.

Mary S. Barlow, 1902. Mary Barlow notes that while Barlow and Rector were exploring the southern flank of Mount Hood for a pass, the remainder of the men cut a track to the head of "Little DesChutes"—White River—and the wagons were moved ahead 12 miles. She says, "We stopped at the long but not very steep hill [Little Laurel Hill, leading down to the White River] and waited . . . for we did not wish to descend it for fear we might have to ascend it again if . . . [it was] 'Thus far and no farther.'" [23: 73-76]

Walter Bailey, 1912. "After several days travel on foot . . . Barlow and Palmer found a passable route for wagons to the western descent. But their own journey was fraught with so much hardship . . . [they were] forced to conclude that the season was too late . . . [It had] been determined that, should the passage prove impossible, the wagons and impedimenta should be cached and the company should proceed with the stock over the mountains. Therefore, on return of the leaders a rude house was constructed about five miles east of the summit. In this were placed the perishables of the company.

"Three young men, William Barlow, John Brown, and William Berry volunteered to remain . . . [It was] found that scarcely any provisions could be left and Berry was left in solitude to keep a long winter's vigil . . ." [19: 291]

William Barlow, 1912. Describes the building of Fort Deposit. [24: 204-05]

Leslie M. Scott, 1918. ". . . the present Barlow Creek, tributary of White River . . . Barlow Camp, on the latter stream, where the Barlow party cached its wagons, in the winter of 1845-46, is some thirteen miles southeast of Government Camp." [348: 75-76]

Oscar O. Winther, 1939. "At a place called Fort Deposit some goods were left to the lonely vigil of William Berry while the remainder of the company, using their oxen and horses as pack animals, moved ahead on foot." [403: 320]

Glen Baker, 1969. Concerning the location of Fort Deposit, "Their records show they were about five miles south of what is now Barlow Pass, and that would put them in the vicinity of Summit Meadows, as we know it today. Here they built a house, cached the wagons and supplies . . ." (The foregoing statement ignores the fact that Summit Meadow is two miles west of Barlow Pass, not five south of it—the wagons were not brought over the summit that fall.) [21: 29]

Author's note, August 15, 1972. Five miles south of Barlow Pass would place Fort Deposit on Barlow Creek, close to its junction with the White River. The distance, by map measure, is correct at the present Barlow Forest Camp, but, with allowance for the deviance of forest travel, the Klingers Camp location, four miles from Barlow Pass, could have been the site. The White River Valley would have been much more habitable and logical.

USGS map, Mt. Wilson, Oreg., 1:62,500, 1956 ed.

BARLOW PASS
Mile 1876.8 — South of Mount Hood, Oregon
Hood River County — SE¼ of NE ¼, Sec. 29, T3S, R9E

The Barlow is not a spectacular pass. It is at the head of Barlow Creek, separating the headwaters of the White River (the "Little DesChutes") from those of the Salmon River, a westward flowing stream. The point where the Barlow Road passed over

This is the Barlow Road west of Barlow Pass—now reopened as a hiking trail.

the divide was about 1,300 feet south of the true pass, or low point, used by the Mount Hood Loop Highway.

The pass was the key to the route over the Cascade Range south of Mount Hood. Joel Palmer was led to it by following an Indian trailway over the mountains. Little notice was taken of the pass itself until later; the naming was also a latter-day development.

Irene D. Paden, 1943. "At the summit of Mount Hood Loop Highway the interested motorist may notice the original road, crossing at the Hood and Clackamas County sign . . . decided to walk down to Government Camp. . . . It was a marvelous hike, short, downhill, and shady. I recommend it . . . comes into the highway at the Pioneer Woman's grave. . . ." [298: 369]

Author's note, August 16, 1972. The Barlow Road is signed where the present Barlow Creek road intersects the Mount Hood Loop Highway; the true crossing is at a parking area south of the pass. From that point, the Barlow Road (which is yet very apparent on the west side of the ridge), has been brushed out down to the Pioneer Woman's grave. That segment will be maintained as a hiking trail and will have appropriate interpretive devices.

USGS map, Mount Hood South, Oreg., 1:24,000, 1962 ed.

CAPE HORN (Upper)
Mile 1877R — North shore of the Columbia River
Skamania County, Washington — Sec. 16, T1N, R5E

The Columbia River flows against this towering cliff on the north shore. Rounding that point when wind and wave were adverse was a perilous undertaking, and many emigrants who came down the river by raft, canoe or barge had lengthy waits before Cape Horn could be passed. It was an awe-inspiring and much-feared landmark.

John C. Fremont, November 1843. ". . . towards sunset we reached a remarkable point of rocks, distinguished, on account of prevailing high winds, and the delay it frequently occasions to the canoe navigation, by the name of *Cape Horn*. It borders the river in a high wall of rock, which comes boldly down into deep water; and in violent gales down the river, and from the opposite shore water is dashed against it with considerable violence . . . a serious obstacle." [202:1, 564]

Overton Johnson, November 1843. He was with the emigrant party which obtained canoes at Fort Walla Walla and descended the Columbia in them. They were ". . . constantly filled with anxiety and dread." Johnson noted Cape Horn. [208: 101]

William D. Stillwell, November 18, 1844. Of his passage through the gorge of the Columbia River, he wrote: "We crossed Hood River at the mouth, coming down Columbia, sometimes over high points. Five or six miles above the Cascades we crossed over to the north side of the Columbia. The Indians ferryed us over and we swam our horses. We followed the Columbia 5 or 6 miles, crossed over the Mt. Hood Cape Horn [and] came down to Washougal. We again crossed the Columbia below the mouth of Sandy . . ." [367: letter]

Loren B. Hastings, November 1847. "We passed a place called Cape Horn, which is the last perpendicular high spar of the Cascade Mountains." [403: 318]

Thompson C. Elliott, 1915. *The James P. Flint*, first steamboat on the waters of the Columbia River above the Cascades, was ". . . sunk on a rock near Cape Horn on September 22nd, 1852 . . .," after returning to the lower reaches of the river. [127: 162]

USGS map, Vancouver, Oreg.-Wash., 1:250,000, 1953 ed.

PIONEER WOMAN'S GRAVE
Mile 1878.0 — ¾ mile west of Barlow Pass, Oregon Clackamas County — SE¼ of NW¼, Sec. 29, T3S, R9E

This grave is marked by a mound of stones 6' wide, 10' long and 4' high. It is on the west side of the Mount Hood Loop Highway, immediately above the crossing of the East Fork of the Salmon River. It is marked by a bronze plaque placed by the Multnomah Chapter, Daughters of the American Revolution, in 1936. No primary documentation on this grave has been found.

Irene D. Paden, 1943. Only a mention of the existence of this grave—no details. [298: 369]

Glen Baker, 1969. Photos, but no details. [21: 27] Author's note, August 16, 1972. An informational sign across the highway from the grave site states: "Pioneer Woman's Grave / The Last Resting Place Of A Pioneer Woman Who / Died in 18____? While Enroute To Western Oregon By / Ox Team Over The Old Barlow Road Which Passed / Near This Spot . . . "

USGS map, Mount Hood, Oreg., 1:24,000, 1962 ed.

BABY MORGAN GRAVE
Mile 1879.0 — Summit Meadow, south of Mount Hood, Oregon Clackamas County — SE¼ of NW¼, Sec. 25, T3S, R8½E

This infant was killed accidentally while an emigrant party was halted at Summit Meadow, on October 24, 1847. A bronze plaque on a half-exposed glacial boulder on the edge of the meadow marks the burial place. There are three other burials within a 20-foot square fencing nearby.

The child's death was a particularly poignant incident of the early Oregon Trail period. The other burials were made after the pioneer years.

Wallace Stegner, 1964. "While they [John Brown and Wilford Woodruff] were on top [of Independence Rock], a party of Missourians came to the foot of the rock and dug a hole and

Above: A huge mound of boulders, one of which holds a plaque, marks the location of the Pioneer Woman's Grave. Below: The grave of Baby Morgan at Summit Meadow, on the Barlow Road.

buried somebody. They noted the name later: Rachel Morgan, aged twenty-five . . ." [363: 151]

Glen Baker, 1969. "There is a cemetery at the west edge of the meadows that has several graves. One is that of a baby born shortly before starting across the Barlow Road and dying at Summit Meadows." [21: 32]

W. W. Morrison, July 10, 1972. Oral comment. Rachel Morgan died at Independence Rock—her grave has not been located. The child born at the time of her death died on the Barlow Road in Oregon—the infant's bed had been placed behind the wagon, in the shade. In adjusting the loading, the tailgate fell and killed the baby. [272: interview]

Author's note, August 16, 1972. A bronze plaque on a boulder in the edge of the forest on the west side of Summit Meadow, states: "This Marks The Grave / Of / Baby Morgan / Infant Daughter Of / Daniel And Rachel Woodsides Morgan / Born Near Independence Rock, June 1847. / The Baby Died As A Result Of An Accident And / Was Buried Here At Summit Meadows Oct. 24, 1847. / Burial Witnessed By Jacob And Sarah Woodsides Caplinger / 'Sweetly Rests Our Baby Dear / All The Labor Ceases Here / Far From Home Though Laid To Sleep / Loving Hearts Thy Memory Keep' / Dedicated By Descendent Relatives, Aug. 20, 1957."

The other burials are: one unidentified, grave of "P. Vickers," and grave of "Beeb / Infant son / of WL Bat. / bar Barclay / Born Jul. 15 / Died Sep 14 / 1882."

USGS map, Mount Hood South, Oreg., 1:24,000, 1962 ed.

VICKER'S "SUMMIT HOUSE"
Mile 1879.1 — One mile south of Government Camp, Oregon
Clackamas County — NE¼ of NW¼, Sec. 25, T3S, R8½E

This is the site of the Barlow Road toll gate during the years 1866-1870. The foundation of the building, on the west side of Summit Meadows, indicates the plan size was at least 12' by 18'. A rock at the site bears the inscription: "J PAWSON / 48-9-50-1-2-3." Presumably, the "P. Vickers" buried in the small cemetery 500 feet to the south was associated with this structure.

USGS map, Mount Hood South, Oreg., 1:24,000, 1962 ed.

LAUREL HILL
Mile 1884.0 — 2¼ miles west of Government Camp, Oregon
Clackamas County — NE¼ of SE¼, Sec. 15, T3S, R8E

This is an extended feature consisting of two drops: the first, of 240 feet vertical and the second of 60 feet vertical, with a right angle turn between them. The upper remains visible as an eroded chute, flanked by several stumps which still show scars from rope burns; the lower is hidden beneath a heavy growth of brush.

This probably was the most difficult hill on the entire Oregon Trail, and so much of an obstacle that the Barlow Road remained a one-way artery—for westbound traffic only—to the end of its useful life as a toll road.

William Barlow, 1912. The descent of the hill by the original party is described. [24: 265]

Walter Bailey, 1912. "Of Laurel Hill an emigrant of 1853 complains: 'The road on this hill is something terrible. It is worn down into the soil from five to seven feet, leaving steep banks on both sides, and so narrow that it is almost impossible to walk alongside of the cattle for any distance without leaning against the oxen . . . cut down a small tree about ten inches in diameter and about forty feet long, and the more limbs it has on it the better. This tree they fasten to the rear axle with chains or ropes, top end foremost, making an excellent brake.'" [19: 249]

Walter E. Meacham, 1947. ". . . the toughest section of the Old Oregon Trail was Laurel Hill, a long, high, broken ridge about four miles in length . . . the oxen could not hold back the wagons, even when rough-locked. Some . . . took their wagons apart and slid them down . . . others cut trees and dragged them behind. . . . others tied long ropes to the rear axle and wound one end around a tree, letting the rope out . . . [if] a rope broke, then there was a broken wagon to mend or abandon. The grooves worn on the trees by the ropes remained visible as long as the trees stood." P. 15: "For many years the Barlow Road was a one-way road, for all the travel headed west. There was none so foolhardy as to attempt the ascent of Big and Little Laurel Hills with wagons." [258: 14, 15]

Glen Baker, 1969. "As soon as the snow melted the following year [1846], Samuel Barlow and his crew returned to complete the road. Wagons were lowered down Laurel Hill one by one, held back by ropes . . . On the route they followed there were

Above: Rope burns remain on a snubbing tree at the top of the Laurel Hill "chute" on the Barlow Road. Several scarred stumps remain where the emigrant wagons were lowered. Below: This is a facsimile of the western gate on the Barlow Road, a half-mile east of Rhododendron, Oregon.

spots where the grade was as much as 60%.

"The technique used in succeeding years was to zigzag across the face of the slope with all wheels locked . . ." (Impossible, as will be explained.) [21: 30]

Oregon State Highway Department, 1970. "Wagon tracks visible on west end Laurel Hill viaduct, a few feet north of U.S. 26 opposite a modest safety refuge, or turn-off. 'The Chute' and rope-burned trees accessible from old Mt. Hood Loop Highway south of turn-off for rustic Oregon History marker east end of Laurel Hill viaduct. Wagon ruts visible on north side of highway at Forest Service access to Pioneer Bridle Trail." [295:1, 12-13]

Author's note, August 16, 1972. The chute by which the upper slope was descended is now about 30 feet wide and up to seven feet deep toward the top. It is composed mainly of scree—loose pieces of flat stone—which has found its angle of repose at about 45 percent (originally, the slope was steeper, but use wore the chute in at the top while building up a debris mound at the bottom, thus lessening the grade). A number of rope-burned stumps stand along the upper portion of the chute, their shell of outer wood charred by fire and yet quite hard.

At the bottom of the upper hill, the wagons were turned sharply to the right, taken over a saddle in the ridge and then directly down the small hill. There, rough-locking the wheels was probably a sufficient precaution to get the vehicles safely down to the flat beside the Zig Zag River, where the Barlow Campground is now.

Concerning the statement that vehicles zig-zagged the face of the big hill, it could not have been managed that way. Top-heavy emigrant wagons were limited to nearly straight-up or straight-down travel, for their center of gravity was far too high for successful negotiation of such a side-slope. Undoubtedly, the reference to zig-zagging the face of the slope has developed from the right-angle turn at the bottom of the upper slope. There was also a right-angle turn in the opposite direction at the bottom of the lower slope.

USGS map, Government Camp, Oreg., 1:24,000, 1962 ed.

BARLOW TOLL GATE (Western)
Mile 1889.1 — ½ mile east of Rhododendron, Oregon
Clackamas County — NE¼ of SE¼, Sec. 11, T3S, R7E

This was the most recent of the four toll gates used on the

west end of the Barlow Road—it operated from 1879 to 1915. The reconstructed gate at this site was designed from photographs of the original structure. There is a roadside turn-out and information panel provided by the U.S. Forest Service.

This site is of greater significance to that period when freighters hauled to the Willamette Valley from Eastern Oregon.

Cranson Fosburg, 1969. This is a recreation area plan prepared by the Forest Service, Mt. Hood National Forest, covering the present installations at this site and proposals for its future management. There are photographs, maps and ground plans. [139: passim]

Clackamas County Planning Board (undated). The map of the Clackamas County Planning Department, showing the relationship of the toll gate site to other Barlow Road sites within the County. [74: map]

Claire S. Belsher, 1972. A listing of Barlow Road sites within Clackamas County shows this toll gate as No. 8: "#5 [fifth] Toll Gate Site—1879-1915 (1mi. E. Rhododendron)." [33: list]

USGS map, Rhododendron, Oreg., 1:24,000, 1962 ed.

FORT VANCOUVER
Mile 1901.8 — in present Vancouver, Washington
Clark County — SE¼ of SE¼, Sec. 27, T2N, R1E

Fort Vancouver was a stockaded post established by the Hudson's Bay Company in 1824. It served as the headquarters for the company's trade in the Pacific Northwest and the interior basin drained by the Columbia River. It was the largest trading center in the West prior to the California gold rush.

The assistance rendered emigrants by Dr. John McLaughlin did much to facilitate their establishment in Oregon. They were given direct aid in transportation, lodging and subsistence, and were extended credit until they could raise a crop.

James W. Nesmith, October 24, 1843. "Arrived at the Hudson Bay Company's mill about seven miles above the fort . . . at Fort Vancouver . . . [we were] kindly treated by Dr. McLaughlin . . ." [290: 359]

John Boardman, November 3, 1843. "Fort Vancouver . . . well received by Doct. McLaughlin, who charged nothing for the use of his boat sent up for us, nor for the provisions, but not satisfied with that sent us plenty of salmon and potatoes, furnished us house room, and wood free of charge, and was very

Above: Osborne Cross made this sketch of the landing place near the Cascades as he saw it in 1849. Below: Dr. John McLoughlin built this house in Oregon City. It is now open as a museum.

anxious that all should get through safe." [37: 118]

Rev. Samuel Parker, October 16, 1835. "Fort Vancouver is situated on the north side of the Columbia River about 60 rods from the shore upon a prairie of some few hundred acres surrounded with dense woods. The country around for a great distance is generally level and of good soil covered with heavy forest, excepting some prairies interspersed and has a pleasant aspect . . . The enclosure is strongly stockaded, 37 rods long and 18 rods wide, facing the south. There are about 100 white persons belonging to this establishment, and an Indian population of 300 in a small compass contiguous. There are eight substantial buildings within the enclosure and a great number of small ones without." [301: 149]

Oscar O. Winther, 1948. A brief description of Fort Vancouver at the time of the emigration. [404: 59-61, 74]

John A. Hussey, 1957. A thorough study of Fort Vancouver based upon archaeological and historical research. [191: passim]

Burt Brown Barker, 1959. A biography of Dr. John McLoughlin. [22: 21-51]

Herbert M. Hart, 1963. Information on the military posts which replaced the Hudson's Bay Company post. [167: 17-18]

Author's note, August 17, 1972. The site of Fort Vancouver became a unit of the National Park System on July 9, 1954.

USGS map, Vancouver, Oreg.-Wash., 1:250,000, 1953 ed.

OLD OREGON TRAIL MONUMENT
Mile 1932.2 — SW corner of Kelly Field, Oregon City, Oregon
Clackamas County — Sec. 29, T2S, R2E

This granite monument is at the intersection of Holcomb Road and Oregon State Route 213. On it is a plaque stating: "Old Oregon Trail / 1846 / Erected By / Willamette Chapter / Daughters Of The American Revolution / Portland, Oregon / 1917."

This monument marks the end of the Oregon Trail, as it was extended from The Dalles to Oregon City by the opening of the Barlow Road in 1846.

Osborne Russell, September 26, 1842. "I started with them [the emigrant party of Dr. Elijah White, which Osborne Russell had joined at Fort Hall] and arrived at the Falls of the Willamette River on the 26 day of Septr. 1842 . . . I found a number of Methodist Missionaries and American Farmers had formed themselves into a Company for the purpose of Erecting Mills and a Sawmill was then building on an Island standing on the brink of the Falls which went into operation in about 2 months after I arrived In the meantime Dr John McLoughlin a chief Factor of the Hudson Bay Co. who contemplated leaving the service of the Company and permanently settling with his family and Fortune in the Willamette Valley laid off a town [the present Oregon City] on the east side of the falls and began erecting a sawmill on a site he had prepared some years previous by cutting a race thro. the rock to let the water on to his works when they should be constructed." [337: 125-26]

Fr. M. Blanchet, March 8, 1843. "M. McLoughlin . . . He has just founded a village at the falls of the Walamette, the City Of Oregon; the streets are drawn, the building grounds divided; they are acquired eagerly. . . ." [221: 171]

Overton Johnson, November 13, 1843. ". . . at Oregon City . . . our destination . . . We found, at the Falls, a small village of about one hundred inhabitants. Lots were laid out on both sides of the River . . . on East, by Dr. McLaughlin . . . on the West by H. Burns, and called Multnomah." [208: 103-04]

Maria P. Belshaw, September 30, 1853. ". . . came to the long expected City . . . worst looking place for a City I ever saw . . ." [132: 330]

Oscar O. Winther, 1948. Footnote 2: "These towns were very small. The 1850 census places the population of Oregon City, the largest in the Territory, at 697 . . . A decade later, 1860 . . . Oregon City, 889 . . ." [404: 169]

Burt Brown Barker, 1959. "Dr. McLoughlin, in an effort to protect the interests of the company, had offered to effect a paper transfer of title to the mills at Oregon City from the Hudson's Bay Company to himself, in the hope that the move would lessen the settler's antagonism. The plan proved to be a trap. Sir George Simpson sprang it, and on his recommendation the Honorable Company [Hudson's Bay Co.] sold Dr. McLoughlin the mills against his wishes and over his strenuous protests. When it became evident to Dr. McLoughlin that he would be forced to quit his position in the Hudson's Bay Company and manage the mills as his private enterprise, he resigned . began to build a home in Oregon City. This he occupied from 1846 until his death on September 3, 1857." Pp. 330-333 provide details on Dr. McLoughlin's Oregon City land claim and his involvement with American settlers there, including a letter of July 15, 1851, stating: ". . . in 1829 I took Oregon City Claim, and made improvements on it. In 1842 I began to erect Mills—in 1843 I had it surveyed by Jesse Applegate Esquire and recorded in the record Book of Land Claims in Oregon Territory . . . Since 1845 I have permanently resided on it. . . ." [22: 49, 330-33]

This monument, which marked the end of the Oregon Trail on the bank of Abernethy Creek at Oregon City, has been replaced by another nearby.

Gregory M. Franzwa, 1972. "By 1845, the little town of Oregon City had a Methodist church, a Catholic chapel, two grist mills (including one owned by Dr. McLaughlin) with a sawmill at each, four stores, two taverns, a hatter, a tanner, a physician, three lawyers, a printing office and newspaper, a lath machine and a good brickyard. There were plenty of carpenters and masons . . . The house [Dr. McLoughlin's] stands now on ground he donated to the city in 1850 as a park. It was moved from the original location in 1909, after much damage from flooding. His claim to citizenship was recognized in 1851, six years before his death. The house is open to the public daily except Mondays." [141: 378]

USGS map, Oregon City, Oreg., 1:62,500, 1961 ed.

Bibliography

The date in [brackets] is the relevant time, when that date is not given elsewhere in the bibliographic reference.

1. Abbey, James. *California: A Trip Across the Plains in the Spring of 1850.* . . . New Albany, Ind.: Kent & Norman and J. R. Nunemacher, 1850.
2. Adams, Cecilia E. McM. Diary, 1852. Misc. Overland Journeys to the Pacific. Portland: Oregon Historical Society.
3. Adams, Claude. "Porter's Rock." *Annals of Wyoming*, 42 (Oct. 1970): 254.
4. Adkinson, John R. "Massacre at Salmon Falls." In *Indian Braves and Battles.* . . . Edited by Norman B. Adkinson. Grangeville: *Idaho County Free Press*, 1967.
5. Akin, James Jr. Diary, 1852. Misc. Overland Journeys to the Pacific. Portland: Oregon Historical Society.
6. Allen, A. J. (comp.) *Ten Years in Oregon; Travels and Adventures of Doctor E. White and Lady, West of the Rocky Mountains.* Ithaca, N.Y.: Andrus, Gauntlett & Co., 1850.
7. Allen, Eleanor W. *Canvas Caravans.* Portland, Oreg.: Binsford & Mort, 1946.
8. Allen, O. *Guide Book to the Gold Fields of Kansas & Nebraska and Great Salt Lake City, 1858-9.* Washington, D.C.: R. A. Walters, 1859.
9. Allyn, Henry A. Diary, 1853. Misc. Overland Journeys to the Pacific), 2 parts. Portland: Oregon Historical Society.
10. Alter, J. Cecil. *James Bridger, Trapper, Frontiersman, Scout and Guide.* . . . Columbus, Ohio: Long's College Book Co., 1951.
11. Altrocchi, Julia C. *The Old California Trail.* Caldwell, Idaho: The Caxton Printers, 1945.
12. Anderson, Sylvia F. (Ed.) *Westward to Oregon.* Boston: Heath, 1958.
13. Anonymous. "Seminoe vs. Seminole." *Annals of Wyoming*, 6 (July-October 1929): 237-38.
14. Anonymous. "Landmarks." *Annals of Wyoming*, 21 (July-October 1949): 223.
15. Anonymous. "Fort Hall, 1834-56," *Idaho Yesterdays*, 12 (Summer 1968): 28-31.
16. Applegate, Lindsay. "Notes and Reminiscences of Laying Out and Establishing the Old Emigrant Road into Southern Oregon in the Year 1846." *Oregon Historical Quarterly*, 22 (March 1921): 12-45.
17. Applegate, Jesse. *A Day With the Cow Column in 1843.* Intro. by Dr. Dorothy Johansen. Portland, Oreg.: Champoeg Press, 1952.

18. Bailey, Betsey (Mrs. D. D.) [1845]. Letter. Misc. Overland Journeys to the Pacific. Portland: Oregon Historical Society.

19. Bailey, Walter. "The Barlow Road." *Oregon Historical Quarterly*, 13 (September 1912): 285-96.

20. Bain, Read. "Educational Plans and Efforts by Methodists in Oregon to 1860." *Oregon Historical Quarterly*, 21 (June 1920): 63-94.

21. Baker, Glen, et. al. "Barlow Road Unusual Interest Area." National Forest Recreation Area Plan (mimeographed). Mt. Hood National Forest, Oreg., 1969.

22. Barker, Burt Brown. *The McLoughlin Empire and Its Rulers*. Glendale, Calif.: The Arthur H. Clark Co., 1959.

23. Barlow, Mary S. "History of the Barlow Road." *Oregon Historical Quarterly*, 3 (March 1902): 71-81.

24. Barlow, William. "Reminiscences of Seventy Years," *Oregon Historical Quarterly*, 13 (September 1912): 240-86.

25. Barney, Lewis. "History of Lewis Barney, 1847-82." Salt Lake City: LDS Church Historian's Office.

26. Barrett, James T. "Cholera in Missouri." *Missouri Historical Review*, 55 (July 1961): 344-54.

27. Barrett, Francis A. "The Greatest Ride in Wyoming History," *Annals of Wyoming*, 38 (October 1966): 223-28.

28. Beal, Josiah [1847]. Account. Misc. Overland Journeys to the Pacific. Portland: Oregon Historical Society.

29. Beard, John W. *Saddles East: Horseback over the Old Oregon Trail*. Portland, Oreg.: Binsford & Mort, 1946.

30. Beidleman, Richard G. "Nathaniel Wyeth's Fort Hall." *Oregon Historical Quarterly*, 58 (September 1957): 197-250.

31. Belshaw, Maria A. Parsons [1853]. Diary. Misc. Overland Journey to the Pacific. Portland: Oregon Historical Society.

32. Belshaw, George [1853]. *The Diary of George Belshaw*. Eugene, Oreg.: Lane Co. Pioneer Historical Society, 1960.

33. Belsher, Claire S. "Barlow Road Trek (Clackamas County Only)." Mimeographed list of sites with a map, 1972.

34. Bidwell, John [1841]. "The First Emigrant Train to California," *Century Magazine*, 41 (November 1890): 106-30.

35. Bidwell, John, et. al. *First Three Trains: to California, 1841, to Oregon, 1842, to Washington, 1853*. Portland, Oreg.: Binsford & Mort, 1961.

36. Bishop, L. C., and Henderson, Paul C. "Pony Express Route; 1860—Centennial—1960." Salt Lake City: National Pony Express Centennial Association, 1960.

37. Boardman, John. "The Journal of John Boardman, An Overland Journey from Kansas to Oregon in 1843." *Utah Historical Quarterly*, 2 (October 1929): 99-121.

38. Bond, Jesse W. [1852] Letter. Misc. Overland Journeys to the Pacific. Portland: Oregon Historical Society.

39. Boone, George L. [1848]. Account recorded in 1904. Misc. Overland Journeys to the Pacific. Portland: Oregon Historical Society.

40. Booth, Margaret (Ed.) "Overland from Indiana to Oregon, the Dinwidde Journal." Reprinted from Frontier 8 (March 1928), as *Sources of Northwest History*, No. 2. Missoula: State University of Montana, 1928.

41. Boyack, Hazel Noble. "Historic Fort Laramie, The Hub of Early Western History, 1834-49." *Annals of Wyoming*, 21 (July-October 1949): 170-80.

42. Bozarth, L.A. (Mrs. John Springer). Account of an 1852 journey across the plains. Misc. Overland Journeys to the Pacific. Portland: Oregon Historical Society.

43. Brady, William. Letter. Kansas Historical Society Collections, 2 (1909-1910): 459-60.

44. Bragg, Bill, Jr. "Handcarts to Heaven." *Annals of Wyoming*, 44 (Fall 1972): 271-73.

45. Branch, E. Douglas. "Frederick West Lander, Road-builder." *Mississippi Valley Historical Review*, 16 (September 1929): 174-75.

46. Brooks, Quincy A. [1851]. Letter. Misc. Overland Journeys to the Pacific. Portland: Oregon Historical Society.

47. Brooks, Quincy A. "Letter of Quincy Adams Brooks." *Oregon Historical Quarterly*, 15 (September 1914): 210-15.

48. Brown, Jennie Broughton. *Fort Hall on the Oregon Trail . . .* Caldwell, Idaho: The Caxton Printers, 1932.

49. Brown, Jennie Broughton. "Colorful Characters of the Snake River Country." *Idaho Yesterdays, Souvenir Handbook, 1834-1934.* Pocatello, Idaho: Graves & Potter, 1934.

50. Bruce, Max. "Crossroads of the Pioneers." reprinted from *Our Public Lands*, (Summer 1970).

51. Bryant, Edwin [1846]. *What I Saw in California . . .* New York: D. Appleton & Co., 1948.

52. Bruff, J. Goldsborough [1849]. *Gold Rush.* Edited by Georgia Willis Read and Ruth Gaines. New York: Columbia University Press, 1949.

53. Buck, Karen. "Names at Emigrant Springs and Johnston's Scout Rock." 1972.

54. Bureau of Land Management. *Lander Cut-off—Oregon Trail.* Ogden, Utah: BLM, 1967.

55. Burnett, Peter H. [1843]. "Recollections and Opinions of an Old Pioneer." *Oregon Historical Quarterly*, 5 (March 1904): 64-79.

56. Burton, Sir Richard Francis [1860]. *The City of the Saints, and Across the Rocky Mountains.* Edited by Fawn M. Brodie. New York: Alfred M. Knopf, 1963.

57. Campbell, Mrs. Paul. "Benoni Morgan Hudspeth." *Idaho Yesterdays,* 12 (Fall 1968): 9-13.

58. Cannon, Miles. *Waiilatpu, Its Rise and Fall, 1836-1847.* Boise, Idaho: *Capital News,* 1915.

59. Cannon, Miles. *Toward the Setting Sun.* Portland, Oreg.: Columbian Press, 1953.

60. Case, William M. "Recollections of His Trip Across the Plains in 1844." *Oregon Historical Quarterly*, 1 (September 1900): 269-95.

61. Case, Robert O. *The Empire Builders*. Portland, Oreg.: Binsford & Mort, 1949.

62. Condie, Gibson. Journal, 1847-1909. Salt Lake City: LDS Church Historian's Office. Microfilm f-22.

63. Canfield, Robert [1848]. Letter. Misc. Overland Journeys to the Pacific. Portland: Oregon Historical Society.

64. Callison, John Joseph. *The Diary of John Joseph Callison, Oregon Trail 1832*. Eugene, Oreg.: Lane County Pioneer Historical Society, 1959.

65. Casler, Melyer. *A Journal, Giving the Incidents of a Journey to California in the Summer of 1859, by the Overland Route*. Toledo, Ohio: Commercial Steam, 1863.

66. Castle, Gwen. "Belshaw Journey, Oregon Trail, 1853." *Oregon Historical Quarterly*, 32 (September 1912): 216-39.

67. Chandless, William. *A Visit to Salt Lake*. London: Smith, Elder and Co., 1857.

68. Chapman, Arthur. *The Pony Express*. New York: G. P. Putnam's Sons, 1932.

69. Child, Andrew [1842]. *Overland Route to California*. Milwaukee: Daily Sentinel Steam Power Press, 1852.

70. Chittenden, Hiram M. *The American Fur Trade of the Far West*, 3 vols. New York: Francis P. Harper, 1902.

71. Christy, Thomas [1850]. *Thomas Christy's Road Across the Plains . . .* Denver, Colo.: Old West Publishing Co., 1969.

72. Churchill, Claire W. "The Journey to Oregon—A Pioneer Girl's Diary." *Oregon Historical Quarterly*, 29 (March 1928): 77-98.

73. Cipriani, Leonetto. *California and Overland Diaries from 1853 through 1871. . . .* Translated and edited by Ernest Falbo. Portland, Oreg.: Champoeg Press, 1962.

74. Clackamas County Planning Department. Map of the Barlow Road and historic sites along it. Oregon City, n.d.

75. Clark, John H. [1852]. "Overland to the Gold Fields. . . ." Edited by Louise Barry, *Kansas Historical Quarterly*, II (August 1942): 227-96.

76. Clark, Roland K., and Tiller, Lowell. *Terrible Trail: The Meek Cutoff, 1843*. Caldwell, Idaho: The Caxton Printers, 1966.

77. Clarke, Dwight L. *Stephen Watts Kearny, Soldier of the West*. Norman, Okla.: University of Oklahoma Press, 1961.

78. Clayton, William [1847]. *The Latter-Day Saints' Emigrants' Guide*. St. Louis: Missouri Republican / Chambers & Knapp, 1848.

79. Clayton, William. [1847]. *Journal: A Daily Record of the Journey of the Original Company of "Mormon" Pioneers from Nauvoo, Ill., to the Valley of the Great Salt Lake*. Salt Lake City, Utah: Clayton Family Association, 1921.

80. Clinkinbeard, Philura V. *Across the Plains in '64, by Prairie Schooner to Oregon*. New York City: Exposition Press, 1953.

81. Clyman, James. James Clyman: *American Frontiersman, 1792-1887*, ed. by C. L. Camp. San Francisco: California Historical Society, 1928.

82. Coans, C. F. "The Adoption of the Reservation Policy in the Pacific Northwest, 1853-55." *Oregon Historical Quarterly*, 23 (March 1922): 1-38.

83. Coke, Henry J. [1850]. *A Ride Over the Rocky Mountains to Oregon and California, etc.* London: Richard Bentley, 1852.

84. Colton, J. H. *Map of California, Oregon, Texas and the Territories Adjoining, with Routes, etc.* Scale, 1:6,500,000, New York City, 1849.

85. Colton, J. H. *The Territories of Washington and Oregon* (Map). Scale, 1:4,000,000, New York City, 1855.

86. Connelley, William E. "The Prairie Band Of Pottawatomie Indians." Kansas Historical Collections, 14 (1915-18): 488-570.

87. Conner, J. J. [1853]. Diary (copy). Misc. Overland Journeys to the Pacific. Portland: Oregon Historical Society.

88. Conyers, W. H. [1852]. Diary (copy). Misc. Overland Journeys to the Pacific. Portland: Oregon Historical Society.

89. Coons, Frederica B. *The Trail to Oregon.* Portland, Oreg.: Binsford & Mort, 1954.

90. Cooper, A. A. [1863] Account of a journey across the plains. Misc. Overland Journeys to the Pacific. Portland: Oregon Historical Society.

91. Copperthwait, Thomas & Co. *A New Map of Texas, Oregon and California,* Scale 1:6,500,000, Philadelphia, 1849.

92. Copperthwait, Thomas. *A New Map of the State of California, The territories of Oregon & Utah . . .,* Scale 1:6,500,000, Philadelphia, 1850.

93. Corthell, Robert A. *An Appraisal of Potentials for Outdoor Recreational Development, Union County, Oregon.* Portland, Oreg.: U.S. Soil Conservation Service, 1972.

94. Cosgrove, Hugh. "Reminiscences of the Emigrant Trail of 1847." *Oregon Historical Quarterly*, 1 (September 1900): 253-69.

95. Couper, J. C. [1857] Account of a journey across the plains. Misc. Overland Journeys to the Pacific. Portland: Oregon Historical Society.

96. Coutant, Charles G. *History of Wyoming from the Earliest Known Discoveries,* Vol. I. Laramie, Wyo.: Chaplin, Spafford & Mathison, 1899.

97. Cramer, Howard R. "The Oregon Trail—Hudspeth's Cutoff." A research report for the Bureau of Land Management, Burley, Idaho, September 1959.

98. Crawford, Medorem. *Journal Written While Commanding the Emigrant Escort to Oregon and Washington Territory, 1862.* Printed by order of the United States Senate, January 6, 1863, 37th Congress, 3rd session. Senate Executive Document 17.

99. Crawford, Charles H. [1851]. *Scenes of Earlier Days in Crossing the Plains to Oregon and Experiences of Western Life.* Chicago: Quadrangle Books, 1962.

100. Crawford, P. V. "Journal of a Trip Across the Plains, 1851." *Oregon Historical Quarterly*, 25 (June 1924): 136-69.

101. Cross, Osborne [1849]. *The March of the Mounted Riflemen. . . .*

Edited by Raymond W. Settle. Glendale, Calif.: The Arthur H. Clark Co., 1940.

102. Cummins, Sarah J. *Autobiography and Reminiscences: Memories of the Oregon Trail in 1845.* LaGrande, Oreg.: LaGrande Printing Co., 1914.

103. Dale, Harrison C. "Organization of the Oregon Emigrating Companies." *Oregon Historical Quarterly,* 16 (September 1915): 205-27.

104. Damon, Samuel C. *A Journey to Lower Oregon and Upper California, 1848-49.* San Francisco, Calif.: J. J. Newbegin, 1927.

105. David, Robert B. *Finn Burnett, Frontiersman* . . . Glendale, Calif.: The Arthur H. Clark Co., 1937.

106. Davidson, A. F. "Collection of Oregon Trail maps by A. F. Davidson, a Pioneer of 1845. Drawn on the way East in 1846." 8½" x 14", no scale, unnumbered and mostly undated. Originals in the Coe Collection, Yale University, New Haven, Conn.

107. Dawson, Nicholas. "Cheyenne." Itinerary of Nicholas Dawson, 1841. Original in the Bancroft Library, Berkeley, Calif.

108. Dawson, Charles. *Pioneer Tales of the Oregon Trail and Jefferson County.* Topeka, Kans.: Crane & Company, 1912.

109. Decker, Peter. *The Diaries of Peter Decker: Overland to California in 1849* . . . Georgetown, Calif.: Talisman, 1966.

110. Defenbach, Byron. "Chronology of Fort Hall and the Oregon Trail." *Idaho Yesterdays, Souvenir Handbook, 1834-1934.* Pocatello, Idaho: Graves & Potter, 1934.

111. Delano, Alonzo [1849]. *Life on the Plains and Among the Diggings.* Ann Arbor, Mich.: University Microfilms, 1966.

112. DeSmet, Pierre Jean. "Letters and Sketches, 1841-1842." In *Early Western Travels,* Vol. 27. Edited by R. G. Thwaites. Cleveland, Ohio: The Arthur H. Clark Co., 1906.

113. DeSmet, Pierre Jean. "Oregon Missions and Travels Over the Rocky Mountains in 1845-1846." In *Early Western Travels,* Vol. 29. Edited by R. G. Thwaites. Cleveland, Ohio: The Arthur H. Clark Co., 1906.

114. DeVoto, Bernard. *The Year of Decision: 1846.* Boston: Little Brown and Company, 1943.

115. DeVoto, Bernard. *Across the Wide Missouri.* Boston: Houghton Mifflin, 1947.

116. Dickenson, Luella. *Reminiscences of a Trip Across the Plains in 1846.* San Francisco, Calif.: The Whitaker & Ray Company, 1904.

117. Dickson, Albert J. [1864]. *Covered Wagon Days* . . . From the private journals of Albert Jerome Dickson. Edited by Arthur Jerome Dickson, Cleveland, Ohio: The Arthur H. Clark Co., 1929.

118. Dickinson, Norman. "Story of South Pass." *Annals of Wyoming,* 44 (Fall 1972): 283-86.

119. Drago, Harry S. *Roads to Empire* . . . New York: Dodd, Mead, 1968.

120. Drew, Susan [1853]. Account of journey across the plains. Misc. Overland Journeys to the Pacific. Portland: Oregon Historical Society.

121. Dudley, Mary F. [1852]. Diary. Misc. Overland Journeys to the Pacific. Portland: Oregon Historical Society.

122. Dunbar, Seymour. *A History of Travel in America* . . . 4 vols. Indianapolis, Ind.: Bobbs-Merrill, 1915.

123. Dunlop, Richard. *Great Trails of the West.* Nashville, Tenn.: Abingdon Press, 1971.

124. Edwards, P. L. *Sketch of the Oregon Territory; or, Emigrant's Guide.* Liberty, Mo.: The Herald, 1842.

125. Elliott, Thompson C. "'Doctor' Robert Newell." *Oregon Historical Quarterly,* 9 (June 1908): 103-26.

126. Elliott, Thompson C. "The Peter Skene Ogden Journals." *Oregon Historical Quarterly,* 10 (December 1909): 331-65.

127. Elliott, Thompson C. "The Dalles—Celilo Portage; Its History and Influence." *Oregon Historical Quarterly,* 16 (June 1915): 133-74.

128. Elliott, Thompson C. "Richard 'Capt. Johnny' Grant." *Oregon Historical Quarterly,* 36 (March 1935): 1-13.

129. Ellis, H. C. [undated]. Letter to Alvin Zaring concerning the Massacre Rocks State Park, Idaho

130. Ellison, Robert S. *Independence Rock, The Great Register of the Desert.* Casper, Wyo.: Natrona County Historical Society, 1930.

131. Ellison, Robert S. *Fort Bridger, Wyoming.* Casper, Wyo.: The Historical Landmark Commission of Wyoming, 1931.

132. Ellison, Joseph W. "Diary of Maria Parsons Belshaw, 1853." *Oregon Historical Quarterly,* 33 (December 1932): 318-33.

133. Farley, Angelina. Diary of Angelina Farley, 1847-1888. Salt Lake City: LDS Church Historian's Office. Microfilm f-262.

134. Farnham, Thomas J. *Travels in the Great Western Prairies, The Anahuac and Rocky Mountains, and in the Oregon Territory.* Poughkeepsie, N.Y.: Killey and Lossing, Printers, 1841.

135. Farrington, Mrs. E. J. (Galtra) [1853]. Diary (copy). Misc. Overland Journeys to the Pacific. Portland: Oregon Historical Society.

136. Fenex, Jim. "Little Ada Magill." *Annals of Wyoming,* 43 (Fall 1971): 279-81.

137. Field, Matthew C. [1843]. *Prairie and Mountain Sketches.* Norman: University of Oklahoma Press, 1957.

138. Fleming, L. A., and Standing, A. R. "The Road to 'Fortune': The Salt Lake Cut-off," *Utah,* 33 (Summer 1965): 248-71.

139. Fosburg, Cranson, and Busher, Richard. "Barlow Toll Gate Historical Area." National Forest Recreation Area Plan—Mt. Hood National Forest, Oregon (mimeographed), 1969.

140. Fox, George W. [1866]. "George W. Fox Diary." *Annals of Wyoming,* 8 (January 1932): 580-601.

141. Franzwa, Gregory M. *The Oregon Trail Revisited.* St. Louis: The Patrice Press, 1972.

142. Frazer, Robert W. *Forts of the West.* Norman: University of Oklahoma Press, 1965.

143. Fremont, John C. *Report of an Exploring Expedition to the Rocky Mountains . . . 1842.* Washington, D.C.: Blair & Rives, 1845.

144. Frost, Donald M. *Notes on General Ashley, the Overland Trail, and*

South Pass, reprinted from *Proceedings of the American Antiquarian Society,* October 1944. Worcester, Mass.: American Antiquarian Society, 1945.

145. Furniss, Norman F. *The Mormon Conflict, 1850-1859.* New Haven: Yale University Press, 1960.

146. Federal WPA Writers' Project. The *Oregon Trail; The Missouri River to the Pacific Ocean,* sponsored by the Oregon Trail Memorial Association. New York: Hastings House, 1939.

147. Gaston, Joseph. *The Centennial History of Oregon, 1811-1912.* 4 vols. Chicago: The S. J. Clarke Pub. Co., 1912.

148. Gailland, Rev. Maurice. "Early Years at St. Mary's Pottawatomie Mission." *Kansas Historical Quarterly* 20 (August 1953): 501-29.

149. Ghent, William J. *The Road to Oregon, A Chronicle . . .* New York City: Tudor, 1934.

150. Geiger, Vincent E., and Bryarly, Wakeman. [1849]. *Trail to California; The Overland Journal of Vincent Geiger and Wakeman Bryarly.* Edited by David M. Potter. New Haven: Yale University Press, 1945.

151. Gould, Jane A. (Holbrook; Toustillot). "Jane A. Gould; Her Journal 1862." Bancroft Library, Berkeley, Calif.

152. Grange, Roger. "Digging at Fort Kearny." *Nebraska History,* 44 (June 1963): 101-22.

153. Green, T. L. "A Forgotten Fur Trade Post in Scotts Bluff County." *Nebraska History,* 15 (March 1934): 38-46.

154. Green, T. L. "Scotts Bluff, Fort John." *Nebraska History,* 19 (September 1938): 175-90.

155. Gregg, Jacob R. *A History of the Oregon Trail, Santa Fe, and Others . . .* Portland, Oreg.: Binsford & Mort, 1955.

156. Hafen, Leroy R., and Young, Francis M. (Eds.) *Fort Laramie and the Pageant of the West, 1834-1890.* Glendale, Calif.: Arthur H. Clark Co., 1938.

157. Hafen, Leroy R. (Ed.) *To the Rockies and Oregon, 1839-1842 . . .* Glendale, Calif.: The Arthur H. Clark Co., 1955.

158. Hafen, Leroy R., and Hafen, Ann W. *The Utah Expedition of 1857-1858.* Glendale, Calif.: The Arthur H. Clark Co., 1958.

159. Hafen, Leroy R. (Ed.) *Handcarts to Zion.* Glendale, Calif.: The Arthur H. Clark Co., 1960.

160. Hafen, Leroy R. (Ed.) *The Mountain Men and the Fur Trade of the Far West.* 10 vols. Glendale, Calif.: The Arthur H. Clark Co., 1965-72.

161. Haines, Aubrey L. Topographic Map of the Site of Fort Hall on the Oregon Trail, drawn from the notes of a survey made August 23-24, 1958, by Alan A. and Aubrey L. Haines, and drafted 1959.

162. Hancock, Samuel. *Samuel Hancock, 1845-1860,* introd. by Arthur D. Howden-Smith . . . New York City: R. M. McBride & Co., 1927.

163. Hanna, Esther B. [1853]. Journal (copy) Misc. Overland Journeys to the Pacific. Portland: Oregon Historical Society.

164. Hannon, Jessie G. *The Boston-Newton Company Venture; From Massachusetts to California in 1849.* Lincoln: University of Nebraska

Press, 1969.

165. Harrison, J. M. [1846]. Reminiscence, c.1870. Misc. Journeys to the Pacific. Portland: Oregon Historical Society.

166. Harstad, Peter T. "The Lander Trail." *Idaho Yesterdays,* 12 (Fall 1968): 14-28.

167. Hart, Herbert M. *Old Forts of the Northwest.* Seattle, Wash.: Superior Publishing Co., 1963.

168. Hartman, Amos W. "The California and Oregon Trails, 1849-1860." *Oregon Historical Quarterly,* 25 (March 1924): 1-35.

169. Harty, James N. [1847]. Letter. Misc. Overland Journeys to the Pacific. Portland: Oregon Historical Society.

170. Hastings, Loren B. [1847]. "Diary of . . . ." *Transactions of the Fifty-first Annual Reunion of the Oregon Pioneers' Association* (1926): 23-26.

171. Hastings, Lansford W. *The Emigrant's Guide to Oregon and California.* Facsimile (1845 edition) with historical notes and bibliography by Charles H. Carey. Princeton, N. J.: Princeton University Press, 1932.

172. Hecox, Margaret M. *California Caravan; The 1846 Overland Trail . . .* Edited by Richard Dillon. San Jose, Calif.: Harlan-Young Press, 1966.

173. Henderson, Paul C. *Landmarks on the Oregon Trail.* New York: Peter Decker, 1957.

174. Henderson, Paul C. "Willow Springs." *Annals of Wyoming,* 43 (Fall 1971): 284-87.

175. Herr, Henry R. [1862]. Diary (copy). Misc. Overland Journeys to the Pacific. Portland: Oregon Historical Society.

176. Hickman, Richard O. *An Overland Journey to California in 1852.* Edited by M. Catherine White. Missoula, Mont.: Montana State University reprints *Sources of Northwest History,* No. 6, 1929.

177. Hieb, David L. *Fort Laramie,* National Park Service Handbook Series, No. 20. Washington, D.C.: GPO, 1954.

178. Hildebrand, Lyle. "La Bonte Station." *Annals of Wyoming,* 42 (October 1970): 266-67.

179. Hill, Almon, and Hill, Sarah [1843]. Ms. with typed commentary. Misc. Overland Journeys to the Pacific. Portland: Oregon Historical Society.

180. Hill, John B. "Gold." *Annals of Wyoming,* 9 (April 1933-January 1935): 35-42.

181. Hilman, John C. Letter written August 11, 1862, to "Mrs. Bronson." concerning the Massacre Rocks incident. (Copy obtained from Massacre Rocks State Park, Idaho).

182. Hite, Joseph [1853]. Diary (copy) Misc. Overland Journeys to the Pacific. Portland: Oregon Historical Society.

183. Holden, Ella. "The Valley of the Fontenelle." *Annals of Wyoming,* 5 (October 1927-January 1928): 45-71.

184. Holman, Frederick V. "Oregon Counties." *Oregon Historical Quarterly,* II (March 1910): 1-81.

185. Horn, Hosea B. *Horn's Overland Guide, from the U.S. Indian Subagency, Council Bluffs, on the Missouri River, to the City of Sacramento . . .* New

York: J. H. Colton, 1852.)

186.   Howard, Minnie. "Fort Hall, Place of Destiny." in *Idaho Yesterdays, Souvenir Handbook, 1834-1934*. Pocatello, Idaho: Graves & Potter, 1934.

187.   Hulbert, Archer B. (Ed.) [1926]. *The American Transcontinental Trails*, Crown Collection of American Maps, Series IV, Vols. 1-3. Colorado Springs: The Stewart Commission on Western History.

188.   Hulbert, Archer B. *Forty-niners; The Chronicle of the California Trail*. Boston, Mass.: Little Brown and Co., 1931.

189.   Hulbert, Archer B. (Ed.) *The Call of the Columbia* . . . Colorado Springs: The Stewart Commission of Colorado College and Denver Public Library, 1934.

190.   Hull, Lewis B. "Soldiering on the High Plains . . .1864-1868." *Kansas Historical Quarterly*, 7 (February 1938): 3-53.

191.   Hussey, John A. *The History of Fort Vancouver and Its Physical Structure*. Tacoma: Washington State Historical Society, 1957.

192.   Hutawa, Edward. *Map of the Oregon Territory of the United States*, compiled from the report of John C. Fremont, 1842, by Edward Hutawa. St. Louis, Mo., 1843.

193.   Idaho Department of Highways. *Route of the Oregon Trail in Idaho*, from historical data furnished by the Idaho Historical Society. Boise: Idaho Department of Highways, 1967.

194.   Idaho Department of Highways. *The Historical Sign Program in the State Of Idaho*, prepared by the Public Information Section. Boise: Idaho Department of Highways, 1968.

195.   Idaho Historical Society. The Reference Series, n.d.
       No. 29, "Location of Fort Boise, 1834-1855."
       No. 50, "The Oregon Trail in Idaho."
       No. 51, "Goodale's Cutoff."
       No. 52, "The California Trail in Idaho."
       No. 62, "Fur Trade Posts in Idaho."
       No. 63, "Idaho Military Posts and Camps."
       No. 74, "The Kelton Road."
       No. 75, "The Toano Route."
       No. 121, "Fort Hall."
       No. 126, "City of Rocks & Granite Pass."
       No. 182, "Soda Springs."
       No. 184, "Salmon Falls and Thousand Springs."
       No. 185, "Three Island Crossing."
       No. 232, "Almo Massacre."
       No. 233, "Otter Massacre."
       No. 234, "Massacre Rocks."
       No. 235, "Battle of Bear River."
       No. 290, "Hudspeth's Cutoff."
       No. 356, "Fort Boise" (Army).
       No. 357, "Camp Lyon."
       No. 358, "Camp Three Forks."

196.   Ingalls, Eleazer S. *Journal of a Trip to California, by the Overland Route Across the Plains in 1850-1851*. Waukegan, Ill.: Tobey & Co.,

1852.

197. Ingersoll, Chester. *Overland to California in 1847* . . . with an intro. by Douglas C. McMurtrie. Chicago: Black Cat Press, 1937.

198. Irvin, Margaret E. [1864]. Account (copy). Misc. Overland Journeys to the Pacific. Portland: Oregon Historical Society.

199. Irving, Washington. "Astoria." In *The Works of Washington Irving, Vol. II.* New York: Pollard & Moss, 1882.

200. Irving, Washington. "Adventures of Captain Bonneville." In *The Works of Washington Irving, Vol. III.* New York: Pollard & Moss, 1882.

201. Jackson, William H. *Time Exposure.* New York: G. P. Putnam's Sons, 1940.

202. Jackson, Donald, and Spence, Mary L. (Eds.) *The Expeditions of John Charles Fremont.* Vol. I, Travels from 1833 to 1844. Urbana: University of Illinois Press, 1970.

203. James, Samuel. Diary 1850-1851 (copy). Misc. Overland Journeys to the Pacific. Portland: Oregon Historical Society.

204. Jefferson, T. H. *Accompaniment to the Map of the Emigrant Road from Independence to San Francisco,* California. New York: Author, 1849.

205. Jensen, Henry. "Robert Stuart." *Annals of Wyoming,* 43 (Fall 1971): 293-94.

206. Jensen, Henry. "Castle Rock." *Annals of Wyoming,* 44 (Fall 1972): 274-75.

207. Jenson, Andrew. "History of Fort Bridger and Fort Supply." *The Utah Genealogical and Historical Magazine,* 4 (1913): 32-39.

208. Johnson, Overton, and Winters, Wm. H. "Migration of 1843." *Oregon Historical Quarterly,* 7 (March 1906): 62-104.

209. Journal History. Salt Lake City: LDS Church Historian's Office.

210. Judge, William. "Fort Caspar." *Annals of Wyoming,* 43 (Fall 1971): 281-83.

210A. Judson, Henry M. [1862]. Diary (Omaha to Oregon). Lincoln: Nebraska State Historical Society.

211. Kahler, William [1852]. Diary. Misc. Overland Journeys to the Pacific. Portland: Oregon Historical Society.

212. Keenan, Joe. "Deer Creek Station." *Annals of Wyoming,* 43 (Fall 1971): 277-79.

213. Keenan, Joe. "Joel J. Hembree's Grave, 1843." *Annals of Wyoming,* 43 (Fall 1971): 271-72.

214. Kelly, William. *Across the Rocky Mountains, from New York to California.* . . . London: Simms and McIntyre, 1852.

215. Kelly, Charles. *Old Greenwood: The Story of Caleb Greenwood: Trapper, Pathfinder and Early Pioneer.* Edited by Dale L. Morgan. Georgetown, Calif.: Talisman Press, 1965.

216. Keller, George [1850]. *A Trip Across the Plains, and Life in California* . . . Massillon, Ohio: White's Press, 1851.

217. Kerns, John T. [1852]. Journal (copy). Misc. Overland Journeys to the Pacific. Portland: Oregon Historical Society.

218. King, Stephen, and King, Mariah [no date]. Obituary. Misc. Overland Journeys to the Pacific. Portland: Oregon Historical

Society.

219. Kirk, Florence. "The Three Crossings of the Sweetwater." *Annals of Wyoming*, 44 (Fall 1972): 275-76.

220. Korns, J. Roderick. "West from Fort Bridger." *Utah Historical Quarterly*, 19 (January-October 1951): 1-268.

221. Landerholm, Carl (transl.) *Notices & Voyages of the Famed Quebec Mission to the Pacific Northwest . . . 1838-1847.* Portland, Oreg.: Champoeg Press, 1956.

222. Langworthy, Franklin [1850]. *Scenery of the Plains, Mountains and Mines. Edited* by Paul C. Phillips from the edition of 1855. Princeton, N.J.: Princeton University Press, 1932.

223. Larpenteur, Charles. *Forty Years a Fur Trader on the Upper Missouri, 1833-1872.*, intro. by Milo M. Quaife. Chicago: R. R. Donnelley & Sons Co., 1933.

224. Lavender, David S. *Westward Vision: The Story of the Oregon Trail.* New York: McGraw-Hill, 1963.

225. Lee, Jason [1834]. "Diary of Rev. Jason Lee." *Oregon Historical Quarterly*, 17 (June 1916): 116-46; (September 1916): 240-66; (December 1916): 397-430.

226. Lee, Willis T., et. al. *Guidebook of the Western U.S., Part B, The Overland Route with a side trip to Yellowstone Park . . .* Washington, D.C.: GPO, 1916.

227. Leonard, Peg L. *Wyoming, La Bonte Country 1820-1872.* Lakeville, Mass.: Cranberry Press, 1972.

228. Lewis, Ila. "The Story of Fort Stambaugh." *Annals of Wyoming*, 44 (Fall 1972): 277-81.

229. Lienhard, Heinrich. *From St. Louis to Sutter's Fort, 1846.* Norman: University of Oklahoma Press, 1961.

230. Lockley, Fred [1845]. "Recollections of Benjamin Franklin Bonney." *Oregon Historical Quarterly*, 24 (March 1923): 36-55.

231. Longworth, Basil N. *Diary of Basil Nelson Longworth, March 15, 1853, to January 22, 1854 . . .* Portland, Oreg.: WPA, 1938.

232. Love, Helen M. *Diary of Helen Stewart, 1853.* Eugene, Oreg.: Lane County Pioneer-Historical Society, 1961.

233. Lyman, H. S. (Ed.) [undated]. "Reminiscences of James Jory." *Oregon Historical Quarterly*, 3 (September 1912): 271-86.

234. Ludlow, Fitz Hugh [1863]. *The Heart Of the Continent; A Record of Travel Across the Plains and in Oregon. . .* New York: Hurd and Houghton, 1870.

235. Maley, W. B. [1852]. Letter (copy). Misc. Overland Journeys to the Pacific. Portland: Oregon Historical Society.

236. Manning, B. F. Ed. "Recollections of a Pioneer of 1859, Lawson Stockman." *Oregon Historical Quarterly*, II (June 1910): 162-76.

237. Mantor, Lyle E. "Fort Kearny and the Westward Movement." *Nebraska History*, 29 (September 1948): 175-207.

238. Marshall, Thomas M. (Ed.) [1850]. "The Road to California: Letters of Joseph Price." *The Mississippi Valley Historical Review*, 11 (September 1924): 237-55.

239. Martin, George W. *How the Oregon Trail Became a Road.* Salt Lake

City: *The Deseret News,* 1906.

240. Masters, Joseph G., et. al. "Pony Express Stations in Nebraska." A listing compiled by the Pony Express Committee, 1930-32.

241. Masters, Joseph G. "The Romance of the Old Oregon Trail." *Idaho Yesterdays, Souvenir Handbook, 1834-1934.* Pocatello, Idaho: Graves & Potter, 1934.

242. Mattes, Merrill J. "Hiram Scott, Fur Trader." *Nebraska History,* 26 (July-September 1945): 127-62.

243. Mattes, Merrill J. "The Sutler's Store at Fort Laramie." *Annals of Wyoming,* 18 (July 1946): 92-123.

244. Mattes, Merrill J. and Thor Borreson. "The Historic Approaches to Fort Laramie." A report submitted to the Regional Director, National Park Service Region 11, October 24, 1947.

245. Mattes, Merrill J. "Robidoux's Trading Post as 'Scott's Bluffs,' and the California Gold Rush." *Nebraska History,* 30 (June 1949): 95-138.

246. Mattes, Merrill J. "Chimney Rock on the Oregon Trail." *Nebraska History,* 36 (March 1955): 1-26.

247. Mattes, Merrill J. *Scotts Bluff National Monument, Nebraska,* National Park Service Historical Handbook Series No. 28. Washington, D.C.: GPO, 1958.

248. Mattes, Merrill J., and Paul C. Henderson. *The Pony Express: Across Nebraska from St. Joseph to Fort* Laramie. Reprinted from *Nebraska History,* 41 (June 1960): 83-122.

249. Mattes, Merrill J. *The Great Platte River Road.* Lincoln: Nebraska State Historical Society, 1969.

250. McArthur, Lewis A. "Oregon Geographic Names." *Oregon Historical Quarterly,* 26 (December 1925): 309-423.

251. McClung, J. S. [1862]. Diary. Misc. Overland Journeys to the Pacific. Portland: Oregon Historical Society.

252. McComas, Evans S. *A Journal of Travel by E. S. McComas . . .* Portland, Ore.: Champoeg Press, 1954.

253. McIntosh, Walter H. *Allen and Rachel; An Overland Honeymoon in 1853. . .* Caldwell, Idaho: The Caxton Printers, 1938.

254. McKimmey, N. Letter relating to 1845. Misc. Overland Journeys to the Pacific. Portland: Oregon Historical Society.

255. McNary, Lawrence A. "Route of Meek's Cut-off, 1845." *Oregon Historical Quarterly,* 35 (March 1934): 1-9.

256. McNeil, Wm. H. [undated]. "History of Wasco County, Oregon." (Mimeographed.)

257. Meacham, Walter E. *Applegate Trail.* Portland, Ore., 1947.

258. Meacham, Walter E. *Barlow Road.* Portland, Ore., 1947.

259. Meacham, Walter E. *Old Oregon Trail, Roadway to American* Home *Builders.* Sponsored by the American Trails Assoc. Manchester, N.H.: The Clarke Press, 1948.

260. Meeker, Ezra. *The Ox Team; or, The Old Oregon Trail, 1852-1906.* Omaha, Nebr.: E. Meeker, 1906.

261. Meeker, Ezra. *The Busy Life of Eighty-five Years of Ezra Meeker.* Seattle, Wash.: E. Meeker, 1916.

262. Meeker, Ezra [1852]. *Ox Team Days on the Oregon Trail* . . . with drawings and photos. Yonkers-on-Hudson, N.Y.: World Book Co., 1922.

263. Meeker, Ezra. *Kate Mulhall; A Romance of the Oregon Trail* . . . New York: E. Meeker, 1926.

264. Meyers, E. L. "A Story of Two Men from Fort Deposit: Samuel K. Barlow and Philip Foster. 1957.

265. Miller, James K. P. *The Road to Virginia City.* Edited by Andrew F. Rolle. Norman: University of Oklahoma Press, 1960.

266. Minto, John. "Reminiscences of Experiences on the Oregon Trail in 1844." *Oregon Historical Quarterly*, 2 (June 1901): 119-67; (September 1901): 209-54.

267. Monaghan, James. *The Overland Trail.* Indianapolis, Ind.: Bobbs Merrill Co., 1947.

268. Moody, Ralph. *The Old Trails West.* New York: Thomas Y. Crowell Co., 1963.

269. Moore, Leroy. "The Unthank Story." *Annals of Wyoming*, 43 (Fall 1971): 276-77.

270. Moreland, Jesse [1852]. Diary. Misc. Overland Journeys to the Pacific. Portland: Oregon Historical Society.

271, Morrill, William [1847]. Reminiscence. Misc. Overland Journeys to the Pacific. Portland: Oregon Historical Society.

272, Morgan, Martha M. *A Trip Across the Plains in the Year 1849* . . . San Francisco: Pioneer Press, 1864.

273. Morgan, Dale L. "The Mormon Ferry on the North Platte." *Annals of Wyoming*, 21 (July-October, 1949): 111-67.

274. Morgan, Dale L. "The Ferries of the Forty-Niners, " *Annals of Wyoming*, 31 (April 1959): 4-31; (October 1959): 145-89; 32 (April 1960): 51-69; (October 1960): 167-203.

275. Morgan, Dale L. (Ed.) Overland *in 1846: Diaries and Letters of the California Oregon Trail.* 2 vols. Georgetown, Calif.: Talisman Press, 1963.

276. Morley, Gregory H. "Map References (Oregon Trail)." With typescript comments, Oregon Parks and Recreation Department, 1971.

277. Morrison, W. W. "Quotes from Various Diaries About the 'Red Earth Country.' " *Annals of Wyoming*, 42 (October 1970): 268-69.

278. Morrison, W. W. "Story of Little Mary Kelly." *Annals of Wyoming*, 43 (Fall 1971): 272-75.

279. Morrison, W. W. Oral information on pioneer gravesites on the Oregon Trail. Cheyenne, Wyo., July 10, 1972.

280. Mossman, Isaac Van D. *A Pony Expressman's Recollections.* Portland, Ore.: Champoeg Press, 1955.

281. Morrow, Honoré (McCue) W. *On to Oregon! The Story of a Pioneer Boy.* New York: W. Morrow and Co., 1926.

282. Mullan, John. "Report of a Reconnaissance from the Bitter Root Valley to Fort Hall . . ." In *Report of Exploration of a Route for the Pacific Railroad, Near the Forty-seventh and Forty-ninth Parallels, from St. Paul to Puget Sound. Gov. Stevens' Report to the Hon. Secretary of*

War. Washington, D.C.: GPO, 1854.

283. Mullan, John. "Map of a Military Reconnaissance from Fort Dalles, Oregon, Via Fort Wallah-Wallah to Fort Taylor, Washington Territory, by Lt. John Mullan, 1858." Scale, 1:300,000.

284. Munkres, Robert L. "Independence Rock and Devil's Gate," *Annals of Wyoming,* 40 (April 1968): 23-40.

285. Nadeau, Remi A. *Fort Laramie and the Sioux Indians.* Englewood Cliffs, N.J.: Prentice-Hall, c. 1967.

286. National Park Service. *Whitman National Monument,* Washington. Washington, D.C.: GPO, 1947.

287. National Register of Historic Places. "Midway Pony Express Station, Nebraska." Inventory nomination form, n.d.

288. Nebraska State Historical Society. "Chimney Rock." Mimeographed, n.d.

289. Nebraska Game and Parks Commission. "Ash Hollow State Historical Park." Mimeographed, n.d.

290. Nesmith, James W. "Diary of the Emigration of 1843." *Oregon Historical Quarterly,* 7 (December 1906): 329-59.

291. Newby, William T. [1843]. "Diary of the Emigration." *Oregon Historical Quarterly,* 40 (September 1939): 219-42.

292. Newley, William T. Diary of William Thompson Newley, July 23-August 23, 1843. Copied from an extract in the possession of Charles F. Guild, Evanston, Wyo.

293. Nichols, Tom. "Story of Sergeant Custard's Fight." *Annals of Wyoming,* 43 (Fall 1971): 294-95.

294. Ogden, Peter S. "The Peter Skene Ogden Journals." Edited by T. C. Elliott, *Oregon Historical Quarterly,* 10 (December 1909): 331-65.

295. Oregon State Highway Department. "Oregon Trail Reconnaissance—Part 1." Typescript. Salem, Oregon, June-July, 1970.

296. Oregon State Highway Department. *The Route of the Oregon Trail,* informational booklet, Salem, Oregon, n.d.

297. Owyhee Historical Society. "The Otter Massacre." Leaflet No. 12, December 1968.

298. Paden, Irene D. *The Wake of the Prairie Schooner.* New York: The MacMillan Company, 1943.

299. Page, Elizabeth [1849]. *Wagons West; A Story of the Oregon Trail.* New York: Farrar & Rinehart, 1930.

300. Palmer, Joel. Journal *of Travels over the Rocky Mountains, to the Mouth of the Columbia River, Made During the Years 1845 and 1846.* Cincinnati: J. A. & U. P. James, 1847.

301. Parker, Rev. Samuel [1835]. *Journal of an Exploring Tour Beyond the Rocky Mountains.* Ithaca, N.Y.: Andrus, Woodruff & Gauntlett, 1844.

302. Parker, Samuel [1845]. Diary (copy). Misc. Overland Journeys to the Pacific. Portland: Oregon Historical Society.

303. Parker, Armeda J. [1878]. Diary (copy). Misc. Overland Journeys to the Pacific. Portland: Oregon Historical Society.

304. Parkman, Francis [1846]. *The Oregon Trail.* Garden City, N.Y.: Doubleday & Company, 1946.

305. Parrish, Edward [1844]. "Crossing The Plains." In *Transactions of the Oregon Pioneer Association* (1888): 82-121.

306. Parrish, Phillip H. *Wagons West; "The Great Migration—1843."* Sponsored by the Old Oregon Trail Centennial Commmission. Portland, Ore.: James, Kerns & Abbott Co., 1943.

307. Parsons, Mary C. Reminiscence of 1852 (copy). Misc. Overland Journeys to the Pacific. Portland: Oregon Historical Society.

308. Partoli, Albert J. (Ed.) *Anderson's Narrative of a Ride to the Rocky Mountains in 1834.* University of Montana historical reprint No. 27. Missoula: State University of Montana, 1938.

309. Partoll, Albert J. "Angus McDonald, Frontier Fur Trader." *The Pacific Northwest Quarterly,* 42 (April 1951): 138-46.

310. Pelzer, Louis. *Marches of the Dragoons in the Mississippi Valley . . .* Iowa City: The State Historical Society of Iowa, 1917.

311. Penter, Samuel. "Recollections of an Oregon Pioneer of 1843." *Oregon Historical Quarterly,* 7 (March 1906): 56-61.

312. Perkins, Elisha D. *Gold Rush Diary, Being the Journal of Elisha Douglas Perkins on the Overland Trail in the Spring and Summer of 1849.* Edited by Thomas D. Clark. Lexington: University of Kentucky Press, 1967.

313. Porter, Elizabeth Lee [1864]. Diary (copy). Misc. Overland Journeys to the Pacific. Portland: Oregon Historical Society.

314. Powers, Kate N.B. [1832]. "Across the Continent Seventy Years Ago." Excerpts from the diary of John Ball. *Oregon Historical Quarterly,* 3 (March 1902): 86-106.

315. Preuss, Charles [1842]. *Topographical Map of the Road from Missouri to Oregon,* compiled by Charles Preuss from the field notes and journals of Capt. J. C. Fremont, at the scale of 10 miles to the inch. Baltimore, Md.: E. Weber & Co., 1846.

316. Pringle, Catherine S. [1854] "Letter of Catherine Sager Pringle." *Oregon Historical Quarterly,* 37 (December 1936): 354-60.

317. Pritchard, James A. *The Overland Diary of James A. Pritchard from Kentucky to California in 1849 . . .* Denver, Colo.: F. A. Rosenstock, 1959.

318. Raynor, James [1847]. Journal (copy). Misc. Overland Journeys to the Pacific. Portland: Oregon Historical Society.

319. Reading, Pierson B. "Journal of Pierson Barton Reading in His Journey of 123 Days Across the Rocky Mountains . . . in 1843." *Quarterly of the Society of California Pioneers,* 6 (September 1930): 148-98.

320. Reasoner, Henry A. [1852]. Account (copy). Misc. Overland Journeys to the Pacific. Portland: Oregon Historical Society.

321. Renshaw, Robert H. [1851]. Diary (copy). Misc. Overland Journeys to the Pacific. Portland: Oregon Historical Society.

322. Richardson, Albert D. *Beyond the Mississippi: From the Great River to the Great Ocean.* Hartford, Conn.: American Pub. Co., 1867.

323. Richardson, Marvin M. *The Whitman Mission, The Third Station on the Oregon Trail.* Walla Walla, Wash.: Whitman Pub. Co., 1940.

324. Rickey, James [18521. Ms. account and letters (typed). Misc.

Overland Journeys to the Pacific. Portland: Oregon Historical Society.

325. Riker, John F. *Journal of a Trip to California, by the Overland Route . . .* Urbana, Ill., 1855.

326. Ritz, Philip [1850]. Reminiscence. Misc. Overland Journeys to the Pacific. Portland: Oregon Historical Society.

327. Robertson, Frank C. *Fort Hall, Gateway to the Oregon Country.* New York: Hastings House, 1963.

328. Robidoux, Orral M. *Memorial to the Robidoux Brothers.* Kansas City, Mo.: Smith Grieves Co., 1924.

329. Rogerson, Josiah, Sr. "Tells Story of Trials of the Handcart Pioneers." *Salt Lake Tribune* (Utah), November 30, 1913.

330. Rogerson, Josiah, Sr. "Strong Men, Brave Women and Sturdy Children Crossed the Wilderness Afoot." *Salt Lake Tribune* (Utah), January 4, 1914.

331. Rollins, Phillip A. (Ed.) *The Discovery of the Oregon Trail; Robert Stuart's Narrative . . . 1812-1813.* New York: C. Scribners Sons, 1935.

332. Root, George A. "Ferries in Kansas." *Kansas Historical Quarterly,* 2 (November 1933): 363-65; 3 (February 1934): 3

333. Root, Riley [1848]. *Journal of Travels from St. Joseph to Oregon with Observations of that Country . . .* foreword by Joseph A. Sullivan. Oakland, Calif.: Biobooks, 1955.

334. Ross, Edith C. *The Old Shawnee Mission.* Topeka: Kansas State Printing Plant, 1928.

335. Rucker, Maude A. *The Oregon Trail and Some of Its Blazes.* New York: W. Neele, 1930.

336. Ruddell, W. H. [1850]. Letter. Misc. Overland Journeys to the Pacific. Portland: Oregon Historical Society.

337. Russell, Osborne [1834]. *Journal of a Trapper.* Edited by Aubrey L. Haines. Portland, Ore.: Oregon Historical Society, 1955.

338. Sage, Rufus B. *Rufus B. Sage, His Letters and Papers, 1836-1847,* Vols. IV & V in *The Far West and The Rockies* series. Edited by Leroy R. Hafen. Glendale, Calif.: The Arthur H. Clark Co., 1956.

339. Salisbury, Albert and Jane. *Here Rolled the Covered Wagons.* Seattle: Superior Publishing Co., 1948.

340. Santee, J. F. "Letters of John R. Tice." *Oregon Historical Quarterly,* 37 (March 1936): 24-44.

341. Sawyer, Lorenzo. "Way Sketches. Containing Incidents of Travel Across the Plains from St. Joseph to California." *Family Visitor,* 1 (1850-51).

342. Scamehorn, Howard L. (Ed.) [1849]. *The Buckeye Rovers in the Gold Rush.* Athens: Ohio University Press, 1965.

343. Schell, H. S. "Report of Assistant Surgeon H. S. Schell, United States Army: Fort Laramie, Wyoming Territory." Circular No. 4, War Department, Surgeon General's Office, Washington, D.C., December 8, 1870.

344. Schiel, Jacob H. *Journey Through the Rocky Mountains and the Humboldt Mountains to the Pacific Ocean.* Translated and edited by

Thomas N. Bonner. Norman: University of Oklahoma Press, 1959.

345. Scofield, W. M. *Oregon's Historical Markers.* Portland: Oregon Historical Society, 1966.

346. Scoll, Levi [1852]. Letter (photostat). Misc. Overland Journeys to the Pacific. Portland: Oregon Historical Society.

347. Scott, Hamilton. "Diary of Hamilton Scott, Covering His Trip Across the Plains in 1862." Entries for August 9 through August 13, 1862, from a copy in the possession of Tom Dilly, American Falls, Idaho.

348. Scott, Leslie M. "News and Comments." *Oregon Historical Quarterly,* 19 (March 1918): 73-87.

349. Scott, Leslie M. "News and Comments." *Oregon Historical Quarterly,* 19 (December 1918): 335-44.

350. Scott, Mary H. Oregon *Trail Through Wyoming: A Century of History, 1812-1912.* Aurora, Colo.: Powder River Publishers, 1958.

351. Seely, Sarah T. [1882]. Reminiscence (copy). Misc. Overland Journeys to the Pacific. Portland: Oregon Historical Society.

352. Seymore, E. Sanford. *Emigrant's Guide to the Gold Mines of Upper California* . . . Chicago: R. L. Wilson, Daily Journal Office, 1849.

353. Shaffer, Tom. "The Story of Atlantic City." *Annals of Wyoming,* 44 (Fall 1972): 282-83.

354. Shaw, Reuben C. *Across the Plains in '49.* Edited by Milo M. Quaife. New York: Citadel Press, 1966.

355. Shay, Bill. "Horseshoe Crossing and Stage Station." *Annals of Wyoming,* 42 (October 1970): 259-63.

356. Shively, J. M. [1845]. *Route and Distances to Oregon and California, With a Description of Watering Places, Dangerous Indians, etc.* Washington, D.C.: W. Greer, 1846.

357. Smitton, Larry. "Dead Man's Pass—Fact and Legend." Typed resume prepared for the Oregon Department of Highways, 1972.

358. Snowden, Clinton A. *History of Washington.* 6 vols. New York: The Century History Co., 1901.

359. Spaulding, Kenneth A. (Ed.) On *the Oregon Trail; Robert Stuart's Journey* . . . Norman: University of Oklahoma Press, 1953.

360. Stansbury, Howard. *Map of a Reconnaisance Between Fort Leavenworth on the Missouri River and the Great Salt Lake in the Territory of Utah, Made in 1849 and 1850, Under the orders of Col. J. J. Abert, Chief of the Topographical Bureau.* Drawn by Lt. Gunnison and Charles Preuss. New York: Ackerman Lith., 1850.

361. Stansbury, Howard [1849]. *Exploration and Survey of the Valley of the Great Salt Lake* . . . Philadelphia: Lippincott, Grambo & Co., 1852.

362. Steele, John. *Across the Plains in 1850.* Edited by Joseph Schafer. Chicago: The Caxton Club, 1930.

363. Stegner, Wallace. *The Gathering of Zion; The Story of the Mormon Trail.* New York: McGraw-Hill, 1964.

364. Stevens, Charles [1852]. "Letters of Charles Stevens." Edited by E. Ruth Rockwell. *Oregon Historical Quarterly,* 37 (June 1936): 137-59.

365. Stewart, Agnes [1853]. Diary (copy). Misc. Overland Journeys to the Pacific. Portland: Oregon Historical Society.

366. Stewart, George R. *The California Trail, An Epic with Many Heroes.* New York: McGraw Hill, 1962.

367. Stillwell, William D. Letter concerning an 1844 journey. Misc. Overland Journeys to the Pacific. Portland: Oregon Historical Society.

368. Stone, Elizabeth A. *Uinta County, Its Place in History.* Laramie, Wyo.: Laramie Printing Co., 1924.

369. Stowell, George [1856]. Reminiscence (copy). Misc. Overland Journeys to the Pacific. Portland: Oregon Historical Society.

370. Stowers, Robert E., and John E. Mills. "Charles A. Scott's Diary of the Utah Expedition, 1857-1861." *Utah Historical Quarterly*, 28 (April 1960): 155-76.

371. Strahorn, Carrie A. *Fifteen Thousand Miles by Stage.* 2nd ed. New York: G.P. Putnam's Sons, 1915.

372. Sudsweeks, Leslie L. "The Raft River in Idaho History." *Pacific Northwest Quarterly*, 32 (July 1941): 289-305.

373. Sun, Mrs. Tom, Jr. "The Story of the Sun Ranch." *Annals of Wyoming*, 44 (Fall 1972): 269-71.

374. Talbot, Theodore. *The Journals of Theodore Talbot, 1843 and 1849-1852.* Edited by Charles H. Carey. Portland, Ore.: Metropolitan Press, 1931.

375. Taylor, George N. [1853-55]. Diary (copy). Misc. Overland Journeys to the Pacific. Portland: Oregon Historical Society.

376. Thompson, Erwin N. *Whitman Mission: National Historic Site.* Washington, D.C.: GPO, 1964.

377. Thompson, Origen [1856]. *"Across the Plains,"* (copy). Misc. Overland Journeys to the Pacific. Portland: Oregon Historical Society.

378. Tobie, Harvey E. *No Man Like Joe: The Life and Times of Joseph L. Meek.* Portland, Ore.: Binsford & Mort, 1949.

379. Townsend, John K. [1832]. "Narrative of a Journey Across the Rocky Mountains to the Columbia River, etc." In *Early Western Travels*, 21. Edited by Reuben G. Thwaites. Cleveland, Ohio: The Arthur H. Clark Co., 1905.

380. Trenholm, Virginia C. "Twin Springs," *Annals of Wyoming*, 42 (October 1970): 256-57.

381. Udell, John. *Incidents of Travel to California, Across the Great Plains* . . . Jefferson, Ohio: The author, 1856.

382. U.S. Army. "Department of Oregon, Map of the State of Oregon and Washington Territory." Compiled in the Bureau of Topographical Engineers, chiefly for military purposes, by order of Hon. John B. Floyd, Secretary of War, 1859. Scale 1:1,500,000.

383. U.S. Congress. House Committee on the Library. *To Mark the Route of the Oregon Trail.* . . , a report to accompany H.R. 20477. Washington: GPO, 1908.

384. U.S. Congress. House Committee on Roads. *The Old Oregon Trail,* a report on House Joint Resolution 232, HJR 328 and Senate Bill 2053, January 23, February 13, 19 and 21, 1925. Washington: GPO, 1925.

385. U.S. Department of the Interior [1959]. Western Museum Laboratory. "Overland Migrations West of the Mississippi." The National Survey of Historic Sites, Theme XV, Westward Expansion and the Extension of the National Boundaries to the Pacific 1830-1898, U.S.D.I. (Typescript)

386. Walker, Beulah. "The Split Rock Telegraph and Pony Express Station, *Annals of Wyoming,* 44 (Fall 1972): 274.

387. Ward, Dillis B. *Across the Plains in 1853* (facsimile). Seattle, Wash,: Shorey Book Store, 1965.

388. Ware, Joseph E. [1848]. *The Emigrants' Guide to California . . .* With an intro. and notes by John W. Caughey. Princeton, N.J.: Princeton University Press, 1932.

389. Ware, Eugene F. *The Indian War of 1864.* With an intro. by Clyde C. Walton. New York: St. Martin's Press, 1960.

390. Watson, William J. *Journal of an Overland Journey to Oregon, Made in the Year 1849.* Jacksonville, Ore.: E. R. Roe, 1851.

391. Webb, Walter P. *The Great Plains.* Boston: Ginn and Co., 1931.

392. Webb, Todd. *The Gold Rush Trail and the Road to Oregon.* Garden City, N.Y.: Doubleday, 1963.

393. West, George M. [1852]. Account (copy). Misc. Overland Journeys to the Pacific. Portland: Oregon Historical Society.

394. White, Thomas. *To Oregon in 1852: Letter of Dr. Thomas White.* Edited by Oscar O. Winther and Gayle Thornburgh. Indianapolis: Indianapolis Historical Society, 1964.

395. White, Thomas E. *Garrison Life Trail: An Illustrated Guide to Historic Fort Laramie.* Fort Laramie NHS, Wyo.: Fort Laramie Historical Association, 1972.

396. Wilkes, George. *History of Oregon . . . to which is Added a Journal of the Events of the Celebrated Emigrating Expedition of 1843.* New York: Wm. H. Colyer, 1845.

397. Wilkins, Edness K. "Sweetwater Station," *Annals of Wyoming,* 43 (Fall 1971): 287-93.

398. Williams, Joseph. *Narrative of a Tour from the State of Indiana to the Oregon Territory in the Years 1841-2.* Cincinnati: J. B. Wilson, 1843.

399. Williams, Velina A. [1853]. Journal. Misc. Overland Journeys to the Pacific. Portland: Oregon Historical Society.

400. Williams, W. T. [1843]. Letter. Misc. Overland Journeys to the Pacific. Portland: Oregon Historical Society.

401. Williams, Joseph. *Narrative of a Tour from the State of Indiana to the Oregon Territory in the Years 1841-2. . . .* Intro. by James C. Bell Jr. New York: The Cadmus Book Shop, 1921.

402. Wilson, Margaret. "The Elkhorn Wagon Train Encounter." *Annals of Wyoming,* 42 (October 1970): 263-65.

403. Winther, Oscar O. "The Development of Transportation in Oregon, 1843-49." *Oregon Historical Quarterly,* 40 (December 1939): 315-26.

404. Winther, Oscar O. *The Great Northwest.* New York: Alfred A. Knopf, 1948.

405. Wislizenus, F. A. *A Journey to the Rocky Mountains in the Year 1839.* Trans. from the German by Frederick A. Wislizenus. St. Louis:

Missouri Historical Society, 1912.
406. Wyeth, Nathaniel J. "The Correspondence and Journals of Captain Nathanial J. Wyeth, 1831-6." Edited by F. G. Young. *Sources of the History of Oregon,* Vol. 1, Parts 3-6. Eugene, Ore.: University Press, 1899.
407. Young, George C. [1850]. "Diary . . ." Reprinted in the Horse Cave, Ky., *Hart County Herald,* August 29, 1940.
408. Young, Lorenzo D. [1847]. "Diary . . .," *Utah Historical Quarterly,* 14 (January-October 1946): 133-70.
409. Young, Will H. [1865] "Journals . . ." *Annals of Wyoming,* 7 (October 1930): 378-82.
410. Zaring, Alvin [undated]. Signed account concerning the Massacre Rocks incident (1862). Copy obtained from Massacre Rocks State Park, Idaho.
411. Zieber, John S. [1851]. Diary (copy). Misc. Overland Journeys to the Pacific. Portland: Oregon Historical Society.

Map List

Maps published by the U.S. Geological Survey may be purchased over the counter at the following offices of the Survey:

Arlington, Virginia — 1200 South Eads Street.

Washington, D.C. — General Services Building, Room 1028, 19th and F Streets NW.

Denver, Colorado — Federal Building, Room 169, 1961 Stout Street, or Building 41, Denver Federal Center

Dallas, Texas — Federal Building, Room IC45, 1100 Commerce Street.

Los Angeles, California — Federal Building, Room 7638, 300 North Los Angeles Street.

Menlo Park, California — Building 3, (Stop 33), Room 122, 345 Middlefield Road.

Reston, Virginia — 302 National Center, Room 1C402, 12201 Sunrise Valley Drive.

Salt Lake City, Utah — Federal Building, Room 8105, 125 South State Street.

San Francisco, California — Customhouse, Room 504, 555 Battery Street.

Spokane, Washington — U.S. Courthouse, Room 678, West 920 Riverside Avenue.

Rolla, Missouri — 1400 Independence Road.

Anchorage, Alaska — Skyline Building, Room 108, 508 2nd Ave.

Fairbanks, Alaska — Federal Building, 101 Twelfth Avenue.

All mail orders for maps of areas west of the Mississippi River should be addressed to:

Distribution Section, U.S. Geological Survey
Box 25286, Federal Center
Denver, CO 80225

Orders should list, individually, the maps required, giving the name and series of each. This list is arranged by states, in the order of progression westward. Include a check or money order for the total number of maps purchased. The current price is $2.50 per map. There is a 50 percent discount on orders totaling more than $500.

These maps are often available locally from private outlets, but the price usually is higher.

All maps listed here are in the 7½-minute series except those marked with an asterisk, which are in the 15-minute series.

Liberty, Mo.
Independence, Mo.
Lees Summit, Mo.
Grandview, Mo.

Kansas City, Mo./Kans.
Shawnee, Kans.
Lenexa, Kans.
Stillwell, Kans.
Ocheltree, Kans.
Gardner, Kans.
Edgerton, Kans.
Eudora, Kans.
Lawrence East, Kans.
Lawrence West, Kans.
Clinton, Kans.
Perry, Kans.
Grantville, Kans.
Topeka, Kans.
Silver Lake, Kans.
Willard, Kans.
Rossville, Kans.
St. Marys, Kans.
Belvue, Kans.
LaClede, Kans.
Louisville, Kans.
Flush, Kans.
Westmoreland, Kans.
Frankfort SW, Kans.
Frankfort, Kans.
Blue Rapids NE, Kans.
Blue Rapids, Kans.
Marysville, Kans.
Hanover SE, Kans.
Hanover East, Kans.
Hanover West, Kans.

Diller, Nebr.
Endicott, Nebr.

Jansen, Nebr.
Fairbury, Nebr.
Gladstone, Nebr.
Alexandria, Nebr.
Hebron, Nebr.
Deshler, Nebr.
Ruskin, Nebr.
Oak, Nebr.
Edgar, Nebr.
Fairfield SE, Nebr.
Deweese, Nebr.
Fairfield NW, Nebr.
Pauline, Nebr.
Ayr, Nebr.
Hastings West, Nebr.
Juniata, Nebr.
Kenesaw, Nebr.
Denman, Nebr.
Gibbon South, Nebr.
Newark, Nebr.
Kearney, Nebr.
Alfalfa Center, Nebr.
Elm Creek East, Nebr.
Elm Creek West, Nebr.
Overton, Nebr.
Bertrand NW, Nebr.
Johnson Lake, Nebr.
Lexington West, Nebr.
Cozad, Nebr.
Gothenburg SE, Nebr.
Gothenburg SW, Nebr.
Gothenburg, Nebr.
Jeffrey Reservoir NE, Nebr.
Jeffrey Reservoir, Nebr.
Brady SW, Nebr.
Maxwell, Nebr.
Maxwell SW, Nebr.
Lake Maloney, Nebr.
North Platte SW, Nebr.

Hershey East, Nebr.
Hershey West, Nebr.
Sutherland Reservoir NW, Nebr.
Sutherland Reservoir, Nebr.
Paxton South, Nebr.
Paxton SW, Nebr.
Ogallala SE, Nebr.
Ogallala SW, Nebr.
Brule SE, Nebr.
Brule, Nebr.
Big Springs, Nebr.
Big Springs NE, Nebr.
Ruthton, Nebr.
Lewellen, Nebr.
Barn Butte, Nebr.
Oshkosh, Nebr.
Coumbe Bluff, Nebr.
Lisco, Nebr.
Lisco NW, Nebr.
Tar Valley SW, Nebr.
Broadwater, Nebr.
Broadwater SW, Nebr.
Courthouse Rock, Nebr.
Bridgeport, Nebr.
Bridgeport NW, Nebr.
South Bayard, Nebr.
McGrew, Nebr.
Bayard SW, Nebr.
Minatare, Nebr.
Scottsbluff South, Nebr.
Roubadeau Pass, Nebr.
Stegall, Nebr.
Morrill, Nebr.
Scottsbluff North, Nebr.
Mitchell, Nebr.

Lyman, Wyo.
Torrington SE, Wyo.
Torrington, Wyo.
Cottier, Wyo.
Habig Spring, Wyo.
Barnes, Wyo.
Fort Laramie, Wyo.
Register Cliff, Wyo.
Guernsey, Wyo.
Guernsey Reservoir, Wyo.
Herman Ranch, Wyo.
Cassa, Wyo.
Sibley Peak, Wyo.
Spring Creek, Wyo.
Cedar Hill, Wyo.
Dilts Ranch, Wyo.
Poison Lake, Wyo.
Chalk Buttes, Wyo.

La Prele Reservoir, Wyo.
Orpha, Wyo.
Careyhurst, Wyo.
Glenrock, Wyo.
Parkerton, Wyo.
Lockett, Wyo.
Brookhurst, Wyo.
Casper, Wyo.
Goose Egg, Wyo.
Emigrant Gap, Wyo.
Oil Mountain, Wyo.
Clarkson Hill, Wyo.
Benton Basin NE, Wyo.
McCleary Reservoir, Wyo.
Benton Basin SW, Wyo.
Sanford Ranch, Wyo.
Fort Ridge, Wyo.
Independence Rock, Wyo.
Savage Peak, Wyo.
Bucklin Reservoir, Wyo.
Split Rock, Wyo.
Split Rock NW, Wyo.
Black Rock Gap, Wyo.
Stampede Meadow, Wyo.
Graham Ranch, Wyo.
Myers Ranch, Wyo.
Sweetwater Station, Wyo.
Red Canyon, Wyo.
Barras Springs, Wyo.
Lewiston Lakes, Wyo.
Radium Springs, Wyo.
Atlantic City, Wyo.
Continental Peak, Wyo.
Dickie Springs, Wyo.
Pacific Springs, Wyo.
Hay Meadow Reservoir, Wyo.
Parting of the Ways, Wyo.
Tule Butte, Wyo.
Eden Reservoir East, Wyo.
Eden Reservoir West, Wyo.
Farson, Wyo.
Simpson Gulch SE, Wyo.
Pittman Well, Wyo.
Gasson Bridge, Wyo.
Thoman School, Wyo.
Lombard Buttes, Wyo.
Blue Point, Wyo.
Sevenmile Gulch, Wyo.
Granger, Wyo.
Verne, Wyo.
Church Butte, Wyo.
Millersville, Wyo.
Turtle Hill, Wyo.
Mountain View, Wyo.

Fort Bridger, Wyo.
Carter, Wyo.
Mulkay Spring, Wyo.
Cumberland Gap, Wyo.
Elkol SW, Wyo.
Warfield Creek, Wyo.
Bell Butte NE, Wyo.
Windy Point, Wyo.
Sage, Wyo.*
Cokeville, Wyo.
Marse, Wyo.

Border, Idaho
Pegram, Idaho
Montpelier Canyon, Idaho
Montpelier, Idaho
Georgetown, Idaho
Nounan, Idaho
Fossil Canyon, Idaho
Soda Springs, Idaho*
Bancroft, Idaho*
Portneuf, Idaho*
Jeff Cabin Creek, Idaho
South Putnam Mountain, Idaho
Yandell Springs, Idaho
Buckskin Basin, Idaho
Fort Hall, Idaho
Pingree, Idaho
Springfield, Idaho
Schiller, Idaho
Wheatgrass Bench, Idaho
American Falls, Idaho
American Falls SW, Idaho
Neeley, Idaho
Yale, Idaho*
Lake Walcott, Idaho*
Rupert SE, Idaho
Rupert SW Idaho
Burley SE, Idaho
Burley SW, Idaho
Milner, Idaho
Milner Butte, Idaho
Murtaugh, Idaho
Stricker Butte, Idaho
Hub Butte, Idaho
Twin Falls, Idaho
Filer, Idaho
Jerome, Idaho
Niagara Springs, Idaho
Thousand Springs, Idaho
Tuttle, Idaho
Hagerman, Idaho
Indian Butte, Idaho
Pasadena Valley, Idaho

Glenns Ferry, Idaho
Bennett Mountain, Idaho
Mountain Home, Idaho
Danskin Peak, Idaho*
Mayfield, Idaho*
Indian Creek Reservoir, Idaho
Lucky Peak, Idaho
Boise South, Idaho
Boise North, Idaho
Eagle, Idaho
Star, Idaho
Middleton, Idaho
Caldwell, Idaho
Notus, Idaho
Parma, Idaho
Owyhee, Idaho
Hammett, Idaho
Indian Cove, Idaho
Sand Dunes, Idaho
Bruneau, Idaho
C. J. Stricker Dam, Idaho
Grand View, Idaho
Dorsey Butte, Idaho
Jackass Butte, Idaho
Castle Butte, Idaho
Wild Horse Butte, Idaho
Sinker Butte, Idaho
Silver City, Idaho*
Walters Butte, Idaho
Wilson Peak, Idaho
Givens Hot Springs, Idaho
Opalene Gulch, Idaho
Marsing, Idaho
Homedale, Idaho
Wilder, Idaho
Adrian, Idaho

Mitchell Butte, Oreg.
Vale East, Oreg.
Moores Hollow, Oreg.*
Jamieson, Oreg.*
Olds Ferry, Oreg.
Huntington, Oreg.*
Durkee, Oreg.*
Lost Basin, Oreg.
Oxman, Oreg.
Encina, Oreg.
Virtue Flat, Oreg.
Baker, Oreg.
Magpie Peak, Oreg.
Haines, Oreg.
North Powder, Oreg.
Craig Mountain, Oreg.
Glass Hill, Oreg.

La Grande SE, Oreg.
Hilgard, Oreg.
Kamela SE, Oreg.
Huron, Oreg.
Meacham Lake, Oreg.
Meacham, Oreg.
Cabbage Hill, Oreg.
Cayuse, Oreg.
Mission, Oreg.
Pendleton, Oreg.
Barnhart, Oreg.
Nolin, Oreg.
Echo, Oreg.
Service Buttes, Oreg.
Service Buttes NW, Oreg.
Strawberry Canyon NE, Oreg.
Well Spring, Oreg.
Ella, Oreg.
Ione North, Oreg.
Cecil, Oreg.
Dalreed Butte, Oreg.
Hickland Butte, Oreg.
Horn Butte, Oreg.
Shutler Flat, Oreg.
Turner Butte, Oreg.
McDonald, Oreg.
Klondike, Oreg.
Quinton, Oreg.
Rufus, Oreg.
Wasco, Oreg.
Locust Grove, Oreg.
Biggs Junction, Oreg.
Wishram, Oreg.
Emerson, Oreg.

Petersburg, Oreg.
The Dalles South, Oreg.
The Dalles North, Oreg.
Lyle, Oreg.
White Salmon, Oreg.
Hood River, Oreg.*
Bonneville Dam, Oreg.*
Bridal Veil, Oreg.*
Washougal, Oreg.
Camas, Oreg.
Mt. Tabor, Oreg.
Portland, Oreg.
Vancouver, Oreg.
Sauvie Island, Oreg.
Linnton, Oreg.
Lake Oswego, Oreg.
Dufur East, Oreg.
Dufur West, Oreg.
Postage Stamp Butte, Oreg.
Tygh Valley, Oreg.
Wamic, Oreg.
Rock Creek Reservoir, Oreg.
Mt. Wilson, Oreg.*
Mount Hood South, Oreg.
Government Camp, Oreg.
Rhododendron, Oreg.
Cherryville, Oreg.*
Sandy, Oreg.
Estacada, Oreg.
Redland, Oreg.
Damascus, Oreg.
Gladstone, Oreg.
Oregon City, Oreg.

Index to Sites

Explore the
Oregon Trail

BY AUTOMOBILE OR ARMCHAIR
WITH THE AWARD WINNING

THE OREGON
TRAIL REVISITED

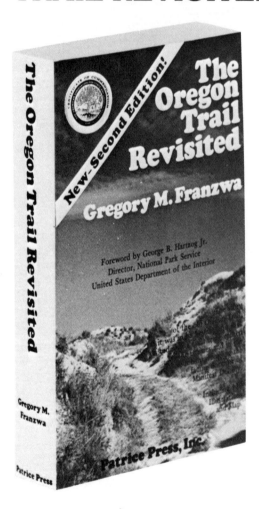

MAPS OF THE OREGON TRAIL

GREGORY M. FRANZWA

A collection of 133 current county maps showing the route of the Oregon Trail

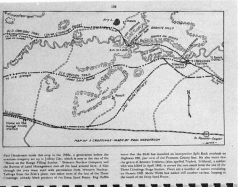

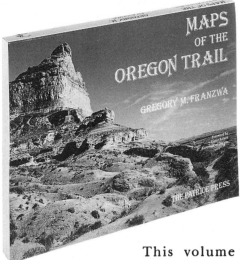

This volume reproduces the route of the Oregon Trail as a thin line over a base of county maps, on a scale of ½" : 1 mile. The route is from Independence, Missouri to Oregon City, Oregon, with the Barlow Cutoff and the South Snake River routes included as alternates. Also in this book are the Sublette Cutoff and several of its branches.

33 Full Page Trail Maps
99 Pages
Detail Maps
Photographs

Paperback, $18.95
Spiral (with removable pages), $24.95
plus $2.95 shipping

The Patrice Press
1810 W. Grant Rd., Suite 108
Tucson AZ 85745
Toll-Free—1-800-367-9242
Order from your favorite bookseller

Other Exciting Books On America's Covered Wagon Roads

(1993 Prices)

Oregon Trail

Discover The Oregon Trail. An adult-child interactive book of puzzles, games, maps, and activities produc by the Jefferson National Expansion Historical Association. A fun way to involve children in the mystiq of the Oregon Trail. 32 pp., 8½"x 11", pb only. **$3.**

The Great Platte River Road, by Merrill J. Mattes. A comprehensive study of the history and geography the Oregon-California Trail from the Missouri River to South Pass. 607 pp, 33 photos, 10 maps, bibliograp citing nearly 1,000 diaries, pb only. **$16.**

Old Oregon Trail Wall Map, This colorful map shows the routes of 13 western trails, including the Orege California, Barlow, Lewis & Clark, Santa Fe, Overland Stage, Pony Express, and many others. 17" x 2₄ Shipped in mailing tube. **$2.**

Trail to Oregon, by Gene & Betty Comfort. Two high school teachers with a talent for scriptwriting and videotap produced this 50-minute VHS videotape of the Oregon Trail as it appears today. **$29.**

Exploring the American West, by William H. Goetzmann. A masterful interpretation of the explorations wh opened the West—pathfinders, mountain men, European visitors, others. Published by the National P₄ Service. 129 pp, 46 color illustrations, 9 color maps, pb only. **$7.**

Platte River Road Narratives, by Merrill J. Mattes. An annotated bibliography of more than 2,000 emigr₄ diaries. Each entry identifies the author, describes the nature of the diary, shows the routes taken, and giv a "star system" rating to the diary. 632 pp., hardcover only. **$95.**

The Overland Migrations, by David Lavender. The greatest mass migration in America is described in de in this colorful book. 112 pp., 45 color illustrations, pb only. **$7.**

The Plains Across, by John D. Unruh, Jr. Dr. Ray Allen Billington called this book "a majesterial history the Oregon-California Trail," and Merrill J. Mattes calls it a "tour de force." It is without a doubt the b book ever written on the western American migration. 382 pp, pb only. **$12.**

"Powerful Rockey"; The Blue Mountains & the Oregon Trail, by John W. Evans. The definitive book the trail through the dreaded Blue Mountains, from Farewell Bend to west of Pendleton. The wagon rc is covered in minute detail. Diary entries, large-scale USGS maps, and photos by the author compared w historic sketches. 394 pp. **$22.**

March of the Mounted Riflemen, by Osborn Cross. A fascinating daily journal of an 1849 military expedit over the Oregon Trail, from Fort Leavenworth to Fort Vancouver. 378 pp, map, sketches, pb only. **$10.**

Prairie Schooner Detours, by Irene D. Paden. A thorough research job on the Hastings Cutoff across the s desert to the Humboldt River, and the Applegate-Lassen Road, which took forty-niners more than 100 mi off their course to California. 311 pp., 9 sketches, maps, pb only. **$12.**

Santa Fe Trail

The Santa Fe Trail Revisited, by Gregory M. Franzwa. Follow the old wagon road from Franklin, Mo., to Sa Fe via the Cimarron Cutoff, then back to the Mountain Branch via Raton Pass. 304 pp., 165 photos, pb or **$12.**

Maps of the Santa Fe Trail, by Gregory M. Franzwa. The route of the Santa Fe Trail is reproduced ove background of current county maps, from Franklin, Mo., to Santa Fe by way of both the Cimarron Cu and the Mountain Branch. 209 pp, 99 full-page map panels, 11 area maps, 29 photos.
$29.95 looseleaf; $24.95 hardco

Images of the Santa Fe Trail, by Gregory M. Franzwa. The author was a member of the National Park Serv team which explored the Santa Fe Trail in 1988. This is his photographic log of the journey—dramatic ρ tures of the most storied sites along the wagon road. 140 pp., 112 photos.
$29.95 hardcover, $19.95

Impressions of the Santa Fe Trail, by Gregory M. Franzwa. The author kept a detailed diary during the 19 National Park Service survey of the Santa Fe Trail. In it he recorded the exhilaration of discovery and ' enjoyment of friendship. 208 pp., 64 photos, hardcover only. **$14.**

The Santa Fe Trail; the National Park Service 1963 Historic Sites Survey, by William E. Brown. A maste work on both the history and the historic sites along the Santa Fe Trail. 240 pp., 82 photos, 20 maps
$17.95 hardcover. $12.95

Santa Fe Trail Wall Map. This beautiful map of the old Santa Fe Trail is now in full color. 24" x 17", includ full-color reproduction of the burlap mat. Shipped in a mailing tube. **$2**

Shipping: $3.95 for first book; 95¢ for each additional book.

Call Toll-free for the latest catalog: 1-800-367-9242

THE AUTHOR

 Aubrey L. Haines attended high school in Seattle, Washington, and obtained a BS degree in Forestry from the College of Technology of the University of Washington. He became a park ranger at Yellowstone National Park in 1938, and following a four-year period of service with the U.S. Army Corps of Engineers during World War II, was made assistant park engineer at Yellowstone in 1946. He obtained an MS degree in Forestry form the University of Montana in 1949, was transferred to Mount Rainier National Park, and returned to Yellowstone where he became part historian in 1960. He edited Osborne Russell's *Journal of A Trapper* (1956), and wrote *Mountain Fever — Historic Conquests of Rainier* (1963), *Valley of the Upper Yellowstone* (1965), *Yellowstone National Park: Its Exploration and Establishment* (1974); and *The Yellowstone Story*, 2 vols. (1977).

Haines and his wife Wilma now live in retirement in Tucson, Arizona.

3 may 2002

Col. Byron H. Gilmore, Ret
1708 Carmel Dr.
Lawrence, KS 66047-1840